SOFTWARE TESTING

A Craftsman's Approach

THIRD EDITION

Other Auerbach Publications in
Software Development, Software Engineering,
and Project Management

SOFTWARE TESTING

A Craftsman's Approach

THIRD EDITION

Paul C. Jorgensen

Auerbach Publications
Taylor & Francis Group
Boca Raton   New York

Auerbach Publications is an imprint of the
Taylor & Francis Group, an **informa** business

Visual Basic, Visual FoxPro, and Windows are registered trademarks of Microsoft Corporation.

Java is a trademark of Sun Microsystems, Inc.

ColdFusion is a registered trademark of Adobe Systems Incorporated.

Auerbach Publications
Taylor & Francis Group
6000 Broken Sound Parkway NW, Suite 300
Boca Raton, FL 33487-2742

© 2008 by Taylor & Francis Group, LLC
Auerbach is an imprint of Taylor & Francis Group, an Informa business

No claim to original U.S. Government works
Printed in the United States of America on acid-free paper
10 9 8 7 6 5

International Standard Book Number-13: 978-0-8493-7475-3 (Hardcover)

Library of Congress Cataloging-in-Publication Data

Jorgensen, Paul.
   Software testing : a craftsman's approach / Paul C. Jorgensen. -- 3rd ed.
     p. cm.
   Includes bibliographical references and index.
   ISBN-13: 978-0-8493-7475-3 (hardcover : alk. paper)
   ISBN-10: 0-8493-7475-8 (hardcover : alk. paper)
   1. Computer software--Testing. I. Title.

QA76.76.T48J67 2007
005.1'4--dc22
                                               2007017469

Visit the Taylor & Francis Web site at
http://www.taylorandfrancis.com

and the Auerbach Web site at
http://www.auerbach-publications.com

Dedication

To Carol, Kirsten, and Katia

Contents

PART III: STRUCTURAL TESTING

Preface to the Third Edition

Five years have passed since the second edition appeared, and software testing has seen a renaissance of renewed interest and technology. The biggest change is the growing prominence and acceptance of agile programming. The various flavors of agile programming have interesting and serious implications for software testing. Almost as a reaction to agile programming, the model-based approaches to both development and testing have also gained adherents. Part VI of the third edition analyzes the testing methods that are gaining acceptance in the new millennium. Except for correction of errors, the first five parts are generally unchanged.

Over the years, several readers have been enormously helpful in pointing out defects — both typos and more serious faults. Particular thanks go to Neil Bitzenhofer (Minnesota), Han Ke (Beijing), Jacob Minidor (Illinois), and Jim Davenport (Ohio). In addition, many of my graduate students have made helpful suggestions in the past 15 years. Special mention goes to two valued colleagues, Dr. Roger Ferguson and Dr. Christian Trefftz, for their help.

This book is now used as a text for formal courses in software testing in dozens of countries. To support both instructors and students, I have added more exercises, and faculty adopters can get a package of support materials from CRC Press.

I, too, have changed in the past five years. I now count several Lakota people among my friends. There is an interesting bit of their influence in Chapter 23, and just one word here — Hecatuyelo!

Paul C. Jorgensen
Rockford, Michigan
December 2007

Preface to the Second Edition

Seven years have passed since I wrote the preface to the first edition. Much has happened in that time, hence this new edition. The most significant change is the dominance of the unified modeling language (UML) as a standard for the specification and design of object-oriented software. The main changes in this edition are the five chapters in Part V that deal with testing object-oriented software. Nearly all the material in Part V is UML-based.

The second major change is that the Pascal examples of the first edition are replaced by a language-neutral pseudocode. Most of the examples have been elaborated, and they are supported by Visual Basic executable modules available on the CRC Press Web site (www.crcpress.com). Several new examples illustrate some of the issues of testing object-oriented software. Dozens of other changes have been made; the most important additions include an improved description of equivalence class testing, a continuing case study, and more details about integration testing.

I am flattered that the first edition is one of the primary references on software testing in the trial–use standard Software Engineering Body of Knowledge jointly produced by the ACM and IEEE Computer Society (www.swebok.org). This recognition makes the problem of uncorrected mistakes more of a burden. A reader in South Korea sent me a list of 38 errors in the first edition, and students in my graduate class on software testing have gleefully contributed others. There is a nice analogy with testing here: I have fixed all the known errors, and my editor tells me it is time to stop looking for others. If you find any, please let me know — they are my responsibility. My e-mail address is: jorgensp@gvsu.edu.

I need to thank Jerry Papke and Helena Redshaw at CRC Press for their patience. I also want to thank my friend and colleague, Prof. Roger Ferguson, for his continued help with the new material in Part V, especially the continuing object-oriented calendar example. In a sense, Roger has been a tester of numerous drafts of Chapters 16 through 20.

Paul C. Jorgensen
Rockford, Michigan
May 2002

Preface to the First Edition

We huddled around the door to the conference room, each taking a turn looking through the small window. Inside, a recently hired software designer had spread out source listings on the conference table, and carefully passed a crystal hanging from a long chain over the source code. Every so often, the designer marked a circle in red on the listing. Later, one of my colleagues asked the designer what he had been doing in the conference room. The nonchalant reply: "Finding the bugs in my program." This is a true story, it happened in the mid-1980s when people had high hopes for hidden powers in crystals.

In a sense, the goal of this book is to provide you with a better set of crystals. As the title suggests, I believe that software (and system) testing is a craft, and I think I have some mastery of that craft. Out of a score of years developing telephone switching systems, I spent about a third of that time on testing: defining testing methodologies and standards, coordinating system testing for a major international telephone toll switch, specifying and helping build two test execution tools (now we would call them CASE tools), and a fair amount of plain, hands-on testing. For the past seven years, I have been teaching software engineering at the university graduate level. My academic research centers on specification and testing. Adherents to the Oxford Method claim that you never really learn something until you have to teach it — I think they're right. The students in my graduate course on testing are all full-time employees in local industries. Believe me, they keep you honest. This book is an outgrowth of my lectures and projects in that class.

I think of myself as a software engineer, but when I compare the level of precision and depth of knowledge prevalent in my field to those of more traditional engineering disciplines, I am uncomfortable with the term. A colleague and I were returning to our project in Italy when Myers' book, *The Art of Software Testing*, first came out. On the way to the airport, we stopped by the MIT bookstore and bought one of the early copies. In the intervening 15 years, I believe we have moved from an art to a craft. I had originally planned to title this book "The Craft of Software Testing," but as I neared the final chapters, another book with that title appeared. Maybe that's confirmation that software testing is becoming a craft. There's still a way to go before it is a science.

Part of any craft is knowing the capabilities and limitations of both the tools and the medium. A good woodworker has a variety of tools and, depending on the item being made and the wood being used, knows which tool is the most appropriate. Of all the phases of the traditional Waterfall Model of the software development life cycle, testing is the most amenable to precise analysis. Elevating software testing to a craft requires that the testing craftsperson know the basic tools. To this end, Chapters 3 and 4 provide mathematical background that is used freely in the remainder of the text.

Mathematics is a descriptive device that helps us better understand software to be tested. Precise notation, by itself, is not enough. We must also have good technique and judgment to identify appropriate testing methods and to apply them well. These are the goals of Parts II and III, which deal with fundamental functional and structural testing techniques. These techniques are applied to the continuing examples, which are described in Chapter 2. In Part IV, we apply these techniques to the integration and system levels of testing, and to object-oriented testing. At these levels, we are more concerned with what to test than how to test it, so the discussion moves toward requirements specification. Part IV concludes with an examination of testing interactions in a software controlled system, with a short discussion of client–server systems.

It is ironic that a book on testing contains faults. Despite the conscientious efforts of reviewers and editors, I am confident that faults persist in the text. Those that remain are my responsibility.

In 1977, I attended a testing seminar given by Edward Miller, who has since become one of the luminaries in software testing circles. In that seminar, Miller went to great lengths to convince us that testing need not be bothersome drudgery, but can be a very creative, interesting part of software development. My goal for you, the reader of this book, is that you will become a testing craftsperson, and that you will be able to derive the sense of pride and pleasure that a true craftsperson realizes from a job well done.

Paul C. Jorgensen
Rockford, Michigan
January 1995

The Author

Paul C. Jorgensen, Ph.D., spent 20 years of his first career developing, supporting, and testing telephone switching systems. Since 1986, he has been teaching graduate courses in software engineering, first at Arizona State University, and then at Grand Valley State University. His consulting practice, Software Paradigms, hibernates during the Michigan winter when he is teaching and returns to life (along with everything else in Michigan) during the summer months.

Living and working for 3 years in Italy made him a confirmed "Italophile." He frequently travels to Italy with his wife, Carol, and daughters, Kirsten and Katia. In the summer, Paul sails his "Rebel" as often as possible. He is a year-round swimmer. His e-mail address is jorgensp@ gvsu.edu.

A MATHEMATICAL CONTEXT

Chapter 1

A Perspective on Testing

Why do we test? The two main reasons are to make a judgment about quality or acceptability and to discover problems. We test because we know that we are fallible — this is especially true in the domain of software and software-controlled systems. The goal of this chapter is to create a perspective (or context) on software testing. We will operate within this context for the remainder of the text.

1.1 Basic Definitions

Much of testing literature is mired in confusing (and sometimes inconsistent) terminology, probably because testing technology has evolved over decades and via scores of writers. The terminology here (and throughout this book) is taken from standards developed by the Institute of Electronics and Electrical Engineers (IEEE) Computer Society. To get started, let us look at a useful progression of terms:

Error — People make errors. A good synonym is *mistake*. When people make mistakes while coding, we call these mistakes *bugs*. Errors tend to propagate; a requirements error may be magnified during design and amplified still more during coding.

Fault — A fault is the result of an error. It is more precise to say that a fault is the representation of an error, where representation is the mode of expression, such as narrative text, dataflow diagrams, hierarchy charts, source code, and so on. Defect is a good synonym for fault, as is bug. Faults can be elusive. When a designer makes an error of omission, the resulting fault is that something is missing that should be present in the representation. This suggests a useful refinement; to borrow from the church, we might speak of faults of commission and faults of omission. A fault of commission occurs when we enter something into a representation that is incorrect. Faults of omission occur when we fail to enter correct information. Of these two types, faults of omission are more difficult to detect and resolve.

Failure — A failure occurs when a fault executes. Two subtleties arise here: (1) Failures only occur in an executable representation, which is usually taken to be source code, or more precisely, loaded object code. (2) This definition relates failures only to faults of commission. How can we deal with failures that correspond to faults of omission? We can push this still further: What about faults that never happen to execute, or perhaps do not execute for a long time? The Michelangelo virus is an example of such a fault — it does not execute until March 6. Reviews prevent many failures by finding faults; in fact, well-done reviews can find faults of omission.

Incident — When a failure occurs, it may or may not be readily apparent to the user (or customer or tester). An incident is the symptom associated with a failure that alerts the user to the occurrence of a failure.

Test — Testing is obviously concerned with errors, faults, failures, and incidents. A test is the act of exercising software with test cases. A test has two distinct goals: to find failures and to demonstrate correct execution.

Test case — Test case has an identity and is associated with a program behavior. A test case also has a set of inputs and expected outputs.

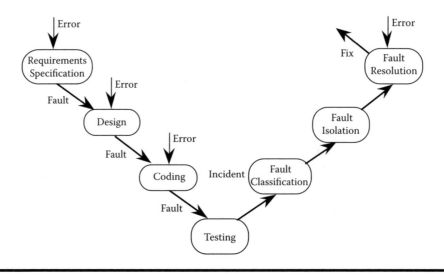

Figure 1.1 A testing life cycle.

Figure 1.1 portrays a life cycle model for testing. Notice that, in the development phases, three opportunities arise for errors to be made, resulting in faults that propagate through the remainder of the development process. One prominent tester summarizes this life cycle as follows: the first three phases are Putting Bugs IN; the testing phase is Finding Bugs; and the last three phases are Getting Bugs OUT (Poston, 1990). The Fault Resolution step is another opportunity for errors (and new faults). When a fix causes formerly correct software to misbehave, the fix is deficient. We will revisit this when we discuss regression testing.

From this sequence of terms, we see that test cases occupy a central position in testing. The process of testing can be subdivided into separate steps: test planning, test case development, running test cases, and evaluating test results. The focus of this book is how to identify useful sets of test cases.

1.2   Test Cases

The essence of software testing is to determine a set of test cases for the item to be tested. Before going on, we need to clarify what information should be in a test case:

>Inputs, really of two types: preconditions (circumstances that hold prior to test case execution) and the actual inputs that were identified by some testing method
>Expected outputs, again of two types: postconditions and actual outputs

The output portion of a test case is frequently overlooked, which is unfortunate because this is often the hard part. Suppose, for example, you were testing software that determined an optimal route for an aircraft, given certain FAA air corridor constraints and the weather data for a flight day. How would you know what the optimal route really is? Various responses can address this problem. The academic response is to postulate the existence of an oracle who "knows all the answers." One industrial response to this problem is known as reference testing, where the system is tested in the presence of expert users. These experts make judgments as to whether outputs of an executed set of test case inputs are acceptable.

The act of testing entails establishing the necessary preconditions, providing the test case inputs, observing the outputs, comparing these with the expected outputs, and then ensuring that the expected postconditions exist to determine whether the test passed.

The remaining information (Figure 1.2) in a well-developed test case primarily supports testing management. Test cases should have an identity and a reason for being (requirements tracing is a fine reason). It is also useful to record the execution history of a test case, including when and by whom it was run, the pass/fail result of each execution, and the version (of software) on which it was run. From all of this it becomes clear that test cases are valuable — at least as valuable as source code. Test cases need to be developed, reviewed, used, managed, and saved.

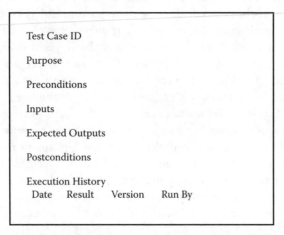

Figure 1.2   Typical test case information.

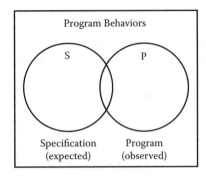

Figure 1.3   Specified and implemented program behaviors.

1.3   Insights from a Venn Diagram

Testing is fundamentally concerned with behavior, and behavior is orthogonal to the structural view common to software (and system) developers.

A quick differentiation is that the structural view focuses on what it is and the behavioral view considers what it does. One of the continuing sources of difficulty for testers is that the base documents are usually written by and for developers; the emphasis is therefore on structural, instead of behavioral, information. In this section, we develop a simple Venn diagram that clarifies several nagging questions about testing.

Consider a universe of program behaviors. (Notice that we are forcing attention on the essence of testing.) Given a program and its specification, consider the set S of specified behaviors and the set P of programmed behaviors. Figure 1.3 shows the relationship among our universe of discourse as well as the specified and programmed behaviors. Of all the possible program behaviors, the specified ones are in the circle labeled S, and all those behaviors actually programmed (note the slight difference between P and U, the universe) are in P. With this diagram, we can see more clearly the problems that confront a tester. What if certain specified behaviors have not been programmed? In our earlier terminology, these are faults of omission. Similarly, what if certain programmed (implemented) behaviors have not been specified? These correspond to faults of commission and to errors that occurred after the specification was complete. The intersection of S and P (the football-shaped region) is the "correct" portion, that is, behaviors that are both specified and implemented. A very good view of testing is that it is the determination of the extent of program behavior that is both specified and implemented. (As an aside, note that correctness only has meaning with respect to a specification and an implementation. It is a relative term, not an absolute.)

The new circle in Figure 1.4 is for test cases. Notice the slight discrepancy with our universe of discourse and the set of program behaviors. Because a test case causes a program behavior, the mathematicians might forgive us. Now, consider the relationships among the sets S, P, and T. There may be specified behaviors that are not tested (regions 2 and 5), specified behaviors that are tested (regions 1 and 4), and test cases that correspond to unspecified behaviors (regions 3 and 7).

Similarly, there may be programmed behaviors that are not tested (regions 2 and 6), programmed behaviors that are tested (regions 1 and 3), and test cases that correspond to unprogrammed behaviors (regions 4 and 7). Each of these regions is important. If specified behaviors exist for which no test cases are available, the testing is necessarily incomplete. If certain test cases correspond to unspecified behaviors, some possibilities arise: either such a test case is unwarranted, the specification is deficient, or the tester wishes to determine that specified nonbehavior does not

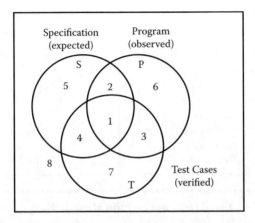

Figure 1.4 Specified, implemented, and tested behaviors.

occur. (In my experience, good testers often postulate test cases of this last type. This is a fine reason to have good testers participate in specification and design reviews.)

We are already at a point where we can see some possibilities for testing as a craft: What can a tester do to make the region where these sets all intersect (region 1) as large as possible? Another approach is to ask how the test cases in the set T are identified. The short answer is that test cases are identified by a testing method. This framework gives us a way to compare the effectiveness of diverse testing methods, as we shall see in Chapters 8 and 11.

1.4 Identifying Test Cases

Two fundamental approaches are used to identify test cases, known as functional and structural testing. Each of these approaches has several distinct test case identification methods, more commonly called testing methods.

1.4.1 Functional Testing

Functional testing is based on the view that any program can be considered to be a function that maps values from its input domain to values in its output range. (Function, domain, and range are defined in Chapter 3.) This notion is commonly used in engineering, when systems are considered to be black boxes. This leads to the term black box testing, in which the content (implementation) of a black box is not known, and the function of the black box is understood completely in terms of its inputs and outputs (see Figure 1.5). In *Zen and the Art of Motorcycle Maintenance*, Pirsig refers

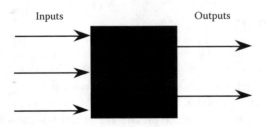

Figure 1.5 An engineer's black box.

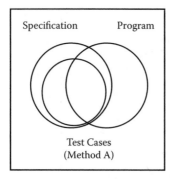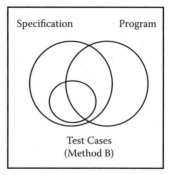

Figure 1.6 Comparing functional test case identification methods.

to this as "romantic" comprehension (Pirsig, 1973). Many times, we operate very effectively with black box knowledge; in fact, this is central to object orientation. As an example, most people successfully operate automobiles with only black box knowledge.

With the functional approach to test case identification, the only information used is the specification of the software.

Functional test cases have two distinct advantages: (1) they are independent of how the software is implemented, so if the implementation changes, the test cases are still useful; and (2) test case development can occur in parallel with the implementation, thereby reducing the overall project development interval. On the negative side, functional test cases frequently suffer from two problems: significant redundancies may exist among test cases, compounded by the possibility of gaps of untested software.

Figure 1.6 shows the results of test cases identified by two functional methods. Method A identifies a larger set of test cases than does Method B. Notice that, for both methods, the set of test cases is completely contained within the set of specified behavior. Because functional methods are based on the specified behavior, it is hard to imagine these methods identifying behaviors that are not specified. In Chapter 8, we will see direct comparisons of test cases generated by various functional methods for the examples defined in Chapter 2.

In Part II, we will examine the mainline approaches to functional testing, including boundary value analysis, robustness testing, worst-case analysis, special value testing, input (domain) equivalence classes, output (range) equivalence classes, and decision table-based testing. The common thread running through these techniques is that all are based on definitional information of the item tested. The mathematical background presented in Chapter 3 applies primarily to the functional approaches.

1.4.2 Structural Testing

Structural testing is the other fundamental approach to test case identification. To contrast it with functional testing, it is sometimes called white box (or even clear box) testing. The clear box metaphor is probably more appropriate, because the essential difference is that the implementation (of the black box) is known and used to identify test cases. The ability to "see inside" the black box allows the tester to identify test cases based on how the function is actually implemented.

Structural testing has been the subject of some fairly strong theory. To really understand structural testing, familiarity with the concepts of linear graph theory (Chapter 4) is essential.

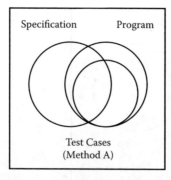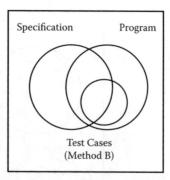

Figure 1.7   Comparing structural test case identification methods.

With these concepts, the tester can rigorously describe exactly what is tested. Because of its strong theoretical basis, structural testing lends itself to the definition and use of test coverage metrics. Test coverage metrics provide a way to explicitly state the extent to which a software item has been tested, and this in turn makes testing management more meaningful.

Figure 1.7 shows the results of test cases identified by two structural methods. As before, Method A identifies a larger set of test cases than does Method B. Is a larger set of test cases necessarily better? This is an excellent question, and structural testing provides important ways to develop an answer. Notice that, for both methods, the set of test cases is completely contained within the set of programmed behavior. Because structural methods are based on the program, it is hard to imagine these methods identifying behaviors that are not programmed. It is easy to imagine, however, that a set of structural test cases is relatively small with respect to the full set of programmed behaviors. In Chapter 11 we will see direct comparisons of test cases generated by various structural methods.

1.4.3 The Functional versus Structural Debate

Given two fundamentally different approaches to test case identification, it is natural to question which is better. If you read much of the literature, you will find strong adherents to either choice. Referring to structural testing, Robert Poston writes, "This tool has been wasting tester's time since the 1970s … [it] does not support good software testing practice and should not be in the tester's toolkit" (Poston, 1991). In defense of structural testing, Edward Miller writes, "Branch coverage [a structural test coverage metric], if attained at the 85% or better level, tends to identify twice the number of defects that would have been found by 'intuitive' [functional] testing" (Miller, 1991).

The Venn diagrams presented earlier yield a strong resolution to this debate. Recall that the goal of both approaches is to identify test cases. Functional testing uses only the specification to identify test cases, while structural testing uses the program source code (implementation) as the basis of test case identification. Our earlier discussion forces the conclusion that neither approach alone is sufficient. Consider program behaviors: if all specified behaviors have not been implemented, structural test cases will never be able to recognize this. Conversely, if the program implements behaviors that have not been specified, this will never be revealed by functional test cases. (A Trojan horse is a good example of such unspecified behavior.) The quick answer is that both approaches are needed; the testing craftsperson's answer is that a judicious combination will provide the confidence of functional testing and the measurement of structured testing. Earlier,

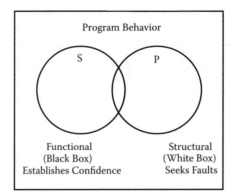

Figure 1.8 Sources of test cases.

we asserted that functional testing often suffers from twin problems of redundancies and gaps. When functional test cases are executed in combination with structural test coverage metrics, both of these problems can be recognized and resolved (see Figure 1.8).

The Venn diagram view of testing provides one final insight. What is the relationship between the set T of test cases and the sets S and P of specified and implemented behaviors? Clearly, the test cases in T are determined by the test case identification method used. A very good question to ask is how appropriate (or effective) is this method? To close a loop from an earlier discussion, recall the causal trail from error to fault, failure, and incident. If we know what kind of errors we are prone to make, and if we know what kinds of faults are likely to reside in the software to be tested, we can use this to employ more appropriate test case identification methods. This is the point at which testing really becomes a craft.

1.5 Error and Fault Taxonomies

Our definitions of error and fault hinge on the distinction between process and product: process refers to how we do something, and product is the end result of a process. The point at which testing and software quality assurance (SQA) meet is that SQA typically tries to improve the product by improving the process. In that sense, testing is clearly more product oriented. SQA is more concerned with reducing errors endemic in the development process, while testing is more concerned with discovering faults in a product. Both disciplines benefit from a clearer definition of types of faults.

Faults can be classified in several ways: the development phase in which the corresponding error occurred, the consequences of corresponding failures, difficulty to resolve, risk of no resolution, and so on. My favorite is based on anomaly occurrence: one time only, intermittent, recurring, or repeatable. Figure 1.9 contains a fault taxonomy (Beizer, 1984) that distinguishes faults by the severity of their consequences.

For a comprehensive treatment of types of faults, see the *IEEE Standard Classification for Software Anomalies* (IEEE, 1993). (A software anomaly is defined in that document as "a departure from the expected," which is pretty close to our definition.) The IEEE standard defines a detailed anomaly resolution process built around four phases (another life cycle): recognition, investigation, action, and disposition. Some of the more useful anomalies are given in Table 1.1 through Table 1.5; most of these are from the IEEE standard, but I have added some of my favorites.

1. Mild	Misspelled word
2. Moderate	Misleading or redundant information
3. Annoying	Truncated names, bill for $0.00
4. Disturbing	Some transaction(s) not processed
5. Serious	Lose a transaction
6. Very serious	Incorrect transaction execution
7. Extreme	Frequent "very serious" errors
8. Intolerable	Database corruption
9. Catastrophic	System shutdown
10. Infectious	Shutdown that spreads to others

Figure 1.9 **Faults classified by severity. (From Beizer, B.,** *Software System Testing and Quality Assurance*, **Van Nostrand Reinhold, New York, 1984.)**

Table 1.1 Input/Output Faults

Type	Instances
Input	Correct input not accepted
	Incorrect input accepted
	Description wrong or missing
	Parameters wrong or missing
Output	Wrong format
	Wrong result
	Correct result at wrong time (too early, too late)
	Incomplete or missing result
	Spurious result
	Spelling/grammar
	Cosmetic

Table 1.2 Logic Faults

Missing case(s)
Duplicate case(s)
Extreme condition neglected
Misinterpretation
Missing condition
Extraneous condition(s)
Test of wrong variable
Incorrect loop iteration
Wrong operator (e.g., < instead of ≤)

Table 1.3   Computation Faults

Incorrect algorithm
Missing computation
Incorrect operand
Incorrect operation
Parenthesis error
Insufficient precision (round-off, truncation)
Wrong built-in function

Table 1.4   Interface Faults

Incorrect interrupt handling
I/O timing
Call to wrong procedure
Call to nonexistent procedure
Parameter mismatch (type, number)
Incompatible types
Superfluous inclusion

Table 1.5   Data Faults

Incorrect initialization
Incorrect storage/access
Wrong flag/index value
Incorrect packing/unpacking
Wrong variable used
Wrong data reference
Scaling or units error
Incorrect data dimension
Incorrect subscript
Incorrect type
Incorrect data scope
Sensor data out of limits
Off by one
Inconsistent data

1.6   Levels of Testing

Thus far, we have said nothing about one of the key concepts of testing — levels of abstraction. Levels of testing echo the levels of abstraction found in the waterfall model of the software development life cycle. Although this model has its drawbacks, it is useful for testing as a means of identifying distinct levels of testing and for clarifying the objectives that pertain to each level. A

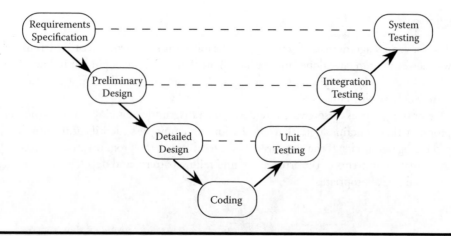

Figure 1.10   Levels of abstraction and testing in the waterfall model.

diagrammatic variation of the waterfall model is given in Figure 1.10; this variation emphasizes the correspondence between testing and design levels. Notice that, especially in terms of functional testing, the three levels of definition (specification, preliminary design, and detailed design) correspond directly to three levels of testing — system, integration, and unit testing.

A practical relationship exists between levels of testing versus functional and structural testing. Most practitioners agree that structural testing is most appropriate at the unit level, while functional testing is most appropriate at the system level. This is generally true, but it is also a likely consequence of the base information produced during the requirements specification, preliminary design, and detailed design phases. The constructs defined for structural testing make the most sense at the unit level, and similar constructs are only now becoming available for the integration and system levels of testing. We develop such structures in Part IV to support structural testing at the integration and system levels for both traditional and object-oriented software.

References

Beizer, B., *Software System Testing and Quality Assurance*, Van Nostrand Reinhold, New York, 1984.

IEEE Computer Society, *IEEE Standard Glossary of Software Engineering Terminology*, 1983, ANSI/IEEE Std. 729-1983.

IEEE Computer Society, *IEEE Standard Classification for Software Anomalies*, 1993, IEEE Std. 1044-1993.

Miller, E.F., Jr., Automated software testing: a technical perspective, *American Programmer*, Vol. 4, No. 4, April 1991, pp. 38–43.

Pirsig, R.M., *Zen and the Art of Motorcycle Maintenance*, Bantam Books, New York, 1973.

Poston, R.M., *T: Automated Software Testing Workshop*, Programming Environments, Inc., Tinton Falls, NJ, 1990.

Poston, R.M., A complete toolkit for the software tester, *American Programmer*, Vol. 4, No. 4, April 1991, pp. 28–37. Reprinted in CrossTalk, a USAF publication.

Exercises

1. Make a Venn diagram that reflects a part of the following statement: "We have left undone that which we ought to have done, and we have done that which we ought not to have done."
2. Describe each of the eight regions in Figure 1.4. Can you recall examples of these in software you have written?
3. One of the folktales of software lore describes a disgruntled employee who writes a payroll program that contains logic that checks for the employee's identification number before producing paychecks. If the employee is ever terminated, the program creates havoc. Discuss this situation in terms of the error, fault, and failure pattern, and decide which form of testing would be appropriate.

Chapter 2

Examples

Three examples will be used throughout Parts II and III to illustrate the various unit testing methods. They are the triangle problem (a venerable example in testing circles); a logically complex function, NextDate; and an example that typifies Management Information Systems (MIS) applications, known here as the commission problem. Taken together, these examples raise most of the issues that testing craftspersons will encounter at the unit level. The discussion of integration and system testing in Part IV uses three other examples: a simplified version of an automated teller machine (ATM), known here as the simple ATM (SATM) system; the currency converter, an event-driven application typical of graphical user interface (GUI) applications; and the windshield wiper control device from the Saturn™ automobile. Finally, an object-oriented version of NextDate is provided, called o-oCalendar, which is used to illustrate aspects of testing object-oriented software in Part V.

For the purposes of structural testing, pseudocode implementations of the three unit-level examples are given in this chapter. System-level descriptions of the SATM system, the currency converter, and the Saturn windshield wiper system are given in Part IV. These applications are described both traditionally (with E/R diagrams, dataflow diagrams, and finite state machines) and with the de facto object-oriented standard, the Unified Modeling Language (UML), in Part V.

2.1 Generalized Pseudocode

Pseudocode provides a "language neutral" way to express program source code. This version is loosely based on Visual Basic and has constructs at two levels: unit and program components. Units can be interpreted either as traditional components (procedures and functions) or as object-oriented components (classes and objects). This definition is somewhat informal; terms such as *expression, variable list,* and *field description* are used with no formal definition. Items in angle brackets indicate language elements that can be used at the identified positions. Part of the value of any pseudocode is the suppression of unwanted detail; here, we illustrate this by allowing natural language phrases in place of more formal, complex conditions (see Table 2.1).

Table 2.1 Generalized Pseudocode

Language Element	Generalized Pseudocode Construct
Comment	` <text>
Data structure declaration	Type <type name><list of field descriptions>End <type name>
Data declaration	Dim <variable> As <type>
Assignment statement	<variable> = <expression>
Input	Input (<variable list>)
Output	Output (<variable list>)
Condition	<expression> <relational operator> <expression>
Compound condition	<Condition> <logical connective> <Condition>
Sequence	Statements in sequential order
Simple selection	If <condition> Then <then clause>EndIf
Selection	If <condition>

Multiple selection	Case <variable> Of
	    Case 1: <predicate>
	      <Case clause>
	
	    …
	    Case n: <predicate>
	      <Case clause>
	EndCase

Counter-controlled repetition	For <counter> = <start> To <end>
Pretest repetition	While <condition> … End While
Posttest repetition	Do … until <condition>
Procedure definition (similarly for functions and o-o methods)	<procedure name>(Input: <list of variables>;Output: <list of variables>)
Interunit communication	Call <procedure name> (<list of variables>; <list of variables>)
Class/object definition	<name> (<attribute list>; <method list>, <body>)End <name>
Interunit communication	msg <destination object name>.<method name> (<list of variables>)
Object creation	Instantiate <class name>.<object name> (list of attribute values)
Object destruction	Delete <class name>.<object name>
Program	Program <program name>

2.2 The Triangle Problem

The triangle problem is the most widely used example in software testing literature. Some of the more notable entries in three decades of testing literature are Gruenberger (1973), Brown and Lipov (1975), Myers (1979), Pressman (1982, and subsequent editions), Clarke (1983, 1984), Chellappa (1987), and Hetzel (1988). There are others, but this list makes the point.

2.2.1 Problem Statement

Simple version: The triangle program accepts three integers, a, b, and c, as input. These are taken to be sides of a triangle. The output of the program is the type of triangle determined by the three sides: Equilateral, Isosceles, Scalene, or Not A Triangle. Sometimes this problem is extended to include right triangles as a fifth type; we will use this extension in some of the exercises.

Improved version: The triangle program accepts three integers, a, b, and c, as input. These are taken to be sides of a triangle. The integers a, b, and c must satisfy the following conditions:

c1. $1 \leq a \leq 200$ c4. $a < b + c$
c2. $1 \leq b \leq 200$ c5. $b < a + c$
c3. $1 \leq c \leq 200$ c6. $c < a + b$

The output of the program is the type of triangle determined by the three sides: Equilateral, Isosceles, Scalene, or NotATriangle. If an input value fails any of conditions c1, c2, or c3, the program notes this with an output message, for example, "Value of b is not in the range of permitted values." If values of a, b, and c satisfy conditions c1, c2, and c3, one of four mutually exclusive outputs is given:

1. If all three sides are equal, the program output is Equilateral.
2. If exactly one pair of sides is equal, the program output is Isosceles.
3. If no pair of sides is equal, the program output is Scalene.
4. If any of conditions c4, c5, and c6 is not met, the program output is NotATriangle.

2.2.2 Discussion

Perhaps one of the reasons for the longevity of this example is that it contains clear but complex logic. It also typifies some of the incomplete definitions that impair communication among customers, developers, and testers. The first specification presumes the developers know some details about triangles, particularly the triangle inequality: the sum of any pair of sides must be strictly greater than the third side. The upper limit of 200 is both arbitrary and convenient; it will be used when we develop boundary value test cases in Chapter 5.

2.2.3 Traditional Implementation

The "traditional" implementation of this grandfather of all examples has a rather Fortran-like style. The flowchart for this implementation appears in Figure 2.1. The flowchart box numbers correspond to comment numbers in the (Fortran-like) pseudocode program given next. (These numbers correspond exactly to those in Pressman (1982).) I do not really like this implementation very much, so a more structured implementation is given in Section 2.2.4.

```
Program triangle1 'Fortran-like version
'
Dim a,b,c,match As INTEGER
'
Output("Enter 3 integers which are sides of a triangle")
Input(a,b,c)
Output("Side A is ",a)
Output("Side B is ",b)
Output("Side C is ",c)
match = 0
If a = b                                                 '(1)
   Then match = match + 1                                '(2)
EndIf
```

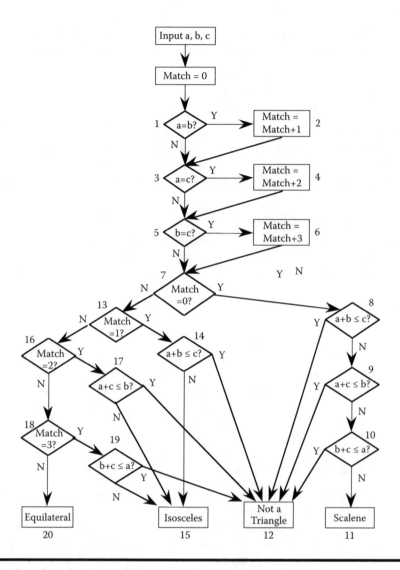

Figure 2.1 Flowchart for the traditional triangle program implementation.

```
If a = c                                                        '(3)
   Then match = match + 2                                       '(4)
EndIf
If b = c                                                        '(5)
   Then match = match + 3                                       '(6)
EndIf
If match = 0                                                    '(7)
   Then    If (a+b)<=c                                          '(8)
      Then    Output ("NotATriangle")                        '(12.1)
      Else    If (b+c)<=a                                       '(9)
         Then    Output ("NotATriangle")                     '(12.2)
```

```
      Else       If (a+c)<=b                                    '(10)
            Then       Output ("NotATriangle")                  '(12.3)
            Else        Output ("Scalene")                      '(11)
                  EndIf
            EndIf
         EndIf
Else   If match=1                                               '(13)
   Then       If (a+c) <=b                                      '(14)
         Then       Output ("NotATriangle")                     '(12.4)
         Else       Output ("Isosceles")                        '(15.1)
      EndIf
   Else       If match=2                                        '(16)
            Then   If (a+c)<=b
                  Then  Output ("NotATriangle")                 '(12.5)
                  Else  Output ("Isosceles")                    '(15.2)
                  EndIf
            Else   If match=3                                   '(18)
                  Then   If (b+c)<=a                            '(19)
                        Then  Output ("NotATriangle") '(12.6)
                        Else  Output ("Isosceles") '  '(15.3)
                        EndIf
                  Else  Output ("Equilateral")                  '(20)
                  EndIf
            EndIf
      EndIf
EndIf
'
End Triangle1
```

The variable "match" is used to record equality among pairs of the sides. A classical intricacy of the Fortran style is connected with the variable "match": notice that all three tests for the triangle inequality do not occur. If two sides are equal, say, a and c, it is only necessary to compare a + c with b. (Because b must be greater than zero, a + b must be greater than c, because c equals a.) This observation clearly reduces the number of comparisons that must be made. The efficiency of this version is obtained at the expense of clarity (and ease of testing). We will find this version useful later in Part III when we discuss infeasible program execution paths. That is the only reason for perpetuating this version.

Notice that six ways are used to reach the NotATriangle box (12.1 to 12.6), and three ways are used to reach the Isosceles box (15.1 to 15.3).

2.2.4 Structured Implementation

Figure 2.2 is a dataflow diagram description of the triangle program. We could implement it as a main program with the three indicated procedures. We will use this example later for unit testing; therefore, the three procedures have been merged into one pseudocode program. Comment lines relate sections of the code to the decomposition given in Figure 2.2.

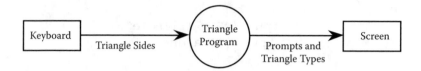

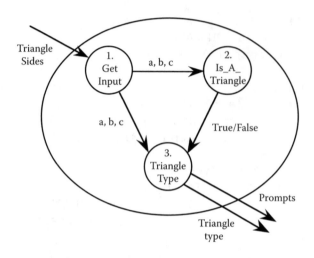

Figure 2.2   Dataflow diagram for a structured triangle program implementation.

```
Program triangle2 'Structured programming version of simpler
specification
'
Dim a,b,c As Integer
Dim IsATriangle As Boolean
'
'Step 1: Get Input
Output("Enter 3 integers which are sides of a triangle")
Input(a,b,c)
Output("Side A is ",a)
Output("Side B is ",b)
Output("Side C is ",c)
'
'Step 2: Is A Triangle?
If (a < b + c) AND (b < a + c) AND (c < a + b)
      Then IsATriangle = True
      Else IsATriangle = False
EndIf
'
'Step 3: Determine Triangle Type
If IsATriangle
```

```
      Then    If (a = b) AND (b = c)
                Then Output ("Equilateral")
                Else    If (a ≠ b) AND (a ≠ c) AND (b ≠ c)
                          Then    Output ("Scalene")
                          Else    Output ("Isosceles")
                        EndIf
              EndIf
      Else      Output ("Not a Triangle")
EndIf
'
End triangle2

Program triangle3 'Structured programming version of improved
specification
'
Dim a,b,c As Integer
Dim c1, c2, c3, IsATriangle As Boolean
'
'Step 1: Get Input
Do
      Output("Enter 3 integers which are sides of a triangle")
      Input(a,b,c)
      c1 = (1 <= a) AND (a <= 200)
      c2 = (1 <= b) AND (b <= 200)
      c3 = (1 <= c) AND (c <= 200)
      If NOT(c1)
        Then  Output("Value of a is not in the range of
        permitted values")
      EndIf
      If NOT (c2)
        Then  Output("Value of b is not in the range of
        permitted values")
      EndIf
      If NOT(c3)
        Then  Output ("Value of c is not in the range of
        permitted values")
      EndIf
Until c1 AND c2 AND c3
Output("Side A is ",a)
Output("Side B is ",b)
Output("Side C is ",c)
'
'Step 2: Is A Triangle?
If (a < (b + c)) AND (b < (a + c)) AND (c < (a + b))
      Then IsATriangle = True
      Else IsATriangle = False
EndIf
```

```
'
'Step 3: Determine Triangle Type
If IsATriangle
    Then  If (a = b) AND (b = c)
            Then Output ("Equilateral")
            Else  If (a ≠ b) AND (a ≠ c) AND (b ≠ c)
                    Then  Output ("Scalene")
                    Else  Output ("Isosceles")
                  EndIf
         EndIf
    Else  Output ("Not a Triangle")
EndIf
'
End triangle3
```

2.3 The NextDate Function

The complexity in the triangle program is due to relationships between inputs and correct outputs. We will use the NextDate function to illustrate a different kind of complexity — logical relationships among the input variables.

2.3.1 Problem Statement

NextDate is a function of three variables: month, day, and year. It returns the date of the day after the input date. The month, day, and year variables have integer values subject to these conditions:

c1.	$1 \leq month \leq 12$	
c2.	$1 \leq day \leq 31$	
c3.	$1812 \leq year \leq 2012$	

As we did with the triangle program, we can make our specification stricter. This entails defining responses for invalid values of the input values for the day, month, and year. We can also define responses for invalid combinations of inputs, such as June 31 of any year. If any of conditions c1, c2, or c3 fails, NextDate produces an output indicating the corresponding variable has an out-of-range value — for example, "Value of month not in the range 1..12." Because numerous invalid day-month-year combinations exist, NextDate collapses these into one message: "Invalid Input Date."

2.3.2 Discussion

Two sources of complexity exist in the NextDate function: the complexity of the input domain discussed previously, and the rule that determines when a year is a leap year. A year is 365.2422 days long; therefore, leap years are used for the "extra day" problem. If we declared a leap year every fourth year, a slight error would occur. The Gregorian calendar (after Pope Gregory) resolves this by adjusting leap years on century years. Thus, a year is a leap year if it is divisible by 4, unless it is a century year. Century years are leap years only if they are multiples of 400 (Inglis, 1961), so 1992, 1996, and 2000 are leap years, while the year 1900 is not. The NextDate function also illustrates a sidelight of software testing. Many times, we find examples of Zipf's law, which states that 80% of the activity occurs in 20% of the space. Notice how much of the source code is devoted to leap year considerations. In the second implementation, notice how much code is devoted to input value validation.

2.3.3 Implementation

```
Program NextDate1        'Simple version
'
Dim tomorrowDay,tomorrowMonth,tomorrowYear As Integer
Dim day,month,year As Integer
'
Output ("Enter today's date in the form MM DD YYYY")
Input (month,day,year)
Case month Of
Case 1: month Is 1,3,5,7,8, Or 10: '31 day months (except Dec.)
   If day < 31
     Then tomorrowDay = day + 1
     Else
        tomorrowDay = 1
        tomorrowMonth = month + 1
   EndIf
Case 2: month Is 4,6,9, Or 11 '30 day months
   If day < 30
     Then tomorrowDay = day + 1
     Else
        tomorrowDay = 1
        tomorrowMonth = month + 1
   EndIf
Case 3: month Is 12: 'December
   If day < 31
     Then tomorrowDay = day + 1
     Else
        tomorrowDay = 1
        tomorrowMonth = 1
        If year = 2012
           Then Output ("2012 is over")
           Else tomorrow.year = year + 1
        EndIf
   EndIf
Case 4: month is 2: 'February
   If day < 28
     Then tomorrowDay = day + 1
     Else
        If day = 28
          Then
             If ((year is a leap year)
                Then tomorrowDay = 29 'leap year
```

```
                    Else    'not a leap year
                        tomorrowDay = 1
                        tomorrowMonth = 3
              EndIf
          Else  If day = 29
                  Then tomorrowDay = 1
                       tomorrowMonth = 3
                  Else Output ("Cannot have Feb.", day)
              EndIf
          EndIf
      EndIf
EndCase
Output ("Tomorrow's date is", tomorrowMonth, tomorrowDay,
tomorrowYear)
'
End NextDate

Program NextDate2       Improved version
'
Dim tomorrowDay,tomorrowMonth, tomorrowYear As Integer
Dim day,month,year As Integer
Dim c1, c2, c3 As Boolean
'
Do
    Output ("Enter today's date in the form MM DD YYYY")
    Input (month,day,year)
    c1 = (1 <= day) AND (day <= 31)
    c2 = (1 <= month) AND (month <= 12)
    c3 = (1812 <= year) AND (year <= 2012)
    If NOT(c1)
      Then      Output ("Value of day not in the range 1..31")
    EndIf
    If NOT (c2)
    EndIf
      Then      Output ("Value of month not in the range 1..12")
    If NOT(c3)
      Then   Output ("Value of year not in the range 1812..2012")
    EndIf
Until c1 AND c2 AND c3
Case month Of
Case 1: month Is 1,3,5,7,8, Or 10: '31 day months (except Dec.)
    If day < 31
      Then tomorrowDay = day + 1
      Else
         tomorrowDay = 1
         tomorrowMonth = month + 1
    EndIf
```

```
Case 2: month Is 4,6,9, Or 11 '30 day months
   If day < 30
      Then tomorrowDay = day + 1
      Else
         If day =30
            Then  tomorrowDay = 1
                     tomorrowMonth = month + 1
            Else  Output ("Invalid Input Date")
         EndIf
   EndIf
Case 3: month Is 12: 'December
   If day < 31
      Then tomorrowDay = day + 1
      Else
         tomorrowDay = 1
         tomorrowMonth = 1
         If year = 2012
           Then Output ("Invalid Input Date")
           Else tomorrow.year = year + 1
         EndIf
   EndIf
Case 4: month is 2: 'February
   If day < 28
      Then tomorrowDay = day + 1
      Else
         If day = 28
            Then
               If (year is a leap year)
               Then tomorrowDay = 29 'leap day
               Else  'not a leap year
                  tomorrowDay = 1
                     tomorrowMonth = 3
               EndIf
            Else
               If day = 29
                  Then
                     If (Year is a leap year)
                        Then tomorrowDay = 1
                             tomorrowMonth = 3
                  Else
                     If day > 29
                        Then Output ("Invalid Input Date")
                     EndIf
                  EndIf
               EndIf
            EndIf
   EndIf
```

```
EndCase
Output ("Tomorrow's date is", tomorrowMonth, tomorrowDay,
tomorrowYear)
'
End NextDate2
```

2.4 The Commission Problem

Our third example is more typical of commercial computing. It contains a mix of computation and decision making, so it leads to interesting testing questions.

2.4.1 Problem Statement

A rifle salesperson in the former Arizona Territory sold rifle locks, stocks, and barrels made by a gunsmith in Missouri. Locks cost $45, stocks cost $30, and barrels cost $25. The salesperson had to sell at least one complete rifle per month, and production limits were such that the most the salesperson could sell in a month was 70 locks, 80 stocks, and 90 barrels. After each town visit, the salesperson sent a telegram to the Missouri gunsmith with the number of locks, stocks, and barrels sold in that town. At the end of a month, the salesperson sent a very short telegram showing –1 lock sold. The gunsmith then knew the sales for the month were complete and computed the salesperson's commission as follows: 10% on sales up to (and including) $1000, 15% on the next $800, and 20% on any sales in excess of $1800. The commission program produced a monthly sales report that gave the total number of locks, stocks, and barrels sold, the salesperson's total dollar sales, and, finally, the commission.

2.4.2 Discussion

This example is somewhat contrived to make the arithmetic quickly visible to the reader. It might be more realistic to consider some other additive function of several variables, such as various calculations found in filling out a U.S. 1040 income tax form. (We will stay with rifles.) This problem separates into three distinct pieces: the input data portion, in which we could deal with input data validation (as we did for the triangle and NextDate programs); the sales calculation; and the commission calculation portion. This time, we will omit the input data validation portion. We will replicate the telegram convention with a sentinel-controlled While loop that is typical of MIS data gathering applications.

2.4.3 Implementation

```
Program Commission (INPUT,OUTPUT)
'
Dim locks, stocks, barrels As Integer
Dim lockPrice, stockPrice, barrelPrice As Real
Dim totalLocks, totalStocks,totalBarrels As Integer
Dim lockSales, stockSales, barrelSales As Real
Dim sales,commission : REAL
'
lockPrice = 45.0
stockPrice = 30.0
```

```
barrelPrice = 25.0
totalLocks = 0
totalStocks = 0
totalBarrels = 0
`
Input(locks)
While NOT(locks = -1)    'Input device uses -1 to indicate end of
data
    Input(stocks, barrels)
    totalLocks = totalLocks + locks
    totalStocks = totalStocks + stocks
    totalBarrels = totalBarrels + barrels
    Input(locks)
EndWhile
`
Output("Locks sold: ", totalLocks)
Output("Stocks sold: ", totalStocks)
Output("Barrels sold: ",totalBarrels)
`
lockSales = lockPrice * totalLocks
stockSales = stockPrice * totalStocks
barrelSales = barrelPrice * totalBarrels
sales = lockSales + stockSales + barrelSales
Output("Total sales: ", sales)
`
If (sales > 1800.0)
    Then
        commission = 0.10 * 1000.0
        commission = commission + 0.15 * 800.0
        commission = commission + 0.20 *(sales-1800.0)
    Else If (sales > 1000.0)
            Then
                commission = 0.10 * 1000.0
                commission = commission + 0.15*(sales-1000.0)
            Else commission = 0.10 * sales
          EndIf
EndIf
Output("Commission is $",commission)
`
End Commission
```

2.5   The SATM System

To better discuss the issues of integration and system testing, we need an example with larger scope. The automated teller machine described here is a refinement of that in Topper (1993); it contains an interesting variety of functionality and interactions that typify the client side of client/server systems.

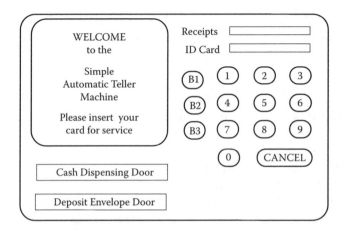

Figure 2.3　The SATM terminal.

2.5.1　*Problem Statement*

The SATM system communicates with bank customers via the 15 screens shown in Figure 2.4. Using a terminal with features as shown in Figure 2.3, SATM customers can select any of three transaction types: deposits, withdrawals, and balance inquiries. These transactions can be done on two types of accounts: checking and savings.

When a bank customer arrives at an SATM station, screen 1 is displayed. The bank customer accesses the SATM system with a plastic card encoded with a personal account number (PAN), which is a key to an internal customer account file, containing, among other things, the customer's name and account information. If the customer's PAN matches the information in the customer account file, the system presents screen 2 to the customer. If the customer's PAN is not found, screen 4 is displayed, and the card is kept.

At screen 2, the customer is prompted to enter his or her personal identification number (PIN). If the PIN is correct (i.e., matches the information in the customer account file), the system displays screen 5; otherwise, screen 3 is displayed. The customer has three chances to get the PIN correct; after three failures, screen 4 is displayed, and the card is kept.

On entry to screen 5, the system adds two pieces of information to the customer's account file: the current date and an increment to the number of ATM sessions. The customer selects the desired transaction from the options shown on screen 5; then the system immediately displays screen 6, where the customer chooses the account to which the selected transaction will be applied.

If balance is requested, the system checks the local ATM file for any unposted transactions and reconciles these with the beginning balance for that day from the customer account file. Screen 14 is then displayed.

If a deposit is requested, the status of the deposit envelope slot is determined from a field in the terminal control file. If no problem is known, the system displays screen 7 to get the transaction amount. If a problem occurs with the deposit envelope slot, the system displays screen 12. Once the deposit amount has been entered, the system displays screen 13, accepts the deposit envelope, and processes the deposit. The deposit amount is entered as an unposted amount in the local ATM file, and the count of deposits per month is incremented. Both of these (and other information) are processed by the master ATM (centralized) system once a day. The system then displays screen 14.

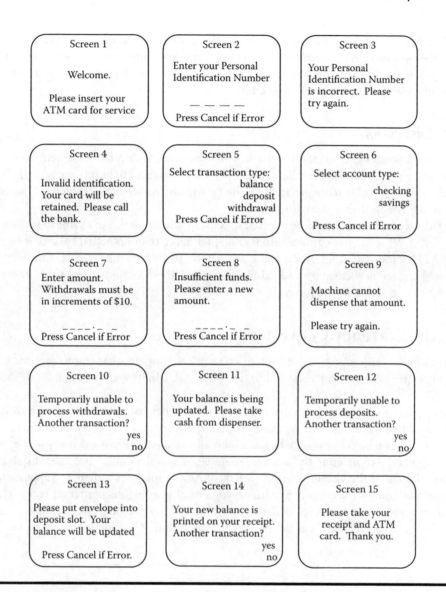

Figure 2.4   SATM screens.

If a withdrawal is requested, the system checks the status (jammed or free) of the withdrawal chute in the terminal control file. If jammed, screen 10 is displayed; otherwise, screen 7 is displayed so the customer can enter the withdrawal amount. Once the withdrawal amount is entered, the system checks the terminal status file to see if it has enough money to dispense. If it does not, screen 9 is displayed; otherwise, the withdrawal is processed. The system checks the customer balance (as described in the balance request transaction); if the funds are insufficient, screen 8 is displayed. If the account balance is sufficient, screen 11 is displayed and the money is dispensed. The withdrawal amount is written to the unposted local ATM file, and the count of withdrawals per month is incremented. The balance is printed on the transaction receipt as it is for a balance request transaction. After the cash has been removed, the system displays screen 14.

When the "No" button is pressed in screen 10, 12, or 14, the system presents screen 15 and returns the customer's ATM card. Once the card is removed from the card slot, screen 1 is displayed. When the "Yes" button is pressed in screen 10, 12, or 14, the system presents screen 5 so the customer can select additional transactions.

2.5.2 Discussion

A surprising amount of information is "buried" in the system description just given. For instance, if you read it closely, you can infer that the terminal only contains $10 bills (see screen 7). This textual definition is probably more precise than what is usually encountered in practice. The example is deliberately simple (hence the name).

A plethora of questions could be resolved by a list of assumptions. For example: Is there a borrowing limit? What keeps a customer from taking out more than his actual balance if he goes to several ATM terminals? A lot of start-up questions are used: How much cash is initially in the machine? How are new customers added to the system? These and other real-world refinements are eliminated to maintain simplicity.

2.6 The Currency Converter

The currency conversion program is another event-driven program that emphasizes code associated with a graphical user interface (GUI). A sample GUI built with Visual Basic is shown in Figure 2.5.

The application converts U.S. dollars to any of four currencies: Brazilian reals, Canadian dollars, European Union euros, and Japanese yen. Currency selection is governed by the radio buttons (Visual Basic option buttons), which are mutually exclusive. When a country is selected, the system responds by completing the label; for example, "Equivalent in ..." becomes "Equivalent in Canadian dollars" if the Canada button is clicked. Also, a small Canadian flag appears next to the output position for the equivalent currency amount. Either before or after currency selection, the user inputs an amount in U.S. dollars. Once both tasks are accomplished, the user can click on the Compute button, the Clear button, or the Quit button. Clicking on the Compute button

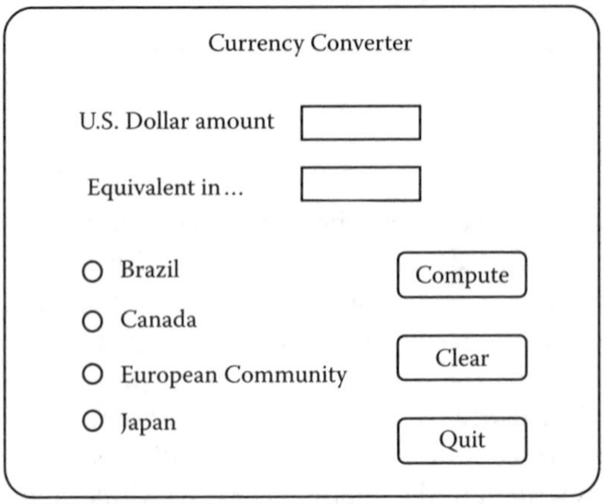

Figure 2.5 Currency converter GUI.

results in the conversion of the U.S. dollar amount to the equivalent amount in the selected currency. Clicking on the Clear button resets the currency selection, the U.S. dollar amount, and the equivalent currency amount and the associated label. Clicking on the Quit button ends the application. This example nicely illustrates a description with UML and an object-oriented implementation we will use in Part V.

2.7 Saturn Windshield Wiper Controller

The windshield wiper on some Saturn automobiles is controlled by a lever with a dial. The lever has four positions — OFF, INT (for intermittent), LOW, and HIGH — and the dial has three positions, numbered simply 1, 2, and 3. The dial positions indicate three intermittent speeds, and the dial position is relevant only when the lever is at the INT position. The decision table below shows the windshield wiper speeds (in wipes per minute) for the lever and dial positions.

c1.	Lever	OFF	INT	INT	INT	LOW	HIGH
c2.	Dial	n/a	1	2	3	n/a	n/a
a1.	Wiper	0	4	6	12	30	60

We will use this example in our discussion of interaction testing in Chapter 15.

References

Brown, J.R. and Lipov, M., Testing for software reliability, *Proceedings of the International Symposium on Reliable Software*, Los Angeles, April 1975, pp. 518–527.

Chellappa, M., Nontraversible paths in a program, *IEEE Transactions on Software Engineering*, Vol. SE-13, No. 6, June 1987, pp. 751–756.

Clarke, L.A. and Richardson, D.J., The application of error sensitive strategies to debugging, *ACM SIGSOFT Software Engineering Notes*, Vol. 8, No. 4, August 1983.

Clarke, L.A. and Richardson, D.J., A reply to Foster's comment on "The Application of Error Sensitive Strategies to Debugging," *ACM SIGSOFT Software Engineering Notes*, Vol. 9, No. 1, January 1984.

Gruenberger, F., Program testing, the historical perspective, in *Program Test Methods*, William C. Hetzel, Ed., Prentice-Hall, New York, 1973, pp. 11–14.

Hetzel, B., *The Complete Guide to Software Testing*, 2nd ed., QED Information Sciences, Inc., Wellesley, MA, 1988.

Inglis, Stuart J., *Planets, Stars, and Galaxies*, 4th ed., John Wiley & Sons, New York, 1961.

Myers, G.J., *The Art of Software Testing*, Wiley Interscience, New York, 1979.

Pressman, R.S., *Software Engineering: A Practitioner's Approach*, McGraw-Hill, New York, 1982.

Topper, A. et al., *Structured Methods: Merging Models, Techniques, and CASE*, McGraw-Hill, New York, 1993.

Exercises

1. Revisit the traditional triangle program flowchart in Figure 2.1. Can the variable match ever have the value of 4? Of 5? Is it ever possible to "execute" the following sequence of numbered boxes: 1, 2, 5, 6?

2. Recall the discussion from Chapter 1 about the relationship between the specification and the implementation of a program. If you study the implementation of NextDate carefully, you will see a problem. Look at the CASE clause for 30-day months (4, 6, 9, 11). There is no special action for day = 31. Discuss whether this implementation is correct. Repeat this discussion for the treatment of values of day 29 in the CASE clause for February.

3. In Chapter 1, we mentioned that part of a test case is the expected output. What would you use as the expected output for a NextDate test case of June 31, 1812? Why?

4. One common addition to the triangle problem is to check for right triangles. Three sides constitute a right triangle if the Pythagorean relationship is satisfied: $c^2 = a^2 + b^2$. This change makes it convenient to require that the sides be presented in increasing order, i.e., $a \leq b \leq c$. Extend the Triangle3 program to include the right triangle feature. We will use this extension in the exercise sections in Parts II and III.

5. What will the Triangle2 program do for the sides −3, −3, 5? Discuss this in terms of the considerations we made in Chapter 1.

6. The function YesterDate is the inverse of NextDate. Given a month, day, year, YesterDate returns the date of the day before. Develop a program in your favorite language (or our generalized pseudocode) for YesterDate. We will also use this as a continuing exercise.

7. Part of the art of GUI design is to prevent user input errors. Event-driven applications are particularly vulnerable to input errors because events can occur in any order. As the given pseudocode definition stands, a user could enter a U.S. dollar amount and then click on the compute button without selecting a country. Similarly, a user could select a country and then click on the compute button without inputting a dollar amount. GUI designers use the concept of "forced navigation" to avoid such situations. In Visual Basic, this can be done using the visibility properties of various controls. Discuss how you could do this.

8. The CRC Press Web site (http://www.crcpress.com) contains some software supplements for this book. There is a series of exercises that I use in my graduate class in software testing; the first part of a continuing exercise is to use the naive.xls (runs in most versions of Microsoft Excel) program to test the Triangle, NextDate, and Commission problems. The spreadsheet lets you postulate test cases and then run them simply by clicking on the "Run Test Cases" button. As a start to becoming a testing craftsperson, use naive.xls to test our three examples in an intuitive (hence naive) way. There are faults inserted into each program. If (when) you find failures, try to hypothesize the underlying fault. Keep your results for comparison to ideas in Chapters 5, 6, and 9.

Chapter 3

Discrete Math for Testers

More than any other life cycle activity, testing lends itself to mathematical description and analysis. In this chapter and in the next, testers will find the mathematics they need. Following the craftsperson metaphor, the mathematical topics presented here are tools; a testing craftsperson should know how to use them well. With these tools, a tester gains rigor, precision, and efficiency—all of which improve testing. The "for testers" part of the chapter title is important: this chapter is written for testers who either have a sketchy math background or have forgotten some of the basics. Serious mathematicians (or maybe just those who take themselves seriously) will likely be annoyed by the informal discussion here. If you are already comfortable with the topics in this chapter, skip to the next chapter and start right in on graph theory.

In general, discrete mathematics is more applicable to functional testing, while graph theory pertains more to structural testing. "Discrete" raises a question: What might be indiscrete about mathematics? The mathematical antonym is continuous, as in calculus, which software developers (and testers) seldom use. Discrete math includes set theory, functions, relations, propositional logic, and probability theory, each of which is discussed here.

3.1 Set Theory

How embarrassing to admit, after all the lofty expiation of rigor and precision, that no explicit definition of a set exists. This is really a nuisance because set theory is central to these two chapters on math. At this point, mathematicians make an important distinction: naive versus axiomatic set theory. In naive set theory, a set is recognized as a primitive term, much like point and line are primitive concepts in geometry. Here are some synonyms for *set*: *collection, group, bunch* — you get the idea. The important thing about a set is that it lets us refer to several things as a group, or a whole. For example, we might wish to refer to the set of months that have exactly 30 days (we need this set when we test the NextDate function from Chapter 2). In set theory notation, we write:

M1 = {April, June, September, November}

and we read this notation as "M1 is the set whose elements are the months April, June, September, November."

3.1.1 Set Membership

The items in a set are called elements or members of the set, and this relationship is denoted by the symbol ∈. Thus, we could write April ∈ M1. When something is not a member of a set, we use the symbol ∉, so we might write December ∉ M1.

3.1.2 Set Definition

A set is defined in three ways: by simply listing its elements, by giving a decision rule, or by constructing a set from other sets. The listing option works well for sets with only a few elements as well as for sets in which the elements obey an obvious pattern. We used this method in defining M1 above. We might define the set of allowable years in the NextDate program as follows:

$$Y = \{1812, 1813, 1814, \ldots, 2011, 2012\}$$

When we define a set by listing its elements, the order of the elements is irrelevant. We will see why when we discuss set equality. The decision rule approach is more complicated, and this complexity carries both advantages and penalties. We could define the years for NextDate as

$$Y = \{year : 1812 \leq year \leq 2012\}$$

which reads "Y is the set of all years such that [the colon is "such that"] the years are between 1812 and 2012 inclusive." When a decision rule is used to define a set, the rule must be unambiguous. Given any possible value of year, we can therefore determine whether that year is in our set Y.

The advantage of defining sets with decision rules is that the unambiguity requirement forces clarity. Experienced testers have encountered "untestable requirements." Many times, the reason that such requirements cannot be tested boils down to an ambiguous decision rule. In our triangle program, for example, suppose we defined a set as follows:

$$N = \{t : t \text{ is a nearly equilateral triangle}\}$$

We might say that the triangle with sides (500, 500, 501) is an element of N, but how would we treat the triangles with sides (50, 50, 51) or (5, 5, 6)?

A second advantage of defining sets with decision rules is that we might be interested in sets where the elements are difficult to list. In the commission problem, for example, we might be interested in the following set:

$$S = \{sales : the 15\% commission rate applies to the total sale\}$$

We cannot easily write down the elements of this set, but given a particular value for sale, we can easily apply the decision rule.

The main disadvantage of decision rules is that they can become logically complex, particularly when they are expressed with the predicate calculus quantifiers ∃ ("there exists") and ∀ ("for all"). If everyone understands this notation, the precision is helpful. Too often customers are overwhelmed by statements with these quantifiers. A second problem with decision rules has to do with self-reference. This is interesting, but it really has very little application for testers.

The problem arises when a decision rule refers to itself, which is a circularity. As an example, the Barber of Seville "is the man who shaves everyone who does not shave himself."

3.1.3 The Empty Set

The empty set, denoted by the symbol ∅, occupies a special place in set theory. The empty set contains no elements. At this point, mathematicians will digress to prove a lot of facts about empty sets:

- The empty set is unique; that is, there cannot be two empty sets (we will take their word for it).
- ∅, {∅}, {{∅}}, are all different sets (we will not need this).

It is useful to note that when a set is defined by a decision rule that is always false, the set is empty. For instance,

$$\varnothing = \{ \text{year} : 2012 \leq \text{year} \leq 1812 \}$$

3.1.4 Venn Diagrams

Sets are commonly pictured by Venn diagrams, as in Chapter 1, when we discussed sets of specified and programmed behaviors. In a Venn diagram, a set is depicted as a circle; points in the interior of the circle correspond to elements of the set. Then, we might draw our set M1 of 30-day months as in Figure 3.1.

Venn diagrams communicate various set relationships in an intuitive way, but some picky questions arise. What about finite versus infinite sets? Both can be drawn as Venn diagrams; in the case of finite sets, we cannot assume that every interior point corresponds to a set element. We do not need to worry about this, but it is helpful to know the limitations. Sometimes, we will find it helpful to label specific elements.

Another sticking point has to do with the empty set. How do we show that a set, or maybe a portion of a set, is empty? The common answer is to shade empty regions, but this is often contradicted by other uses in which shading is used to highlight regions of interest. The best practice is to provide a legend that clarifies the intended meaning of shaded areas.

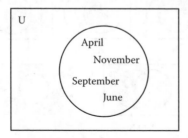

Figure 3.1   Venn diagram of the set of 30-day months.

It is often helpful to think of all the sets in a discussion as subsets of some larger set, known as the universe of discourse. We did this in Chapter 1 when we chose the set of all program behaviors as our universe of discourse. The universe of discourse can usually be guessed from given sets. In Figure 3.1, most people would take the universe of discourse to be the set of all months in a year. Testers should be aware that assumed universes of discourse are often sources of confusion. As such, they constitute a subtle point of miscommunication between customers and developers.

3.1.5 Set Operations

Much of the expressive power of set theory comes from basic operations on sets: union, intersection, and complement. Other handy operations are used: relative complement, symmetric difference, and Cartesian product. Each of these is defined next. In each of these definitions, we begin with two sets, A and B, contained in some universe of discourse U. The definitions use logical connectives from propositional calculus: and ($\wedge$), or ($\vee$), exclusive-or ($\oplus$), and not ($\neg$).

Definition
Given sets A and B,

> Their *union* is the set $A \cup B = \{x : x \in A \vee x \in B\}$
> Their *intersection* is the set $A \cap B = \{x : x \in A \wedge x \in B\}$
> The *complement* of A is the set $A' = \{x : x \notin A\}$
> The *relative complement of B with respect to A* is the set $A - B = \{x : x \in A \wedge x \notin B\}$
> The *symmetric difference of A and B* is the set $A \oplus B = \{x : x \in A \oplus x \in B\}$

Venn diagrams for these sets are shown in Figure 3.2.

The intuitive expressive power of Venn diagrams is very useful for describing relationships among test cases and among items to be tested. Looking at the Venn diagrams in Figure 3.2, we might guess that

$$A \oplus B = (A \cup B) - (A \cap B)$$

This is the case, and we could prove it with propositional logic.

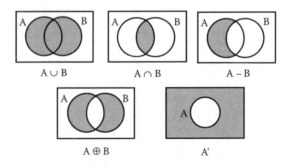

Figure 3.2   Venn diagrams of basic sets.

Venn diagrams are used elsewhere in software development: together with directed graphs, they are the basis of the StateCharts notation, which is among the most rigorous specification techniques supported by CASE technology. StateCharts are also the control notation chosen for the Unified Modeling Language (UML) from IBM Corp. and the Object Management Group.

The Cartesian product (also known as the cross-product) of two sets is more complex; it depends on the notion of ordered pairs, which are two element sets in which the order of the elements is important. The usual notation for unordered and ordered pairs is:

Unordered pair: (a, b)
Ordered pair: < a, b >

The difference is that, for a ≠ b,

$$(a, b) = (b, a)$$

but

$$< a, b > \neq < b, a >$$

This distinction is important to the material in Chapter 4; as we shall see, the fundamental difference between ordinary and directed graphs is exactly the difference between unordered and ordered pairs.

Definition

The *Cartesian product of two sets A and B* is the set

$$A \times B = \{<x, y> : x \in A \land y \in B\}$$

Venn diagrams do not show Cartesian products, so we will look at a short example. The Cartesian product of the sets A = {1, 2, 3} and B = {w, x, y, z} is the set

$$A \times B = \{<1, w>, <1, x>, <1, y>, <1, z>, <2, w>, <2, x>,$$
$$<2, y>, <2, z>, <3, w>, <3, x>, <3, y>, <3, z>\}$$

The Cartesian product has an intuitive connection with arithmetic. The cardinality of a set A is the number of elements in A and is denoted by |A|. (Some authors prefer Card(A).) For sets A and B, $|A \times B| = |A| \times |B|$. When we study functional testing in Chapter 5, we will use the Cartesian product to describe test cases for programs with several input variables. The multiplicative property of the Cartesian product means that this form of testing generates a very large number of test cases.

3.1.6 Set Relations

We use set operations to construct interesting new sets from existing sets. When we do, we often would like to know something about the way the new and the old sets are related. Given two sets, A and B, we define three fundamental set relationships:

Definition

A is a *subset* of B, written A ⊆ B, if and only if (iff) a ∈ A ⟹ a ∈ B
A is a *proper subset* of B, written A ⊂ B, iff A ⊆ B ∧ B − A ≠ ∅
A and B are *equal sets*, written A = B, iff A ⊆ B ∧ B ⊆ A

In plain English, set A is a subset of set B if every element of A is also an element of B. To be a proper subset of B, A must be a subset of B and there must be some element in B that is not an element of A. Finally, the sets A and B are equal if each is a subset of the other.

3.1.7 Set Partitions

A partition of a set is a very special situation that is extremely important for testers. Partitions have several analogs in everyday life: we might put up partitions to separate an office area into individual offices; we also encounter political partitions when a state is divided up into legislative districts. In both of these, notice that the sense of "partition" is to divide up a whole into pieces such that everything is in some piece and nothing is left out. More formally:

Definition

Given a set A, and a set of subsets $A_1, A_2, \ldots, A_n$ of A, the subsets are a *partition of A* iff

$$A_1 \cup A_2 \cup \ldots \cup A_n = A$$

and

$$i \neq j \Rightarrow A_i \cap A_j = \emptyset$$

Because a partition is a set of subsets, we frequently refer to individual subsets as elements of the partition.

The two parts of this definition are important for testers. The first part guarantees that every element of B is in some subset, while the second part guarantees that no element of B is in two of the subsets.

This corresponds well with the legislative districts example: everyone is represented by some legislator, and nobody is represented by two legislators. A jigsaw puzzle is another good example of a partition; in fact, Venn diagrams of partitions are often drawn like puzzles, as in Figure 3.3.

Partitions are helpful to testers because the two definitional properties yield important assurances: completeness (everything is somewhere) and nonredundancy. When we study functional

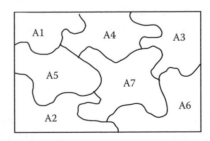

Figure 3.3   Venn diagram of a partition.

testing, we shall see that its inherent weakness is the vulnerability to both gaps and redundancies: some things may remain untested, while others are tested repeatedly. One of the difficulties of functional testing centers on finding an appropriate partition. In the triangle program, for example, the universe of discourse is the set of all triplets of positive integers. (Note that this is actually a Cartesian product of the set of positive integers with itself three times.) We might partition this universe three ways:

1. Into triangles and nontriangles
2. Into equilateral, isosceles, scalene, and nontriangles
3. Into equilateral, isosceles, scalene, right, and nontriangles

At first these partitions seem okay, but there is a problem with the last partition. The sets of scalene and right triangles are not disjoint (the triangle with sides 3, 4, 5 is a right triangle that is scalene).

3.1.8 Set Identities

Set operations and relations, when taken together, yield an important class of set identities that can be used to algebraically simplify complex set expressions. Math students usually have to derive all these; we will just list them and (occasionally) use them.

Name	Expression
Identity laws	$A \cup \varnothing = A$
	$A \cap U = A$
Domination laws	$A \cup U = U$
	$A \cap \varnothing = \varnothing$
Idempotent laws	$A \cup A = A$
	$A \cap A = A$
Complementation laws	$(A')' = A$
Commutative laws	$A \cup B = B \cup A$
	$A \cap B = B \cap A$
Associative laws	$A \cup (B \cup C) = (A \cup B) \cup C$
	$A \cap (B \cap C) = (A \cap B) \cap C$
Distributive laws	$A \cup (B \cap C) = (A \cup B) \cap (A \cup C)$
	$A \cap (B \cup C) = (A \cap B) \cup (A \cap C)$
DeMorgan's laws	$(A \cup B)' = A' \cap B'$
	$(A \cap B)' = A' \cup B'$

3.2 Functions

Functions are a central notion to software development and testing. The whole functional decomposition paradigm, for example, implicitly uses the mathematical notion of a function. We make this notion explicit here because all functional testing is based on it.

Informally, a function associates elements of sets. In the NextDate program, for example, the function of a given date is the date of the following day, and in the triangle problem, the function of three input integers is the kind of triangle formed by sides with those lengths. In the commission problem, the salesperson's commission is a function of sales, which in turn is a function of the number of locks, stocks, and barrels sold. Functions in the ATM system are much more complex; not surprisingly, this will add complexity to the testing.

Any program can be thought of as a function that associates its outputs with its inputs. In the mathematical formulation of a function, the inputs are the domain and the outputs are the range of the function.

Definition

Given sets A and B, a *function* f is a subset of $A \times B$ such that, for a_i, $a_j \in A$, b_i, $b_j \in B$, and $f(a_i) = b_i$, $f(a_j) = b_j$, $b_i \neq b_j \Rightarrow a_i \neq a_j$.

Formal definitions like this one are notoriously terse, so let us take a closer look. The inputs to the function f are elements of the set A, and the outputs of f are elements of B. What the definition says is that the function f is "well behaved" in the sense that an element in A is never associated with more than one element of B. (If this could happen, how would we ever test such a function? This is an example of nondeterminism.)

3.2.1 Domain and Range

In the definition just given, the set A is the domain of the function f, and the set B is the range. Because input and output have a "natural" order, it is an easy step to say that a function f is really a set of ordered pairs in which the first element is from the domain and the second element is from the range. Here are two common notations for function:

$$f : A \rightarrow B$$

$$f \subseteq A \times B$$

We have not put any restrictions on the sets A and B in this definition. We could have A = B, and either A or B could be a Cartesian product of other sets.

3.2.2 Function Types

Functions are further described by particulars of the mapping. In the definition below, we start with a function $f : A \rightarrow B$, and we define the set:

$$f(A) = \{b_i \in B : b_i = f(a_i) \text{ for some } a_i \in A\}$$

This set is sometimes called the image of A under f.

Definition

f is a *function from A onto B* iff f(A) = B.
f is a *function from A into B* iff $f(A) \subset B$ (note the proper subset here).
f is a *one-to-one function from A to B* iff, for all a_i, $a_j \in A$, $a_i \neq a_j \Rightarrow f(a_i) \neq f(a_j)$.
f is a *many-to-one function from A to B* iff there exists a_i, $a_j \in A$, $a_i \neq a_j$ such that $f(a_i) = f(a_j)$.

Back to plain English, if f is a function from A onto B, we know that every element of B is associated with some element of A. If f is a function from A into B, we know that there is at least one element of B that is not associated with an element of A. One-to-one functions guarantee a form of uniqueness: distinct domain elements are never mapped to the same range element. (Notice this is the inverse of the well-behaved attribute described earlier.) If a function is not one-to-one, it is many-to-one; that is, more than one domain element can be mapped to the same range element. In these terms, the well-behaved requirement prohibits functions from being one-to-many. Testers familiar with relational databases will recognize that all these possibilities (one-to-one, one-to-many, many-to-one, and many-to-many) are allowed for relations.

Referring again to our testing examples, suppose we take A, B, and C to be sets of dates for the NextDate program, where:

$$A = \{date : 1 \text{ January } 1812 \leq date \leq 31 \text{ December } 2012\}$$

$$B = \{date : 2 \text{ January } 1812 \leq date \leq 1 \text{ January } 2013\}$$

$$C = A \cup B$$

Now, NextDate : A → B is a one-to-one onto function, and NextDate : A → C is a one-to-one into function.

It makes no sense for NextDate to be many-to-one, but it is easy to see how the triangle problem can be many-to-one. When a function is one-to-one and onto, such as NextDate : A → B previously, each element of the domain corresponds to exactly one element of the range; conversely, each element of the range corresponds to exactly one element of the domain. When this happens, it is always possible to find an inverse function (see the YesterDate exercise in Chapter 2) that is one-to-one from the range back to the domain.

All this is important for testing. The into versus onto distinction has implications for domain- and range-based functional testing, and one-to-one functions may require much more testing than many-to-one functions.

3.2.3 Function Composition

Suppose we have sets and functions such that the range of one is the domain of the next:

$$f : A \to B$$

$$g : B \to C$$

$$h : C \to D$$

When this occurs, we can compose the functions. To do this, let us refer to specific elements of the domain and range sets $a \in A$, $b \in B$, $c \in C$, $d \in D$, and suppose that $f(a) = b$, $g(b) = c$, and $h(c) = d$. Now the composition of functions h, g, and f is

$$
\begin{aligned}
h \circ g \circ f(a) &= h(g(f(a))) \\
&= h(g(b)) \\
&= h(c) \\
&= d
\end{aligned}
$$

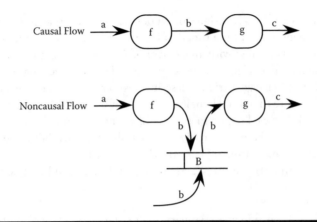

Figure 3.4 Causal and noncausal flows in a dataflow diagram.

Function composition is a very common practice in software development; it is inherent in the process of defining procedures and subroutines. We have an example of it in the commission program, in which

$$f_1(\text{locks, stocks, barrels}) = \text{sales}$$

$$f_2(\text{sales}) = \text{commission}$$

so

$$f_2(f_1(\text{locks, stocks, barrels}) = \text{commission}$$

Composed chains of functions can be problematic for testers, particularly when the range of one function is a proper subset of the domain of the next function in the chain. Figure 3.4 shows how this can happen in a program defined by a dataflow diagram.

In the causal flow, the composition $g \circ f(a)$ (which we know to be $g(b)$, which yields c) is a rather assembly line-like process. In the noncausal flow, the possibility of more than one source of b values for the data store B raises two problems for testers. Multiple sources of b values might raise problems of domain/range compatibility, and even if this is not a problem, there might be timing anomalies with respect to b values. (What if g used an "old" b value?)

A special case of composition can be used, which helps testers in a curious way. Recall we discussed how one-to-one onto functions always have an inverse function. It turns out that this inverse function is unique and is guaranteed to exist (again, the math folks would prove this). If f is a one-to-one function from A onto B, we denote its unique inverse by f^{-1}. It turns out that for $a \in A$ and $b \in B$, $f^{-1} \circ f(a) = a$ and $f \circ f^{-1}(b) = b$. The NextDate and YesterDate programs are such inverses. The way this helps testers is that, for a given function, its inverse acts as a cross-check, and this can often expedite the identification of functional test cases.

3.3 Relations

Functions are a special case of a relation: both are subsets of some Cartesian product, but in the case of functions, we have the well-behaved requirement that says that a domain element cannot be associated with more than one range element. This is borne out in everyday usage: when we say something "is a function" of something else, our intent is that there is a deterministic relationship present. Not all relationships are strictly functional. Consider the mapping between a set of patients and a set of physicians. One patient may be treated by several physicians, and one physician may treat several patients — a many-to-many mapping.

3.3.1 Relations among Sets

Definition
Given two sets A and B, a *relation R* is a subset of the Cartesian product A × B.

Two notations are popular; when we wish to speak about the entire relation, we usually just write $R \subseteq A \times B$; for specific elements $a_i \in A$, $b_i \in B$, we write $a_i \, R \, b_i$. Most math texts omit treatment of relations; we are interested in them because they are essential to both data modeling and object-oriented analysis.

Next, we have to explain an overloaded term — cardinality. Recall that, as it applies to sets, cardinality refers to the number of elements in a set. Because a relation is also a set, we might expect that the cardinality of a relation refers to how many ordered pairs are in the set $R \subseteq A \times B$. Unfortunately, this is not the case.

Definition
Given two sets A and B, a relation $R \subseteq A \times B$, the *cardinality of relation R* is:

> One-to-one iff R is a one-to-one function from A to B
> Many-to-one iff R is a many-to-one function from A to B
> One-to-many iff at least one element $a \in A$ is in two ordered pairs in R, that is, $<a, b_j> \in$ R and $<a, b_j> \in R$
> Many-to-many iff at least one element $a \in A$ is in two ordered pairs in R, that is, $<a, b_j> \in R$ and $<a, b_j> \in R$, and at least one element $b \in B$ is in two ordered pairs in R, that is, $<a_i, b> \in R$ and $<a_j, b> \in R$

The distinction between functions into and onto their range has an analog in relations — the notion of participation.

Definition
Given two sets A and B, a relation $R \subseteq A \times B$, the *participation of relation R* is:

> Total iff every element of A is in some ordered pair in R
> Partial iff some element of A is not in some ordered pair in R
> Onto iff every element of B is in some ordered pair in R
> Into iff some element of B is not in some ordered pair in R

In plain English, a relation is total if it applies to every element of A and partial if it does not apply to every element. Another term for this distinction is mandatory versus optional participation. Similarly, a relation is onto if it applies to every element of B and into if it does not. The parallelism between total/partial and onto/into is curious and deserves special mention here. From the standpoint of relational database theory, no reason exists for this; in fact, a compelling reason exists to avoid this distinction. Data modeling is essentially declarative, while process modeling is essentially imperative. The parallel sets of terms force a direction on relations, when in fact no need exists for the directionality. Part of this is a likely holdover from the fact that Cartesian products consist of ordered pairs, which clearly have a first and second element.

So far, we have only considered relations between two sets. Extending relations to three or more sets is more complicated than simply the Cartesian product. Suppose, for example, we had three sets, A, B, and C, and a relation $R \subseteq A \times B \times C$. Do we intend the relation to be strictly among three elements, or is it between one element and an ordered pair (there would be three possibilities here)? This line of thinking also needs to be applied to the definitions of cardinality and participation. It is straightforward for participation, but cardinality is essentially a binary property. (Suppose, for example, the relation is one-to-one from A to B and is many-to-one from A to C.) We discussed a three-way relation in Chapter 1, when we examined the relationships among specified, implemented, and tested program behaviors. We would like to have some form of totality between test cases and specification–implementation pairs; we will revisit this when we study functional and structural testing.

Testers need to be concerned with the definitions of relations because they bear directly on software properties to be tested. The onto/into distinction, for example, bears directly on what we will call output-based functional testing. The mandatory–optional distinction is the essence of exception handling, which also has implications for testers.

3.3.2 Relations on a Single Set

Two important mathematical relations are used, both of which are defined on a single set: ordering relations and equivalence relations. Both are defined with respect to specific properties of relations.

Let A be a set, and let $R \subseteq A \times A$ be a relation defined on A, with <a, a>, <a, b>, <b, a>, <b, c>, <a, c> ∈ R. Relations have four special attributes:

Definition
A relation $R \subseteq A \times A$ is:

> *Reflexive* iff for all a ∈ A, <a, a> ∈ R
> *Symmetric* iff <a, b> ∈ R ⟹ <b, a> ∈ R
> *Antisymmetric* iff <a, b>, <b, a> ∈ R ⟹ a = b
> *Transitive* iff <a, b>, <b, c> ∈ R ⟹ <a, c> ∈ R

Family relationships are nice examples of these properties. You might want to think about the following relationships and decide for yourself which attributes apply: brother of, sibling of, and ancestor of. Now we can define the two important relations.

Definition
A relation $R \subseteq A \times A$ is an *ordering relation* if R is reflexive, antisymmetric, and transitive.

Ordering relations have a sense of direction; some common ordering relations are older than, ≥, ⟹, and ancestor of. (The reflexive part usually requires some fudging — we really should say not younger than and not a descendant of.) Ordering relations are a common occurrence in software: data access techniques, hashing codes, tree structures, and arrays are all situations in which ordering relations are used.

The power set of a given set is the set of all subsets of the given set. The power set of the set A is denoted P(A). The subset relation ⊆ is an ordering relation on P(A), because it is reflexive (any set is trivially a subset of itself), antisymmetric (the definition of set equality), and transitive.

Definition

A relation $R \subseteq A \times A$ is an *equivalence relation* if R is reflexive, symmetric, and transitive.

Mathematics is full of equivalence relations: equality and congruence are two quick examples. A very important connection exists between equivalence relations and partitions of a set. Suppose we have some partition A_1, A_2, ..., A_n of a set B, and we say that two elements, b_1 and b_2 of B, are related (i.e., b_1 R b_2) if b_1 and b_2 are in the same partition element. This relation is reflexive (any element is in its own partition), symmetric (if b_1 and b_2 are in a partition element, then b_2 and b_1 are), and transitive (if b_1 and b_2 are in the same set, and if b_2 and b_3 are in the same set, then b_1 and b_2 are in the same set). The relation defined from the partition is called the equivalence relation induced by the partition. The converse process works in the same way. If we start with an equivalence relation defined on a set, we can define subsets according to elements that are related to each other. This turns out to be a partition and is called the partition induced by the equivalence relation. The sets in this partition are known as equivalence classes. The end result is that partitions and equivalence relations are interchangeable, and this becomes a powerful concept for testers. Recall that the two properties of a partition are notions of completeness and nonredundancy. When translated into testing situations, these notions allow testers to make powerful, absolute statements about the extent to which a software item has been tested. In addition, great efficiency follows from testing just one element of an equivalence class and assuming that the remaining elements will behave similarly.

3.4 Propositional Logic

We have already been using propositional logic notation; if you were perplexed by this usage definition before, you are not alone. Set theory and propositional logic have a chicken-and-egg relationship — it is hard to decide which should be discussed first. Just as sets are taken as primitive terms and are therefore not defined, we take propositions to be primitive terms. A proposition is a sentence that is either true or false, and we call these the truth values of the proposition. Furthermore, propositions are unambiguous: given a proposition, it is always possible to tell whether it is true or false. The sentence "Mathematics is difficult" would not qualify as a proposition because of the ambiguity. There are also temporal and spatial aspects of propositions. For example, "It is raining" may be true at some times and false at others. In addition, it may be true for one person and false for another at the same time but different locations.

We usually denote propositions with lowercase letters p, q, and r. Propositional logic has operations, expressions, and identities that are very similar (in fact, they are isomorphic) to set theory.

3.4.1 Logical Operators

Logical operators (also known as logical connectives or operations) are defined in terms of their effect on the truth values of the propositions to which they are applied. This is easy; only two values are used: T (for true) and F (for false). Arithmetic operators could also be defined this way (in fact, that is how they are taught to children), but the tables become too large. The three basic logical operators are and (∧), or (∨), and not (¬); these are sometimes called conjunction, disjunction, and negation. Negation is the only unary (one operand) logical operator; the others are all binary.

p	q	p ∧ q	p ∨ q	¬p
T	T	T	T	F
T	F	F	T	F
F	T	F	T	T
F	F	F	F	T

Conjunction and disjunction are familiar in everyday life: a conjunction is true only when all components are true, and a disjunction is true if at least one component is true. Negations also behave as we expect. Two other common connectives are used: exclusive-or (⊕) and IF-THEN (→). They are defined as follows:

p	q	p ⊕ q	p → q
T	T	F	T
T	F	T	F
F	T	T	T
F	F	F	T

An exclusive-or is true only when one of the propositions is true, while a disjunction (or inclusive-or) is true when both propositions are true. The IF-THEN connective usually causes the most difficulty. The easy view is that this is just a definition, but because the other connectives all transfer nicely to natural language, we have similar expectations for IF-THEN. The quick answer is that the IF-THEN connective is closely related to the process of deduction: in a valid deductive syllogism, we can say "if premises, then conclusion" and the IF-THEN statement will be a tautology.

3.4.2 Logical Expressions

We use logical operators to build logical expressions in exactly the same way that we use arithmetic operators to build algebraic expressions. We can specify the order in which operators are applied with the usual conventions on parentheses, or we can employ a precedence order (negation first, then conjunction followed by disjunction). Given a logical expression, we can always find its truth table by "building up" to it following the order determined by the parentheses. For example, the expression ¬ ((p → q) ∧ (q → p)) has the following truth table:

p	q	p → q	q → p	(p → q) ∧ (q → p)	¬((p → q) ∧ (q → p))
T	T	T	T	T	F
T	F	F	T	F	T
F	T	T	F	F	T
F	F	T	T	T	F

3.4.3 *Logical Equivalence*

The notions of arithmetic equality and identical sets have analogs in propositional logic. Notice that the expressions $\neg((p \rightarrow q) \wedge (q \rightarrow p))$ and $p \oplus q$ have identical truth tables. This means that no matter what truth values are given to the base propositions p and q, these expressions will always have the same truth value. This property can be defined in several ways; we use the simplest.

Definition

Two propositions *p and q are logically equivalent* (denoted $p \Leftrightarrow q$) iff their truth tables are identical.

By the way, the curious "iff" abbreviation we have been using for "if and only if" is sometimes called the biconditional, so the proposition p iff q is really $(p \rightarrow q) \wedge (q \rightarrow p)$, which is denoted $p \leftrightarrow q$.

Definition

A proposition that is always true is a *tautology*; a proposition that is always false is a *contradiction*.

To be a tautology or a contradiction, a proposition must contain at least one connective and two or more primitive propositions. We sometimes denote a tautology as a proposition T and a contradiction as a proposition F. We can now state several laws that are direct analogs of the ones we had for sets.

Law	Expression
Identity	$p \wedge T \Leftrightarrow p$
	$p \vee F \Leftrightarrow p$
Domination	$p \vee T \Leftrightarrow T$
	$p \wedge F \Leftrightarrow F$
Idempotent	$p \wedge p \Leftrightarrow p$
	$p \vee p \Leftrightarrow p$
Complementation	$\neg (\neg p) \Leftrightarrow p$
Commutative	$p \wedge q \Leftrightarrow q \wedge p$
	$p \vee q \Leftrightarrow q \vee p$
Associative	$p \wedge (q \wedge r) \Leftrightarrow (p \wedge q) \wedge r$
	$p \vee (q \vee r) \Leftrightarrow (p \vee q) \vee r$
Distributive	$p \wedge (q \vee r) \Leftrightarrow (p \wedge q) \vee (p \wedge r)$
	$p \vee (q \wedge r) \Leftrightarrow (p \vee q) \wedge (p \vee r)$
DeMorgan's	$\neg (p \wedge q) \Leftrightarrow \neg p \vee \neg q$
	$\neg (p \vee q) \Leftrightarrow \neg p \subseteq \neg q$

3.5 Probability Theory

We will have two occasions to use probability theory in our study of software testing: one deals with the probability that a particular path of statements executes, and the other generalizes this to a popular industrial concept called an operational profile (see Chapter 14). Because of this limited use, we will only cover the rudiments here.

As with both set theory and propositional logic, we start out with a primitive concept — the probability of an event. Here is the definition provided by a classic textbook (Rosen, 1991):

> The probability of an event E, which is a subset of a finite sample space S of equally likely outcomes, is $p(E) = |E|/|S|$, where $|E|$ is the cardinality of set E, and $|S|$ is the cardinality of set S.

This definition hinges on the idea of an experiment that results in an outcome, the sample space is the set of all possible outcomes, and an event is a subset of outcomes. This definition is circular: What are equally likely outcomes? We assume these have equal probabilities, but then probability is defined in terms of itself.

The French mathematician Laplace had a reasonable working definition of probability two centuries ago. To paraphrase it, the probability that something occurs is the number of favorable ways it can occur divided by the total number of ways (favorable and unfavorable). Laplace's definition works well when we are concerned with drawing colored marbles out of a bag (probability folks are unusually concerned with their marbles; maybe there is a lesson here), but it does not extend well to situations in which it is hard to enumerate the various possibilities.

We will use our (refurbished) capabilities in set theory and propositional logic to arrive at a more cohesive formulation. As testers, we will be concerned with things that happen; we will call these events and say that the set of all events is our universe of discourse. Next, we will devise propositions about events, such that the propositions refer to elements in the universe of discourse. Now, for some universe U and some proposition p about elements of U, we make a definition:

Definition

The *truth set T of a proposition p*, written T(p), is the set of all elements in the universe U for which p is true.

Propositions are either true or false; therefore, a proposition p divides the universe of discourse into two sets, $T(p)$ and $(T(p))'$, where $T(p) \cup (T(p))' = U$. Notice that $(T(p))'$ is the same as $T(\neg p)$. Truth sets facilitate a clear mapping among set theory, propositional logic, and probability theory.

Definition

The *probability that a proposition p is true*, denoted Pr(p), is $|T(p)|/|U|$.

With this definition, Laplace's "number of favorable ways" becomes the cardinality of the truth set T(p), and the total number of ways becomes the cardinality of the universe of discourse. This forces one more connection: because the truth set of a tautology is the universe of discourse, and the truth set of a contradiction is the empty set, the probabilities of $\varnothing$ and U are, respectively, 0 and 1.

The NextDate problem is a good source of examples. Consider the month variable and the proposition

$$p(m) : m \text{ is a 30-day month}$$

The universe of discourse is the set U = {Jan., Feb., ..., Dec.}, and the truth set of p(m) is the set

$$T(p(m)) = \{Apr., June, Sept., Nov.\}$$

Now, the probability that a given month is a 30-day month is

$$Pr(p(m)) = |T(p(m))|/|U| = 4/12$$

A subtlety exists in the role of the universe of discourse; this is part of the craft of using probability theory in testing — choosing the right universe. Suppose we want to know the probability that a month is February. The quick answer: 1/12. Now, suppose we want the probability of a month with exactly 29 days. Less easy — we need a universe that includes both leap years and common years. We could use congruence arithmetic and choose a universe that consists of months in a period of four consecutive years — say 1991, 1992, 1993, and 1994. This universe would contain 48 months, and in this universe the probability of a 29-day month is 1/48. Another possibility would be to use the full two-century range of the NextDate program, in which the year 1900 is not a leap year. This would slightly reduce the probability of a 29-day month. One conclusion: getting the right universe is important. A bigger conclusion: it is even more important to avoid "shifting universes."

Here are some facts about probabilities that we will use without proof. They refer to a given universe, propositions p and q, with truth sets $T(p)$ and $T(q)$:

$$Pr(\neg p) = 1 - Pr(p)$$

$$Pr(p \wedge q) = Pr(p) \times Pr(q)$$

$$Pr(p \vee q) = Pr(p) + Pr(q) - Pr(p \wedge q)$$

These facts, together with the tables of set theory and propositional identities, provide a strong algebraic capability to manipulate probability expressions.

Reference

Rosen, K.H., *Discrete Mathematics and Its Applications*, McGraw-Hill, New York, 1991.

Exercises

1. A very deep connection (an isomorphism) exists between set operations and the logical connectives in the propositional logic.

Operation	Propositional Logic	Set Theory
Disjunction	Or	Union
Conjunction	And	Intersection
Negation	Not	Complement
Implication	If, Then	Subset
	Exclusive or	Symmetric difference

    a. Express $A \oplus B$ in words.

    b. Express $(A \cup B) - (A \cap B)$ in words.

    c. Convince yourself that $A \oplus B$ and $(A \cup B) - (A \cap B)$ are the same set.

    d. Is it true that $A \oplus B = (A - B) \cup (B - A)$?

    e. What name would you give to the blank entry in the previous table?

2. In many parts of the United States, real estate taxes are levied by different taxing bodies, for example, a school district, a fire protection district, a township, and so on. Discuss whether these taxing bodies form a partition of a state. Do the 50 states form a partition of the United States of America? (What about the District of Columbia?)

3. Is brotherOf an equivalence relation on the set of all people? How about siblingOf?

Chapter 4

Graph Theory for Testers

Graph theory is a branch of topology that is sometimes referred to as "rubber sheet geometry." Curious, because the rubber sheet parts of topology have little to do with graph theory; furthermore, the graphs in graph theory do not involve axes, scales, points, and curves as you might expect. Whatever the origin of the term, graph theory is probably the most useful part of mathematics for computer science — far more useful than calculus — yet it is not commonly taught. Our excursion into graph theory will follow a "pure math" spirit: definitions are as devoid of specific interpretations as possible. Postponing interpretations results in maximum latitude in interpretations later, much like well-defined abstract data types promote reuse.

Two basic kinds of graphs are used: undirected and directed. Because the latter are a special case of the former, we begin with undirected graphs. This will allow us to inherit many concepts when we get to directed graphs.

4.1 Graphs

A graph (also known as a linear graph) is an abstract mathematical structure defined from two sets — a set of nodes and a set of edges that form connections between nodes. A computer network is a fine example of a graph. More formally:

Definition

A *graph* $G = (V, E)$ is composed of a finite (and nonempty) set V of nodes and a set E of unordered pairs of nodes.

$$V = \{n_1, n_2, \ldots, n_m\}$$

and

$$E = \{e_1, e_2, \ldots, e_p\}$$

where each edge $e_k = \{n_i, n_j\}$ for some nodes $n_i, n_j \in V$. Recall from Chapter 3 that the set $\{n_i, n_j\}$ is an unordered pair, which we sometimes write as (n_i, n_j).

Nodes are sometimes called vertices; edges are sometimes called arcs; and we sometimes call nodes the endpoints of an arc. The common visual form of a graph shows nodes as circles and edges as lines

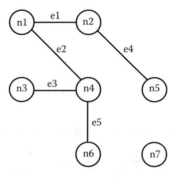

Figure 4.1   A graph with seven nodes and five edges.

connecting pairs of nodes, as in Figure 4.1. We will use this figure as a continuing example, so take a minute to become familiar with it.

In the graph in Figure 4.1 the node and edge sets are

$$V = \{n_1, n_2, n_3, n_4, n_5, n_6, n_7\}$$
$$E = \{e_1, e_2, e_3, e_4, e_5\}$$
$$= \{(n_1, n_2), (n_1, n_4), (n_3, n_4), (n_2, n_5), (n_4, n_6)\}$$

To define a particular graph, we must first define a set of nodes and then define a set of edges between pairs of nodes. We usually think of nodes as program statements, and we have various kinds of edges, representing, for instance, flow of control or define/use relationships.

4.1.1   Degree of a Node

Definition

The *degree of a node in a graph* is the number of edges that have that node as an endpoint. We write deg(n) for the degree of node n.

We might say that the degree of a node indicates its "popularity" in a graph. In fact, social scientists use graphs to describe social interactions, in which nodes are people, and edges often refer to things like "friendship," "communicates with," and so on. If we make a graph in which objects are nodes and edges are messages, the degree of a node (object) indicates the extent of integration testing that is appropriate for the object.

The degrees of the nodes in Figure 4.1 are

$$deg(n_1) = 2$$
$$deg(n_2) = 2$$
$$deg(n_3) = 1$$
$$deg(n_4) = 3$$
$$deg(n_5) = 1$$
$$deg(n_6) = 1$$
$$deg(n_7) = 0$$

4.1.2 Incidence Matrices

Graphs need not be represented pictorially — they can be fully represented in an incidence matrix. This concept becomes very useful for testers, so we will formalize it here. When graphs are given a specific interpretation, the incidence matrix always provides useful information for the new interpretation.

Definition

The *incidence matrix of a graph* $G = (V, E)$ with m nodes and n edges is an $m \times n$ matrix, where the element in row i, column j is a 1 if and only if node i is an endpoint of edge j; otherwise, the element is 0.

The incidence matrix of the graph in Figure 4.1 is:

	e1	e2	e3	e4	e5
n1	1	1	0	0	0
n2	1	0	0	1	0
n3	0	0	1	0	0
n4	0	1	1	0	1
n5	0	0	0	1	0
n6	0	0	0	0	1
n7	0	0	0	0	0

We can make some observations about a graph by examining its incidence matrix. First, notice that the sum of the entries in any column is 2. That is because every edge has exactly two endpoints. If a column sum in an incidence matrix is ever something other than 2, there is a mistake somewhere. Thus, forming column sums is a form of integrity checking similar in spirit to that of parity checks. Next, we see that the row sum is the degree of the node. When the degree of a node is zero, as it is for node n_7, we say the node is isolated. (This might correspond to unreachable code, or to objects that are included but never used.)

4.1.3 Adjacency Matrices

The adjacency matrix of a graph is a useful supplement to the incidence matrix. Because adjacency matrices deal with connections, they are the basis of many later graph theory concepts.

Definition

The *adjacency matrix of a graph* $G = (V, E)$ with m nodes is an $m \times m$ matrix, where the element in row i, column j is a 1 if and only if an edge exists between node i and node j; otherwise, the element is 0.

The adjacency matrix is symmetric (element i, j always equals element j, i), and a row sum is the degree of the node (as it was in the incidence matrix).

The adjacency matrix of the graph in Figure 4.1 is:

	n1	n2	n3	n4	n5	n6	n7
n1	0	1	0	1	0	0	0
n2	1	0	0	0	1	0	0
n3	0	0	0	1	0	0	0
n4	1	0	1	0	0	1	0
n5	0	1	0	0	0	0	0
n6	0	0	0	1	0	0	0
n7	0	0	0	0	0	0	0

4.1.4 Paths

As a preview of how we will use graph theory, the structural approaches to testing (see Part III) all center on types of paths in a program. Here, we define (interpretation-free) paths in a graph.

Definition

A *path* is a sequence of edges such that, for any adjacent pair of edges e_i, e_j in the sequence, the edges share a common (node) endpoint.

Paths can be described either as sequences of edges or as sequences of nodes; the node sequence choice is more common.

Some paths in the graph in Figure 4.1 are:

Path	Node Sequence	Edge Sequence
Between n1 and n5	n1, n2, n5	e1, e4
Between n6 and n5	n6, n4, n1, n2, n5	e5, e2, e1, e4
Between n3 and n2	n3, n4, n1, n2	e3, e2, e1

Paths can be generated directly from the adjacency matrix of a graph using a binary form of matrix multiplication and addition. In our continuing example, edge e_1 is between nodes n_1 and n_2, and edge e_4 is between nodes n_2 and n_5. In the product of the adjacency matrix with itself, the element in position (1, 2) forms a product with the element in position (2, 5), yielding an element in position (1, 5), which corresponds to the two-edge path between n_1 and n_5. If we multiplied the product matrix by the original adjacency matrix again, we would get all three edge paths, and so on. At this point, the pure math folks go into a long digression to determine the length of the longest path in a graph; we will not bother. Instead, we focus our interest on the fact that paths connect "distant" parts of a graph.

The graph in Figure 4.1 predisposes a problem. It is not completely general, because it does not show all the situations that might occur in a graph. In particular, no paths exist in which a node occurs twice in the path. If it did, the path would be a loop (or circuit). We could create a circuit by adding an edge between nodes n_3 and n_6.

4.1.5 Connectedness

Paths let us speak about nodes that are connected; this leads to a powerful simplification device that is very important for testers.

Definition

Nodes n_i and n_j are connected if and only if they are in the same path.

Connectedness is an equivalence relation (see Chapter 3) on the node set of a graph. To see this, we can check the three defining properties of equivalence relations:

1. Connectedness is reflexive, because every node is, by default, in a path of length 0 with itself. (Sometimes, for emphasis, an edge is shown that begins and ends on the same node.)
2. Connectedness is symmetric, because if nodes n_i and n_j are in a path, then nodes n_j and n_i are in the same path.
3. Connectedness is transitive (see the discussion of adjacency matrix multiplication for paths of length 2).

Equivalence relations induce a partition (see Chapter 3 if you need a reminder); therefore, we are guaranteed that connectedness defines a partition on the node set of a graph. This permits the definition of components of a graph:

Definition

A *component of a graph* is a maximal set of connected nodes.

Nodes in the equivalence classes are components of the graph. The classes are maximal due to the transitivity part of the equivalence relation. The graph in Figure 4.1 has two components: $\{n_1, n_2, n_3, n_4, n_5, n_6\}$ and $\{n_7\}$.

4.1.6 Condensation Graphs

We are finally in a position to formalize an important simplification mechanism for testers.

Definition

Given a graph $G = (V, E)$, its *condensation graph* is formed by replacing each component by a condensing node.

Developing the condensation graph of a given graph is an unambiguous (i.e., algorithmic) process. We use the adjacency matrix to identify path connectivity, and then use the equivalence relation to identify components. The absolute nature of this process is important: the condensation graph of a given graph is unique. This implies that the resulting simplification represents an important aspect of the original graph.

The components in our continuing example are $S_1 = \{n_1, n_2, n_3, n_4, n_5, n_6\}$ and $S_2 = \{n_7\}$.

No edges can be present in a condensation graph of an ordinary (undirected) graph. Two reasons are:

1. Edges have individual nodes as endpoints, not sets of nodes. (Here, we can finally use the distinction between n_7 and $\{n_7\}$.)
2. Even if we fudge the definition of edge to ignore this distinction, a possible edge would mean that nodes from two different components were connected, thus in a path, thus in the same (maximal) component.

The implication for testing is that components are independent in an important way; thus, they can be tested separately.

4.1.7 Cyclomatic Number

Another property of graphs has deep implications for testing: cyclomatic complexity.

Definition

The *cyclomatic number of a graph* G is given by $V(G) = e - n + p$, where e is the number of edges in G, n is the number of nodes in G, and p is the number of components in G.

$V(G)$ is the number of distinct regions in a strongly connected directed graph. In Chapter 9 we will examine a formulation of structural testing that considers all the paths in a program graph to be a vector space. There are $V(G)$ elements in the set of basis vectors for this space. The cyclomatic number of our example graph is $V(G) = 5 - 7 + 2 = 0$. This is not a very good example for cyclomatic complexity. When we use cyclomatic complexity in testing, we will (usually) have strongly connected graphs, which will have a larger cyclomatic complexity than this small example.

4.2 Directed Graphs

Directed graphs are a slight refinement to ordinary graphs: edges acquire a sense of direction. Symbolically, the unordered pairs (n_i, n_j) become ordered pairs $<n_i, n_j>$, and we speak of a directed edge going from node n_i to n_j, instead of being between the nodes.

Definition

A *directed graph* (*or digraph*) $D = (V, E)$ consists of a finite set $V = \{n_1, n_2, ..., n_m\}$ of nodes and a set $E = \{e_1, e_2, ..., e_p\}$ of edges, where each edge $e_k = <n_i, n_j>$ is an ordered pair of nodes $n_i, n_j \in V$.

In the directed edge $e_k = <n_i, n_j>$, n_i is the initial (or start) node and n_j is the terminal (or finish) node. Edges in directed graphs fit naturally with many software concepts: sequential behavior, imperative programming languages, time-ordered events, define/reference pairings, messages, function and procedure calls, and so on. Given this, you might ask why we spent (wasted?) so much time on ordinary graphs. The difference between ordinary and directed graphs is very analogous to the difference between declarative and imperative programming languages. In imperative languages (e.g., COBOL, Fortran, Pascal, C, Ada®), the sequential order of source language statements determines the execution time order of compiled code. This is not true for declarative languages (such as Prologue). The most common declarative situation for most software developers is entity/relationship (E/R) modeling. In an E/R model, we choose entities as nodes and identify relationships as edges. (If a relationship involves three or more entities, we need the notion of a "hyper-edge" that has three or more

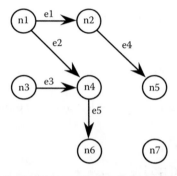

Figure 4.2   A directed graph.

endpoints.) The resulting graph of an E/R model is more properly interpreted as an ordinary graph. Good E/R modeling practice suppresses the sequential thinking that directed graphs promote.

When testing a program written in a declarative language, the only concepts available to the tester are those that follow from ordinary graphs. Fortunately, most software is developed in imperative languages; so testers usually have the full power of directed graphs at their disposal.

The next series of definitions roughly parallels the ones for ordinary graphs. We modify our now familiar continuing example to the one shown in Figure 4.2.

We have the same node set $V = \{n_1, n_2, n_3, n_4, n_5, n_6, n_7\}$, and the edge set appears to be the same: $E = \{e_1, e_2, e_3, e_4, e_5\}$. The difference is that the edges are now ordered pairs of nodes in V:

$$E = \{<n_1, n_2>, <n_1, n_4>, <n_3, n_4>, <n_2, n_5>, <n_4, n_6>\}$$

4.2.1 Indegrees and Outdegrees

The degree of a node in an ordinary graph is refined to reflect direction, as follows:

Definition

The *indegree of a node* in a directed graph is the number of distinct edges that have the node as a terminal node. We write indeg(n) for the indegree of node n.

The *outdegree of a node* in a directed graph is the number of distinct edges that have the node as a start point. We write outdeg(n) for the outdegree of node n.

The nodes in the digraph in Figure 4.2 have the following indegrees and outdegrees:

$$\text{indeg}(n_1) = 0 \; \text{outdeg}(n_1) = 2$$
$$\text{indeg}(n_2) = 1 \; \text{outdeg}(n_2) = 1$$
$$\text{indeg}(n_3) = 0 \; \text{outdeg}(n_3) = 1$$
$$\text{indeg}(n_4) = 2 \; \text{outdeg}(n_4) = 1$$
$$\text{indeg}(n_5) = 1 \; \text{outdeg}(n_5) = 0$$
$$\text{indeg}(n_6) = 1 \; \text{outdeg}(n_6) = 0$$
$$\text{indeg}(n_7) = 0 \; \text{outdeg}(n_7) = 0$$

Ordinary and directed graphs meet through definitions that relate obvious correspondences, such as deg(n) = indeg(n) + outdeg(n).

4.2.2 Types of Nodes

The added descriptive power of directed graphs lets us define different kinds of nodes:

Definition

> A node with indegree = 0 is a *source node.*
> A node with outdegree = 0 is a *sink node.*
> A node with indegree ≠ 0 and outdegree ≠ 0 is a *transfer node.*

Source and sink nodes constitute the external boundary of a graph. If we made a directed graph of a context diagram (from a set of dataflow diagrams produced by structured analysis), the external entities would be source and sink nodes.

In our continuing example, n_1, n_3, and n_7 are source nodes; n_5, n_6, and n_7 are sink nodes; and n_2 and n_4 are transfer (also known as interior) nodes. A node that is both a source and a sink node is an isolated node.

4.2.3 Adjacency Matrix of a Directed Graph

As we might expect, the addition of direction to edges changes the definition of the adjacency matrix of a directed graph. (It also changes the incidence matrix, but this matrix is seldom used in conjunction with digraphs.)

Definition

The *adjacency matrix of a directed graph* $D = (V, E)$ with m nodes is an m × m matrix: A = (a(i, j)), where a(i, j) is a 1 if and only if there is an edge from node i to node j; otherwise, the element is 0.

The adjacency matrix of a directed graph is not necessarily symmetric. A row sum is the out-degree of the node; a column sum is the indegree of a node. The adjacency matrix of our continuing example is:

	n1	n2	n3	n4	n5	n6	n7
n1	0	1	0	1	0	0	0
n2	0	0	0	0	1	0	0
n3	0	0	0	1	0	0	0
n4	0	0	0	0	0	1	0
n5	0	0	0	0	0	0	0
n6	0	0	0	0	0	0	0
n7	0	0	0	0	0	0	0

One common use of directed graphs is to record family relationships, in which siblings, cousins, and so on, are connected by an ancestor; and parents, grandparents, and so on, are connected by a descendant. Entries in powers of the adjacency matrix now show existence of directed paths.

4.2.4 Paths and Semipaths

Direction permits a more precise meaning to paths that connect nodes in a directed graph. As a handy analogy, you may think in terms of one-way and two-way streets.

Definition

A (*directed*) *path* is a sequence of edges such that, for any adjacent pair of edges e_i, e_j in the sequence, the terminal node of the first edge is the initial node of the second edge.
A *cycle* is a directed path that begins and ends at the same node.
A (*directed*) *semipath* is a sequence of edges such that, for at least one adjacent pair of edges e_i, e_j in the sequence, the initial node of the first edge is the initial node of the second edge, or the terminal node of the first edge is the terminal node of the second edge.

Directed paths are sometimes called chains; we will use this concept in Chapter 9. Our continuing example contains the following paths and semipaths (not all are listed):

A path from n_1 to n_6
A semipath between n_1 and n_3
A semipath between n_2 and n_4
A semipath between n_5 and n_6

4.2.5 Reachability Matrix

When we model an application with a digraph, we often ask questions that deal with paths that let us reach (or "get to") certain nodes. This is an extremely useful capability and is made possible by the reachability matrix of a digraph.

Definition

The *reachability matrix of a directed graph* $D = (V, E)$ with m nodes is an m × m matrix R = (r(i, j)), where r(i, j) is a 1 if and only if there is a path from node i to node j; otherwise, the element is 0.

The reachability matrix of a directed graph D can be calculated from the adjacency matrix A as follows:

$$R = I + A + A^2 + A^3 + \cdots + A^k$$

where k is the length of the longest path in D and I is the identity matrix. The reachability matrix for our continuing example is:

	n1	n2	n3	n4	n5	n6	n7
n1	1	1	0	1	1	1	0
n2	0	1	0	0	1	0	0
n3	0	0	1	1	0	1	0
n4	0	0	0	1	0	1	0
n5	0	0	0	0	1	0	0
n6	0	0	0	0	0	1	0
n7	0	0	0	0	0	0	1

The reachability matrix tells us that nodes n_2, n_4, n_5, and n_6 can be reached from n_1, node n_5 can be reached from n_2, and so on.

4.2.6 n-Connectedness

Connectedness of ordinary graphs extends to a rich, highly explanatory concept for digraphs.

Definition

Two nodes n_i and n_j in a directed graph are:

> *0-connected* iff no path exists between n_i and n_j
> *1-connected* iff a semipath but no path exists between n_i and n_j
> *2-connected* iff a path exists between n_i and n_j
> *3-connected* iff a path goes from n_i to n_j and a path goes from n_j to n_i

No other degrees of connectedness exist.

We need to modify our continuing example to show 3-connectedness. The change is the addition of a new edge e_6 from n_6 to n_3, so the graph contains a cycle.

With this change, we have the following instances of n-connectivity in Figure 4.3 (not all are listed):

> n_1 and n_7 are 0-connected
> n_2 and n_6 are 1-connected
> n_1 and n_6 are 2-connected
> n_3 and n_6 are 3-connected

In terms of one-way streets, you cannot get from n_2 to n_6.

4.2.7 Strong Components

The analogy continues. We get two equivalence relations from n-connectedness: 1-connectedness yields what we might call weak connection, and this in turn yields weak components. (These turn out to be the same as we had for ordinary graphs, which is what should happen, because 1-connectedness effectively ignores direction.) The second equivalence relation, based on 3-connectedness, is

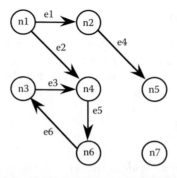

Figure 4.3   A directed graph with a cycle.

more interesting. As before, the equivalence relation induces a partition on the node set of a digraph, but the condensation graph is quite different. Nodes that previously were 0-, 1-, or 2-connected remain so. The 3-connected nodes become the strong components.

Definition

A *strong component of a directed graph* is a maximal set of 3-connected nodes.

In our amended example, the strong components are the sets $\{n_3, n_4, n_6\}$ and $\{n_7\}$. The condensation graph for our amended example is shown in Figure 4.4.

Strong components let us simplify by removing loops and isolated nodes. Although this is not as dramatic as the simplification we had in ordinary graphs, it does solve a major testing problem. Notice that the condensation graph of a digraph will never contain a loop. (If it did, the loop would have been condensed by the maximal aspect of the partition.) These graphs have a special name: directed acyclic graphs, sometimes written as DAGs.

Many papers on structured testing make quite a point of showing how relatively simple programs can have millions of distinct execution paths. The intent of these discussions is to convince us that exhaustive testing is exactly that — exhaustive. The large number of execution paths comes from nested loops. Condensation graphs eliminate loops (or at least condense them down to a single node); therefore, we can use this as a strategy to simplify situations that otherwise are computationally untenable.

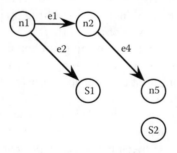

Figure 4.4   Condensation graph of the digraph in Figure 4.3.

4.3 Graphs for Testing

We conclude this chapter with four special graphs that are widely used for testing. The first of these, the program graph, is used primarily at the unit testing level. The other three, finite state machines, state charts, and Petri nets, are best used to describe system-level behavior, although they can be used at lower levels of testing.

4.3.1 Program Graphs

At the beginning of this chapter, we made a point of avoiding interpretations on the graph theory definitions to preserve latitude in later applications. Here, we give the most common use of graph theory in software testing — the program graph. To better connect with existing testing literature, the traditional definition is given, followed by an improved definition.

Definition

Given a program written in an imperative programming language, the *program graph* is a directed graph in which:

1. (Traditional definition) Nodes are program statements, and edges represent flow of control (there is an edge from node i to node j iff the statement corresponding to node j can be executed immediately after the statement corresponding to node i).
2. (Improved definition) Nodes are either entire statements or fragments of a statement, and edges represent flow of control (there is an edge from node i to node j iff the statement or statement fragment corresponding to node j can be executed immediately after the statement or statement fragment corresponding to node i).

It is cumbersome to always say "statement or statement fragment," so we adopt the convention that a statement fragment can be an entire statement. The directed graph formulation of a program enables a very precise description of testing aspects of the program. For one thing, a very satisfying connection exists between this formulation and the precepts of structured programming. The basic structured programming constructs (sequence, selection, and repetition) all have clear, directed graphs, as shown in Figure 4.5.

When these constructs are used in a structured program, the corresponding graphs are either nested or concatenated. The single entrance and single exit criteria result in unique source and sink nodes in the program graph. In fact, the old (nonstructured) "spaghetti code" resulted in very complex program graphs. GOTO statements, for example, introduce edges, and when these are used to branch into or out of loops, the resulting program graphs become even more complex. One of the pioneering analysts of this is Thomas McCabe, who popularized the cyclomatic number of a graph as an indicator of program complexity (McCabe, 1976). When a program executes, the statements that execute comprise a path in the program graph. Loops and decisions greatly increase the number of possible paths, and therefore similarly increase the need for testing.

One of the problems with program graphs is how to treat nonexecutable statements such as comments and data declaration statements. The simplest answer is to ignore them. A second problem has to do with the difference between topologically possible and semantically feasible paths. We will discuss this in more detail in Part III.

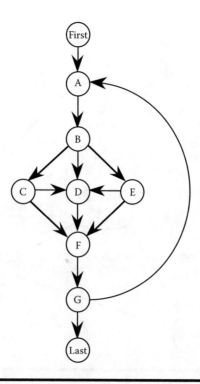

Figure 4.5   Digraphs of the structured programming constructs.

4.3.2 Finite State Machines

Finite state machines have become a fairly standard notation for requirements specification. All the real-time extensions of structured analysis use some form of finite state machine, and nearly all forms of object-oriented analysis require them. A finite state machine is a directed graph in which states are nodes and transitions are edges. Source and sink states become initial and terminal nodes, sequences of transitions are modeled as paths, and so on. Most finite state machine notations add information to the edges (transitions) to indicate the cause of the transition and actions that occur as a result of the transition.

Figure 4.6 is a finite state machine for the personal identification number (PIN) try portion of the simple automated teller machine (SATM) system. This machine contains five states (Idle, Awaiting First PIN Try, and so on) and eight transitions, which are shown as edges. The labels on the transitions follow a convention that the numerator is the event that causes the transition and the denominator is the action that is associated with the transition. The events are mandatory — transitions do not just happen, but the actions are optional. Finite state machines are simple ways to represent situations in which a variety of events may occur, and their occurrences have different consequences. In the PIN entry portion of the SATM system, for example, a customer has three chances to enter the correct PIN digits. If the correct PIN is entered on the first try, the SATM system exhibits the output action of displaying screen 5 (which invites the customer to choose a transaction type). If an incorrect PIN is entered, the machine goes to a different state, one in which it awaits a second PIN attempt. Notice that the same events and actions occur on the transitions from the Awaiting Second PIN Try state. This is the way in which finite state machines can keep a history of past events.

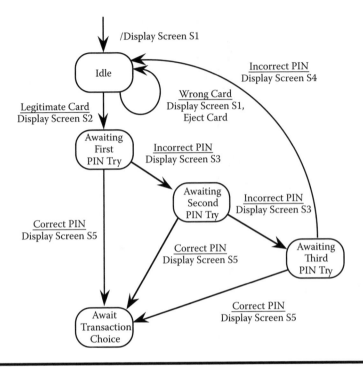

Figure 4.6 Finite state machine for PIN tries.

Finite state machines can be executed, but a few conventions are needed first. One is the notion of the active state. We speak of a system being "in" a certain state; when the system is modeled as a finite state machine, the active state refers to the state "we are in." Another convention is that finite state machines may have an initial state, which is the state that is active when a finite state machine is first entered. (The Idle state is the initial state in Figure 4.6; this is indicated by the transition that comes from nowhere. Final states are recognized by the absence of outgoing transitions.) Exactly one state can be active at any time. We also think of transitions as instantaneous occurrences, and the events that cause transitions also occur one at a time. To execute a finite state machine, we start with an initial state and provide a sequence of events that causes state transitions. As each event occurs, the transition changes the active state and a new event occurs. In this way, a sequence of events selects a path of states (or equivalently, of transitions) through the machine.

4.3.3 Petri Nets

Petri nets were the topic of Carl Adam Petri's Ph.D. dissertation in 1963; today, they are the accepted model for protocols and other applications involving concurrency and distributed processing. Petri nets are a special form of directed graph: a bipartite directed graph. (A bipartite graph has two sets of nodes, V_1 and V_2, and a set of edges E, with the restriction that every edge has its initial node on one of the sets V_1, V_2, and its terminal node in the other set.) In a Petri net, one of the sets is referred to as "places," and the other is referred to as "transitions." These sets are usually denoted as P and T, respectively. Places are inputs to and outputs of transitions; the input and output relationships are functions, and they are usually denoted as In and Out, as in the following definition.

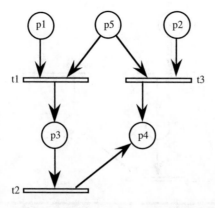

Figure 4.7   A Petri net.

Definition

A *Petri net* is a bipartite directed graph (P, T, In, Out), in which P and T are disjoint sets of nodes, and In and Out are sets of edges, where In ⊆ P × T, and Out ⊆ T × P.

For the sample Petri net in Figure 4.7, the sets P, T, In, and Out are

$$P = \{p_1, p_2, p_3, p_4, p_5\}$$

$$T = \{t_1, t_2, t_3\}$$

$$In = \{<p_1, t_1>, <p_5, t_1>, <p_5, t_3>, <p_2, t_3>, <p_3, t_2>\}$$

$$Out = \{<t_1, p_3>, <t_2, p_4>, <t_3, p_4>\}$$

Petri nets are executable in more interesting ways than finite state machines. The next few definitions lead us to Petri net execution.

Definition

A *marked Petri net* is a 5-tuple (P, T, In, Out, M) in which (P, T, In, Out) is a Petri net and M is a set of mappings of places to positive integers.

The set M is called the marking set of the Petri net. Elements of M are n-tuples, where n is the number of places in the set P. For the Petri net in Figure 4.7, the set M contains elements of the form $<n_1, n_2, n_3, n_4, n_5>$, where the n's are the integers associated with the respective places. The number associated with a place refers to the number of tokens that are said to be "in" the place. Tokens are abstractions that can be interpreted in modeling situations. For example, tokens might refer to the number of times a place has been used, or the number of things in a place, or whether the place is true. Figure 4.8 shows a marked Petri net.

The marking tuple for the marked Petri net in Figure 4.8 is <1, 1, 0, 2, 0>. We need the concept of tokens to make two essential definitions.

Definition

A *transition in a Petri net is enabled* if at least one token is in each of its input places.

No enabled transitions are in the marked Petri net in Figure 4.8. If we put a token in place p_3, then transition t_2 would be enabled.

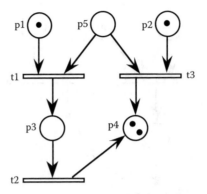

Figure 4.8   A marked Petri net.

Definition

When an enabled Petri net *transition fires*, one token is removed from each of its input places and one token is added to each of its output places.

In Figure 4.9, transition t_2 is enabled in the upper net and has been fired in the lower net.

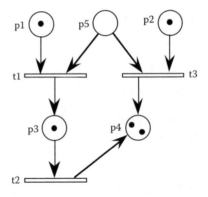

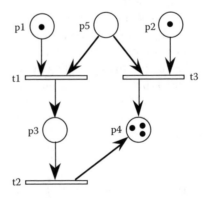

Figure 4.9   Before and after firing t_2.

The marking set for the net in Figure 4.9 contains two tuples — the first shows the net when t_2 is enabled, and the second shows the net after t_2 has fired.

$$M = \{<1, 1, 1, 2, 0>, <1, 1, 0, 3, 0>\}$$

Tokens may be created or destroyed by transition firings. Under special conditions, the total number of tokens in a net never changes; such nets are called conservative. We usually do not worry about token conservation. Markings let us execute Petri nets in much the same way that we execute finite state machines. (It turns out that finite state machines are a special case of Petri nets.) Suppose we had a different marking of the net in Figure 4.7; in this new marking, places p_1, p_2, and p_5 are all marked. With such a marking, transitions t_1 and t_3 are both enabled. If we choose to fire transition t_1, the token in place p_5 is removed and t_3 is no longer enabled. Similarly, if we choose to fire t_3, we disable t_1. This pattern is known as Petri net conflict. More specifically, we say that transitions t_1 and t_3 are in conflict with respect to place p_5. Petri net conflict exhibits an interesting form of interaction between two transitions; we will revisit this (and other) interactions in Chapter 15.

4.3.4 *Event-Driven Petri Nets*

Basic Petri nets need two slight enhancements to become event-driven Petri nets (EDPNs). The first enables them to express more closely event-driven systems, and the second deals with Petri net markings that express event quiescence, an important notion in object-oriented applications. Taken together, these extensions result in an effective, operational view of software requirements; elsewhere they are known as OSD nets (for operational software development) (Jorgensen, 1989).

Definition

An *EDPN* is a tripartite-directed graph (P, D, S, In, Out) composed of three sets of nodes, P, D, and S, and two mappings, In and Out, where

> P is a set of port events
> D is a set of data places
> S is a set of transitions
> In is a set of ordered pairs from $(P \cup D) \times S$
> Out is a set of ordered pairs from $S \times (P \cup D)$

EDPNs express four of the five basic system constructs defined in Chapter 14; only devices are missing. The set S of transitions corresponds to ordinary Petri net transitions, which are interpreted as actions.

Two kinds of places, port events and data places, are inputs to or outputs of transitions in S as defined by the input and output functions In and Out. A thread is a sequence of transitions in S, so we can always construct the inputs and outputs of a thread from the inputs and outputs of the transitions in the thread. EDPNs are graphically represented in much the same way as ordinary Petri nets; the only difference is the use of triangles for port event places. The EDPN in Figure 4.10 has four transitions, s_7, s_8, s_9, and s_{10}; two port input events, p_3 and p_4; and three data places, d_5, d_6, and d_7. It does not have port output events.

This is the EDPN that corresponds to the finite state machine developed for the dial portion of the Saturn windshield wiper system in Chapter 15 (see Figure 15.10). The components of this net are described in Table 4.1.

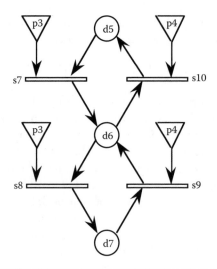

Figure 4.10   An EDPN.

Markings for an EDPN are more complicated because we want to be able to deal with event quiescence.

Definition

A *marking M of an EDPN* (P, D, S, In, Out) is a sequence M = <m1, m2, ...> of p-tuples, where p = k + n, and k and n are the number of elements in the sets P and D, and individual entries in a p-tuple indicate the number of tokens in the event or data place.

By convention, we will put the input places first, followed by the data places and then the output event places. An EDPN may have any number of markings; each corresponds to an execution of the net. Table 4.2 shows a sample marking of the EDPN in Figure 4.10.

The rules for transition enabling and firing in an EDPN are exact analogs of those for traditional Petri nets; a transition is enabled if there is at least one token in each input place, and when an enabled transition fires, one token is removed from each of its input places and one token is placed in each of its output places. Table 4.3 follows the marking sequence given in Table 4.2, showing which transitions are enabled and fired.

Table 4.1   EDPN Elements in Figure 4.10

Element	Type	Description
p3	Port input event	Rotate dial clockwise
p4	Port input event	Rotate dial counterclockwise
d5	Data place	Dial at position 1
d6	Data place	Dial at position 2
d7	Data place	Dial at position 3
s7	Transition	State transition: d5 to d6
s8	Transition	State transition: d6 to d7
s9	Transition	State transition: d7 to d6
s10	Transition	State transition: d6 to d5

Table 4.2   A Marking of the EDPN in Figure 4.10

Tuple	(p3, p4, d5, d6, d7)	Description
m1	(0, 0, 1, 0, 0)	Initial condition, in state d5
m2	(1, 0, 1, 0, 0)	p3 occurs
m3	(0, 0, 0, 1, 0)	In state d6
m4	(1, 0, 0, 1, 0)	p3 occurs
m5	(0, 0, 0, 0, 1)	In state d7
m6	(0, 1, 0, 0, 1)	p4 occurs
m7	(0, 0, 0, 1, 0)	In state d6

The important difference between EDPNs and traditional Petri nets is that event quiescence can be broken by creating a token in a port input event place. In traditional Petri nets, when no transition is enabled, we say that the net is deadlocked. In EDPNs, when no transition is enabled, the net is at a point of event quiescence. (Of course, if no event occurs, this is the same as deadlock.) Event quiescence occurs four times in the thread in Table 4.3, at m_1, m_3, m_5, and m_7.

The individual members in a marking can be thought of as snapshots of the executing EDPN at discrete points in time; these members are alternatively referred to as time steps, p-tuples, or marking vectors. This lets us think of time as an ordering that allows us to recognize "before" and "after." If we attach instantaneous time as an attribute of port events, data places, and transitions, we obtain a much clearer picture of thread behavior. One awkward part to this is how to treat tokens in a port output event place. Port output places always have outdegree = 0; in an ordinary Petri net, tokens cannot be removed from a place with a zero outdegree. If the tokens in a port output event place persist, this suggests that the event occurs indefinitely. Here again, the time attributes resolve the confusion; this time we need a duration of the marked output event. (Another possibility is to remove tokens from a marked output event place after one time step; this works reasonably well.)

4.3.5 StateCharts

David Harel had two goals when he developed the StateChart notation: he wanted to devise a visual notation that combined the ability of Venn diagrams to express hierarchy and the ability of directed graphs to express connectedness (Harel, 1988). Taken together, these capabilities provide

Table 4.3   Enabled and Fired Transitions in Table 4.2

Tuple	(p3, p4, d5, d6, d7)	Description
m1	(0, 0, 1, 0, 0)	Nothing enabled
m2	(1, 0, 1, 0, 0)	s7 enabled; s7 fired
m3	(0, 0, 0, 1, 0)	Nothing enabled
m4	(1, 0, 0, 1, 0)	s8 enabled; s8 fired
m5	(0, 0, 0, 0, 1)	Nothing enabled
m6	(0, 1, 0, 0, 1)	s9 enabled; s9 fired
m7	(0, 0, 0, 1, 0)	Nothing enabled

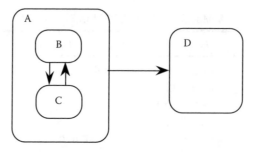

Figure 4.11   Blobs in a StateChart.

an elegant answer to the "state explosion" problem of ordinary finite state machines. The result is a highly sophisticated and very precise notation that is supported by commercially available CASE tools, notably the StateMate system from Telelogic. StateCharts are now the control model of choice for the Unified Modeling Language (UML) from IBM. (See http://www-306.ibm.com/software/rational/uml/ for more details.)

Harel uses the methodology-neutral term *blob* to describe the basic building block of a State-Chart. Blobs can contain other blobs in the same way that Venn diagrams show set containment. Blobs can also be connected to other blobs with edges in the same way that nodes in a directed graph are connected. In Figure 4.11, blob A contains two blobs (B and C), and they are connected by edges. Blob A is also connected to blob D by an edge.

As Harel intends, we can interpret blobs as states, and edges as transitions. The full StateChart system supports an elaborate language that defines how and when transitions occur (their training course runs for a full week, so this section is a highly simplified introduction). StateCharts are executable in a much more elaborate way than ordinary finite state machines. Executing a State-Chart requires a notion similar to that of Petri net markings. The initial state of a StateChart is indicated by an edge that has no source state.

When states are nested within other states, the same indication is used to show the lower-level initial state. In Figure 4.12, state A is the initial state, and when it is entered, state B is also entered

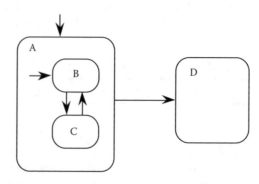

Figure 4.12   Initial states in a StateChart.

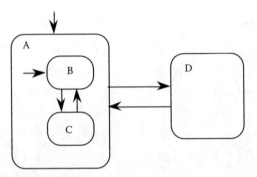

Figure 4.13   Default entry into substates.

at the lower level. When a state is entered, we can think of it as active in a way analogous to a marked place in a Petri net. (The StateChart tool uses colors to show which states are active, and this is equivalent to marking places in a Petri net.) A subtlety exists in Figure 4.12: the transition from state A to state D seems ambiguous at first because it has no apparent recognition of states B and C. The convention is that edges must start and end on the outline of a state. If a state contains substates, as state A does, the edge "refers" to all substates. Thus, the edge from A to D means that the transition can occur either from state B or from state C. If we had an edge from state D to state A, as in Figure 4.13, the fact that state B is indicated as the initial state means that the transition is really from state D to state B. This convention greatly reduces the tendency of finite state machines to look like spaghetti code.

The last aspect of StateCharts we will discuss is the notion of concurrent StateCharts. The dotted line in state D (see Figure 4.14) is used to show that state D really refers to two concurrent states, E and F. (Harel's convention is to move the state label of D to a rectangular tag on the perimeter of the state.) Although not shown here, we can think of E and F as parallel machines that execute concurrently. Because the edge from state A terminates on the perimeter of state D, when that transition occurs, both machines E and F are active (or marked, in the Petri net sense).

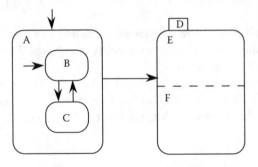

Figure 4.14   Concurrent states.

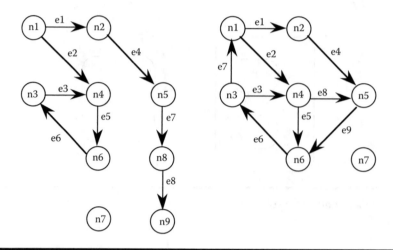

Figure 4.15   Directed graphs for exercise 5.

References

Harel, D., On visual formalisms, *Communications of the ACM*, Vol. 31, No. 5, May 1988, pp. 514–530.
Jorgensen, Paul C., An operational common denominator to the structured real-time methods, *Proceedings of the Fifth Structural Techniques Association (STA-5) Conference*, Chicago, May 11, 1989.
McCabe, Thomas J., A complexity metric, *IEEE Transactions of Software Engineering*, SE-2, 4, December 1976, pp. 308–320.

Exercises

1. Propose a definition for the length of a path in a graph.
2. What loop(s) is created if an edge is added between nodes n_5 and n_6 in the graph in Figure 4.1?
3. Convince yourself that 3-connectedness is an equivalence relation on the nodes of a digraph.
4. Compute the cyclomatic complexity for each of the structured programming constructs in Figure 4.5.
5. The digraphs in Figure 4.15 were obtained by adding nodes and edges to the digraph in Figure 4.3. Compute the cyclomatic complexity of each new digraph, and explain how the changes affected the complexity.
6. Suppose we make a graph in which nodes are people and edges correspond to some form of social interaction, such as "talks to" or "socializes with." Find graph theory concepts that correspond to social concepts such as popularity, cliques, and hermits.

FUNCTIONAL TESTING   II

Chapter 5

Boundary Value Testing

In Chapter 3, we saw that a function maps values from one set (its domain) to values in another set (its range) and that the domain and range can be cross-products of other sets. Any program can be considered to be a function in the sense that program inputs form its domain and program outputs form its range. Input domain testing is the best-known functional testing technique. In this and the next two chapters, we examine how to use knowledge of the functional nature of a program to identify test cases for the program. Historically, this form of testing has focused on the input domain, but it is often a good supplement to apply many of these techniques to develop range-based test cases.

5.1 Boundary Value Analysis

For the sake of comprehensible drawings, the discussion relates to a function, F, of two variables, x_1 and x_2. When the function F is implemented as a program, the input variables x_1 and x_2 will have some (possibly unstated) boundaries:

$$a \leq x_1 \leq b$$
$$c \leq x_2 \leq d$$

Unfortunately, the intervals [a, b] and [c, d] are referred to as the ranges of x_1 and x_2, so right away we have an overloaded term. The intended meaning will always be clear from its context. Strongly typed languages (such as Ada® and Pascal) permit explicit definition of such variable ranges. In fact, part of the historical reason for strong typing was to prevent programmers from making the kinds of errors that result in faults that are easily revealed by boundary value testing. Other languages (such as COBOL, Fortran, and C) are not strongly typed, so boundary value testing is more appropriate for programs coded in such languages. The input space (domain) of our function F is shown in Figure 5.1. Any point within the shaded rectangle is a legitimate input to the function F.

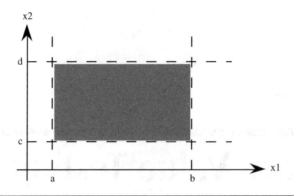

Figure 5.1   Input domain of a function of two variables.

Boundary value analysis focuses on the boundary of the input space to identify test cases. The rationale behind boundary value testing is that errors tend to occur near the extreme values of an input variable. Loop conditions, for example, may test for < when they should test for ≤, and counters are often "off by 1." The desktop publishing program with which this manuscript is written has an interesting boundary value problem. Two modes of textual display are used: one indicates new pages by a dotted line, and the other displays a page image showing where the text is placed on the page. If the cursor is at the last line of a page and new text is added, an anomaly occurs: in the first mode, the new line(s) simply appears, and the dotted line (page break) is adjusted. In the page display mode, however, the new text is lost—it does not appear on either page.

The basic idea of boundary value analysis is to use input variable values at their minimum, just above the minimum, a nominal value, just below their maximum, and their maximum. A commercially available testing tool (originally named T) generates such test cases for a properly specified program. This tool has been successfully integrated with two popular front-end CASE tools (Teamwork from Cadre Systems, and Software through Pictures from Aonix, http://www.aonix.com/pdf/2140-AON.pdf). The T tool refers to these values as min, min+, nom, max−, and max. We will use these conventions here.

The next part of boundary value analysis is based on a critical assumption; it is known as the single fault assumption in reliability theory. This says that failures are only rarely the result of the simultaneous occurrence of two (or more) faults. Thus, the boundary value analysis test cases are obtained by holding the values of all but one variable at their nominal values, and letting that variable assume its extreme values. The boundary value analysis test cases for our function F of two variables (illustrated in Figure 5.2) are

$$\{<x_{1nom}, x_{2min}>, <x_{1nom}, x_{2min+}>, <x_{1nom}, x_{2nom}>, <x_{1nom}, x_{2max-}>, <x_{1nom}, x_{2max}>,$$
$$<x_{1min}, x_{2nom}>, <x_{1min+}, x_{2nom}>, <x_{1max-}, x_{2nom}>, <x_{1max}, x_{2nom}>\}$$

5.1.1 Generalizing Boundary Value Analysis

The basic boundary value analysis technique can be generalized in two ways: by the number of variables and by the kinds of ranges. Generalizing the number of variables is easy: if we have a function of n variables, we hold all but one at the nominal values and let the remaining variable assume the

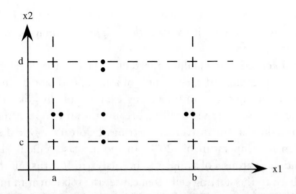

Figure 5.2   Boundary value analysis test cases for a function of two variables.

min, min+, nom, max–, and max values, repeating this for each variable. Thus, for a function of n variables, boundary value analysis yields 4n + 1 unique test cases.

Generalizing ranges depends on the nature (or more precisely, the type) of the variables themselves. In the NextDate function, for example, we have variables for the month, the day, and the year. In a Fortran-like language, we would most likely encode these, so that January would correspond to 1, February to 2, and so on. In a language that supports user-defined types (like Pascal or Ada), we could define the variable month as an enumerated type {Jan., Feb.,..., Dec.}. Either way, the values for min, min+, nom, max–, and max are clear from the context. When a variable has discrete, bounded values, as the variables in the commission problem have, the min, min+, nom, max–, and max are also easily determined. When no explicit bounds are present, as in the triangle problem, we usually have to create artificial bounds. The lower bound of side lengths is clearly 1 (a negative side length is silly), but what might we do for an upper bound? By default, the largest representable integer (called MAXINT in some languages) is one possibility, or we might impose an arbitrary upper limit such as 200 or 2000.

Boundary value analysis does not make much sense for Boolean variables; the extreme values are TRUE and FALSE, but no clear choice is available for the remaining three. We will see in Chapter 7 that Boolean variables lend themselves to decision table-based testing. Logical variables also present a problem for boundary value analysis. In the ATM example, a customer's PIN is a logical variable, as is the transaction type (deposit, withdrawal, or inquiry). We could "go through the motions" of boundary value analysis testing for such variables, but the exercise is not very satisfying to the tester's intuition.

5.1.2 Limitations of Boundary Value Analysis

Boundary value analysis works well when the program to be tested is a function of several independent variables that represent bounded physical quantities. The key words here are *independent* and *physical quantities*. A quick look at the boundary value analysis test cases for Next-Date (in Section 5.5) shows them to be inadequate. Very little stress occurs on February and on leap years, for example. The real problem here is that interesting dependencies exist among the month, day, and year variables. Boundary value analysis presumes the variables to be truly independent. Even so, boundary value analysis happens to catch end-of-month and end-of-year faults. Boundary value analysis test cases are derived from the extrema of bounded, independent variables that refer to physical quantities, with no consideration of the nature of the function, or of the semantic meaning of the variables. We see boundary value analysis test cases to be rudimentary because they are obtained with very little insight and imagination. As with so many things, you get what you pay for.

The physical quantity criterion is equally important. When a variable refers to a physical quantity, such as temperature, pressure, air speed, angle of attack, load, and so forth, physical boundaries can be extremely important. (In an interesting example of this, Sky Harbor International Airport in Phoenix had to close on June 26, 1992, because the air temperature was 122°F. Aircraft pilots were unable to make certain instrument settings before take-off: the instruments could only accept a maximum air temperature of 120°F.) In another case, a medical analysis system uses stepper motors to position a carousel of samples to be analyzed. It turns out that the mechanics of moving the carousel back to the starting cell often causes the robot arm to miss the first cell.

As an example of logical (versus physical) variables, we might look at PINs or telephone numbers. It is hard to imagine what faults might be revealed by testing PIN values of 0000, 0001, 5000, 9998, and 9999.

5.2 Robustness Testing

Robustness testing is a simple extension of boundary value analysis: in addition to the five boundary value analysis values of a variable, we see what happens when the extrema are exceeded with a value slightly greater than the maximum (max+) and a value slightly less than the minimum (min–). Robustness test cases for our continuing example are shown in Figure 5.3.

Most of the discussion of boundary value analysis applies directly to robustness testing, especially the generalizations and limitations. The most interesting part of robustness testing is not with the inputs, but with the expected outputs. What happens when a physical quantity exceeds its maximum? If it is the angle of attack of an airplane wing, the aircraft might stall. If it is the load capacity of a public elevator, we hope nothing special would happen. If it is a date, like May 32, we would expect an error message. The main value of robustness testing is that it forces attention on exception handling. With strongly typed languages, robustness testing may be very awkward. In Pascal, for example, if a variable is defined to be within a certain range, values outside that range result in runtime errors that abort normal execution. This raises an interesting question of implementation philosophy: Is it better to perform explicit range checking and use exception handling to deal with robust values, or is it better to stay with strong typing? The exception handling choice mandates robustness testing.

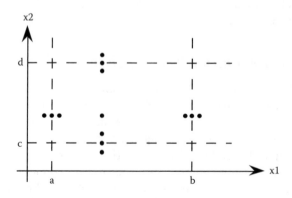

Figure 5.3   Robustness test cases for a function of two variables.

5.3 Worst-Case Testing

Boundary value analysis, as we said earlier, makes the single fault assumption of reliability theory. Rejecting this assumption means that we are interested in what happens when more than one variable has an extreme value. In electronic circuit analysis, this is called worst-case analysis; we use that idea here to generate worst-case test cases. For each variable, we start with the five-element set that contains the min, min+, nom, max–, and max values. We then take the Cartesian product (see Chapter 3) of these sets to generate test cases. The result of the two-variable version of this is shown in Figure 5.4.

Worst-case testing is clearly more thorough in the sense that boundary value analysis test cases are a proper subset of worst-case test cases. It also represents much more effort: worst-case testing for a function of n variables generates 5^n test cases, as opposed to $4n + 1$ test cases for boundary value analysis.

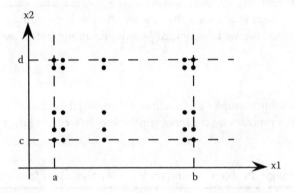

Figure 5.4   Worst-case test cases for a function of two variables.

Worst-case testing follows the generalization pattern we saw for boundary value analysis. It also has the same limitations, particularly those related to independence. Probably the best application for worst-case testing is where physical variables have numerous interactions, and where failure of the function is extremely costly. For really paranoid testing, we could go to robust worst-case testing. This involves the Cartesian product of the seven-element sets we used in robustness testing resulting in 7^n test cases. Figure 5.5 shows the robust worst-case test cases for our two variable functions.

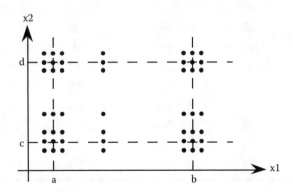

Figure 5.5   Robust worst-case test cases for a function of two variables.

5.4 Special Value Testing

Special value testing is probably the most widely practiced form of functional testing. It also is the most intuitive and least uniform. Special value testing occurs when a tester uses domain knowledge, experience with similar programs, and information about "soft spots" to devise test cases. We might also call this ad hoc testing or "seat-of-the-pants (or -skirt)" testing. No guidelines are used other than to use "best engineering judgment." As a result, special value testing is very dependent on the abilities of the tester.

Despite all the apparent negatives, special value testing can be very useful. In the next section, you will find test cases generated by the methods we just discussed for three of our examples. If you look carefully at these, especially for the NextDate function, you find that none is very satisfactory. If an interested tester defined special value test cases for NextDate, we would see several test cases involving February 28, February 29, and leap years. Even though special value testing is highly subjective, it often results in a set of test cases that is more effective in revealing faults than the test sets generated by the other methods we have studied—testimony to the craft of software testing.

5.5 Examples

Each of the three continuing examples is a function of three variables. Printing all the test cases from all the methods for each problem is very space consuming, so we have just selected examples.

Table 5.1 Triangle Problem Boundary Value Analysis Test Cases

Case	a	b	c	Expected Output
1	100	100	1	Isosceles
2	100	100	2	Isosceles
3	100	100	100	Equilateral
4	100	100	199	Isosceles
5	100	100	200	Not a Triangle
6	100	1	100	Isosceles
7	100	2	100	Isosceles
8	100	100	100	Equilateral
9	100	199	100	Isosceles
10	100	200	100	Not a Triangle
11	1	100	100	Isosceles
12	2	100	100	Isosceles
13	100	100	100	Equilateral
14	199	100	100	Isosceles
15	200	100	100	Not a Triangle

5.5.1 Test Cases for the Triangle Problem

In the problem statement, no conditions are specified on the triangle sides, other than being integers. Obviously, the lower bounds of the ranges are all 1. We arbitrarily take 200 as an upper bound. Table 5.1 contains boundary value test cases using these ranges. Notice that test cases 3, 8, and 13 are identical; two should be deleted.

Table 5.2 shows the worst case test cases in just "one corner" of the input space cube. (The remaining test cases are in the spread sheet for Exercise 5 at the end of this chapter.)

Table 5.2 Triangle Problem Worst-Case Test Cases

Case	a	b	c	Expected Output
1	1	1	1	Equilateral
2	1	1	2	Not a Triangle
3	1	1	100	Not a Triangle
4	1	1	199	Not a Triangle
5	1	1	200	Not a Triangle
6	1	2	1	Not a Triangle
7	1	2	2	Isosceles
8	1	2	100	Not a Triangle
9	1	2	199	Not a Triangle
10	1	2	200	Not a Triangle
11	1	100	1	Not a Triangle
12	1	100	2	Not a Triangle
13	1	100	100	Isosceles
14	1	100	199	Not a Triangle
15	1	100	200	Not a Triangle
16	1	199	1	Not a Triangle
17	1	199	2	Not a Triangle
18	1	199	100	Not a Triangle
19	1	199	199	Isosceles
20	1	199	200	Not a Triangle
21	1	200	1	Not a Triangle
22	1	200	2	Not a Triangle
23	1	200	100	Not a Triangle
24	1	200	199	Not a Triangle
25	1	200	200	Isosceles

5.5.2 Test Cases for the NextDate Function

Table 5.3 contains the worst case test cases for the NextDate function. As before only one corner of the input space cube B is shown.

Table 5.3 NextDate Worst-Case Test Cases

Case	Month	Day	Year	Expected Output
1	1	1	1812	January 2, 1812
2	1	1	1813	January 2, 1813
3	1	1	1912	January 2, 1912
4	1	1	2011	January 2, 2011
5	1	1	2012	January 2, 2012
6	1	2	1812	January 3, 1812
7	1	2	1813	January 3, 1813
8	1	2	1912	January 3, 1912
9	1	2	2011	January 3, 2011
10	1	2	2012	January 3, 2012
11	1	15	1812	January 16, 1812
12	1	15	1813	January 16, 1813
13	1	15	1912	January 16, 1912
14	1	15	2011	January 16, 2011
15	1	15	2012	January 16, 2012
16	1	30	1812	January 31, 1812
17	1	30	1813	January 31, 1813
18	1	30	1912	January 31, 1912
19	1	30	2011	January 31, 2011
20	1	30	2012	January 31, 2012
21	1	31	1812	February 1, 1812
22	1	31	1813	February 1, 1813
23	1	31	1912	February 1, 1912
24	1	31	2011	February 1, 2011
25	1	31	2012	February 1, 2012

5.5.3 Test Cases for the Commission Problem

Instead of going through 125 boring test cases again, we will look at some more interesting test cases for the commission problem. This time, we will look at boundary values for the output range, especially near the threshold points of $1000 and $1800. The output space of the commission is shown in Figure 5.6. The intercepts of these threshold planes with the axes are shown.

Table 5.4   Commission Problem Output Boundary Value Analysis Test Cases

Case	Locks	Stocks	Barrels	Sales	Commission	Comment
1	1	1	1	100	10	Output minimum
2	1	1	2	125	12.5	Output minimum +
3	1	2	1	130	13	Output minimum +
4	2	1	1	145	14.5	Output minimum +
5	5	5	5	500	50	Midpoint
6	10	10	9	975	97.5	Border point −
7	10	9	10	970	97	Border point −
8	9	10	10	955	95.5	Border point −
9	10	10	10	1000	100	Border point
10	10	10	11	1025	103.75	Border point +
11	10	11	10	1030	104.5	Border point +
12	11	10	10	1045	106.75	Border point +
13	14	14	14	1400	160	Midpoint
14	18	18	17	1775	216.25	Border point −
15	18	17	18	1770	215.5	Border point −
16	17	18	18	1755	213.25	Border point −
17	18	18	18	1800	220	Border point
18	18	18	19	1825	225	Border point +
19	18	19	18	1830	226	Border point +
20	19	18	18	1845	229	Border point +
21	48	48	48	4800	820	Midpoint
22	70	80	89	7775	1415	Output maximum −
23	70	79	90	7770	1414	Output maximum −
24	69	80	90	7755	1411	Output maximum −
25	70	80	90	7800	1420	Output maximum

Table 5.4 shows the worst case test cases in the output space for the commission problem. These test cases exercise the points at which the commission percentage changes.

The volume below the lower plane corresponds to sales below the $1000 threshold. The volume between the two planes is the 15% commission range. Part of the reason for using the output range to determine test cases is that cases from the input range are almost all in the 20% zone. We want to find input variable combinations that stress the boundary values: $100, $1000, $1800, and $7800. These test cases were developed with a spreadsheet, which saves a lot of calculator pecking. The minimum and maximum were easy, and the numbers happen to work out so that the border points are easy to generate. Here is where it gets interesting: test case 9 is the $1000 border point. If we tweak the input variables, we get values just below and just above the border (cases 6 to 8 and 10 to 12). If we wanted

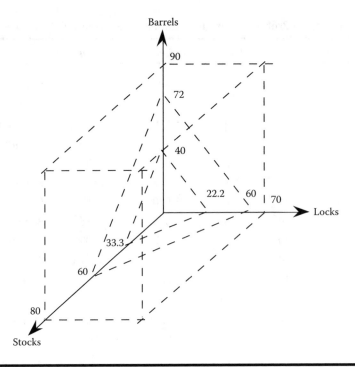

Figure 5.6 Input space of the commission problem.

to, we could pick values near the intercepts such as (22, 1, 1) and (21, 1, 1). As we continue in this way, we have a sense that we are exercising interesting parts of the code. We might claim that this is really a form of special value testing, because we used our mathematical insight to generate test cases.

Table 5.5 contains some typical special value test cases for the commission problem.

Table 5.5 Output Special Value Test Cases

Case	Locks	Stocks	Barrels	Sales	Commission	Comment
1	10	11	9	1005	100.75	Border point +
2	18	17	19	1795	219.25	Border point −
3	18	19	17	1805	221	Border point +

5.6 Random Testing

At least two decades of discussion of random testing are included in the literature. Most of this interest is among academics, and in a statistical sense, it is interesting. Our three sample problems lend themselves nicely to random testing. The basic idea is that, rather than always choose the min, min+, nom, max−, and max values of a bounded variable, use a random number

Table 5.6   Random Test Cases for the Triangle Program

Test Cases	Nontriangles	Scalene	Isosceles	Equilateral
1289	663	593	32	1
15436	7696	7372	367	1
17091	8556	8164	367	1
2603	1284	1252	66	1
6475	3197	3122	155	1
5978	2998	2850	129	1
9008	4447	4353	207	1
Percentage	49.83%	47.87%	2.29%	0.01%

generator to pick test case values. This avoids a form of bias in testing. It also raises a serious question: How many random test cases are sufficient? Later, when we discuss structural test coverage metrics, we will have an elegant answer. For now, Tables 5.6 to Table 5.8 show the results of randomly generated test cases. They are derived from a Visual Basic application that picks values for a bounded variable $a \leq x \leq b$ as follows:

$$x = Int((b - a + 1) * Rnd + a)$$

where the function Int returns the integer part of a floating point number, and the function Rnd generates random numbers in the interval [0, 1]. The program keeps generating random test cases until at least one of each output occurs. In each table, the program went through seven cycles that ended with the hard-to-generate test case. In Table 5.6 and Table 5.7, the last line shows what percentage of the random test cases was generated for each column. In the table for NextDate, the percentages are very close to the computed probability given in the last line of Table 5.8.

Table 5.7   Random Test Cases for the Commission Program

Test Cases	10%	15%	20%
91	1	6	84
27	1	1	25
72	1	1	70
176	1	6	169
48	1	1	46
152	1	6	145
125	1	4	120
Percentage	1.01%	3.62%	95.37%

Table 5.8   Random Test Cases for the NextDate Program

Test Cases	Days 1–30 of 31-Day Months	Day 31 of 31-Day Months	Days 1–29 of 30-Day Months	Days 30 of 30-Day Months
913	542	17	274	10
1101	621	9	358	8
4201	2448	64	1242	46
1097	600	21	350	9
5853	3342	100	1804	82
3959	2195	73	1252	42
1436	786	22	456	13
Percentage	56.76%	1.65%	30.91%	1.13%
Probability	56.45%	1.88%	31.18%	1.88%

Days 1–27 of Feb.	Feb. 28 of a Leap Year	Feb. 28 of a Non-Leap Year	Feb. 29 of a Leap Year	Impossible Days
45	1	1	1	22
83	1	1	1	19
312	1	8	3	77
92	1	4	1	19
417	1	11	2	94
310	1	6	5	75
126	1	5	1	26
7.46%	0.04%	0.19%	0.08%	1.79%
7.26%	0.07%	0.20%	0.07%	1.01%

5.7 Guidelines for Boundary Value Testing

With the exception of special value testing, the test methods based on the input domain of a function (program) are the most rudimentary of all functional testing methods. They share the common assumption that the input variables are truly independent, and when this assumption is not warranted, the methods generate unsatisfactory test cases (such as June 31, 1912, for NextDate). These methods have two other distinctions: normal versus robust values, and the single fault versus the multiple fault assumption. Just using these distinctions carefully will result in better testing. Each of these methods can be applied to the output range of a program, as we did for the commission problem.

Another useful form of output-based test cases is for systems that generate error messages. The tester should devise test cases to check that error messages are generated when they are appropriate, and are not falsely generated. Boundary value analysis can also be used for internal variables, such as loop control variables, indices, and pointers. Strictly speaking, these are not input variables, but errors in the use of these variables are quite common. Robustness testing is a good choice for testing internal variables.

Exercises

1. Develop a formula for the number of robustness test cases for a function of n variables.
2. Develop a formula for the number of robust worst-case test cases for a function of n variables.
3. Make a Venn diagram showing the relationships among test cases from boundary value analysis, robustness testing, worst-case testing, and robust worst-case testing.
4. What happens if we try to do output range robustness testing? Use the commission problem as an example.
5. If you did exercise 8 in Chapter 2, you are already familiar with the CRC Press Web site for downloads (http://www.crcpress.com). There you will find an Excel spreadsheet named specBasedTesting.xls. (It is an extended version of Naive.xls, and it contains the same inserted faults.) Different sheets contain worst-case boundary value test cases for the Triangle, NextDate, and Commission problems, respectively. Run these sets of test cases and compare the results with your naive testing from Chapter 2.

Chapter 6

Equivalence Class Testing

The use of equivalence classes as the basis for functional testing has two motivations: we would like to have a sense of complete testing and, at the same time, we would hope to avoid redundancy. Neither of these hopes is realized by boundary value testing: looking at the tables of test cases, it is easy to see massive redundancy — and looking more closely, serious gaps exist. Equivalence class testing echoes the two deciding factors of boundary value testing, robustness, and the single/multiple fault assumption. Three forms of equivalence class testing were identified in the first edition of this book; here, we identify four. The single versus multiple fault assumption yields the weak/strong distinction made in the first edition. The focus on invalid data yields a new distinction: robust versus normal.

Most of the standard testing texts (Myers, 1979; Mosley, 1993) discuss what we will call weak robust equivalence class testing. This traditional form focuses on invalid data values, and it is (was) a consequence of the dominant style of programming in the 1960s and 1970s. Input data validation was an important issue at the time, and "garbage in, garbage out" was the programmer's watchword. The usual response to this problem was extensive input validation sections of a program. Authors and seminar leaders frequently commented that in the classic afferent/central/efferent architecture of structured programming, the afferent portion often represented 80% of the total source code. In this context, it is natural to emphasize input data validation. The gradual shift to modern programming languages, especially those that feature strong data typing, and then to graphical user interfaces (GUIs) obviated much of the need for input data validation.

6.1 Equivalence Classes

In Chapter 3, we noted that the important aspect of equivalence classes is that they form a partition of a set, where partition refers to a collection of mutually disjoint subsets, the union of which is the entire set. This has two important implications for testing: the fact that the entire set is represented provides a form of completeness, and the disjointedness ensures a form of nonredundancy. Because the subsets are determined by an equivalence relation, the elements of a subset have something in common. The idea of equivalence class testing is to identify test cases by using one element from each equivalence class. If the equivalence classes are chosen wisely, this greatly reduces the potential redundancy among test cases. In the triangle problem, for example, we would certainly have a test case for an equilateral triangle, and we might pick the triple (5, 5, 5) as inputs for a test case. If we did this, we would not expect to learn much from test cases such as (6, 6, 6) and (100, 100, 100). Our intuition tells us that these would be treated the same as the first test case; thus, they would be redundant. When we consider structural testing in Part III, we shall see that "treated the same" maps onto "traversing the same execution path."

The key (and the craft) of equivalence class testing is the choice of the equivalence relation that determines the classes. Very often, we make this choice by second-guessing the likely implementation and thinking about the functional manipulations that must somehow be present in the implementation. We will illustrate this with our continuing examples, but first, we need to make a distinction between weak and strong equivalence class testing. After that, we will compare these to the traditional form of equivalence class testing.

We need to enrich the function we used in boundary value testing. Again, for the sake of comprehensible drawings, the discussion relates to a function, F, of two variables, x_1 and x_2. When F is implemented as a program, the input variables x_1 and x_2 will have the following boundaries, and intervals within the boundaries:

$$a \le x_1 \le d, \text{ with intervals } [a, b), [b, c), [c, d]$$

$$e \le x_2 \le g, \text{ with intervals } [e, f), [f, g]$$

where square brackets and parentheses denote, respectively, closed and open interval endpoints. The intervals presumably correspond to some distinction in the program being tested, for example, the commission ranges in the commission problem. Invalid values of x_1 and x_2 are $x_1 < a$, $x_1 > d$ and $x_2 < e$, $x_2 > g$.

6.1.1 Weak Normal Equivalence Class Testing

With the notation as given previously, weak normal equivalence class testing is accomplished by using one variable from each equivalence class (interval) in a test case. (Note the effect of the single fault assumption.) For the previous example, we would end up with the weak equivalence class test cases shown in Figure 6.1.

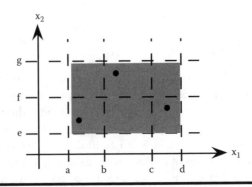

Figure 6.1 Weak normal equivalence class test cases.

These three test cases use one value from each equivalence class. We identify these in a systematic way, thus the apparent pattern. In fact, we will always have the same number of weak equivalence class test cases as classes in the partition with the largest number of subsets.

6.1.2 *Strong Normal Equivalence Class Testing*

Strong equivalence class testing is based on the multiple fault assumption, so we need test cases from each element of the Cartesian product of the equivalence classes, as shown in Figure 6.2.

Notice the similarity between the pattern of these test cases and the construction of a truth table in propositional logic. The Cartesian product guarantees that we have a notion of completeness in two senses: we cover all the equivalence classes, and we have one of each possible combination of inputs.

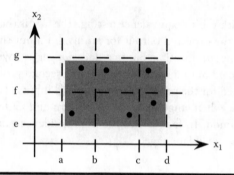

Figure 6.2   Strong normal equivalence class test cases.

As we shall see from our continuing examples, the key to good equivalence class testing is the selection of the equivalence relation. Watch for the notion of inputs being treated the same. Most of the time, equivalence class testing defines classes of the input domain. There is no reason why we could not define equivalence relations on the output range of the program function being tested; in fact, this is the simplest approach for the triangle problem.

6.1.3 *Weak Robust Equivalence Class Testing*

The name for this form is admittedly counterintuitive and oxymoronic. How can something be both weak and robust?

The robust part comes from consideration of invalid values, and the weak part refers to the single fault assumption. (This form was referred to as "traditional equivalence class testing" in the first edition of this book.)

1. For valid inputs, use one value from each valid class (as in what we have called weak normal equivalence class testing. Note that each input in these test cases will be valid.)
2. For invalid inputs, a test case will have one invalid value and the remaining values will all be valid. (Thus, a single failure should cause the test case to fail.)

The test cases resulting from this strategy are shown in Figure 6.3.

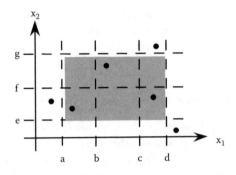

Figure 6.3 Weak robust equivalence class test cases.

Two problems occur with robust equivalence testing. The first is that, very often, the specification does not define what the expected output for an invalid input should be. (We could argue that this is a deficiency of the specification, but that does not get us anywhere.) Thus, testers spend a lot of time defining expected outputs for these cases. The second problem is that strongly typed languages eliminate the need for the consideration of invalid inputs. Traditional equivalence testing is a product of the time when languages such as Fortran and COBOL were dominant; thus, this type of error was common. In fact, it was the high incidence of such errors that led to the implementation of strongly typed languages.

6.1.4 Strong Robust Equivalence Class Testing

At least the name for this form is neither counterintuitive nor oxymoronic, just redundant. As before, the robust part comes from consideration of invalid values, and the strong part refers to the multiple fault assumption. (This form was omitted in the first edition of this book.)

We obtain test cases from each element of the Cartesian product of all the equivalence classes, as shown in Figure 6.4.

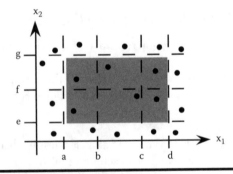

Figure 6.4 Strong robust equivalence class test cases.

6.2   Equivalence Class Test Cases for the Triangle Problem

In the problem statement, we note that four possible outputs can occur: Not a Triangle, Scalene, Isosceles, and Equilateral. We can use these to identify output (range) equivalence classes as follows:

> R1 = {<a, b, c> : the triangle with sides a, b, and c is equilateral}
> R2 = {<a, b, c> : the triangle with sides a, b, and c is isosceles}
> R3 = {<a, b, c> : the triangle with sides a, b, and c is scalene}
> R4 = {<a, b, c> : sides a, b, and c do not form a triangle}

Four weak normal equivalence class test cases, chosen arbitrarily from each class, are:

Test Case	a	b	c	Expected Output
WN1	5	5	5	Equilateral
WN2	2	2	3	Isosceles
WN3	3	4	5	Scalene
WN4	4	1	2	Not a Triangle

Because no valid subintervals of variables a, b, and c exist, the strong normal equivalence class test cases are identical to the weak normal equivalence class test cases.

Considering the invalid values for a, b, and c yields the following additional weak robust equivalence class test cases. (The invalid values could be zero, any negative number, or any number greater than 200.)

Test Case	a	b	c	Expected Output
WR1	−1	5	5	Value of a is not in the range of permitted values
WR2	5	−1	5	Value of b is not in the range of permitted values
WR3	5	5	−1	Value of c is not in the range of permitted values
WR4	201	5	5	Value of a is not in the range of permitted values
WR5	5	201	5	Value of b is not in the range of permitted values
WR6	5	5	201	Value of c is not in the range of permitted values

Here is one "corner" of the cube in 3-space of the additional strong robust equivalence class test cases:

Test Case	a	b	c	Expected Output
SR1	−1	5	5	Value of a is not in the range of permitted values
SR2	5	−1	5	Value of b is not in the range of permitted values
SR3	5	5	−1	Value of c is not in the range of permitted values
SR4	−1	−1	5	Values of a, b are not in the range of permitted values
SR5	5	−1	−1	Values of b, c are not in the range of permitted values
SR6	−1	5	−1	Values of a, c are not in the range of permitted values
SR7	−1	−1	−1	Values of a, b, c are not in the range of permitted values

Notice how thoroughly the expected outputs describe the invalid input values.

Equivalence class testing is clearly sensitive to the equivalence relation used to define classes. Here is another instance of craftsmanship. If we base equivalence classes on the input domain, we obtain a richer set of test cases. What are some of the possibilities for the three integers, a, b, and c? They can all be equal, exactly one pair can be equal (this can happen in three ways), or none can be equal:

$$D1 = \{<a, b, c> : a = b = c\}$$
$$D2 = \{<a, b, c> : a = b, a \neq c\}$$
$$D3 = \{<a, b, c> : a = c, a \neq b\}$$
$$D4 = \{<a, b, c> : b = c, a \neq b\}$$
$$D5 = \{<a, b, c> : a \neq b, a \neq c, b \neq c\}$$

As a separate question, we can apply the triangle property to see if they even constitute a triangle. (For example, the triplet <1, 4, 1> has exactly one pair of equal sides, but these sides do not form a triangle.)

$$D6 = \{<a, b, c> : a \geq b + c\}$$
$$D7 = \{<a, b, c> : b \geq a + c\}$$
$$D8 = \{<a, b, c> : c \geq a + b\}$$

If we wanted to be even more thorough, we could separate the "greater than or equal to" into two distinct cases; thus, the set D6 would become:

$$D6' = \{<a, b, c> : a = b + c\}$$
$$D6'' = \{<a, b, c> : a > b + c\}$$

and similarly for D7 and D8.

6.3 Equivalence Class Test Cases for the NextDate Function

The NextDate function illustrates very well the craft of choosing the underlying equivalence relation. Recall that NextDate is a function of three variables—month, day, and year—and these have intervals of valid values defined as follows:

> M1 = {month : 1 ≤ month ≤ 12}
> D1 = {day : 1 ≤ day ≤ 31}
> Y1 = {year : 1812 ≤ year ≤ 2012}

The invalid equivalence classes are:

> M2 = {month : month < 1}
> M3 = {month : month > 12}
> D2 = {day : day < 1}
> D3 = {day : day > 31}
> Y2 = {year : year < 1812}
> Y3 = {year : year > 2012}

Because the number of valid classes equals the number of independent variables, only one weak normal equivalence class test case occurs, and it is identical to the strong normal equivalence class test case:

Case ID	Month	Day	Year	Expected Output
WN1, SN1	6	15	1912	6/16/1912

Here is the full set of weak robust test cases:

Case ID	Month	Day	Year	Expected Output
WR1	6	15	1912	6/16/1912
WR2	−1	15	1912	Value of month not in the range 1..12
WR3	13	15	1912	Value of month not in the range 1..12
WR4	6	−1	1912	Value of day not in the range 1..31
WR5	6	32	1912	Value of day not in the range 1..31
WR6	6	15	1811	Value of year not in the range 1812..2012
WR7	6	15	2013	Value of year not in the range 1812..2012

As with the triangle problem, here is one corner of the cube in 3-space of the additional strong robust equivalence class test cases:

Case ID	Month	Day	Year	Expected Output
SR1	−1	15	1912	Value of month not in the range 1..12
SR2	6	−1	1912	Value of day not in the range 1..31
SR3	6	15	1811	Value of year not in the range 1812..2012
SR4	−1	−1	1912	Value of month not in the range 1..12 Value of day not in the range 1..31
SR5	6	−1	1811	Value of day not in the range 1..31 Value of year not in the range 1812..2012
SR6	−1	15	1811	Value of month not in the range 1..12 Value of year not in the range 1812..2012
SR7	−1	−1	1811	Value of month not in the range 1..12 Value of day not in the range 1..31 Value of year not in the range 1812..2012

If we more carefully choose the equivalence relation, the resulting equivalence classes will be more useful. Recall that earlier we said that the gist of the equivalence relation is that elements in a class are treated the same way. One way to see the deficiency of the traditional approach is that the treatment is at the valid/invalid level. We next reduce the granularity by focusing on more specific treatment.

What must be done to an input date? If it is not the last day of a month, the NextDate function will simply increment the day value. At the end of a month, the next day is 1 and the month is incremented. At the end of a year, both the day and the month are reset to 1, and the year is incremented. Finally, the problem of leap year makes determining the last day of a month interesting. With all this in mind, we might postulate the following equivalence classes:

M1 = {month : month has 30 days}
M2 = {month : month has 31 days}
M3 = {month : month is February}
D1 = {day : 1 ≤ day ≤ 28}
D2 = {day : day = 29}
D3 = {day : day = 30}
D4 = {day : day = 31}
Y1 = {year : year = 2000}
Y2 = {year : year is a non-century leap year}
Y3 = {year : year is a common year}

By choosing separate classes for 30- and 31-day months, we simplify the question of the last day of the month. By taking February as a separate class, we can give more attention to leap year questions. We also give special attention to day values: days in D1 are (nearly) always incremented, while days in D4 only have meaning for months in M2. Finally, we have three classes of years: the special case of the year 2000, leap years, and non-leap years. This is not a perfect set of equivalence classes, but its use will reveal many potential errors.

6.3.1 Equivalence Class Test Cases

These classes yield the following weak equivalence class test cases. As before, the inputs are mechanically selected from the approximate middle of the corresponding class:

Case ID	Month	Day	Year	Expected Output
WN1	6	14	2000	6/15/2000
WN2	7	29	1996	7/30/1996
WN3	2	30	2002	Invalid Input Date
WN4	6	31	2000	Invalid Input Date

Mechanical selection of input values makes no consideration of our domain knowledge—thus the two impossible dates. This will always be a problem with automatic test case generation, because all of our domain knowledge is not captured in the choice of equivalence classes. The strong normal equivalence class test cases for the revised classes are:

Case ID	Month	Day	Year	Expected Output
SN1	6	14	2000	6/15/2000
SN2	6	14	1996	6/15/1996
SN3	6	14	2002	6/15/2002
SN4	6	29	2000	6/30/2000
SN5	6	29	1996	6/30/1996
SN6	6	29	2002	6/30/2002
SN7	6	30	2000	Invalid Input Date
SN8	6	30	1996	Invalid Input Date
SN9	6	30	2002	Invalid Input Date
SN10	6	31	2000	Invalid Input Date
SN11	6	31	1996	Invalid Input Date
SN12	6	31	2002	Invalid Input Date
SN13	7	14	2000	7/15/2000
SN14	7	14	1996	7/15/1996
SN15	7	14	2002	7/15/2002
SN16	7	29	2000	7/30/2000
SN17	7	29	1996	7/30/1996
SN18	7	29	2002	7/30/2002
SN19	7	30	2000	7/31/2000
SN20	7	30	1996	7/31/1996
SN21	7	30	2002	7/31/2002

(continued from previous page)

Case ID	Month	Day	Year	Expected Output
SN22	7	31	2000	8/1/2000
SN23	7	31	1996	8/1/1996
SN24	7	31	2002	8/1/2002
SN25	2	14	2000	2/15/2000
SN26	2	14	1996	2/15/1996
SN27	2	14	2002	2/15/2002
SN28	2	29	2000	Invalid Input Date
SN29	2	29	1996	3/1/1996
SN30	2	29	2002	Invalid Input Date
SN31	2	30	2000	Invalid Input Date
SN32	2	30	1996	Invalid Input Date
SN33	2	30	2002	Invalid Input Date
SN34	2	31	2000	Invalid Input Date
SN35	2	31	1996	Invalid Input Date
SN36	2	31	2002	Invalid Input Date

Moving from weak to strong normal testing raises some of the issues of redundancy that we saw with boundary value testing. The move from weak to strong, whether with normal or robust classes, always makes the presumption of independence, and this is reflected in the cross-product of the equivalence classes. Three month classes times four day classes times three year classes results in 36 strong normal equivalence class test cases. Adding two invalid classes for each variable will result in 150 strong robust equivalence class test cases (too many to show here).

We could also streamline our set of test cases by taking a closer look at the year classes. If we merge Y1 and Y2 and call the result the set of leap years, our 36 test cases would drop down to 24. This change suppresses special attention to considerations in the year 2000, and it also adds some complexity to the determination of which years are leap years. Balance this against how much might be learned from the present test cases.

6.4 Equivalence Class Test Cases for the Commission Problem

The input domain of the commission problem is naturally partitioned by the limits on locks, stocks, and barrels. These equivalence classes are exactly those that would also be identified by traditional equivalence class testing. The first class is the valid input; the other two are invalid. The input domain equivalence classes lead to very unsatisfactory sets of test cases. Equivalence classes defined on the output range of the commission function will be an improvement.

The valid classes of the input variables are:

L1   = {locks : $1 \leq locks \leq 70$}
L2   = {locks $= -1$} (occurs if locks $= -1$ is used to control input iteration)
S1   = {stocks : $1 \leq stocks \leq 80$}
B1   = {barrels : $1 \leq barrels \leq 90$}

The corresponding invalid classes of the input variables are:

L3	= {locks : locks = 0 OR locks < –1}
L4	= {locks : locks > 70}
S2	= {stocks : stocks < 1}
S3	= {stocks : stocks > 80}
B2	= {barrels : barrels < 1}
B3	= {barrels : barrels > 90}

One problem occurs, however. The variable locks are also used as a sentinel to indicate no more telegrams. When a value of –1 is given for locks, the While loop terminates, and the values of totalLocks, totalStocks, and totalBarrels are used to compute sales, and then commission.

Except for the names of the variables and the interval endpoint values, this is identical to our first version of the NextDate function. Therefore, we will have exactly one weak normal equivalence class test case — and again, it is identical to the strong normal equivalence class test case. Note that the case for locks = –1 just terminates the iteration. We will have eight weak robust test cases.

Case ID	Locks	Stocks	Barrels	Expected Output
WR1	10	10	10	$100
WR2	–1	40	45	Program terminates
WR3	–2	40	45	Value of Locks not in the range 1..70
WR4	71	40	45	Value of Locks not in the range 1..70
WR5	35	–1	45	Value of Stocks not in the range 1..80
WR6	35	81	45	Value of Stocks not in the range 1..80
WR7	35	40	–1	Value of Barrels not in the range 1..90
WR8	35	40	91	Value of Barrels not in the range 1..90

Finally, a corner of the cube will be in 3-space of the additional strong robust equivalence class test cases:

Case ID	Locks	Stocks	Barrels	Expected Output
SR1	–2	40	45	Value of Locks not in the range 1..70
SR2	35	–1	45	Value of Stocks not in the range 1..80
SR3	35	40	–2	Value of Barrels not in the range 1..90
SR4	–2	–1	45	Value of Locks not in the range 1..70 Value of Stocks not in the range 1..80
SR5	–2	40	–1	Value of Locks not in the range 1..70 Value of Barrels not in the range 1..90

Case ID	Locks	Stocks	Barrels	Expected Output
SR6	35	−1	−1	Value of Stocks not in the range 1..80 Value of Barrels not in the range 1..90
SR7	−2	−1	−1	Value of Locks not in the range 1..70 Value of Stocks not in the range 1..80 Value of Barrels not in the range 1..90

6.4.1 Output Range Equivalence Class Test Cases

Notice that of strong test cases—whether normal or robust—only one is a legitimate input. If we were really worried about error cases, this might be a good set of test cases. It can hardly give us a sense of confidence about the calculation portion of the problem, however. We can get some help by considering equivalence classes defined on the output range. Recall that sales is a function of the number of locks, stocks, and barrels sold:

$$sales = 45 \times locks + 30 \times stocks + 25 \times barrels$$

We could define equivalence classes of three variables by commission ranges:

> $S1 = \{<locks, stocks, barrels> : sales \leq 1000\}$
> $S2 = \{<locks, stocks, barrels> : 1000 < sales \leq 1800\}$
> $S3 = \{<locks, stocks, barrels> : sales > 1800\}$

Figure 5.6 helps us get a better feel for the input space. Elements of S1 are points with integer coordinates in the pyramid near the origin. Elements of S2 are points in the triangular slice between the pyramid and the rest of the input space. Finally, elements of S3 are all those points in the rectangular volume that are not in S1 or S2. All the error cases found by the strong equivalence classes of the input domain are outside of the rectangular space shown in Figure 5.6.

As was the case with the triangle problem, the fact that our input is a triplet means that we no longer take test cases from a Cartesian product.

Test Case	Locks	Stocks	Barrels	Sales	Commission
OR1	5	5	5	500	50
OR2	15	15	15	1500	175
OR3	25	25	25	2500	360

These test cases give us some sense that we are exercising important parts of the problem. Together with the weak robust test cases, we would have a pretty good test of the commission problem. We might want to add some boundary checking, just to make sure the transitions at sales of $1000 and $1800 are correct. This is not particularly easy because we can only choose values of locks, stocks, and barrels. It happens that the constants in this example are contrived so that there are nice triplets.

6.5 Guidelines and Observations

Now that we have gone through three examples, we conclude with some observations about, and guidelines for, equivalence class testing:

1. Obviously, the weak forms of equivalence class testing (normal or robust) are not as comprehensive as the corresponding strong forms.
2. If the implementation language is strongly typed (and invalid values cause runtime errors), it makes no sense to use the robust forms.
3. If error conditions are a high priority, the robust forms are appropriate.
4. Equivalence class testing is appropriate when input data is defined in terms of intervals and sets of discrete values. This is certainly the case when system malfunctions can occur for out-of-limit variable values.
5. Equivalence class testing is strengthened by a hybrid approach with boundary value testing. (We can reuse the effort made in defining the equivalence classes.)
6. Equivalence class testing is indicated when the program function is complex. In such cases, the complexity of the function can help identify useful equivalence classes, as in the NextDate function.
7. Strong equivalence class testing makes a presumption that the variables are independent, and the corresponding multiplication of test cases raises issues of redundancy. If any dependencies occur, they will often generate "error" test cases, as they did in the NextDate function. (The decision table technique in Chapter 7 resolves this problem.)
8. Several tries may be needed before the "right" equivalence relation is discovered, as we saw in the NextDate example. In other cases, there is an obvious or natural equivalence relation. When in doubt, the best bet is to try to second-guess aspects of any reasonable implementation.
9. The difference between the strong and weak forms of equivalence class testing is helpful in the distinction between progression and regression testing (see Chapters 12 and 14).

References

Mosley, D.J., *The Handbook of MIS Application Software Testing*, Yourdon Press, Prentice-Hall, Englewood Cliffs, NJ, 1993.
Myers, G.J., *The Art of Software Testing*, Wiley Interscience, New York, 1979.

Exercises

1. Starting with the 36 strong normal equivalence class test cases for the NextDate function, revise the day classes as discussed, and then find the other nine test cases.
2. If you use a compiler for a strongly typed language, discuss how it would react to robust equivalence class test cases.

3. Revise the set of weak normal equivalence classes for the extended triangle problem that considers right triangles.

4. Compare and contrast the single/multiple fault assumption with boundary value and equivalence class testing.

5. The spring and fall changes between standard and daylight savings time create an interesting problem for telephone bills. In the spring, this switch occurs at 2:00 A.M. the Sunday morning (in March) when clocks are reset to 3:00 A.M. The symmetric change takes place usually on the first Sunday in November (The days are different in the European Union Countries) when the clock changes from 2:59:59 back to 2:00:00.

   Develop equivalence classes for a long-distance telephone service function that bills calls using the following rate structure:

   Call duration ≤ 20 minutes charged at $0.05 per each minute or fraction of a minute
   Call duration > 20 minutes charged at $1.00 plus $0.10 per each minute or fraction of a minute in excess of 20 minutes

   Make these assumptions:
   - Chargeable time of a call begins when the called party answers, and ends when the calling party disconnects.
   - Call durations of seconds are rounded up to the next larger minute.
   - No call lasts more than 30 hours.

6. If you did exercise 8 in Chapter 2 and exercise 5 in Chapter 5, you are already familiar with the CRC Press Web site for downloads (http://www. crcpress.com). There you will find an Excel spreadsheet named specBasedTesting.xls. (It is an extended version of Naive.xls, and it contains the same inserted faults.) Different sheets contain strong normal equivalence class test cases for the triangle, NextDate, and commission problems, respectively. Run these sets of test cases and compare the results with your naive testing from Chapter 2 and your boundary value testing from Chapter 5.

Chapter 7

Decision Table–Based Testing

Of all the functional testing methods, those based on decision tables are the most rigorous because decision tables enforce logical rigor. Two closely related methods are used: cause–effect graphing (Elmendorf, 1973; Myers, 1979) and the decision tableau method (Mosley, 1993). These are more cumbersome to use and are fully redundant with decision tables, so we will not discuss them here. Both are covered in Mosley (1993).

7.1 Decision Tables

Decision tables have been used to represent and analyze complex logical relationships since the early 1960s. They are ideal for describing situations in which a number of combinations of actions are taken under varying sets of conditions. Some of the basic decision table terms are illustrated in Table 7.1.

A decision table has four portions: the left-most column is the stub portion; to the right is the entry portion. The the condition portion is noted by c's, the action portion is noted by a's. Thus, we can refer to the condition stub, the condition entries, the action stub, and the action entries. A column in the entry portion is a rule. Rules indicate which actions, if any, are taken for the circumstances indicated in the condition portion of the rule. In the decision table in Table 7.1, when conditions c_1, c_2, and c_3 are all true, actions a_1 and a_2 occur. When c_1 and c_2 are both true and c_3 is false, actions a_1 and a_3 occur. The entry for c_3 in the rule where c_1 is true and c_2 is false is called a "don't care" entry. The don't care entry has two major interpretations: the condition is irrelevant, or the condition does not apply. Sometimes people will enter the "n/a" symbol for this latter interpretation.

When we have binary conditions (true/false, yes/no, 0/1), the condition portion of a decision table is a truth table (from propositional logic) that has been rotated 90°. This structure guarantees that we consider every possible combination of condition values. When we use decision tables for test case identification, this completeness property of a decision table guarantees a form of complete testing. Decision tables in which all the conditions are binary are called limited entry decision tables. If conditions are allowed to have several values, the resulting tables are called extended entry decision tables. We will see examples of both types for the NextDate problem.

Table 7.1   Portions of a Decision Table

Stub	Rule 1	Rule 2	Rules 3, 4	Rule 5	Rule 6	Rules 7, 8
c1	T	T	T	F	F	F
c2	T	T	F	T	T	F
c3	T	F	–	T	F	–
a1	X	X		X		
a2	X				X	
a3		X		X		
a4			X			X

Decision tables are deliberately declarative (as opposed to imperative); no particular order is implied by the conditions, and selected actions do not occur in any particular order.

7.1.1   Technique

To identify test cases with decision tables, we interpret conditions as inputs and actions as outputs. Sometimes conditions end up referring to equivalence classes of inputs, and actions refer to major functional processing portions of the item tested. The rules are then interpreted as test cases. Because the decision table can mechanically be forced to be complete, we know we have a comprehensive set of test cases.

Several techniques that produce decision tables are more useful to testers. One helpful style is to add an action to show when a rule is logically impossible.

In the decision table in Table 7.2, we see examples of don't care entries and impossible rule usage. If the integers a, b, and c do not constitute a triangle, we do not even care about possible equalities, as indicated in the first rule. In rules 3, 4, and 6, if two pairs of integers are equal, by transitivity, the third pair must be equal; thus, the negative entry makes these rules impossible.

Table 7.2   Decision Table for the Triangle Problem

c1: a, b, c form a triangle?	F	T	T	T	T	T	T	T	T
c2: a = b?	–	T	T	T	T	F	F	F	F
c3: a = c?	–	T	T	F	F	T	T	F	F
c4: b = c?	–	T	F	T	F	T	F	T	F
a1: Not a Triangle	X								
a2: Scalene									X
a3: Isosceles						X		X	X
a4: Equilateral		X							
a5: Impossible			X	X		X			

Table 7.3   Refined Decision Table for the Triangle Problem

c1: $a < b + c$?	F	T	T	T	T	T	T	T	T	T	T
c2: $b < a + c$?	—	F	T	T	T	T	T	T	T	T	T
c3: $c < a + b$?	—	—	F	T	T	T	T	T	T	T	T
c4: $a = b$?	—	—	—	T	T	T	T	F	F	F	F
c5: $a = c$?	—	—	—	T	T	F	F	T	T	F	F
c6: $b = c$?	—	—	—	T	F	T	F	T	F	T	F
a1: Not a Triangle	X	X	X								
a2: Scalene											X
a3: Isosceles							X		X	X	
a4: Equilateral				X							
a5: Impossible					X	X		X			

The decision table in Table 7.3 illustrates another consideration related to technique: the choice of conditions can greatly expand the size of a decision table. Here, we expanded the old condition (c1: a, b, c form a triangle?) to a more detailed view of the three inequalities of the triangle property. If any one of these fails, the three integers do not constitute sides of a triangle. We could expand this still further because there are two ways an inequality could fail: one side could equal the sum of the other two, or it could be strictly greater.

When conditions refer to equivalence classes, decision tables have a characteristic appearance. Conditions in the decision table in Table 7.4 are from the NextDate problem; they refer to the mutually exclusive possibilities for the month variable. Because a month is in exactly one equivalence class, we cannot ever have a rule in which two entries are true. The don't care entries (—) really mean "must be false." Some decision table aficionados use the notation F! to make this point.

Use of don't care entries has a subtle effect on the way in which complete decision tables are recognized. For limited entry decision tables, if n conditions exist, there must be 2^n rules. When don't care entries really indicate that the condition is irrelevant, we can develop a rule count as follows: rules in which no don't care entries occur count as one rule, and each don't care entry in

Table 7.4   Decision Table with Mutually Exclusive Conditions

Conditions	R1	R2	R3
c1: month in M1?	T	—	—
c2: month in M2?	—	T	—
c3: month in M3?	—	—	T
a1			
a2			
a3			

Table 7.5 Decision Table for Table 7.3 with Rule Counts

c1: $a < b + c$?	F	T	T	T	T	T	T	T	T	T	T
c2: $b < a + c$?	—	F	T	T	T	T	T	T	T	T	T
c3: $c < a + b$?	—	—	F	T	T	T	T	T	T	T	T
c4: $a = b$?	—	—	—	T	T	T	T	F	F	F	F
c5: $a = c$?	—	—	—	T	T	F	F	T	T	F	F
c6: $b = c$?	—	—	—	T	F	T	F	T	F	T	F
Rule count	32	16	8	1	1	1	1	1	1	1	1
a1: Not a Triangle	X	X	X								
a2: Scalene											X
a3: Isosceles								X		X	X
a4: Equilateral				X							
a5: Impossible					X	X		X			

a rule doubles the count of that rule. The rule counts for the decision table in Table 7.3 are shown in Table 7.5. Notice that the sum of the rule counts is 64 (as it should be).

If we apply this simplistic algorithm to the decision table in Table 7.4, we get the rule counts shown in Table 7.6.

Table 7.6 Rule Counts for a Decision Table with Mutually Exclusive Conditions

Conditions	R1	R2	R3
c1: month in M1	T	—	—
c2: month in M2	—	T	—
c3: month in M3	—	—	T
Rule count	4	4	4
a1			

We should only have eight rules, so we clearly have a problem. To see where the problem lies, we expand each of the three rules, replacing the "—" entries with the T and F possibilities, as shown in Table 7.7.

Notice that we have three rules in which all entries are T: rules 1.1, 2.1, and 3.1. We also have two rules with T, T, F entries: rules 1.2 and 2.2. Similarly, rules 1.3 and 3.2 are identical; so are rules 2.3 and 3.3. If we delete the repetitions, we end up with seven rules; the missing rule is the one in which all conditions are false. The result of this process is shown in Table 7.8. The impossible rules are also shown.

The ability to recognize (and develop) complete decision tables puts us in a powerful position with respect to redundancy and inconsistency. The decision table in Table 7.9 is redundant — three conditions and nine rules exist. (Rule 9 is identical to rule 4.)

Notice that the action entries in rule 9 are identical to those in rules 1 to 4. As long as the actions in a redundant rule are identical to the corresponding part of the decision table, we do

Table 7.7 Expanded Version of Table 7.6

Conditions	1.1	1.2	1.3	1.4	2.1	2.2	2.3	2.4	3.1	3.2	3.3	3.4
c1: mo. in M1	T	T	T	T	T	T	F	F	T	T	F	F
c2: mo. in M2	T	T	F	F	T	T	T	T	T	F	T	F
c3: mo. in M3	T	F	T	F	T	F	T	F	T	T	T	T
Rule count	1	1	1	1	1	1	1	1	1	1	1	1
a1												

Table 7.8 Mutually Exclusive Conditions with Impossible Rules

	1.1	1.2	1.3	1.4	2.3	2.4	3.4	
c1: mo. in M1	T	T	T	T	F	F	F	F
c2: mo. in M2	T	T	F	F	T	T	F	F
c3: mo. in M3	T	F	T	F	T	F	T	F
Rule count	1	1	1	1	1	1	1	1
a1: Impossible	X	X	X		X			X

Table 7.9 A Redundant Decision Table

Conditions	1–4	5	6	7	8	9
c1	T	F	F	F	F	T
c2	—	T	T	F	F	F
c3	—	T	F	T	F	F
a1	X	X	X	—	—	X
a2	—	X	X	X	—	—
a3	X	—	X	X	X	X

Table 7.10 An Inconsistent Decision Table

Conditions	1–4	5	6	7	8	9
c1	T	F	F	F	F	T
c2	—	T	T	F	F	F
c3	—	T	F	T	F	F
a1	X	X	X	—	—	—
a2	—	X	X	X	—	X
a3	X	—	X	X	X	—

not have much of a problem. If the action entries are different, as they are in Table 7.10, we have a bigger problem.

If the decision table in Table 7.10 were to process a transaction in which c1 is true and both c2 and c3 are false, both rules 4 and 9 apply. We can make two observations:

1. Rules 4 and 9 are inconsistent.
2. The decision table is nondeterministic.

Rules 4 and 9 are inconsistent because the action sets are different. The whole table is nondeterministic because there is no way to decide whether to apply rule 4 or rule 9. The bottom line for testers is that care should be taken when don't care entries are used in a decision table.

7.2 Test Cases for the Triangle Problem

Using the decision table in Table 7.3, we obtain 11 functional test cases: 3 impossible cases, 3 ways to fail the triangle property, 1 way to get an equilateral triangle, 1 way to get a scalene triangle, and 3 ways to get an isosceles triangle (see Table 7.11). Of course, we still need to provide actual values

Table 7.11 Test Cases from Table 7.3

Case ID	a	b	c	Expected Output
DT1	4	1	2	Not a Triangle
DT2	1	4	2	Not a Triangle
DT3	1	2	4	Not a Triangle
DT4	5	5	5	Equilateral
DT5	?	?	?	Impossible
DT6	?	?	?	Impossible
DT7	2	2	3	Isosceles
DT8	?	?	?	Impossible
DT9	2	3	2	Isosceles
DT10	3	2	2	Isosceles
DT11	3	4	5	Scalene

for the variables in the conditions. If we extended the decision table to show both ways to fail an inequality, we would pick up three more test cases (where one side is exactly the sum of the other two). Some judgment is required in this because of the exponential growth of rules. In this case, we would end up with many more don't care entries and more impossible rules.

7.3 Test Cases for the NextDate Function

The NextDate function was chosen because it illustrates the problem of dependencies in the input domain. This makes it a perfect example for decision table-based testing, because decision tables can highlight such dependencies. Recall that, in Chapter 6, we identified equivalence classes in the input domain of the NextDate function. One of the limitations we found in Chapter 6 was that indiscriminate selection of input values from the equivalence classes resulted in "strange" test cases, such as finding the next date to June 31, 1812. The problem stems from the presumption that the variables are independent. If they are, a Cartesian product of the classes makes sense. When logical dependencies exist among variables in the input domain, these dependencies are lost (suppressed is better) in a Cartesian product. The decision table format lets us emphasize such dependencies using the notion of the "impossible" action to denote impossible combinations of conditions (which are actually impossible rules). In this section, we will make three tries at a decision table formulation of the NextDate function.

7.3.1 *First Try*

Identifying appropriate conditions and actions presents an opportunity for craftsmanship. Suppose we start with a set of equivalence classes close to the one we used in Chapter 6:

> M1 = {month : month has 30 days}
> M2 = {month : month has 31 days}
> M3 = {month : month is February}
> D1 = {day : 1 ≤ day ≤ 28}
> D2 = {day : day = 29}
> D3 = {day : day = 30}
> D4 = {day : day = 31}
> Y1 = {year : year is a leap year}
> Y2 = {year : year is not a leap year}

If we wish to highlight impossible combinations, we could make a limited entry decision table with the following conditions and actions. (Note that the equivalence classes for the year variable collapse into one condition in Table 7.12.)

This decision table will have 256 rules, many of which will be impossible. If we wanted to show why these rules were impossible, we might revise our actions to the following:

> a1: Day invalid for this month
> a2: Cannot happen in a non-leap year
> a3: Compute the next date

Table 7.12 First Try Decision Table with 256 Rules

Conditions			
c1: month in M1?	T		
c2: month in M2?		T	
c3: month in M3?			T
c4: day in D1?			
c5: day in D2?			
c6: day in D3?			
c7: day in D4?			
c8: year in Y1?			
a1: impossible			
a2: next date			

7.3.2 Second Try

If we focus on the leap year aspect of the NextDate function, we could use the set of equivalence classes as they were in Chapter 6. These classes have a Cartesian product that contains 36 entries (test cases), with several that are impossible.

To illustrate another decision table technique, this time we will develop an extended entry decision table, and we will take a closer look at the action stub. In making an extended entry decision table, we must ensure that the equivalence classes form a true partition of the input domain. (Recall from Chapter 3 that a partition is a set of disjoint subsets where the union is the entire set.) If there were any overlaps among the rule entries, we would have a redundant case in which more than one rule could be satisfied. Here, Y2 is the set of years between 1812 and 2012, evenly divisible by four, excluding the year 2000:

M1 = {month : month has 30 days}
M2 = {month : month has 31 days}
M3 = {month : month is February}
D1 = {day : 1 ≤ day ≤ 28}
D2 = {day : day = 29}
D3 = {day : day = 30}
D4 = {day : day = 31}
Y1 = {year : year = 2000}
Y2 = {year : year is a non-century leap year}
Y3 = {year : year is a common year}

In a sense, we could argue that we have a "gray box" technique, because we take a closer look at the NextDate problem statement. To produce the next date of a given date, only five possible manipulations can be used: incrementing and resetting the day and month, and incrementing the year. (We will not let time go backward by resetting the year.) To follow the metaphor, we still cannot see inside the implementation box—the implementation could be a table lookup.

These conditions would result in a decision table with 36 rules that correspond to the Cartesian product of the equivalence classes. Combining rules with don't care entries yields the decision

Table 7.13 Second Try Decision Table with 36 Rules

	1	2	3	4	5	6	7	8
c1: month in	M1	M1	M1	M1	M2	M2	M2	M2
c2: day in	D1	D2	D3	D4	D1	D2	D3	D4
c3: year in	—	—	—	—	—	—	—	—
Rule count	3	3	3	3	3	3	3	3
Actions								
a1: impossible				X				
a2: increment day	X	X			X	X	X	
a3: reset day			X					X
a4: increment month			X					?
a5: reset month								?
a6: increment year								?

	9	10	11	12	13	14	15	16
c1: month in	M3	M3	M3	M3	M3	M3	M3	M3
c2: day in	D1	D1	D1	D2	D2	D2	D3	D4
c3: year in	Y1	Y2	Y3	Y1	Y2	Y3	—	—
Rule count	1	1	1	1	1	1	3	3
Actions								
a1: impossible						X	X	X
a2: increment day		X						
a3: reset day	X		X	X	X			
a4: increment month	X		X	X	X			
a5: reset month								
a6: increment year								

table in Table 7.13, which has 16 rules. We still have the problem with logically impossible rules, but this formulation helps us identify the expected outputs of a test case. If you complete the action entries in this table, you will find some cumbersome problems with December (in rule 8) and other problems with February 28 in rules 9, 11, and 12. We fix these next.

7.3.3 Third Try

We can clear up the end-of-year considerations with a third set of equivalence classes. This time, we are very specific about days and months, and we revert to the simpler leap year or non-leap year condition of the first try—so the year 2000 gets no special attention. (We could do a fourth try, showing year equivalence classes as in the second try, but by now you get the point.)

M1 = {month : month has 30 days}
M2 = {month : month has 31 days except December}
M3 = {month : month is December}
M4 = {month : month is February}
D1 = {day : 1 ≤ day ≤ 27}
D2 = {day : day = 28}
D3 = {day : day = 29}
D4 = {day : day = 30}
D5 = {day : day = 31}
Y1 = {year : year is a leap year}
Y2 = {year : year is a common year}

The Cartesian product of these contains 40 elements. The result of combining rules with don't care entries is given in Table 7.14; it has 22 rules, compared with the 36 of the second try. Recall from Chapter 1 the question of whether a large set of test cases is necessarily better than a smaller

Table 7.14   Decision Table for the NextDate Function

	1	2	3	4	5	6	7	8	9	10
c1: month in	M1	M1	M1	M1	M1	M2	M2	M2	M2	M2
c2: day in	D1	D2	D3	D4	D5	D1	D2	D3	D4	D5
c3: year in	—	—	—	—	—	—	—	—	—	—
Actions										
a1: impossible					X					
a2: increment day	X	X	X			X	X	X	X	
a3: reset day				X						X
a4: increment month				X						X
a5: reset month										
a6: increment year										

	11	12	13	14	15	16	17	18	19	20	21	22
c1: month in	M3	M3	M3	M3	M3	M4	M4	M4	M4	M4	M4	M4
c2: day in	D1	D2	D3	D4	D5	D1	D2	D2	D3	D3	D4	D5
c3: year in	—	—	—	—	—	—	Y1	Y2	Y1	Y2	—	—
Actions												
a1: impossible										X	X	X
a2: increment day	X	X	X	X		X	X					
a3: reset day					X			X	X			
a4: increment month								X	X			
a5: reset month					X							
a6: increment year					X							

set. Here, we have a 22-rule decision table that gives a clearer picture of the NextDate function than does the 36-rule decision table. The first five rules deal with 30-day months; notice that the leap year considerations are irrelevant. The next two sets of rules (6 to 15) deal with 31-day months, where rules 6 to 10 deal with months other than December and rules 11 to 15 deal with December. No impossible rules are listed in this portion of the decision table, although there is some redundancy that an efficient tester might question. Eight of the 10 rules simply increment the day. Would we really require eight separate test cases for this subfunction? Probably not; but note the insights we can get from the decision table. Finally, the last seven rules focus on February in common and leap years.

The decision table in Table 7.14 is the basis for the source code for the NextDate function in Chapter 2. As an aside, this example shows how good testing can improve programming. All the decision table analysis could have been done during the detailed design of the NextDate function.

Table 7.15 Reduced Decision Table for the NextDate Function

	1–3	4	5	6–9	10
c1: month in	M1	M1	M1	M2	M2
c2: day in	D1, D2, D3	D4	D5	D1, D2, D3, D4	D5
c3: year in	—	—	—	—	—
Actions					
a1: impossible			X		
a2: increment day	X			X	
a3: reset day		X			X
a4: increment month		X			X
a5: reset month					
a6: increment year					

	11–14	15	16	17	18	19	20	21, 22
c1: month in	M3	M3	M4	M4	M4	M4	M4	M4
c2: day in	D1, D2, D3, D4	D5	D1	D2	D2	D3	D3	D4, D5
c3: year in	—	—	—	Y1	Y2	Y1	Y2	—
Actions								
a1: impossible							X	X
a2: increment day	X		X	X				
a3: reset day		X			X	X		
a4: increment month					X	X		
a5: reset month		X						
a6: increment year		X						

We can use the algebra of decision tables to further simplify these 22 test cases. If the action sets of two rules in a limited entry decision table are identical, there must be at least one condition that allows two rules to be combined with a don't care entry. This is the decision table equivalent of the "treated the same" guideline that we used to identify equivalence classes. In a sense, we are identifying equivalence classes of rules. For example, rules 1, 2, and 3 involve day classes D1, D2, and D3 for 30-day months. These can be combined similarly for day classes D1, D2, D3, and D4 in the 31-day month rules, and D4 and D5 for February. The result is in Table 7.15.

The corresponding test cases are shown in Table 7.16.

Table 7.16 Decision Table Test Cases for NextDate

Case ID	Month	Day	Year	Expected Output
1–3	April	15	2001	April 16, 2001
4	April	30	2001	May 1, 2001
5	April	31	2001	Invalid Input Date
6–9	January	15	2001	January 16, 2001
10	January	31	2001	February 1, 2001
11–14	December	15	2001	December 16, 2001
15	December	31	2001	January 1, 2002
16	February	15	2001	February 16, 2001
17	February	28	2004	February 29, 2004
18	February	28	2001	March 1, 2001
19	February	29	2004	March 1, 2004
20	February	29	2001	Invalid Input Date
21, 22	February	30	2001	Invalid Input Date

7.4 Test Cases for the Commission Problem

The commission problem is not well served by a decision table analysis. This is not surprising because very little decisional logic is used in the problem. Because the variables in the equivalence classes are truly independent, no impossible rules will occur in a decision table in which conditions correspond to the equivalence classes. Thus, we will have the same test cases as we did for equivalence class testing.

7.5 Guidelines and Observations

As with the other testing techniques, decision table-based testing works well for some applications (such as NextDate) and is not worth the trouble for others (such as the commission problem). Not surprisingly, the situations in which it works well are those in which a lot of decision making takes place (such as the triangle problem), and those in which important logical relationships exist among input variables (the NextDate function).

1. The decision table technique is indicated for applications characterized by any of the following:

   Prominent if-then-else logic

   Logical relationships among input variables

   Calculations involving subsets of the input variables

   Cause-and-effect relationships between inputs and outputs

   High cyclomatic complexity (see Chapter 9)

2. Decision tables do not scale up very well (a limited entry table with n conditions has 2^n rules). There are several ways to deal with this: use extended entry decision tables, algebraically simplify tables, "factor" large tables into smaller ones, and look for repeating patterns of condition entries. For more on these techniques, see Topper (1993).

3. As with other techniques, iteration helps. The first set of conditions and actions you identify may be unsatisfactory. Use it as a stepping stone, and gradually improve on it until you are satisfied with a decision table.

References

Elmendorf, W.R., *Cause–Effect Graphs in Functional Testing*, TR-00.2487, IBM System Development Division, Poughkeepsie, NY, 1973.

Mosley, D.J., *The Handbook of MIS Application Software Testing*, Yourdon Press, Prentice-Hall, Englewood Cliffs, NJ, 1993.

Myers, G.J., *The Art of Software Testing*, Wiley Interscience, New York, 1979.

Topper, A. et al., *Structured Methods: Merging Models, Techniques, and CASE*, McGraw-Hill, New York, 1993.

Exercises

1. Develop a decision table and additional test cases for the right triangle addition to the triangle problem (see Chapter 2 exercises). Note that there can be isosceles right triangles, but not with integer sides.

2. Develop a decision table for the "second try" at the NextDate function. At the end of a 31-day month, the day is always reset to 1. For all non-December months, the month is incremented; for December, the month is reset to January and the year is incremented.

3. Develop a decision table for the YesterDate function (see Chapter 2 exercises).

4. Expand the commission problem to consider violations of the sales limits. Develop the corresponding decision tables and test cases for a company-friendly version and a salesperson-friendly version.

5. Discuss how well decision table testing deals with the multiple fault assumption.

6. Develop decision table test cases for the time change problem (Chapter 6, exercise 5).

7. If you did exercise 8 in Chapter 2, exercise 5 in Chapter 5, and exercise 6 in Chapter 6, you are already familiar with the CRC Press Web site for downloads (http://www.crcpress.com). There you will find an Excel spreadsheet named specBasedTesting.xls. (It is an extended version of Naive.xls, and it contains the same inserted faults.) Different sheets contain decision table-based test cases for the triangle, NextDate, and commission problems, respectively. Run these sets of test cases and compare the results with your naive testing from Chapter 2, your boundary value testing from Chapter 5, and your equivalence class testing from Chapter 6.

Chapter 8

Retrospective on Functional Testing

In the preceding three chapters, we studied as many types of functional testing. The common thread among these is that all view a program as a mathematical function that maps its inputs onto its outputs. With the boundary-based approaches, test cases are identified in terms of the boundaries of the ranges of the input variables, and variations give us four techniques—boundary value analysis, robustness testing, worst-case testing, and robust worst-case testing. We then took a closer look at the input variables, defining equivalence classes in terms of values that should receive "similar treatment" from the program tested. Four forms of equivalence class testing are used—weak normal, strong normal, weak robust, and strong robust. The goal of examining similar treatment is to reduce the sheer number of test cases generated by the boundary-based techniques. We pushed this a step further when we used decision tables to analyze the logical dependencies imposed by the function of the program. Whenever we have a choice among alternatives, we naturally want to know which is preferred—or at least how to make an informed choice. In this chapter, we look at questions about testing effort and efficiency, and then try to get a handle on test effectiveness.

8.1 Testing Effort

Let us return to our craftsperson metaphor for a minute. We usually think of such people as knowing their crafts so well that their time is spent very effectively. Even if it takes a little longer, we like to think that the time is well spent. We are finally in a position to see a hint of this as far as testing techniques are concerned. The functional methods we have studied vary in terms of both the number of test cases generated and the effort to develop these test cases. Figure 8.1 and Figure 8.2 show the general trends, but the sophistication axis needs some explanation.

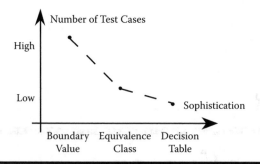

Figure 8.1   Trendline of test cases per testing method.

The boundary-based techniques have no recognition of data or logical dependencies; they are very mechanical in the way they generate test cases. Because of this, they are also easy to automate. The equivalence class techniques pay attention to data dependencies and to the function itself. More thought is required to use these techniques—also more judgment, or craft. The thinking goes into the identification of the equivalence classes; after that, the process is also mechanical. The decision table technique is the most sophisticated, because it requires the tester to consider both data and logical dependencies. As we saw in our examples, you might not get the conditions of a decision table right on the first try, but once you have a good set of conditions, the resulting test cases are both complete and, in some sense, minimal.

The end result is a satisfying trade-off between test identification effort and test execution effort: methods that are easy to use generate numerous test cases, which in turn are more time-consuming to execute. If we shift our effort toward more sophisticated testing methods, we are repaid with less test execution time. This is particularly important because tests are typically executed several times. We might also note that judging testing quality in terms of the sheer number of test cases has drawbacks similar to those of judging programming productivity in terms of lines of code.

Our examples bear out the trends of Figure 8.1 and Figure 8.2. The following three graphs (Figure 8.2 to Figure 8.5) are taken from a spreadsheet that summarized the number of test cases for each of our examples in terms of the various methods. The boundary-based numbers are identical,

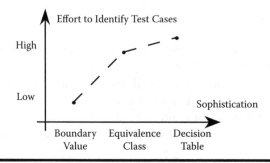

Figure 8.2   Trendline of test case identification effort per testing method.

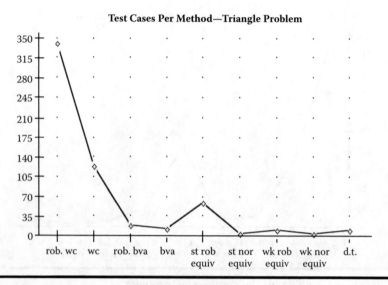

Figure 8.3 Test case trendline for the triangle problem.

reflecting both the mechanical nature of the techniques and the formulas that describe the number of test cases generated by each method. The main differences are seen in strong equivalence class testing and decision table testing. Both of these reflect the logical complexity of the problems, so we would expect to see differences here. When we study structural testing (Chapters 9 and 10), we will see that these distinctions have an important implication for testing. The three graphs are superimposed on each other in Figure 8.6.

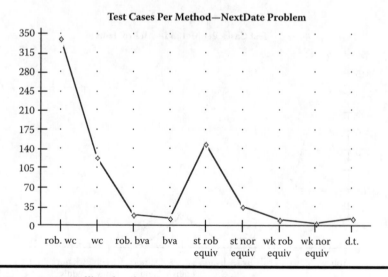

Figure 8.4 Test case trendline for the NextDate problem.

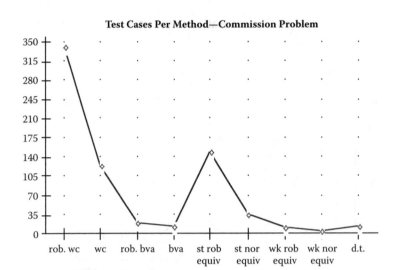

Figure 8.5   Test case trendline for the commission problem.

8.2   Testing Efficiency

If you look closely at these sets of test cases, you can get a feel for the fundamental limitation of functional testing: the twin possibilities of gaps of untested functionality and redundant tests. Consider the NextDate problem, for example. The decision table (which took three tries to get it right) yields 13 test cases. We have confidence that these test cases are complete (in some sense) because the decision table is complete. On the other hand, worst-case boundary value analysis yielded 125 test cases. When we look closely at these, they are not very satisfactory: What do we expect to learn from cases 1 to 5? These test cases check the NextDate function for January 1 in

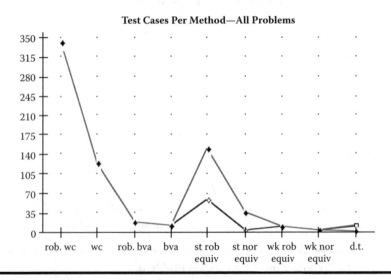

Figure 8.6   Test case trendline for all three problems.

five different years. The year has nothing to do with this part of the calendar, so we would expect that one of these would suffice. If we roughly estimate a "times 10" redundancy, we might expect a reduction to 25 test cases, quite compatible with the 22 from the decision table approach. Looking closer, we find a few cases for February, but none happen to hit February 28 or 29, and no interesting connection is made with leap years. Not only do we have a times 10 redundancy, but we also have some severe gaps around the end of February and leap years.

The strong normal equivalence class test cases move in the right direction: 36 test cases, of which 11 are impossible. Once again, the impossible test cases result from the presumed independence among the equivalence classes. All but six of the decision table test cases (cases 2, 7, 12, 15, 17, and 18 of Table 7.16) map to corresponding strong equivalence class test cases (see Section 6.3.1). Half of these deal with the 28th day of non-February months, so they are not very interesting. The remaining three are useful test cases, especially because they test possibilities that are missed by the strong equivalence class test cases. All this supports two conclusions: gaps occur in the functional test cases, and these gaps are reduced by using more sophisticated techniques.

Can we push this a little further by trying to quantify what we mean by testing efficiency? The intuitive notion is that a set of test cases is just right—that is, no gaps and no redundancy. We can develop various ratios of total number of test cases generated by method A to those generated by method B, or even ratios on a test case basis. This is usually more trouble than it is worth, but sometimes management demands numbers even when they have little real meaning. We will revisit this in Chapter 11, after we complete our study of structural testing. The structural approaches support interesting (and useful) metrics, and these will provide a much better quantification of testing efficiency. Meanwhile, we can help recognize redundancy by annotating test cases with a brief purpose comment. When we see several test cases with the same purpose, we (correctly) sense redundancy. Detecting gaps is harder: If we can only use functional testing, then the best we can do is compare the test cases that result from two methods. In general, the more sophisticated methods will help us recognize gaps with respect to the specification, but nothing is guaranteed. We could develop excellent strong equivalence classes for a program, and then produce a klutzy decision table.

8.3 Testing Effectiveness

What we would really like to know about a set of test cases is how effective they are, but we need to clarify what "effective" means. The easy choice is to be dogmatic: mandate a method, use it to generate test cases, and then run the test cases. This is absolute, and conformity is measurable, so it can be used as a basis for contractual compliance. We can improve on this by relaxing a dogmatic mandate and requiring that testers choose appropriate methods, using the guidelines given at the ends of various chapters here. We can gain another incremental improvement by devising appropriate hybrid methods, as we did with the commission problem in Chapter 5.

Structured testing techniques yield a second choice for test effectiveness. In Chapter 9, we will discuss the notion of program execution paths, which provide a good formulation of test effectiveness. We will be able to examine a set of test cases in terms of the execution paths traversed. When a particular path is traversed more than once, we might question the redundancy. Sometimes such redundancy can have a purpose, as we shall see in Chapter 10.

The best interpretation for testing effectiveness is (no great surprise) the most difficult. We would really like to know how effective a set of test cases is for finding faults present in a program. This is problematic for two reasons: First, it presumes we know all the faults in a program. Quite a circularity—if we did, we would take care of them. Because we do not know all the faults in a program, we could never know if the test cases from a given method revealed them. The second reason is more theoretical: proving that a program is fault-free is equivalent to the famous halting problem of computer science, which is known to be impossible. The best we can do is to work backward from fault types. Given a particular kind of fault, we can choose testing methods (functional and structural) that are likely to reveal faults of that type. If we couple this with knowledge of the most likely kinds of faults, we end up with a pragmatic approach to testing effectiveness. This is improved if we track the kinds (and frequencies) of faults in the software we develop.

8.4   Guidelines

Here is one of my favorite testing stories. An inebriated man was crawling around on the sidewalk beneath a streetlight. When a policeman asked him what he was doing, he replied that he was looking for his car keys. "Did you lose them here?" the policeman asked. "No, I lost them in the parking lot, but the light is better here."

This little story contains an important message for testers: testing for faults that are not likely to be present is pointless. It is far more effective to have a good idea of the kinds of faults that are most likely (or most damaging) and then to select testing methods that are likely to reveal these faults.

Many times, we do not even have a feeling for the kinds of faults that may be prevalent. What then? The best we can do is use known attributes of the program to select methods that deal with the attributes—sort of a "punishment fits the crime" view. The attributes that are most helpful in choosing functional testing methods are:

> Whether the variables represent physical or logical quantities
> Whether dependencies exist among the variables
> Whether single or multiple faults are assumed
> Whether exception handling is prominent

Here is the beginning of an "expert system" on functional testing technique selection:

1. If the variables refer to physical quantities, domain testing and equivalence class testing are indicated.
2. If the variables are independent, domain testing and equivalence class testing are indicated.
3. If the variables are dependent, decision table testing is indicated.
4. If the single fault assumption is warranted, boundary value analysis and robustness testing are indicated.
5. If the multiple fault assumption is warranted, worst-case testing, robust worst-case testing, and decision table testing are indicated.
6. If the program contains significant exception handling, robustness testing and decision table testing are indicated.
7. If the variables refer to logical quantities, equivalence class testing and decision table testing are indicated.

Combinations of these may occur; therefore, the guidelines are summarized as a decision table in Table 8.1.

Table 8.1 Appropriate Choices for Functional Testing

c1	Variables (P, physical; L, logical)	P	P	P	P	P	L	L	L	L	L
c2	Independent variables?	Y	Y	Y	Y	N	Y	Y	Y	Y	N
c3	Single fault assumption?	Y	Y	N	N	—	Y	Y	N	N	—
c4	Exception handling?	Y	N	Y	N	—	Y	N	Y	N	—
a1	Boundary value analysis		x								
a2	Robustness testing	x									
a3	Worst-case testing				x						
a4	Robust worst case			x							
a5	Weak robust equivalence class	x		x			x		x		
a6	Weak normal equivalence class	x	x				x	x			
a7	Strong normal equivalence class			x	x	x			x	x	x
a8	Decision table					x					x

8.5 Case Study

Here is an example that lets us compare functional testing methods and apply the guidelines. A hypothetical insurance premium program computes the semiannual car insurance premium based on two parameters: the policyholder's age and driving record:

$$Premium = BaseRate*ageMultiplier - safeDrivingReduction$$

The ageMultiplier is a function of the policyholder's age, and the safe driving reduction is given when the current points (assigned by traffic courts for moving violations) on the policyholder's driver's license are below an age-related cutoff. Policies are written for drivers in the age range of 16 to 100. Once a policyholder has 12 points, the driver's license is suspended (thus, no insurance is needed). The BaseRate changes from time to time; for this example, it is $500 for a semiannual premium.

Age Range	Age Multiplier	Points Cutoff	Safe Driving Reduction
$16 \le age < 25$	2.8	1	50
$25 \le age < 35$	1.8	3	50
$35 \le age < 45$	1.0	5	100
$45 \le age < 60$	0.8	7	150
$60 \le age < 100$	1.5	5	200

Worst-case boundary value testing, based on the input variables, age, and points, yields the following extreme values. The corresponding 25 test cases are shown in Figure 8.7.

Variable	Min	Min+	Nom.	Max–	Max
Age	16	17	54	99	100
Points	0	1	6	11	12

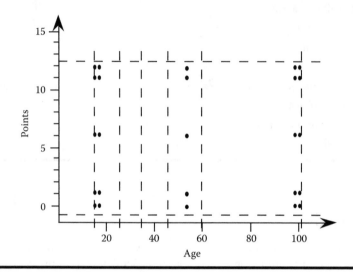

Figure 8.7 Worst-case boundary value test cases for the insurance premium program.

I do not think anyone would be content with these test cases. There is too much of the problem statement missing. The various age cutoffs are not tested, nor are the point cutoffs. We could refine this by taking a closer look at the age ranges and point ranges:

A1 = {age: 16 ≤ age < 25}
A2 = {age: 25 ≤ age < 35}
A3 = {age: 35 ≤ age < 45}
A4 = {age: 45 ≤ age < 60}
A5 = {age: 60 ≤ age < 100}
P1 = {points = 0, 1}
P2 = {points = 2, 3}
P3 = {points = 4, 5}
P4 = {points = 6, 7}
P5 = {points = 8, 9, 10, 11, 12}

Because these ranges meet at endpoints, we would have the worst-case test values shown in Table 8.2. Notice that the discrete values of the point variable do not lend themselves to the min+ and max– convention in some cases.

If we drew the grid, we would get something like the one in Figure 8.8. Each vertical set (in which the age variable is held constant) has 13 points, and we have such a column for each value of the age variable (there are 21 of these); so there would be 273 worst-case boundary value test cases. We are clearly at a point of severe redundancy; time to move on to equivalence class testing.

Table 8.2   Detailed Worst-Case Values

Variable	Min	Min+	Nom.	Max–	Max
Age	16	17	20	24	
Age	25	26	30	34	
Age	35	36	40	44	
Age	45	46	53	59	
Age	60	61	75	99	100
Points	0	n/a	n/a	n/a	1
Points	2	n/a	n/a	n/a	3
Points	4	n/a	n/a	n/a	5
Points	6	n/a	n/a	n/a	7
Points	8	9	10	11	12

The age sets A1 to A5 and the points sets P1 to P5 are natural choices for equivalence classes. The corresponding equivalence class test cases are shown in Figure 8.9; the open circles correspond to strong normal test cases, and the black circles are the weak normal test cases.

Equivalence class testing clearly reduces the redundancy problem, but there still seems to be some excess. Why test all the point classes P2 to P5 for A1? Once the point threshold is exceeded, the safe driving reduction is lost. We can address these dependencies with the extended entry decision table in Table 8.3.

The decision table test cases are shown in Figure 8.10.

Take a look at Figure 8.8 and Figure 8.10; one is overkill and the other is inadequate. We need to find some happy compromise, and this is where the story about the drunkard looking for keys comes in.

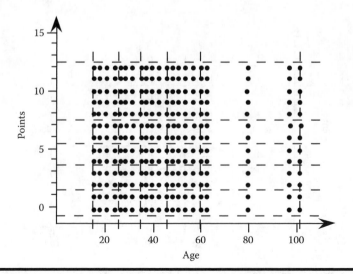

Figure 8.8   Detailed worst-case boundary value test cases for the insurance premium program.

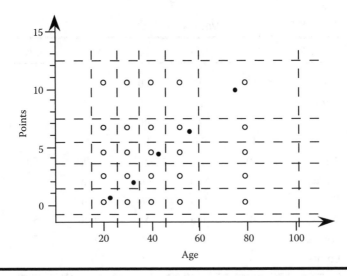

Figure 8.9 Weak and strong equivalence class test cases for the insurance premium program.

Table 8.3 Decision Table Test Cases for the Insurance Premium Program

Age Is	16–25	16–25	25–35	25–35	35–45	35–45	45–60	45–60	60–100	60–100
Points	0	1–12	0–2	3–12	0–4	5–12	0–6	7–12	0–4	5–12
Age multiplier	2.8	2.8	1.8	1.8	1	1	0.8	0.8	1.5	1.5
Safe driving reduction	50	—	50	—	100	—	150	—	200	—

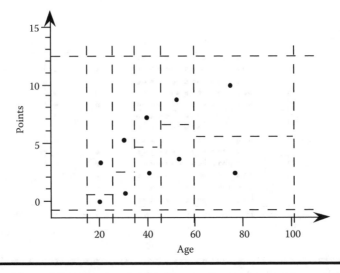

Figure 8.10 Decision table test cases for the insurance premium program.

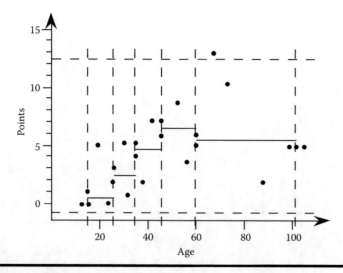

Figure 8.11   Final (hybrid) test cases for the insurance premium program.

What are the error-prone aspects of the insurance premium program? The endpoints of the age ranges appear to be a good place to start, and this puts us back in boundary value mode. Also, we have not considered ages under 16 and over 100, which suggests some element of robust boundary value thinking. Finally, we should probably check the values at which the safe driving reduction is lost, and maybe values of points over 12, when all insurance is lost. (Notice that the responses to these were not in the problem statement, but our testing analysis provokes us to think about them.) Maybe this should be called hybrid functional testing: it uses the advantages of all three forms in a blend that is determined by the nature of the application (shades of special value testing). Hybrid appears appropriate, because such selection is usually done to improve the stock. Hybrid test cases are illustrated in Figure 8.11.

STRUCTURAL TESTING

Chapter 9

Path Testing

The distinguishing characteristic of structural testing methods is that they are all based on the source code of the program tested, and not on the specification. Because of this absolute basis, structural testing methods are very amenable to rigorous definitions, mathematical analysis, and precise measurement. In this chapter, we examine the two most common forms of path testing. The technology behind these has been available since the mid-1970s, and the originators of these methods now have companies that market very successful tools that implement the techniques. Both techniques start with the program graph; we repeat the improved definition from Chapter 4 here.

Definition

Given a program written in an imperative programming language, the *program graph* is a directed graph in which nodes are statement fragments and edges represent flow of control. (A complete statement is a "default" statement fragment.)

If i and j are nodes in the program graph, an edge exists from node i to node j iff the statement fragment corresponding to node j can be executed immediately after the statement fragment corresponding to node i.

Constructing a program graph from a given program is an easy process. It is illustrated here with the pseudocode implementation of the triangle program from Chapter 2. Line numbers refer to statements and statement fragments. An element of judgment can be used here: sometimes it is convenient to keep a fragment as a separate node; other times it seems better to include this with another portion of a statement. We will see that this latitude collapses onto a unique DD-Path graph, so the differences introduced by differing judgments are moot. (A mathematician would make the point that, for a given program, several distinct program graphs might be used, all of which reduce to a unique DD-Path graph.) We also need to decide whether to associate nodes with nonexecutable statements such as variable and type declarations; here we do not.

```
1.    Program triangle 2 'Structured programming version of
      simpler specification
2.    Dim a,b,c As Integer
3.    Dim IsATriangle As Boolean
```

```
            'Step 1: Get Input
4.      Output ("Enter 3 integers which are sides of a triangle")
5.      Input (a,b,c)
6.      Output ("Side A is ",a)
7.      Output ("Side B is ",b)
8.      Output ("Side C is ",c)
            'Step 2: Is A Triangle?
9.      If (a < b + c) AND (b < a + c) AND (c < a + b)
10.         Then IsATriangle = True
11.         Else IsATriangle = False
12.     EndIf
            'Step 3: Determine Triangle Type
13.     If IsATriangle
14.         Then  If (a = b) AND (b = c)
15.                 Then Output ("Equilateral")
16.                 Else  If (a ≠ b) AND (a ≠ c) AND (b ≠ c)
17.                         Then Output ("Scalene")
18.                         Else Output ("Isosceles")
19.                       EndIf
20.               EndIf
21.         Else  Output ("Not a Triangle")
22.     EndIf
23.     End triangle2
```

A program graph of this program is given in Figure 9.1. Examine it closely to find graphs of the structured programming constructs we discussed in Chapter 4.

Nodes 4 through 8 are a sequence, nodes 9 through 12 are an if-then-else construct, and nodes 13 through 22 are nested if-then-else constructs. Nodes 4 and 23 are the program source and sink nodes, corresponding to the single-entry, single-exit criteria. No loops exist, so this is a directed acyclic graph.

The importance of the program graph is that program executions correspond to paths from the source to the sink nodes. Because test cases force the execution of some such program path, we now have a very explicit description of the relationship between a test case and the part of the program it exercises. We also have an elegant, theoretically respectable way to deal with the potentially large number of execution paths in a program. Figure 9.2 is a graph of a simple (but unstructured) program; it is typical of the kind of example used to show the impossibility of completely testing even simple programs (Schach, 1993). In this program, five paths lead from node B to node F in the interior of the loop. If the loop may have up to 18 repetitions, some 4.77 trillion distinct program execution paths exist.

9.1 DD-Paths

The best-known form of structural testing is based on a construct known as a decision-to-decision path (DD-Path) (Miller, 1977). The name refers to a sequence of statements that, in Miller's words, begins with the "outway" of a decision statement and ends with the "inway" of the next decision statement. No internal branches occur in such a sequence, so the corresponding code is like a row of dominoes lined up so that when the first falls, all the rest in the sequence fall. Miller's original

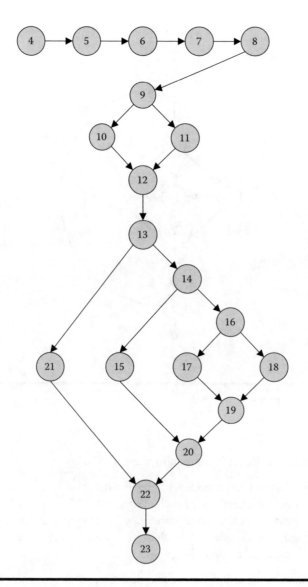

Figure 9.1   Program graph of the triangle program.

definition works well for second-generation languages like Fortran II, because decision-making statements (such as arithmetic IFs and DO loops) use statement labels to refer to target statements. With block-structured languages (e.g., Pascal, Ada®, C, Visual Basic,® Java™), the notion of statement fragments resolves the difficulty of applying Miller's original definition — otherwise, we end up with program graphs in which some statements are members of more than one DD-Path.

We will define DD-Paths in terms of paths of nodes in a directed graph. We might call these paths chains, where a chain is a path in which the initial and terminal nodes are distinct, and every interior node has indegree = 1 and outdegree = 1. Notice that the initial node is 2-connected to every other node in the chain, and no instances of 1- or 3-connected nodes occur, as shown in Figure 9.3. The length (number of edges) of the chain in Figure 9.3 is 6.

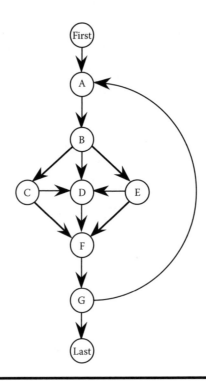

Figure 9.2 Trillions of paths.

Definition

A *DD-Path* is a sequence of nodes in a program graph such that:

        Case 1: It consists of a single node with indeg = 0.
        Case 2: It consists of a single node with outdeg = 0.
        Case 3: It consists of a single node with indeg ≥ 2 or outdeg ≥ 2.
        Case 4: It consists of a single node with indeg = 1 and outdeg = 1.
        Case 5: It is a maximal chain of length ≥ 1.

Cases 1 and 2 establish the unique source and sink nodes of the program graph of a structured program as initial and final DD-Paths. Case 3 deals with complex nodes; it ensures that no node is contained in more than one DD-Path. Case 4 is needed for short branches; it also preserves the one-fragment, one-DD-Path principle. Case 5 is the "normal" case, in which a DD-Path is a single-entry, single-exit sequence of nodes (a chain). The maximal part of the case 5 definition is used to determine the final node of a normal (nontrivial) chain.

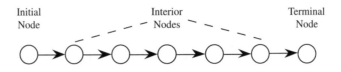

Initial   Interior   Terminal
Node   Nodes   Node

Figure 9.3 A chain of nodes in a directed graph.

Table 9.1 Types of DD-Paths in Figure 9.1

Program Graph Nodes	DD-Path Name	Case of Definition
4	First	1
5–8	A	5
9	B	3
10	C	4
11	D	4
12	E	3
13	F	3
14	H	3
15	I	4
16	J	3
17	K	4
18	L	4
19	M	3
20	N	3
21	G	4
22	O	3
23	Last	2

This is a complex definition, so we will apply it to the program graph in Figure 9.1. Node 4 is a case 1 DD-Path; we will call it first. Similarly, node 23 is a case 2 DD-Path; we will call it last. Nodes 5 through 8 are case 5 DD-Paths. We know that node 8 is the last node in this DD-Path because it is the last node that preserves the 2-connectedness property of the chain. If we go beyond node 8 to include node 9, we violate the indegree = outdegree = 1 criterion of a chain. If we stop at node 7, we violate the "maximal" criterion. Nodes 10, 11, 15, 17, 18, and 21 are case 4 DD-Paths. Nodes 9, 12, 13, 14, 16, 19, 20, and 22 are case 3 DD-Paths. Finally, node 23 is a case 2 DD-Path. All this is summarized in Table 9.1, where the DD-Path names correspond to node names in the DD-Path graph in Figure 9.4.

Part of the confusion with this example is that the triangle problem is logic intensive and computationally sparse. This combination yields many short DD-Paths. If the THEN and ELSE clauses contained blocks of computational statements, we would have longer chains, as we will see in the commission problem. We can now define the DD-Path graph of a program.

Definition

Given a program written in an imperative language, the *DD-Path graph* is the directed graph in which nodes are DD-Paths of its program graph, and edges represent control flow between successor DD-Paths.

In effect, the DD-Path graph is a form of condensation graph (see Chapter 4); in this condensation, 2-connected components are collapsed into individual nodes that correspond to case

5 DD-Paths. The single-node DD-Paths (corresponding to cases 1 to 4) are required to preserve the convention that a statement (or statement fragment) is in exactly one DD-Path. Without this convention, we end up with rather clumsy DD-Path graphs, in which some statement fragments are in several DD-Paths.

This process should not intimidate testers—high-quality commercial tools are available, which generate the DD-Path graph of a given program. The vendors make sure that their products work for a wide variety of programming languages. In practice, it is reasonable to manually create DD-Path graphs for programs up to about 100 source lines. Beyond that, most testers look for a tool.

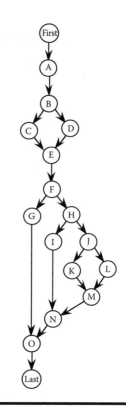

Figure 9.4   DD-Path graph for the triangle program.

9.2   Test Coverage Metrics

The *raison d'être* of DD-Paths is that they enable very precise descriptions of test coverage. Recall (from Chapter 8) that one of the fundamental limitations of functional testing is that it is impossible to know either the extent of redundancy or the possibility of gaps corresponding to the way a set of functional test cases exercises a program. Back in Chapter 1, we had a Venn diagram showing relationships among specified, programmed, and tested behaviors. Test coverage metrics are a device to measure the extent to which a set of test cases covers (or exercises) a program.

Several widely accepted test coverage metrics are used; most of those in Table 9.2 are due to the early work of E.F. Miller (Miller, 1977). Having an organized view of the extent to which

Table 9.2   Structural Test Coverage Metrics

Metric	Description of Coverage
C_0	Every statement
C_1	Every DD-Path (predicate outcome)
C_{1p}	Every predicate to each outcome
C_2	C1 coverage + loop coverage
C_d	C1 coverage + every dependent pair of DD-Paths
C_{MCC}	Multiple condition coverage
C_{ik}	Every program path that contains up to k repetitions of a loop (usually $k = 2$)
C_{stat}	Statistically significant fraction of paths
C_∞	All possible execution paths

a program is tested makes it possible to sensibly manage the testing process. Most quality organizations now expect the C_1 metric (DD-Path coverage) as the minimum acceptable level of test coverage. Less adequate, the statement coverage metric (C_0) is still widely accepted: it is mandated by ANSI Standard 187B and has been used successfully by IBM since the mid-1970s.

These coverage metrics form a lattice (see Chapter 10) in which some are equivalent and some are implied by others. The importance of the lattice is that there are always fault types that can be revealed at one level while escaping detection by inferior levels of testing. E.F. Miller (1991) observes that when DD-Path coverage is attained by a set of test cases, roughly 85% of all faults are revealed.

9.2.1 Metric-Based Testing

The test coverage metrics in Table 9.2 tell us what to test but not how to test it. In this section, we take a closer look at techniques that exercise source code in terms of the metrics in Table 9.2. We must keep an important distinction in mind: Miller's test coverage metrics are based on program graphs in which nodes are full statements, whereas our formulation allows statement fragments (which can be entire statements) to be nodes.

Statement and Predicate Testing

Because our formulation allows statement fragments to be individual nodes, the statement and predicate levels (C_0 and C_1) collapse into one consideration. In our triangle problem (see Figure 9.1), nodes 9, 10, 11, and 12 are a complete if-then-else statement. If we required nodes to correspond to full statements, we could execute just one of the decision alternatives and satisfy the statement coverage criterion. Because we allow statement fragments, it is natural to divide such a statement into three nodes. Doing so results in predicate outcome coverage. Whether or not our convention is followed, these coverage metrics require that we find a set of test cases such that, when executed, every node of the program graph is traversed at least once.

DD-Path Testing

When every DD-Path is traversed (the C_1 metric), we know that each predicate outcome has been executed; this amounts to traversing every edge in the DD-Path graph (or program graph), as opposed to only every node. For if-then and if-then-else statements, this means that both the true and the false branches are covered (C_{1p} coverage). For CASE statements, each clause is covered. Beyond this, it is useful to ask what else we might do to test a DD-Path. Longer DD-Paths generally represent complex computations, which we can rightly consider as individual functions. For such DD-Paths, it may be appropriate to apply a number of functional tests, especially those for boundary and special values.

Dependent Pairs of DD-Paths

The C_d metric foreshadows the topic of Chapter 10 — dataflow testing. The most common dependency among pairs of DD-Paths is the define/reference relationship, in which a variable is defined (receives a value) in one DD-Path and is referenced in another DD-Path. The importance of these dependencies is that they are closely related to the problem of infeasible paths. We have good examples of dependent pairs of DD-Paths: in Figure 9.4, C and H are such a pair, as are DD-Paths D and H. The variable IsATriangle is set to TRUE at node C and FALSE at node D. Node H is the branch taken when IsATriangle is TRUE in the condition at node B, so any path containing

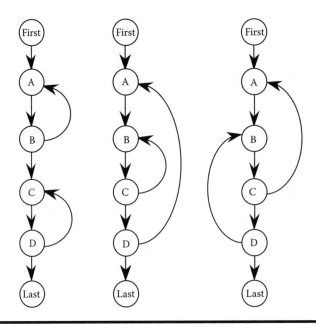

Figure 9.5   Concatenated, nested, and knotted loops.

nodes D and H is infeasible. Simple DD-Path coverage might not exercise these dependencies; thus, a deeper class of faults would not be revealed.

Multiple Condition Coverage

Look closely at the compound conditions in DD-Paths B and H. Instead of simply traversing such predicates to their true and false outcomes, we should investigate the different ways that each outcome can occur. One possibility is to make a truth table; a compound condition of three simple conditions would have eight rows, yielding eight test cases. Another possibility is to reprogram compound predicates into nested simple if-then-else logic, which will result in more DD-Paths to cover. We see an interesting trade-off: statement complexity versus path complexity. Multiple condition coverage ensures that this complexity is not swept under the DD-Path coverage rug.

Loop Coverage

The condensation graphs we studied in Chapter 4 provide us with an elegant resolution to the problems of testing loops. Loop testing has been studied extensively, and with good reason—loops are a highly fault-prone portion of source code. To start, an amusing taxonomy of loops occurs (Beizer, 1984): concatenated, nested, and horrible, shown in Figure 9.5.

Concatenated loops are simply a sequence of disjoint loops, while nested loops are such that one is contained inside another. Knotted loops cannot occur when the structured programming precepts are followed, but they can occur in languages like Java with try/catch. When it is possible to branch into (or out from) the middle of a loop, and these branches are internal to other loops, the result is Beizer's knotted loop. The simple view of loop testing is that every loop involves a decision, and we need to test both outcomes of the decision: one is to traverse the loop, and the other is to exit (or not enter) the loop. This is carefully proved in Huang (1979). We can also take a modified boundary value approach, where the loop index is given its minimum, nominal, and maximum values (see Chapter 5). We can push this further to full boundary value testing and even robustness testing. If the body of a simple loop is a DD-Path that performs a complex calculation, this should also be tested, as discussed previously. Once a loop has been tested, the tester condenses it into a single node. If loops are nested, this process is repeated starting with the innermost loop and working outward. This results in the same multiplicity of test cases we found with boundary value analysis, which makes sense, because each loop index variable acts like an input variable. If loops are knotted, it will be necessary to carefully analyze them in terms of the dataflow methods discussed in Chapter 10. As a preview, consider the infinite loop that could occur if one loop tampers with the value of the other loop's index.

9.2.2 Test Coverage Analyzers

Coverage analyzers are a class of test tools that offer automated support for this approach to testing management. With a coverage analyzer, the tester runs a set of test cases on a program that has been "instrumented" by the coverage analyzer. The analyzer then uses information produced by the instrumentation code to generate a coverage report. In the common case of DD-Path coverage, for example, the instrumentation identifies and labels all DD-Paths in an original program. When the instrumented program is executed with test cases, the analyzer tabulates the DD-Paths traversed by each test case. In this way, the tester can experiment with different sets of test cases to determine the coverage of each set.

9.3 Basis Path Testing

The mathematical notion of a basis has attractive possibilities for structural testing. Certain sets can have a basis, and when they do, the basis has very important properties with respect to the entire set. Mathematicians usually define a basis in terms of a structure called a vector space, which is a set of elements (called vectors) as well as operations that correspond to multiplication and addition defined for the vectors. If a half dozen other criteria apply, the structure is said to be a vector space, and all vector spaces have a basis (in fact, they may have several bases). The basis of a vector space is a set of vectors that are independent of each other and span the entire vector space in the sense that any other vector in the space can be expressed in terms of the basis vectors. Thus, a set of basis vectors somehow represents the essence of the full vector space: everything else in the space can be expressed in terms of the basis, and if one basis element is deleted, this spanning property is lost. The potential value of this theory for testing is that if we can view a program as a vector space, then the basis for such a space would be a very interesting set of elements to test. If the basis is okay, we could hope that everything that can be expressed in terms of the basis is also okay. In this section, we examine the early work of Thomas McCabe, who recognized this possibility in the mid-1970s.

9.3.1 McCabe's Basis Path Method

Figure 9.6 is taken from McCabe (1982). It is a directed graph that we might take to be the program graph (or the DD-Path graph) of some program. For the convenience of readers who have encountered this example elsewhere (McCabe, 1987; Perry, 1987), the original notation for nodes and edges is repeated here. (Notice that this is not a graph derived from a structured program: nodes B and C are a loop with two exits, and the edge from B to E is a branch into the if-then statement in nodes D, E, and F.) The program does have a single entry (A) and a single exit (G). McCabe based his view of testing on a major result from graph theory, which states that the cyclomatic number

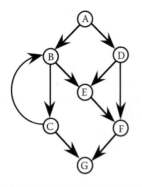

Figure 9.6 McCabe's control graph. (From McCabe, T.J., *Structural Testing: A Software Testing Methodology Using the Cyclomatic Complexity Metric,* **Special Publication 500-99, National Bureau of Standards (now NIST), Washington, DC, 1982.)**

(see Chapter 4) of a strongly connected graph is the number of linearly independent circuits in the graph. (A circuit is similar to a chain: no internal loops or decisions occur, but the initial node is the terminal node. A circuit is a set of 3-connected nodes.)

We can always create a strongly connected graph by adding an edge from the (every) sink node to the (every) source node. (Notice that if the single-entry, single-exit precept is violated, we greatly increase the cyclomatic number, because we need to add edges from each sink node to each source node.) Figure 9.7 shows the result of doing this; it also contains edge labels that are used in the discussion that follows.

Some confusion exists in the literature about the correct formula for cyclomatic complexity. Some sources give the formula as $V(G) = e - n + p$, while others use the formula $V(G) = e - n + 2p$; everyone agrees that e is the number of edges, n is the number of nodes, and p is the number of connected regions. The confusion apparently comes from the transformation of an arbitrary directed graph (such as the one in Figure 9.6) to a strongly connected, directed graph obtained by adding one edge from the sink to the source node (as in Figure 9.7). Adding an edge clearly affects value computed by the formula, but it should not affect the number of circuits. Here is a way to resolve the apparent inconsistency. The number of linearly independent paths from the source node to the sink node in Figure 9.6 is

$$V(G) = e - n + 2p = 10 - 7 + 2(1) = 5$$

and the number of linearly independent circuits in the graph in Figure 9.7 is

$$V(G) = e - n + p = 11 - 7 + 1 = 5$$

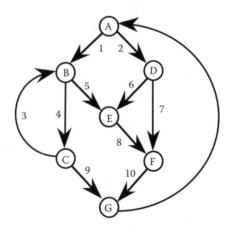

Figure 9.7 McCabe's derived strongly connected graph.

The cyclomatic complexity of the strongly connected graph in Figure 9.7 is 5; thus, there are five linearly independent circuits. If we now delete the added edge from node G to node A, these five circuits become five linearly independent paths from node A to node G. In small graphs, we can visually identify independent paths. Here, we identify paths as sequences of nodes:

    p1: A, B, C, G
    p2: A, B, C, B, C, G
    p3: A, B, E, F, G
    p4: A, D, E, F, G
    p5: A, D, F, G

We can force this to begin to look like a vector space by defining notions of addition and scalar multiplication: path addition is simply one path followed by another path, and multiplication corresponds to repetitions of a path. With this formulation, McCabe arrives at a vector space of program paths. His illustration of the basis part of this framework is that the path A, B, C, B, E, F, G is the basis sum p2 + p3 – p1, and the path A, B, C, B, C, B, C, G is the linear combination 2p2 – p1. It is easier to see this addition with an incidence matrix (see Chapter 4) in which rows correspond to paths, and columns correspond to edges, as in Table 9.3. The entries in this table are obtained by following a path and noting which edges are traversed. Path p1, for example, traverses edges 1, 4, and 9, while path p2 traverses the following edge sequence: 1, 4, 3, 4, 9. Because edge 4 is traversed twice by path p2, that is the entry for the edge 4 column.

Table 9.3 Path/Edge Traversal

Path/Edges Traversed	1	2	3	4	5	6	7	8	9	10
p1: A, B, C, G	1	0	0	1	0	0	0	0	1	0
p2: A, B, C, B, C, G	1	0	1	2	0	0	0	0	1	0
p3: A, B, E, F, G	1	0	0	0	1	0	0	1	0	1
p4: A, D, E, F, G	0	1	0	0	0	1	0	1	0	1
p5: A, D, F, G	0	1	0	0	0	0	1	0	0	1
ex1: A, B, C, B, E, F, G	1	0	1	1	1	0	0	1	0	1
ex2: A, B, C, B, C, B, C, G	1	0	2	3	0	0	0	0	1	0

We can check the independence of paths p1 to p5 by examining the first five rows of this incidence matrix. The bold entries show edges that appear in exactly one path, so paths p2 to p5 must be independent. Path p1 is independent of all of these, because any attempt to express p1 in terms of the others introduces unwanted edges. None can be deleted, and these five paths span the set of all paths from node A to node G. At this point, you should check the linear combinations of the two example paths. (The addition and multiplication are performed on the column entries.)

McCabe next develops an algorithmic procedure (called the baseline method) to determine a set of basis paths. The method begins with the selection of a baseline path, which should correspond to some "normal case" program execution. This can be somewhat arbitrary; McCabe advises choosing a path with as many decision nodes as possible. Next the baseline path is retraced, and in turn each decision is "flipped"; that is, when a node of outdegree ≥ 2 is reached, a different edge must be taken. Here we follow McCabe's example, in which he first postulates the path through nodes A, B, C, B, E, F, G as the baseline. (This was expressed in terms of paths p1 to p5 earlier.) The first decision node (outdegree ≥ 2) in this path is node A; so for the next basis path, we traverse edge 2 instead of edge 1. We get the path A, D, E, F, G, where we retrace nodes E, F, G in path 1 to be as minimally different as possible. For the next path, we can follow the second path, and take the other decision outcome of node D, which gives us the path A, D, F, G. Now, only decision nodes B and C have not been flipped; doing so yields the last two basis paths, A, B, E, F, G and A, B, C, G. Notice that this set of basis paths is distinct from the one in Table 9.3: this is not problematic, because a unique basis is not required.

9.3.2 Observations on McCabe's Basis Path Method

If you had trouble following some of the discussion on basis paths and sums and products of these, you may have felt a haunting skepticism — something along the lines of "Here's another academic oversimplification of a real-world problem." Rightly so, because two major soft spots occur in the McCabe view: one is that testing the set of basis paths is sufficient (it is not), and the other has to do with the yoga-like contortions we went through to make program paths look like a vector space. McCabe's example that the path A, B, C, B, C, B, C, G is the linear combination 2p2 – p1 is very unsatisfactory. What does the 2p2 part mean? Execute path p2 twice? (Yes, according to the math.) Even worse, what does the – p1 part mean? Execute path p1 backward? Undo the most recent execution of p1? Don't do p1 next time? Mathematical sophistries like this are a real turnoff to practitioners looking for solutions to their very real problems. To get a better understanding of these problems, we will go back to the triangle program example.

Start with the DD-Path graph of the triangle program in Figure 9.4. We begin with a baseline path that corresponds to a scalene triangle, for example, with sides 3, 4, 5. This test case will traverse the path p1 (see Table 9.4). Now, if we flip the decision at node B, we get path p2. Continuing the procedure, we flip the decision at node F, which yields the path p3. Now, we continue to flip decision nodes in the baseline path p1; the next node with outdegree = 2 is node H. When we flip node H, we get the path p4. Next, we flip node J to get p5. We know we are done, because there are only five basis paths; they are shown in Table 9.4.

Time for a reality check: if you follow paths p2 and p3, you find that they are both infeasible. Path p2 is infeasible, because passing through node D means the sides are not a triangle; so the outcome of the decision at node F must be node G. Similarly, in p3, passing through node C means the sides do form a triangle; so node G cannot be traversed. Paths p4 and p5 are both feasible and correspond respectively to equilateral and isosceles triangles. Notice that we do not have a basis path for the Not a Triangle case.

Table 9.4 Basis Paths in Figure 9.4

Original	p1: A-B-C-E-F-H-J-K-M-N-O-Last	Scalene
Flip p1 at B	p2: A-B-D-E-F-H-J-K-M-N-O-Last	Infeasible
Flip p1 at F	p3: A-B-C-E-F-G-O-Last	Infeasible
Flip p1 at H	p4: A-B-C-E-F-H-I-N-O-Last	Equilateral
Flip p1 at J	p5: A-B-C-E-F-H-J-L-M-N-O-Last	Isosceles

Recall that dependencies in the input data domain caused difficulties for boundary value testing and that we resolved these by going to decision table-based functional testing, where we addressed data dependencies in the decision table. Here, we are dealing with code-level dependencies, which are absolutely incompatible with the latent assumption that basis paths are independent. McCabe's procedure successfully identifies basis paths that are topologically independent, but when these contradict semantic dependencies, topologically possible paths are seen to be logically infeasible. One solution to this problem is to always require that flipping a decision results in a semantically feasible path. Another is to reason about logical dependencies. If we think about this problem, we can identify two rules:

If node C is traversed, then we must traverse node H.
If node D is traversed, then we must traverse node G.

Taken together, these rules, in conjunction with McCabe's baseline method, will yield the following feasible basis path set. Notice that logical dependencies reduce the size of a basis set when basis paths must be feasible.

p1: A-B-C-E-F-H-J-K-M-N-O-Last	Scalene
p6: A-B-D-E-F-G-O-Last	Not a Triangle
p4: A-B-C-E-F-H-I-N-O-Last	Equilateral
p5: A-B-C-E-F-H-J-L-M-N-O-Last	Isosceles

The triangle problem is atypical in that no loops occur. The program has only eight topologically possible paths, and of these, only the four basis paths listed above are feasible. Thus, for this special case, we arrive at the same test cases as we did with special value testing and output range testing.

For a more positive observation, basis path coverage guarantees DD-Path coverage: the process of flipping decisions guarantees that every decision outcome is traversed, which is the same as DD-Path coverage. We see this by example from the incidence matrix description of basis paths and in our triangle program feasible basis paths. We could push this a step further and observe that the set of DD-Paths acts like a basis because any program path can be expressed as a linear combination of DD-Paths.

9.3.3 Essential Complexity

Part of McCabe's work on cyclomatic complexity does more to improve programming than testing. In this section we take a quick look at this elegant blend of graph theory, structured programming, and the implications these have for testing. This whole package centers on the notion of essential complexity (McCabe, 1982), which is only the cyclomatic complexity of yet another form of condensation graph. Recall that condensation graphs are a way of simplifying an existing graph; so far, our simplifications have been based on removing either strong components or DD-Paths. Here, we condense around the structured programming constructs, which are repeated as Figure 9.8.

The basic idea is to look for the graph of one of the structured programming constructs, collapse it into a single node, and repeat until no more structured programming constructs can be found. This process is followed in Figure 9.9 and Figure 9.10, which starts with the DD-Path

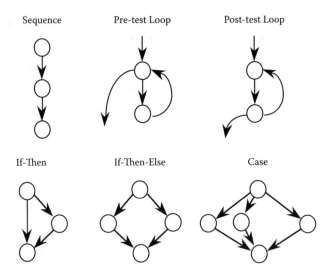

Figure 9.8 Structured programming constructs.

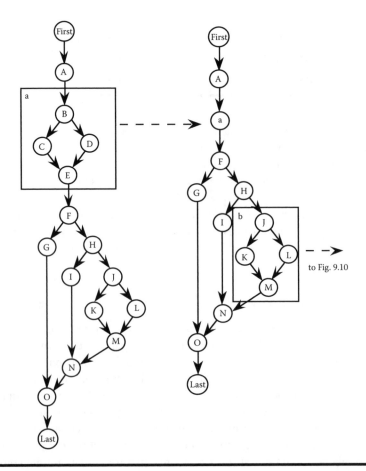

Figure 9.9 Condensing with respect to the structured programming constructs.

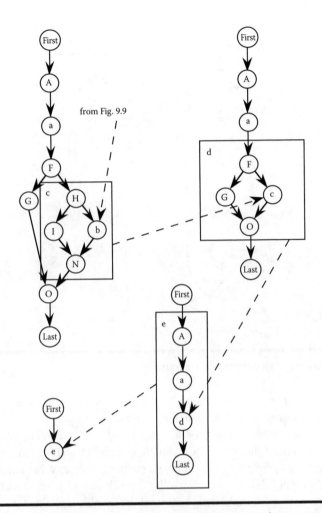

from Fig. 9.9

Figure 9.10 Condensing with respect to the structured programming constructs (continued).

graph of the pseudocode triangle program. The if-then-else construct involving nodes B, C, D, and E is condensed into node a, and then the three if-then constructs are condensed onto nodes b, c, and d. The remaining if-then-else (which corresponds to the IF IsATriangle statement) is condensed into node e, resulting in a condensed graph with cyclomatic complexity $V(G) = 1$. In general, when a program is well structured (i.e., is composed solely of the structured programming constructs), it can always be reduced to a graph with one path.

The graph in Figure 9.6 cannot be reduced in this way (try it!). The loop with nodes B and C cannot be condensed because of the edge from B to E. Similarly, nodes D, E, and F look like an if-then construct, but the edge from B to E violates the structure. McCabe went on to find elemental "unstructures" that violate the precepts of structured programming (McCabe, 1976). These are shown in Figure 9.11.

Each of these unstructures contains three distinct paths, as opposed to the two paths present in the corresponding structured programming constructs; so one conclusion is that such violations increase cyclomatic complexity. The *pièce de resistance* of McCabe's analysis is that these unstructures cannot occur by themselves: if one occurs in a program, there must be at least one more, so a program cannot be only slightly unstructured. Because these increase cyclomatic complexity,

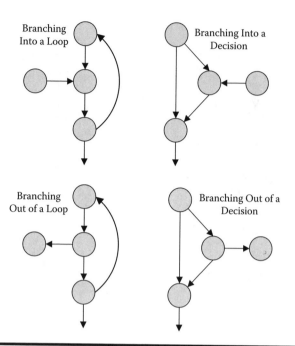

Figure 9.11 Violations of structured programming.

the minimum number of test cases is thereby increased. In the next chapter, we will see that the unstructures have interesting implications for dataflow testing.

The bottom line for testers is this: programs with high cyclomatic complexity require more testing. Of the organizations that use the cyclomatic complexity metric, most set some guideline for maximum acceptable complexity; $V(G) = 10$ is a common choice. What happens if a unit has a higher complexity? Two possibilities: either simplify the unit or plan to do more testing. If the unit is well structured, its essential complexity is 1, so it can be simplified easily. If the unit has an essential complexity that exceeds the guidelines, often the best choice is to eliminate the unstructures.

9.4 Guidelines and Observations

In our study of functional testing, we observed that gaps and redundancies can both exist and, at the same time, cannot be recognized. The problem was that functional testing removes us too far from the code. The path testing approaches to structural testing represent the case where the pendulum has swung too far the other way: moving from code to directed graph representations and program path formulations obscures important information that is present in the code, in particular the distinction between feasible and infeasible paths. In the next chapter, we look at dataflow-based testing. These techniques move closer to the code, so the pendulum will swing back from the path analysis extreme.

McCabe was partly right when he observed, "It is important to understand that these are purely criteria that measure the quality of testing, and not a procedure to identify test cases" (McCabe, 1982). He was referring to the DD-Path coverage metric (which is equivalent to the predicate outcome metric) and the cyclomatic complexity metric (which requires at least the cyclomatic number of distinct program paths be traversed). Basis path testing therefore gives us a lower boundary on how much testing is necessary.

Path–based testing also provides us with a set of metrics that act as cross-checks on functional testing. We can use these metrics to resolve the gaps and redundancies question. When we find that the same program path is traversed by several functional test cases, we suspect that this redundancy is not revealing new faults. When we fail to attain DD-Path coverage, we know that there are gaps in the functional test cases. As an example, suppose we have a program that contains extensive error handling, and we test it with boundary value test cases (min, min+, nom, max–, and max). Because these are all permissible values, DD-Paths corresponding to the error-handling code will not be traversed. If we add test cases derived from robustness testing or traditional equivalence class testing, the DD-Path coverage will improve. Beyond this rather obvious use of coverage metrics, an opportunity exists for real testing craftsmanship. The coverage metrics in Table 9.2 can operate in two ways: as a blanket mandated standard (e.g., all units shall be tested to attain full DD-Path coverage) or as mechanism to selectively test portions of code more rigorously than others. We might choose multiple condition coverage for modules with complex logic, while those with extensive iteration might be tested in terms of the loop coverage techniques. This is probably the best view of structural testing: use the properties of the source code to identify appropriate coverage metrics, and then use these as a cross-check on functional test cases. When the desired coverage is not attained, follow interesting paths to identify additional (special value) test cases.

This is a good place to revisit the Venn diagram view of testing that we used in Chapter 1. Figure 9.12 shows the relationship among specified behaviors (set S), programmed behaviors (set P), and topologically feasible paths in a program (set T). As usual, region 1 is the most desirable — it contains specified behaviors that are implemented by feasible paths. By definition, every feasible path is topologically possible; so the shaded portion (regions 2 and 6) of the set P must be empty. Region 3 contains feasible paths that correspond to unspecified behaviors. Such extra functionality needs to be examined: if useful, the specification should be changed; otherwise, these feasible paths should be removed. Regions 4 and 7 contain the infeasible paths; of these, region 4 is problematic. Region 4 refers to specified behaviors that have almost been implemented — topologically possible yet infeasible program paths. This region very likely corresponds to coding errors, where changes are needed to make the paths feasible. Region 5 still corresponds to specified behaviors that have not been implemented. Path–based testing will never recognize this region. Finally, region 7 is a curiosity: unspecified, infeasible, yet topologically possible paths. Strictly speaking,

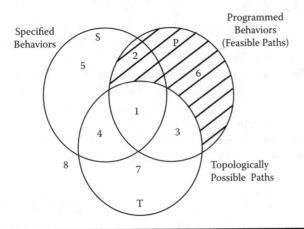

Figure 9.12 Feasible and topologically possible paths.

no problem occurs here because infeasible paths cannot execute. If the corresponding code is incorrectly changed by a maintenance action (maybe by a programmer who does not fully understand the code), these could become feasible paths, as in region 3.

References

Beizer, Boris, *Software System Testing and Quality Assurance*, Van Nostrand Reinhold, New York, 1984.

Huang, J.C., Detection of dataflow anomaly through program instrumentation, *IEEE Transactions on Software Engineering*, SE-5, 1979, pp. 226–236.

McCabe, T.J., A complexity metric, *IEEE Transactions on Software Engineering*, SE-2, 4, December 1976, pp. 308–320.

McCabe, T.J., *Structural Testing: A Software Testing Methodology Using the Cyclomatic Complexity Metric*, Special Publication 500-99, National Bureau of Standards (now NIST), Washington, DC, 1982.

McCabe, T.J., *Structural Testing: A Software Testing Methodology Using the Cyclomatic Complexity Metric*, McCabe and Associates, Baltimore, 1987.

Miller, E.F., Jr., *Tutorial: Program Testing Techniques*, COMPSAC '77 IEEE Computer Society, 1977.

Miller, E.F., Jr., Automated software testing: a technical perspective, *American Programmer*, Vol. 4, No. 4, April 1991, pp. 38–43.

Perry, W.E., *A Structured Approach to Systems Testing*, QED Information Systems, Inc., Wellesley, MA, 1987.

Schach, S.R., *Software Engineering*, 2nd ed., Richard D. Irwin, Inc., and Aksen Associates, Inc. Boston, MA, 1993.

Exercises

1. Find the cyclomatic complexity of the graph in Figure 9.2.
2. Identify a set of basis paths for the graph in Figure 9.2.
3. Discuss McCabe's concept of "flipping" for nodes with outdegree ≥ 3.
4. Suppose we take Figure 9.2 as the DD-Path graph of some program. Develop sets of paths (which would be test cases) for the C_0, C_1, and C_2 metrics.
5. Develop multiple condition coverage test cases for the pseudocode triangle program. (Pay attention to the dependency between statement fragments 14 and 16 with the expression (a = b) AND (b = c).)
6. Rewrite the program segment 14 to 20 such that the compound conditions are replaced by nested if-then-else statements. Compare the cyclomatic complexity of your program with that of the existing version.
7. Look carefully at the original statement fragments 14 to 20. What happens with a test case (e.g., a = 3, b = 4, c = 3) in which a = c? The condition in line 14 uses the transitivity of equality to eliminate the a = c condition. Is this a problem?
8. The codeBasedTesting.xls Excel spreadsheet at the CRC Web site (www.crcpress.com) contains instrumented VBA implementations of the triangle, NextDate, and commission problems that you may have analyzed with the specBasedTesting.xls spreadsheet. The output shows the DD-Path coverage of individual test cases and an indication of any faults revealed by a failing test case. Experiment with various sets of test cases to see if you can devise a set of test cases that has full DD-Path coverage yet does not reveal the known faults.

9. (For mathematicians only) For a set V to be a vector space, two operations (addition and scalar multiplication) must be defined for elements in the set. In addition, the following criteria must hold for all vectors x, y, and z ∈ V, and for all scalars k, l, 0, and 1:

   a. If x, y ∈ V, the vector x + y ∈ V.
   b. x + y = y + x.
   c. (x + y) + z = x + (y + z).
   d. There is a vector 0 ∈ V such that x + 0 = x.
   e. For any x ∈ V, there is a vector −x ∈ V such that x + (−x) = 0.
   f. For any x ∈ V, the vector kx ∈ V.
   g. k(x + y) = kx + ky.
   h. (k + l)x = kx + lx.
   i. k(lx) = (kl)x.
   j. 1x = x.

How many of these 10 criteria hold for the vector space of paths in a program?

Chapter 10

Dataflow Testing

Dataflow testing is an unfortunate term because it suggests some connection with dataflow diagrams; no connection exists. Dataflow testing refers to forms of structural testing that focus on the points at which variables receive values and the points at which these values are used (or referenced). We will see that dataflow testing serves as a reality check on path testing; indeed, many of the dataflow testing proponents (and researchers) see this approach as a form of path testing. We will look at two mainline forms of dataflow testing: one provides a set of basic definitions and a unifying structure of test coverage metrics, while the other is based on a concept called a program slice. Both of these formalize intuitive behaviors (and analyses) of testers, and although they both start with a program graph, both move back in the direction of functional testing.

Most programs deliver functionality in terms of data. Variables that represent data somehow receive values, and these values are used to compute values for other variables. Since the early 1960s, programmers have analyzed source code in terms of the points (statements) at which variables receive values and points at which these values are used. Many times, their analyses were based on concordances that list statement numbers in which variable names occur. Concordances were popular features of second-generation language compilers (they are still popular with COBOL programmers). Early dataflow analyses often centered on a set of faults that are now known as define/reference anomalies:

A variable that is defined but never used (referenced)
A variable that is used before it is defined
A variable that is defined twice before it is used

Each of these anomalies can be recognized from the concordance of a program. Because the concordance information is compiler generated, these anomalies can be discovered by what is known as static analysis: finding faults in source code without executing it.

10.1 Define/Use Testing

Much of the formalization of define/use testing was done in the early 1980s (Rapps and Weyuker, 1985); the definitions in this section are compatible with those in Clarke et al. (1989), which summarizes most define/use testing theory. This body of research is very compatible with the formulation we developed in Chapters 4 and 9. It presumes a program graph in which nodes are statement fragments (a fragment may be an entire statement) and programs that follow the structured programming precepts.

The following definitions refer to a program P that has a program graph G(P) and a set of program variables V. The program graph G(P) is constructed as in Chapter 4, with statement fragments as nodes and edges that represent node sequences. G(P) has a single-entry node and a single-exit node. We also disallow edges from a node to itself. Paths, subpaths, and cycles are as they were in Chapter 4. The set of all paths in P is PATHS(P).

Definition

Node $n \in G(P)$ is a *defining node of the variable* $v \in V$, written as DEF(v, n), iff the value of the variable v is defined at the statement fragment corresponding to node n.

Input statements, assignment statements, loop control statements, and procedure calls are all examples of statements that are defining nodes. When the code corresponding to such statements executes, the contents of the memory location(s) associated with the variables are changed.

Definition

Node $n \in G(P)$ is a *usage node of the variable* $v \in V$, written as USE(v, n), iff the value of the variable v is used at the statement fragment corresponding to node n.

Output statements, assignment statements, conditional statements, loop control statements, and procedure calls are all examples of statements that are usage nodes. When the code corresponding to such statements executes, the contents of the memory location(s) associated with the variables remain unchanged.

Definition

A usage node USE(v, n) is a *predicate use* (denoted as P-use) iff the statement n is a predicate statement; otherwise, USE(v, n) is a *computation use* (denoted C-use).

The nodes corresponding to predicate uses always have an outdegree ≥ 2, and nodes corresponding to computation uses always have an outdegree ≤ 1.

Definition

A *definition-use path with respect to a variable* v (denoted du-path) is a path in PATHS(P) such that for some $v \in V$, there are define and usage nodes DEF(v, m) and USE(v, n) such that m and n are the initial and final nodes of the path.

Definition

A *definition-clear path with respect to a variable* v (denoted dc-path) is a definition-use path in PATHS(P) with initial and final nodes DEF (v, m) and USE (v, n) such that no other node in the path is a defining node of v.

Testers should notice how these definitions capture the essence of computing with stored data values. Du-paths and dc-paths describe the flow of data across source statements from points at which the values are defined to points at which the values are used. Du-paths that are not definition-clear are potential trouble spots.

10.1.1 Example

We will use the commission problem and its program graph to illustrate these definitions. The numbered pseudocode is given next, followed by a program graph constructed according to the procedures we discussed in Chapter 4. This program computes the commission on the sales of the total numbers of locks, stocks, and barrels sold. The While loop is a classical sentinel controlled loop in which a value of −1 for locks signifies the end of the sales data. The totals are accumulated as the data values are read in the While loop. After printing this preliminary information, the sales value is computed, using the constant item prices defined at the beginning of the program. The sales value is then used to compute the commission in the conditional portion of the program:

```
1.      Program Commission (INPUT,OUTPUT)
2.          Dim locks, stocks, barrels As Integer
3.          Dim lockPrice, stockPrice, barrelPrice As Real
4.          Dim totalLocks, totalStocks, totalBarrels As Integer
5.          Dim lockSales, stockSales, barrelSales As Real
6.          Dim sales, commission As Real
7.          lockPrice = 45.0
8.          stockPrice = 30.0
9.          barrelPrice = 25.0
10.         totalLocks = 0
11.         totalStocks = 0
12.         totalBarrels = 0
13.         Input(locks)
14.         While NOT(locks = -1)    'loop condition uses -1 to
                indicate end of data
15.             Input(stocks, barrels)
16.             totalLocks = totalLocks + locks
17.             totalStocks = totalStocks + stocks
18.             totalBarrels = totalBarrels + barrels
19.             Input(locks)
20.         EndWhile
21.         Output("Locks sold: ", totalLocks)
22.         Output("Stocks sold: ", totalStocks)
23.         Output("Barrels sold: ", totalBarrels)
24.         lockSales = lockPrice * totalLocks
25.         stockSales = stockPrice * totalStocks
26.         barrelSales = barrelPrice * totalBarrels
27.         sales = lockSales + stockSales + barrelSales
28.         Output("Total sales: ", sales)
29.         If (sales > 1800.0)
30.             Then
31.                 commission = 0.10 * 1000.0
```

```
32.                    commission = commission + 0.15 * 800.0
33.                    commission = commission + 0.20 *
                       (sales-1800.0)
34.         Else If (sales > 1000.0)
35.             Then
36.                    commission = 0.10 * 1000.0
37.                    commission = commission + 0.15 *
                       (sales-1000.0)
38.             Else
39.                    commission = 0.10 * sales
40.             EndIf
41.         EndIf
42.         Output("Commission is $", commission)
43.         End Commission
```

Figure 10.2 shows the decision-to-decision path (DD-Path) graph of the program graph in Figure 10.1. More compression exists in this DD-Path graph because of the increased computation in the commission problem. Table 10.1 details the statement fragments associated with DD-Paths. Some DD-Paths (per the definition in Chapter 9) are combined to simplify the graph.

Table 10.1   DD-Paths in Figure 10.1

DD-Path	Nodes
A	7, 8, 9, 10, 11, 12, 13
B	14
C	15, 16, 17, 18, 19,20
D	21, 22, 23, 24, 25, 26, 27, 28
E	29
F	30, 31, 32, 33
G	34
H	35, 36, 37
I	38, 39
J	40
K	41, 42, 43

Table 10.2 lists the define and usage nodes for the variables in the commission problem. We use this information in conjunction with the program graph in Figure 10.1 to identify various definition-use and definition-clear paths. It is a judgment call whether nonexecutable statements such as constant and variable declaration statements should be considered as defining nodes. Such nodes are not very interesting when we follow what happens along their du-paths, but if something is wrong, it can be helpful to include them. Take your pick. We will refer to the various paths as sequences of node numbers.

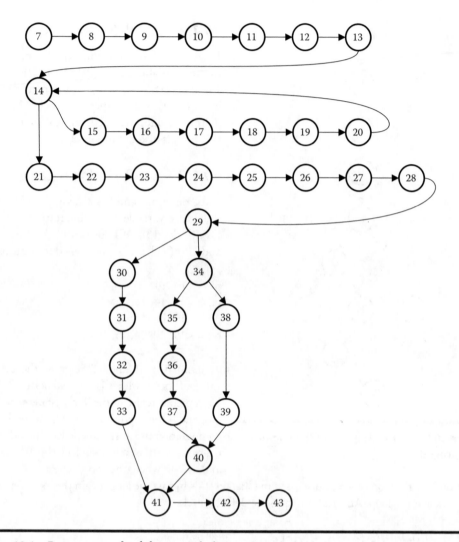

Figure 10.1 Program graph of the commission program.

Table 10.3 presents some of the du-paths in the commission problem; they are named by their beginning and ending nodes (from Figure 10.1). The third column in Table 10.3 indicates whether the du-paths are definition-clear. Some of the du-paths are trivial — for example, those for lockPrice, stockPrice, and barrelPrice. Others are more complex: the While loop (node sequence <14, 15, 16, 17, 18, 19, 20>) inputs and accumulates values for totalLocks, totalStocks, and totalBarrels. Table 10.3 only shows the details for the totalStocks variable. The initial value definition for totalStocks occurs at node 11, and it is first used at node 17. Thus, the path (11, 17), which consists of the node sequence <11, 12, 13, 14, 15, 16, 17>, is definition-clear. The path (11, 22), which consists of the node sequence <11, 12, 13, (14, 15, 16, 17, 18, 19, 20)*, 21, 22>, is not definition-clear because values of totalStocks are defined at node 11 and (possibly several times at) node 17. (The asterisk after the While loop is the Kleene star notation used in both formal logic and regular expressions to denote zero or more repetitions.)

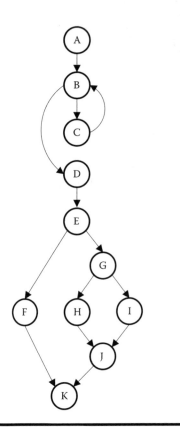

Figure 10.2 DD-Path graph of the commission program.

10.1.2 du-Paths for Stocks

First, let us look at a simple path: the du-path for the variable stocks. We have DEF(stocks, 15) and USE(stocks, 17), so the path <15, 17> is a du-path with respect to stocks. No other defining nodes are used for stocks; therefore, this path is also definition-clear.

10.1.3 du-Paths for Locks

Two defining and two usage nodes make the locks variable more interesting: we have DEF(locks, 13), DEF(locks, 19), USE(locks, 14), and USE(locks, 16). These yield four du-paths:

p1 = <13, 14>
p2 = <13, 14, 15, 16>
p3 = <19, 20, 14>
p4 = <19, 20, 14, 15, 16>

Du-paths p1 and p2 refer to the priming value of locks, which is read at node 13: locks has a predicate use in the While statement (node 14), and if the condition is true (as in path p2), a computation use at statement 16. The other two du-paths start near the end of the While loop and occur when the loop repeats. These four paths provide the loop coverage discussed in Chapter 9 — bypass the loop, begin the loop, repeat the loop, and exit the loop. All these du-paths are definition-clear.

10.1.4 du-Paths for totalLocks

The du-paths for totalLocks will lead us to typical test cases for computations. With two defining nodes (DEF(totalLocks, 10) and DEF(totalLocks, 16)) and three usage nodes (USE(totalLocks, 16), USE(totalLocks, 21), USE(totalLocks, 24)), we might expect six du-paths. Let us take a closer look.

Path p5 = <10, 11, 12, 13, 14, 15, 16> is a du-path in which the initial value of totalLocks (0) has a computation use. This path is definition-clear. The next path is problematic:

p6 = <10, 11, 12, 13, 14, 15, 16, 17, 18, 19, 20, 14, 21>

Path p6 ignores the possible repetition of the While loop. We could highlight this by noting that the subpath <16, 17, 18, 19, 20, 14, 15> might be traversed several times. Ignoring this for now, we still have a du-path that fails to be definition-clear. If a problem occurs with the value of totalLocks at node 21 (the output statement), we should look at the intervening DEF(totalLocks, 16) node.

The next path contains p6; we can show this by using a path name in place of its corresponding node sequence:

Table 10.2   Define/Use Nodes for Variables in the Commission Problem

Variable	Defined at Node	Used at Node
lockPrice	7	24
stockPrice	8	25
barrelPrice	9	26
totalLocks	10, 16	16, 21, 24
totalStocks	11, 17	17, 22, 25
totalBarrels	12, 18	18, 23, 26
locks	13, 19	14, 16
stocks	15	17
barrels	15	18
lockSales	24	27
stockSales	25	27
barrelSales	26	27
sales	27	28, 29, 33, 34, 37, 39
commission	31, 32, 33, 36, 37, 39	32, 33, 37, 42

p7 = <10, 11, 12, 13, 14, 15, 16, 17, 18, 19, 20, 14, 21, 22, 23, 24>
p7 = < p6, 22, 23, 24>

Du-path p7 is not definition-clear because it includes node 16.

Subpaths that begin with node 16 (an assignment statement) are interesting. The first, <16, 16>, seems degenerate. If we "expanded" it into machine code, we would be able to separate the define and usage portions. We will disallow these as du-paths. Technically, the usage on the right-hand side of the assignment refers to a value defined at node 10 (see path p5). The remaining two du-paths are both subpaths of p7:

p8 = <16, 17, 18, 19, 20, 14, 21>
p9 = <16, 17, 18, 19, 20, 14, 21, 22, 23, 24>

Both are definition-clear, and both have the loop iteration problem we discussed before.

10.1.5   du-Paths for Sales

Only one defining node is used for sales; therefore, all the du-paths with respect to sales must be definition-clear. They are interesting because they illustrate predicate and computation uses. The first three du-paths are easy:

p10 = <27, 28>
p11 = <27, 28, 29>
p12 = <27, 28, 29, 30, 31, 32, 33>

Table 10.3   Selected Define/Use Paths

Variable	Path (Beginning, End) Nodes	Definition-Clear?
lockPrice	7, 24	Yes
stockPrice	8, 25	Yes
barrelPrice	9, 26	Yes
totalStocks	11, 17	Yes
totalStocks	11, 22	No
totalStocks	11, 25	No
totalStocks	17, 17	Yes
totalStocks	17, 22	No
totalStocks	17, 25	No
locks	13, 14	Yes
locks	13, 16	Yes
locks	19, 14	Yes
locks	19, 16	Yes
sales	27, 28	Yes
sales	27, 29	Yes
sales	27, 33	Yes
sales	27, 34	Yes
sales	27, 37	Yes
sales	27, 39	Yes

Notice that p12 is a definition-clear path with three usage nodes; it also contains paths p10 and p11. If we were testing with p12, we know we would also have covered the other two paths. We will revisit this toward the end of the chapter.

The IF, ELSE IF logic in statements 29 through 40 highlights an ambiguity in the original research. Two choices for du-paths begin with path p11: one choice is the path <27, 28, 29, 30, 31, 32, 33>, and the other is the path <27, 28, 29, 34>. The remaining du-paths for sales are:

p13 = <27, 28, 29, 34>
p14 = <27, 28, 29, 34, 35, 36, 37>
p15 = <27, 28, 29, 34, 38,39>

Note that the dynamic view is very compatible with the kind of thinking we used for DD-Paths in Chapter 9.

10.1.6   du-Paths for Commission

If you have followed this discussion carefully, you are probably dreading the analysis of du-paths with respect to commission. You are right — it is time for a change of pace. In statements 29

Table 10.4   Define/Use Paths for Commission

Variable	Path (Beginning, End) Nodes	Feasible?	Definition-Clear?
commission	31, 32	Yes	Yes
commission	31, 33	Yes	No
commission	31, 37	No	n/a
commission	31, 42	Yes	No
commission	32, 32	Yes	Yes
commission	32, 33	Yes	Yes
commission	32, 37	No	n/a
commission	32, 42	Yes	No
commission	33, 32	No	n/a
commission	33, 33	Yes	Yes
commission	33, 37	No	n/a
commission	33, 42	Yes	Yes
commission	36, 32	No	n/a
commission	36, 33	No	n/a
commission	36, 37	Yes	Yes
commission	36, 42	Yes	No
commission	37, 32	No	n/a
commission	37, 33	No	n/a
commission	37, 37	Yes	Yes
commission	37, 42	Yes	Yes
commission	38, 32	No	n/a
commission	38, 33	No	n/a
commission	38, 37	No	n/a
commission	38, 42	Yes	Yes

through 41, the calculation of commission is controlled by ranges of the variable sales. Statements 31 to 33 build up the value of commission by using the memory location to hold intermediate values. This is a common programming practice, and it is desirable because it shows how the final value is computed. (We could replace these lines with the statement "commission : = 220 + 0.20*(sales −1800)," where 220 is the value of 0.10*1000 + 0.15*800, but this would be hard for a maintainer to understand.) The "built-up" version uses intermediate values, and these will appear as define and usage nodes in the du-path analysis. We decided to disallow du-paths from assignment statements like 31 and 32, so we will just consider du-paths that begin with the three "real" defining nodes: DEF(commission, 33), DEF(commission, 37), and DEF(commission, 38). Only one usage node is used: USE(commission, 42).

10.1.7 du-Path Test Coverage Metrics

The whole point of analyzing a program with definition-use paths is to define a set of test coverage metrics known as the Rapps–Weyuker dataflow metrics (Rapps and Weyuker, 1985). The first three of these are equivalent to three of E.F. Miller's metrics in Chapter 9: All-Paths, All-Edges, and All-Nodes. The others presume that define and usage nodes have been identified for all program variables, and that du-paths have been identified with respect to each variable. In the following definitions, T is a set of paths in the program graph G(P) of a program P, with the set V of variables. It is not enough to take the cross-product of the set of DEF nodes with the set of USE nodes for a variable to define du-paths. This mechanical approach can result in infeasible paths. In the next definitions, we assume that the define/use paths are all feasible.

Definition

The set T satisfies the *All-Defs criterion* for the program P iff for every variable v ∈ V, T contains definition-clear paths from every defining node of v to a use of v.

Definition

The set T satisfies the *All-Uses criterion* for the program P iff for every variable v ∈ V, T contains definition-clear paths from every defining node of v to every use of v, and to the successor node of each USE(v, n).

Definition

The set T satisfies the *All-P-Uses/Some C-Uses* criterion for the program P iff for every variable v ∈ V, T contains definition-clear paths from every defining node of v to every predicate use of v; if a definition of v has no P-uses, a definition-clear path leads to at least one computation use.

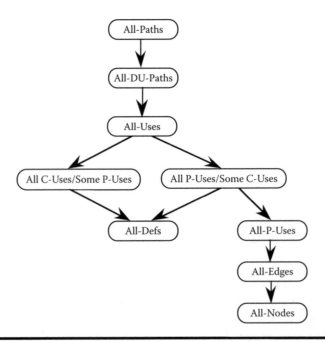

Figure 10.3   Rapps–Weyuker hierarchy of dataflow coverage metrics.

Definition

The set T satisfies the *All-C-Uses/Some P-Uses* criterion for the program P iff for every variable v ∈ V, T contains definition-clear paths from every defining node of v to every computation use of v; if a definition of v has no C-uses, a definition-clear path leads to at least one predicate use.

Definition

The set T satisfies the *All-du-paths criterion* for the program P iff for every variable v ∈ V, T contains definition-clear paths from every defining node of v to every use of v and to the successor node of each USE(v, n), and that these paths are either single-loop traversals or cycle-free.

These test coverage metrics have several set theory-based relationships, which are referred to as "subsumption" in Rapps and Weyuker (1985). These relationships are shown in Figure 10.3.

We now have a more refined view of structural testing possibilities between the extremes of the (typically unattainable) All-Paths metric and the generally accepted minimum, All-Edges. What good is all this? Define/use testing provides a rigorous, systematic way to examine points at which faults may occur.

10.2 Slice-Based Testing

Program slices have surfaced and submerged in software engineering literature since the early 1980s. They were originally proposed in Weiser (1988), used as an approach to software maintenance in Gallagher and Lyle (1991), and more recently used to quantify functional cohesion in Bieman and Ott (1994). Part of this versatility is due to the natural, intuitively clear intent of the program slice concept. Informally, a program slice is a set of program statements that contributes to or affects a value for a variable at some point in the program. This notion of slice corresponds to other disciplines as well. We might study history in terms of slices — U.S. history, European history, Russian history, Far East history, Roman history, and so on. The way in which such historical slices interact turns out to be very analogous to the way program slices interact.

We will start by growing our working definition of a program slice. We continue with the notation we used for define/use paths: a program P that has a program graph G(P) and a set of program variables V. The first try refines the definition in Gallagher and Lyle (1991) to allow nodes in P(G) to refer to statement fragments.

Definition

Given a program P and a set V of variables in P, *a slice on the variable set V at statement* n, written S(V, n), is the set of all statements in P prior to node n that contribute to the values of variables in V at node n.

Listing elements of a slice S(V, n) will be cumbersome because the elements are program statement fragments. It is much simpler to list fragment numbers in P(G), so we make the following trivial change (it keeps the set theory purists happy).

Definition

Given a program P and a program graph G(P) in which statements and statement fragments are numbered, and a set V of variables in P, the *slice on the variable set V at statement fragment n*, written S(V, n), is the set of node numbers of all statement fragments in P prior to and including n that contribute to the values of variables in V at statement fragment n.

The idea of slices is to separate a program into components that have some useful (functional) meaning. First, we need to explain two parts of the definition. Here, we mean "prior to" in the dynamic sense, so a slice captures the execution time behavior of a program with respect to the variable(s) in the slice. Eventually, we will develop a lattice (a directed, acyclic graph) of slices, in which nodes are slices and edges correspond to the subset relationship.

The "contribute" part is more complex. In a sense, data declaration statements have an effect on the value of a variable. For now, we simply exclude all nonexecutable statements. The notion of contribution is partially clarified by the predicate (P-use) and computation (C-use) usage distinction of Rapps and Weyuker (1985), but we need to refine these forms of variable usage. Specifically, the USE relationship pertains to five forms of usage:

P-use	Used in a predicate (decision)
C-use	Used in computation
O-use	Used for output
L-use	Used for location (pointers, subscripts)
I-use	Iteration (internal counters, loop indices)

While we are at it, we identify two forms of definition nodes:

I-def	Defined by input
A-def	Defined by assignment

For now, presume that the slice S(V, n) is a slice on one variable; that is, the set V consists of a single variable, v. If statement fragment n is a defining node for v, then n is included in the slice. If statement fragment n is a usage node for v, then n is not included in the slice. (Notice that this is a subtle refinement of our second definition.) P-uses and C-uses of other variables (not the v in the slice set V) are included to the extent that their execution affects the value of the variable v. As a guideline, if the value of v is the same whether a statement fragment is included or excluded, exclude the statement fragment.

L-use and I-use variables are typically invisible outside their modules, but this hardly precludes the problems such variables often create. Another judgment call: here (with some peril), we choose to exclude these from the intent of "contribute." Thus, O-use, L-use, and I-use nodes are excluded from slices.

10.2.1 Example

The commission problem is used in this book because it contains interesting dataflow properties, and these are not present in the triangle problem (or in NextDate). Follow these examples while looking at the source code for the commission problem that we used to analyze in terms of define/use paths.

Slices on the locks variable show why it is potentially fault-prone. It has a P-use at node 14 and a C-use at node 16 and has two definitions, the I-defs at nodes 13 and 19.

S_1: S(locks, 13) = {13}
S_2: S(locks, 14) = {13, 14, 19, 20}
S_3: S(locks, 16) = {13, 14, 19, 20}

S_4: S(locks, 19) = {19}

The slices for stocks and barrels are boring. They are short, definition-clear paths contained entirely within a loop, so they are not affected by iterations of the loop. (Think of the loop body as a DD-Path.)

S_5: S(stocks, 15) = {13, 14, 15, 19, 20}
S_6: S(stocks, 17) = {13, 14, 15, 19, 20}
S_7: S(barrels, 15) = {13, 14, 15, 19, 20}
S_8: S(barrels, 18) = {13, 14, 15, 19, 20}

The next three slices illustrate how repetition appears in slices. Node 10 is an A-def for total-Locks, and node 16 contains both an A-def and a C-use. The remaining nodes in S_{10} (13, 14, 19, and 20) pertain to the While loop controlled by locks. Slices S_{10} and S_{11} are equal because nodes 21 and 24 are an O-use and a C-use of totalLocks, respectively.

S_9: S(totalLocks, 10) = {10}
S_{10}: S(totalLocks, 16) = {10, 13, 14, 16, 19, 20}
S_{11}: S(totalLocks, 21) = {10, 13, 14, 16, 19, 20}

The slices on totalStocks and totalBarrels are quite similar. They are initialized by A-defs at nodes 11 and 12 and then are redefined by A-defs at nodes 17 and 18. Again, the remaining nodes (13, 14, 19, and 20) pertain to the While loop controlled by locks.

S_{12}: S(totalStocks, 11) = {11}
S_{13}: S(totalStocks, 17) = {11, 13, 14, 15, 17, 19, 20}
S_{14}: S(totalStocks, 22) = {11, 13, 14, 15, 17, 19, 20}
S_{15}: S(totalBarrels, 12) = {12}
S_{16}: S(totalBarrels, 18) = {12, 13, 14, 15, 18, 19, 20}
S_{17}: S(totalBarrels, 23) = {12, 13, 14, 15, 18, 19, 20}

The next six slices demonstrate our convention regarding values defined by assignment statements (A-defs).

S_{18}: S(lockPrice, 24) = {7}
S_{19}: S(stockPrice, 25) = {8}
S_{20}: S(barrelPrice, 26) = {9}
S_{21}: S(lockSales, 24) = {7, 10, 13, 14, 16, 19, 20, 24}
S_{22}: S(stockSales, 25) = {8, 11, 13, 14, 15, 17, 19, 20, 25}
S_{23}: S(barrelSales, 26) = {9, 12, 13, 14, 15, 18, 19, 20, 26}

The slices on sales and commission are the interesting ones. Only one defining node exists for sales, the A-def at node 27. The remaining slices on sales show the P-uses, C-uses, and the O-use in definition-clear paths.

S_{24}: S(sales, 27) = {7, 8, 9, 10, 11, 12, 13, 14, 15, 16, 17, 18, 19, 20, 24, 25, 26, 27}

S_{25}: S(sales, 28) = {7, 8, 9, 10, 11, 12, 13, 14, 15, 16, 17, 18, 19, 20, 24, 25, 26, 27}
S_{26}: S(sales, 29) = {7, 8, 9, 10, 11, 12, 13, 14, 15, 16, 17, 18, 19, 20, 24, 25, 26, 27}
S_{27}: S(sales, 33) = {7, 8, 9, 10, 11, 12, 13, 14, 15, 16, 17, 18, 19, 20, 24, 25, 26, 27}
S_{28}: S(sales, 34) = {7, 8, 9, 10, 11, 12, 13, 14, 15, 16, 17, 18, 19, 20, 24, 25, 26, 27}
S_{29}: S(sales, 37) = {7, 8, 9, 10, 11, 12, 13, 14, 15, 16, 17, 18, 19, 20, 24, 25, 26, 27}
S_{30}: S(sales, 39) = {7, 8, 9, 10, 11, 12, 13, 14, 15, 16, 17, 18, 19, 20, 24, 25, 26, 27}

Think about slice S_{24} in terms of its components, which are the slices on the C-use variables. We can write $S_{24} = S_{10} \cup S_{13} \cup S_{16} \cup S_{21} \cup S_{22} \cup S_{23} \cup$ {27}. Notice how the formalism corresponds to our intuition: if the value of sales is wrong, we first look at how it is computed; if this is OK, we check how the components are computed.

Everything comes together (literally) with the slices on commission. Six A-def nodes are used for commission (corresponding to the six du-paths we identified earlier). Three computations of commission are controlled by P-uses of sales in the IF, ELSE IF logic. This yields three paths of slices that compute commission.

S_{31}: S(commission, 31) = {31}
S_{32}: S(commission, 32) = {31, 32}
S_{33}: S(commission, 33) = {7, 8, 9 10, 11, 12, 13, 14, 15, 16, 17, 18, 19, 20, 24, 25, 26, 27, 29, 30, 31, 32, 33}
S_{34}: S(commission, 36) = {36}
S_{35}: S(commission, 37) = {7, 8, 9 10, 11, 12, 13, 14, 15, 16, 17, 18, 19, 20, 24, 25, 26, 27, 36, 37}
S_{36}: S(commission, 39) = {7, 8, 9 10, 11, 12, 13, 14, 15, 16, 17, 18, 19, 20, 24, 25, 26, 27, 29, 34, 38, 39}

Whichever computation is taken, all come together in the last slice.

S_{37}: S(commission, 41) = {7, 8, 9 10, 11, 12, 13, 14, 15, 16, 17, 18, 19, 20, 24, 25, 26, 27, 29, 30, 31, 32, 33, 34, 35, 36, 37, 38, 39}

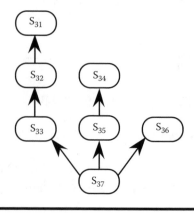

Figure 10.4 Lattice of slices on commission.

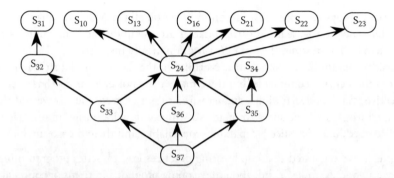

Figure 10.5　Lattice on sales and commission.

The slice information improves our insight. Look at the lattice in Figure 10.4; it is a directed acyclic graph in which slices are nodes and an edge represents the proper subset relationship.

This lattice is drawn so that the position of the slice nodes roughly corresponds with their position in the source code. The definition-clear paths <33, 41>, <37, 41>, and <39, 41> correspond to the edges that show slices S_{33}, S_{35}, and S_{36} are subsets of slice S_{37}. Figure 10.5 shows a lattice of slices for the entire program. Some slices (those that are identical to others) have been deleted for clarity.

10.2.2　Style and Technique

When we analyze a program in terms of interesting slices, we can focus on parts of interest while disregarding unrelated parts. We could not do this with du-paths — they are sequences that include statements and variables that may not be of interest. Before discussing some analytic techniques, we will first look at "good style." We could have built these stylistic precepts into the definitions, but then the definitions become even more cumbersome.

1. Never make a slice S(V, n) for which variables v of V do not appear in statement fragment n. This possibility is permitted by the definition of a slice, but it is bad practice. As an example, suppose we defined a slice on the locks variable at node 27. Defining such slices necessitates tracking the values of all variables at all points in the program.
2. Make slices on one variable. The set V in slice S(V, n) can contain several variables, and sometimes such slices are useful. The slice S(V, 26), where

$$V = \{lockSales, stockSales, barrelSales\}$$

   contains all the elements of the slice S({sales}, 27) except statement 27. These two slices are so similar, so why define the one in terms of C-uses?
3. Make slices for all A-def nodes. When a variable is computed by an assignment statement, a slice on the variable at that statement will include (portions of) all du-paths of the variables used in the computation. Slice ({sales}, 36) is a good example of an A-def slice.
4. Make slices for P-use nodes. When a variable is used in a predicate, the slice on that variable at the decision statement shows how the predicate variable got its value. This is very useful in decision-intensive programs such as the triangle program and NextDate.
5. Slices on non-P-use usage nodes are not very interesting. We discussed C-use slices in point 2, where we saw they were very redundant with the A-def slice. Slices on O-use vari-

ables can always be expressed as unions of slices on all the A-defs (and I-defs) of the O-use variable. Slices on I-use and O-use variables are useful during debugging, but if they are mandated for all testing, the test effort is dramatically increased.

6. Consider making slices compilable. Nothing in the definition of a slice requires that the set of statements is compilable, but if we make this choice, it means that a set of compiler directive and data declaration statements is a subset of every slice. If we add this same set of statements to all the slices we made for the commission program, our lattices remain undisturbed, but each slice is separately compilable (and therefore executable).

In Chapter 1, we suggested that good testing practices lead to better programming practices. Here, we have a good example. Think about developing programs in terms of compilable slices. If we did this, we could code a slice and immediately test it. We can then code and test other slices and merge them (sometimes called slice splicing) into a fairly solid program. Try coding the commission program this way.

10.3 Guidelines and Observations

Dataflow testing is clearly indicated for programs that are computationally intensive. As a corollary, in control-intensive programs, if control variables are computed (P-uses), dataflow testing is also indicated. The definitions we made for define/use paths and slices give us very precise ways to describe parts of a program that we would like to test. Academic tools can be used to support these definitions, but they have not migrated to the commercial marketplace. Some pieces are there; you can find programming language compilers that provide on-screen highlighting of slices, and most debugging tools let you "watch" certain variables as you step through a program execution. Here are some ideas that may prove helpful, particularly when there is a difficult module to test:

1. Slices do not map nicely into test cases (because the other, unrelated code is still in an executable path). On the other hand, they provide a handy way to eliminate interaction among variables. Use the slice composition approach to re-develop difficult sections of code, and test these slices before you splice (compose) them with other slices. There are software tools that will produce compilable slices given the source code to assist with debugging.

2. Relative complements of slices yield a diagnostic capability. The relative complement of a set B with respect to another set A is the set of all elements of A that are not elements of B. It is denoted as A − B. Consider the relative complement set S(commission, 41) − S(sales, 27):

    S(commission, 41) = {7, 8, 9 10, 11, 12, 13, 14, 15, 16, 17, 18, 19, 20, 24, 25, 26, 27, 29, 30, 31, 32, 33, 34, 35, 36, 37, 38, 39}

    S(sales, 27) = {7, 8, 9, 10, 11, 12, 13, 14, 15, 16, 17, 18, 19, 20, 24, 25, 26, 27}

    S(commission, 41) − S(sales, 27) = {29, 30, 31, 32, 33, 34, 35, 36, 37, 38, 39}

    If a problem exists with commission at line 48, we can divide the program into two parts — the computation of sales at line 34, and the computation of commission between lines 35 and 48. If sales is okay at line 34, the problem must lie in the relative complement; if not, the problem may be in either portion.

3. A many-to-many relationship exists between slices and DD-Paths: statements in one slice may be in several DD-Paths, and statements in one DD-Path may be in several slices. Well-chosen relative complements of slices can be identical to DD-Paths. For example, consider S(commission, 40) − S(commission, 37).

4. If you develop a lattice of slices, it is convenient to postulate a slice on the very first statement. This way, the lattice of slices always terminates in one root node. Show equal slices with a two-way arrow.
5. Slices exhibit define/reference information. Consider the following slices on totalLocks:

S_9: S(totalLocks, 10) = {10}
S_{10}: S(totalLocks, 16) = {10, 13, 14, 16, 19, 20}
S_{11}: S(totalLocks, 21) = {10, 13, 14, 16, 19, 20}

When slices are equal, the corresponding paths are definition-clear.

References

Bieman, J.M. and Ott, L.M., Measuring functional cohesion, *IEEE Transactions on Software Engineering*, Vol. SE-20, No. 8, August 1994, pp. 644–657.

Clarke, L.A. et al., A formal evaluation of data flow path selection criteria, *IEEE Transactions on Software Engineering*, Vol. SE-15, No. 11, November 1989, pp. 1318–1332.

Gallagher, K.B. and Lyle, J.R., Using program slicing in software maintenance, *IEEE Transactions on Software Engineering*, Vol. SE-17, No. 8, August 1991, pp. 751–761.

Rapps, S. and Weyuker, E.J., Selecting software test data using data flow information, *IEEE Transactions on Software Engineering*, Vol. SE-11, No. 4, April 1985, pp. 367–375.

Weiser, M.D., Program slicing, *IEEE Transactions on Software Engineering*, Vol. SE-10, No. 4, April 1988, pp. 352–357.

Exercises

1. Think about the static versus dynamic ambiguity of du-paths in terms of DD-Paths. As a start, what DD-Paths are found in the du-paths p12, p13, and p14 for sales?
2. Try to merge some of the DD-Path–based test coverage metrics into the Rapps–Weyuker hierarchy shown in Figure 10.2.
3. List the du-paths for the commission variable.
4. Express slice S_{37} as the union of other pertinent slices.
5. Find the following program slices:
   a. S(commission, 28)
   b. S(sales, 23)
   c. S(commission, 37), S(commission, 29), S(commission, 28)
   d. S(totalLocks, 22)
   e. S(totalStocks, 22)
   f. S(totalBarrels, 22)
6. Find the definition-clear paths (with respect to sales) from lines 27 to 29, 33, 34, 38, 39.
7. Complete the lattice in Figure 10.5.
8. Our discussion of slices in this chapter has actually been about "backward slices" in the sense that we are always concerned with parts of a program that contribute to the value of a variable at a certain point in the program. We could also consider "forward slices" that refer to parts of the program where the variable is used. Compare and contrast forward slices with du-paths.

Chapter 11

Retrospective on Structural Testing

When should testing stop? Here are some possible answers:

1. When you run out of time
2. When continued testing causes no new failures
3. When continued testing reveals no new faults
4. When you cannot think of any new test cases
5. When you reach a point of diminishing returns
6. When mandated coverage has been attained
7. When all faults have been removed

Unfortunately, the first answer is all too common, and the seventh cannot be guaranteed. This leaves the testing craftsperson somewhere in the middle. Software reliability models provide answers that support the second and third choices; both of these have been used with success in industry. The fourth choice is curious: if you have followed the precepts and guidelines we have been discussing, this is probably a good answer. On the other hand, if the reason is due to a lack of motivation, this choice is as unfortunate as the first. The point of diminishing returns choice has some appeal: it suggests that serious testing has continued, and the discovery of new faults has slowed dramatically. Continued testing becomes very expensive and may reveal no new faults. If the cost (or risk) of remaining faults can be determined, the trade-off is clear. (This is a big IF.) We are left with the coverage answer, and it is a pretty good one. In this chapter, we will see how using structural testing as a cross-check on functional testing yields powerful results. First, we demonstrate (by example) the gaps and redundancies problem of functional testing. Next, we develop some metrics of testing efficiency. Because these metrics are expressed in terms of structural coverage, we have an obvious answer to the gaps and redundancies question. Then the question reduces to which coverage metric to use. The answer that is most common in industrial practice is DD-Paths.

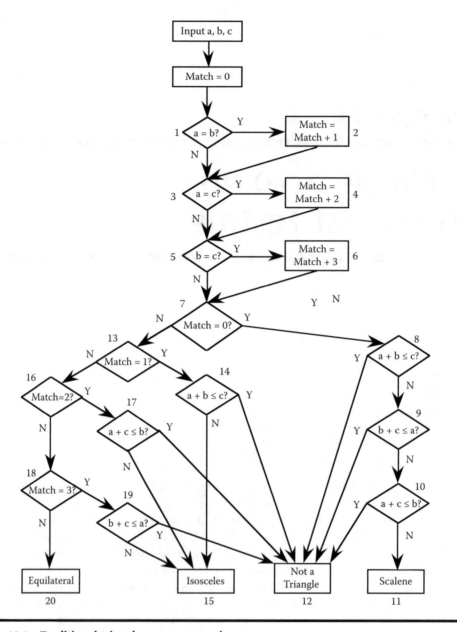

Figure 11.1   Traditional triangle program graph.

11.1   Gaps and Redundancies

The gaps and redundancies problem of functional testing is very prominent in the triangle problem. We use the (klutzy) traditional implementation here, mostly because it is the most frequently used in testing literature (Brown, 1975; Pressman, 1982). Recall that this implementation has exactly 11 feasible paths. They are given in Table 11.1. The path names will be used later; the node numbers are shown in Figure 11.1.

Table 11.1   Paths in the Triangle Program

Path	Node Sequence	Description
p1	1–2–3–4–5–6–7–13–16–18–20	Equilateral
p2	1–3–5–6–7–13–16–18–19–15	Isosceles (b = c)
p3	1–3–5–6–7–13–16–18–19–12	Not a Triangle (b = c)
p4	1–3–4–5–7–13–16–17–15	Isosceles (a = c)
p5	1–3–4–5–7–13–16–17–12	Not a Triangle (a = c)
p6	1–2–3–5–7–13–14–15	Isosceles (a = b)
p7	1–2–3–5–7–13–14–12	Not a Triangle (a = b)
p8	1–3–5–7–8–12	Not a Triangle (a + b ≤ c)
p9	1–3–5–7–8–9–12	Not a Triangle (b + c ≤ a)
p10	1–3–5–7–8–9–10–12	Not a Triangle (a + c ≤ b)
p11	1–3–5–7–8–9–10–11	Scalene

Now, suppose we use boundary value testing to define test cases. We will do this for both the basic and worst-case formulations. Table 11.2 shows the test cases generated using the nominal boundary value form of functional testing. The last column shows the path (in Table 11.1) taken by the test case.

Table 11.2   Path Coverage of Nominal Values

Case	a	b	c	Expected Output	Path
1	100	100	1	Isosceles	p6
2	100	100	2	Isosceles	p6
3	100	100	100	Equilateral	p1
4	100	100	199	Isosceles	p6
5	100	100	200	Not a Triangle	p7
6	100	1	100	Isosceles	p4
7	100	2	100	Isosceles	p4
8	100	100	100	Equilateral	p1
9	100	199	100	Isosceles	p4
10	100	200	100	Not a Triangle	p5
11	1	100	100	Isosceles	p2
12	2	100	100	Isosceles	p2
13	100	100	100	Equilateral	p1
14	199	100	100	Isosceles	p2
15	200	100	100	Not a Triangle	p3

The following paths are covered: p1, p2, p3, p4, p5, p6, p7. Paths p8, p9, p10, p11 are missed. Now, suppose we use a more powerful functional testing technique, worst-case boundary value testing. We saw, in Chapter 5, that this yields 125 test cases; they are summarized in Table 11.3 so you can see the extent of the redundant path coverage.

Taken together, the 125 test cases provide full path coverage, but the redundancy is onerous.

Table 11.3   Path Coverage of Worst-Case Values

	p1	p2	p3	p4	p5	p6	p7	p8	p9	p10	p11
Nominal	3	3	1	3	1	3	1	0	0	0	0
Worst case	5	12	6	11	6	12	7	17	18	19	12

11.2   Metrics for Method Evaluation

Having convinced ourselves that the functional methods are indeed open to the twin problems of gaps and redundancies, we can develop some metrics that relate the effectiveness of a functional technique with the achievement of a structural metric. Functional testing techniques always result in a set of test cases, and the structural metric is always expressed in terms of something countable, such as the number of program paths, the number of decision-to-decision paths (DD-Paths), or the number of slices.

In the following definitions, we assume that a functional testing technique M generates m test cases, and that these test cases are tracked with respect to a structural metric S that identifies s elements in the unit under test. When the m test cases are executed, they traverse n of the s structural elements.

Definition

The *coverage of a methodology M with respect to a metric S* is the ratio of n to s. We denote it as C(M, S).

Definition

The *redundancy of a methodology M with respect to a metric S* is the ratio of m to s. We denote it as R(M, S).

Definition

The *net redundancy of a methodology M with respect to a metric S* is the ratio of m to n. We denote it as NR(M, S).

We interpret these metrics as follows: the coverage metric, C(M, S), deals with gaps. When this value is less than 1, there are gaps in the coverage with respect to the metric. Notice that when C(M, S) = 1, algebra forces R(M, S) = NR(M, S). The redundancy metric is obvious — the bigger it is, the greater the redundancy. Net redundancy is more useful — it refers to things actually

Table 11.4 Metrics for the Triangle Program

Method	m	n	s	C(M, S) = n/s	R(M, S) = m/s	NR(M, S) = m/n
Nominal	15	7	11	0.64	1.36	2.14
Worst-case	125	11	11	1.00	11.36	11.36
Goal	s	s	s	1.00	1.00	1.00

traversed, not to the total space of things to be traversed. Taken together, these three metrics give a quantitative way to evaluate the effectiveness of any functional testing method (except special value testing) with respect to a structural metric. This is only half the battle, however. What we really would like is to know how effective test cases are with respect to kinds of faults. Unfortunately, information such as this simply is not available. We can come close by selecting structural metrics with respect to the kinds of faults we anticipate (or maybe faults we most fear). See the guidelines near the ends of Chapters 9 and 10 for specific advice.

In general, the more sophisticated structural metrics result in more elements (the quantity s); hence, a given functional methodology will tend to become less effective when evaluated in terms of more rigorous structural metrics. This is intuitively appealing, and it is borne out by our examples. These metrics are devised such that the best possible value is 1. Table 11.4 summarizes the application of these definitions to the data in Table 11.3. The structural metric was program paths, and there were 11 of these. (It makes no sense to consider infeasible paths, because a test case can never traverse an infeasible path.) Table 11.5 contains similar results obtained from the commission problem.

Figure 11.2 and Figure 11.3 show, respectively, the trendlines for the number of test coverage items (s in the definitions) and the effort to identify them as functions of structural testing methods. We no longer have the pleasing trade-off that we had for functional testing methods. Instead, these graphs illustrate the importance of choosing an appropriate structural coverage metric. We will see this when we revisit the case study from Chapter 8.

Table 11.5 Metrics for the Commission Problem

Method	m	n	s	C(M, S) = n/s	R(M, S) = m/s
Output bva	25	11	11	1	2.27
Decision table	3	11	11	1	0.27
DD-Path	25	11	11	1	2.27
du-path	25	33	33	1	0.76
Slice	25	40	40	1	0.63

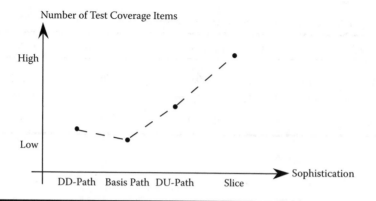

Figure 11.2   Trend of test coverage item(s).

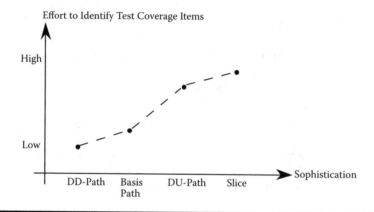

Figure 11.3   Trend of test method effort.

11.3   Case Study Revisited

Here, we continue our case study using the hypothetical insurance premium program example from the retrospective on functional testing (Chapter 8). The pseudocode implementation is minimal in the sense that it does very little error checking. The program graph of this implementation is in Figure 11.4.

```
Pseudo-code for the Insurance Premium Program
        Dim driverAge, points As Integer
        Dim baseRate, premium As Real
1.      Input(baseRate, driverAge, points)
2.      premium = 0
3.      Select Case driverAge
4.      Case 1: 16<= driverAge < 20
5.          ageMultiplier = 2.8
6.          If points < 1 Then
7.              safeDrivingReduction = 50
8.          EndIf
```

```
9.     Case 2: 20<= driverAge < 25
10.         ageMultiplier = 1.8
11.         If points < 3 Then
12.              safeDrivingReduction = 50
13.         EndIf
14.     Case 3: 25<= driverAge < 45
15.         ageMultiplier = 1#
16.         If points < 5 Then
17.              safeDrivingReduction = 100
18.         EndIf
19.     Case 4: 45<= driverAge < 60
20.         ageMultiplier = 0.8
21.         If points < 7 Then
22.              safeDrivingReduction = 150
23.         EndIf
24.     Case 5: 60<= driverAge < 120
25.         ageMultiplier = 1.5
26.         If points < 5 Then
27.              safeDrivingReduction = 200
28.         EndIf
29.     Case 6: Else
30.              Output ("Driver age out of range")
31.     End Select
32.     premium = baseRate * ageMultiplier - safeDrivingReduction
33.     Output (premium)
```

The cyclomatic complexity of the program graph of the insurance premium program is V(G) = 11, and exactly 11 feasible program execution paths exist. They are listed in Table 11.6.

If you take the time to follow the pseudocode for the various sets of functional test cases in Chapter 8, you will find the results shown in Table 11.7.

Now, we can see some of the insights gained from structural testing. For one thing, the problem of gaps and redundancies is obvious. Only the test cases from the hybrid approach yield complete path coverage. It is instructive to compare the results of these 25 test cases with the other two methods yielding the same number of test cases. The 25 boundary value test cases only cover six of the feasible execution paths, while the 25 strong normal equivalence classes test cases cover 10 of the feasible execution paths. The next difference is in the coverage of the conditions in the case statement. Each predicate is a compound condition of the form $a \leq x < b$. The only methods that yield test cases that exercise these extreme values are the worst-case boundary value (273) and hybrid (25) test cases. Quite a difference!

11.3.1 Path–Based Testing

Because the program graph is acyclic, only a finite number of paths exist — in this case, 11. The best choice is simply to have test cases that exercise each path. This automatically constitutes both statement and DD-Path coverage. The compound case predicates indicate multiple condition coverage; this is accomplished only with the worst-case boundary test cases and the hybrid test cases. The remaining path–based coverage metrics are not applicable.

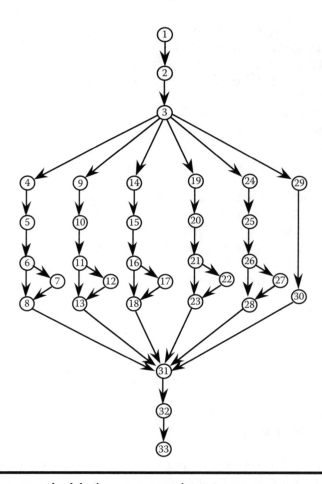

Figure 11.4   Program graph of the insurance premium program.

Table 11.6   Paths in the Insurance Premium Program

Path	Node Sequence
p1	1–2–3–4–5–6–8–31–32–33
p2	1–2–3–4–5–6–7–8–31–32–33
p3	1–2–3–9–10–11–13–31–32–33
p4	1–2–3–9–10–11–12–13–31–32–33
p5	1–2–3–14–15–16–18–31–32–33
p6	1–2–3–14–15–16–17–18–31–32–33
p7	1–2–3–19–20–21–23–31–32–33
p8	1–2–3–19–20–21–22–23–31–32–33
p9	1–2–3–24–25–26–28–31–32–33
p10	1–2–3–24–25–26–27–28–31–32–33
p11	1–2–3–29–30–31–32–33

Table 11.7 Path Coverage of Functional Methods in the Insurance Premium Program

Figure	Method	Test Cases	Paths Covered
8.7	Boundary value	25	p1, p2, p7, p8, p9, p10
8.8	Worst-case boundary value	273	p1, p2, p3, p4, p5, p6, p7, p8, p9, p10
8.9	Weak normal equivalence class	5	p2, p4, p6, p8, p9
8.9	Strong normal equivalence class	25	p1, p2, p3, p4, p5, p6, p7, p8, p9, p10
8.10	Decision table	10	p1, p2, p3, p4, p5, p6, p7, p8, p9, p10
8.11	Hybrid	25	p1, p2, p3, p4, p5, p6, p7, p8, p9, p10, p11

11.3.2 Dataflow Testing

Dataflow testing for this problem is boring. The driverAge, points, and safeDrivingReduction variables all occur in six definition-clear du-paths. The "uses" for driverAge and points are both predicate uses. Recall from Chapter 10 that the All-Paths criterion implies all the lower dataflow coverages.

11.3.3 Slice Testing

Slice testing does not provide much insight either. There are only four interesting slices (the EndIf statements are not listed):

S(safeDrivingReduction, 32) = {1, 3, 4, 6, 7, 9, 11, 12 14, 16, 17, 19, 21, 22, 24, 26, 27, 31}
S(ageMultiplier, 32) = {1, 3, 4, 5, 9, 10, 14, 15, 19, 20, 24, 25, 31}
S(baseRate, 32) = {1}
S(Premium, 31) = {2}

The union of these slices (plus the EndIf statements) is the whole program. The only insight we might get from slice-based testing is that if a failure occurred at line 32, the slices on safeDrivingReduction and ageMultiplier separate the program into two disjoint pieces, and that would simplify fault isolation.

References

Brown, J.R. and Lipov, M., Testing for software reliability, *Proceedings of the International Symposium on Reliable Software*, Los Angeles, April 1975, pp. 518–527.
Pressman, R.S., *Software Engineering: A Practitioner's Approach*, McGraw-Hill, New York, 1982.

Exercises

1. Repeat the gaps and redundancies analysis for the triangle problem using the structured implementation in Chapter 2 and its DD-Path graph in Chapter 9.
2. Compute the coverage, redundancy, and net redundancy metrics for your study in Exercise 1.
3. The pseudocode for the insurance premium program does not check for driver ages under 16 or (unlikely) over 120. The Else clause (case 6) will catch these, but the output message is not very specific. Also, the output statement (33) is not affected by the driver age checks. Which functional testing techniques will reveal this fault? Which structural testing coverage, if not met, will reveal this fault?

INTEGRATION AND SYSTEM TESTING

Chapter 12

Levels of Testing

In this chapter, we build a context for Part IV, in which we examine integration and system testing for traditional software. Our immediate goal is to identify what we mean by these levels of testing. We took a simplistic view in Chapter 1, where we identified three levels (unit, integration, and system) in terms of symmetries in the waterfall model of software development. This view has been relatively successful for decades; however, the advent of alternative life cycle models mandates a second look at these views of testing. We begin with the traditional waterfall model, mostly because it has enormous acceptance and similar expressive power. To ground our discussion in something concrete, we switch to the automated teller machine example.

In Parts IV and V, we also make a major shift in our thinking. We are more concerned with how to represent the item tested, because the representation may limit our ability to identify test cases. Take a look at the papers presented at the leading conferences (professional or academic) on software testing — you will find nearly as many presentations on specification models and techniques as on testing techniques.

12.1 Traditional View of Testing Levels

The traditional model of software development is the waterfall model, which is drawn as a V in Figure 12.1 to emphasize the basic levels of testing. In this view, information produced in one of the development phases constitutes the basis for test case identification at that level. Nothing controversial here: we certainly would hope that system test cases are somehow correlated with the requirements specification, and that unit test cases are derived from the detailed design of the unit. Two observations: a clear presumption of functional testing is used here, and an implied bottom-up testing order is used. Here, bottom-up refers to levels of abstraction; in Chapter 13, bottom-up also refers to a choice of orders in which units are integrated (and tested).

Of the three traditional levels of testing (unit, integration, and system), unit testing is best understood. The testing theory and techniques we worked through in Parts II and III are directly applicable to unit testing. System testing is understood better than integration testing, but both need clarification. The bottom-up approach sheds some insight: test the individual components, and then integrate these into subsystems until the entire system is tested. System testing should be

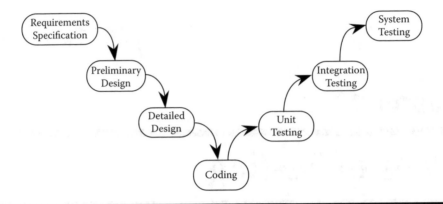

Figure 12.1 The waterfall life cycle.

something that the customer (or user) understands, and it often borders on customer acceptance testing. Generally, system testing is functional instead of structural; this is mostly due to the lack of higher-level structural notations.

The waterfall model is closely associated with top-down development and design by functional decomposition. The end result of preliminary design is a functional decomposition of the entire system into a tree-like structure of functional components. Figure 12.2 contains a partial functional decomposition of our automated teller machine (ATM) system. With this decomposition, top-down integration would begin with the main program, checking the calls to the three next-level procedures (Terminal I/O, ManageSessions, and ConductTransactions). Following the tree, the ManageSessions procedure would be tested, and then the CardEntry, PIN entry, and Select-Transaction procedures. In each case, the actual code for lower-level units is replaced by a stub, which is a throwaway piece of code that takes the place of the actual code. Bottom-up integration would be the opposite sequence, starting with the CardEntry, PIN entry, and SelectTransaction procedures, and working up toward the main program. In bottom-up integration, units at higher levels are replaced by drivers (another form of throwaway code) that emulate the procedure calls. The "big bang" approach simply puts all the units together at once, with no stubs or drivers. Whichever approach is taken, the goal of traditional integration testing is to integrate previously tested units with respect to the functional decomposition tree. Although this describes integration testing as a process, discussions of this type offer little information about the methods or techniques. Before addressing these (real) issues, we need to see if the alternative life cycle models have any consequences for integration testing.

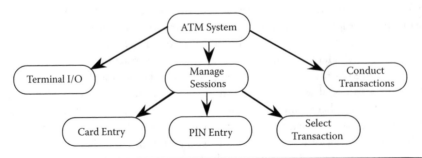

Figure 12.2 Partial functional decomposition of the ATM system.

12.2 Alternative Life Cycle Models

Since the early 1980s, practitioners have devised alternatives in response to shortcomings of the traditional waterfall model of software development (Agresti, 1986). Common to all of these alternatives is the shift away from the functional decomposition to an emphasis on composition. Decomposition is a perfect fit both to the top-down progression of the waterfall model and to the bottom-up testing order. One of the major weaknesses of waterfall development cited by Agresti (1986) is the overreliance on this whole paradigm. Functional decomposition can only be well done when the system is completely understood, and it promotes analysis to the near exclusion of synthesis. The result is a very long separation between requirements specification and a completed system, and during this interval, no opportunity is available for feedback from the customer. Composition, on the other hand, is closer to the way people work: start with something known and understood, then add to it gradually, and maybe remove undesired portions. A very nice analogy can be applied to positive and negative sculpture. In negative sculpture, work proceeds by removing unwanted material, as in the mathematician's view of sculpting Michelangelo's *David*: start with a piece of marble and simply chip away all non-David. Positive sculpture is often done with a medium like wax. The central shape is approximated, and then wax is either added or removed until the desired shape is attained. Think about the consequences of a mistake: with negative sculpture, the whole work must be thrown away and restarted. (A museum in Florence, Italy, contains half a dozen such false starts to David.) With positive sculpture, the erroneous part is simply removed and replaced. The centrality of composition in the alternative models has a major implication for integration testing.

12.2.1 *Waterfall Spin-Offs*

Three mainline derivatives of the waterfall model are used: incremental development, evolutionary development, and the spiral model (Boehm, 1988). Each of these involves a series of increments or builds as shown in Figure 12.3. Within a build, the normal waterfall phases from detailed design through testing occur with one important difference: system testing is split into two steps — regression and progression testing.

It is important to keep preliminary design as an integral phase, rather than to try to amortize such high-level design across a series of builds. (To do so usually results in unfortunate consequences of design choices made during the early builds that are regrettable in later builds.) Because preliminary design remains a separate step, we conclude that integration testing is unaffected in the spin-off models. The main impact of the series of builds is that regression testing becomes necessary. The goal of regression testing is to ensure that things that worked correctly in the previous build still work with the newly added code. Progression testing assumes that regression testing was successful and that the new functionality can be tested. (We like to think that the addition of new code represents progress, not a regression.) Regression testing is an absolute necessity in a series of builds because of the well-known ripple effect of changes to an existing system. (The industrial average is that one change in five introduces a new fault.)

The differences among the three spin-off models are due to how the builds are identified. In incremental development, the motivation for separate builds is usually to level off the staff profile. With pure waterfall development, there can be a huge bulge of personnel for the phases from detailed design through unit testing. Most organizations cannot support such rapid staff fluctuations, so the system is divided into builds that can be supported by existing personnel. In evolutionary development, the

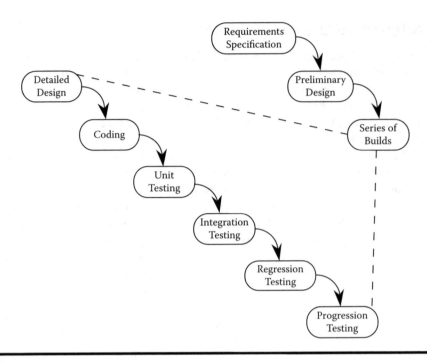

Figure 12.3   Life cycle with a build sequence.

presumption of a build sequence is still made, but only the first build is defined. Based on that, later builds are identified, usually in response to priorities set by the customer/user, so the system evolves to meet the changing needs of the user. The spiral model is a combination of rapid prototyping and evolutionary development, in which a build first is defined in terms of rapid prototyping and then is subjected to a go/no-go decision based on technology-related risk factors. From this, we see that keeping preliminary design as an integral step is difficult for the evolutionary and spiral models. To the extent that this cannot be maintained as an integral activity, integration testing is negatively affected. System testing is not affected.

Because a build is a set of deliverable end user functionalities, one advantage common to all these spin-off models is that all yield earlier synthesis. This also results in earlier customer feedback, so two of the deficiencies of waterfall development are mitigated.

12.2.2 Specification-Based Life Cycle Models

Two other variations are responses to the "complete understanding" problem. (Recall that functional decomposition is successful only when the system is completely understood.) When systems are not fully understood (by either the customer or the developer), functional decomposition is perilous at best. The rapid prototyping life cycle (Figure 12.4) deals with this by drastically reducing the specification-to-customer feedback loop to produce very early synthesis. Rather than build a final system, a quick and dirty prototype is built and then used to elicit customer feedback. Depending on the feedback, more prototyping cycles may occur. Once the developer

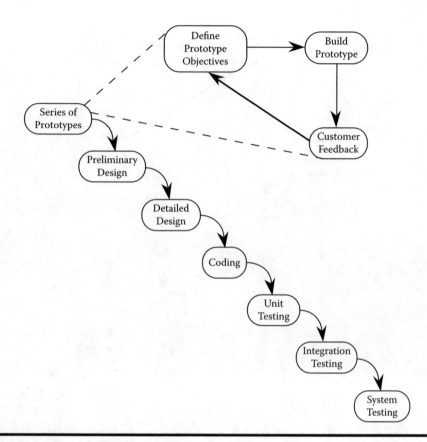

Figure 12.4   Rapid prototyping life cycle.

and the customer agree that a prototype represents the desired system, the developer goes ahead and builds to a correct specification. At this point, any of the waterfall spin-offs might also be used.

Rapid prototyping has no implications for integration testing; it has very interesting implications for system testing. Where are the requirements? Is the last prototype the specification? How are system test cases traced back to the prototype? One good answer to questions such as these is to use the prototyping cycles as information-gathering activities, and then produce a requirements specification in a more traditional manner. Another possibility is to capture what the customer does with the prototypes, define these as scenarios that are important to the customer, and then use these as system test cases. The main contribution of rapid prototyping is that it brings the operational (or behavioral) viewpoint to the requirements specification phase. Usually, requirements specification techniques emphasize the structure of a system, not its behavior. This is unfortunate, because most customers do not care about the structure, and they do care about the behavior.

Executable specifications (Figure 12.5) are an extension of the rapid prototyping concept. With this approach, the requirements are specified in an executable format (such as finite state machines, StateCharts, or Petri nets). The customer then executes the specification to observe the intended system behavior and provides feedback as in the rapid prototyping model.

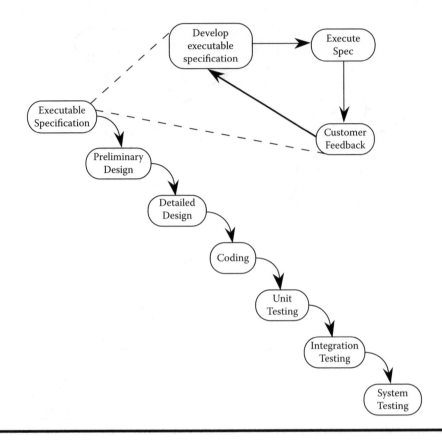

Figure 12.5   Executable specification.

Once again, this life cycle has no implications for integration testing. One big difference is that the requirements specification document is explicit, as opposed to a prototype. More important, it is often a mechanical process to derive system test cases from an executable specification. We will see this in Chapter 15. Although more work is required to develop an executable specification, this is partially offset by the reduced effort to generate system test cases. Here is another important distinction: when system testing is based on an executable specification, we have an interesting form of structural testing at the system level.

12.3   The SATM System

In Part IV, we will relate our discussion to a higher-level example, the simple automatic teller machine (SATM) system. The version developed here is a revision of that found in Topper et al. (1993); it is built around the 15 screens shown in Figure 12.6. This is a greatly reduced system; commercial ATM systems have hundreds of screens and numerous time-outs.

The SATM terminal is sketched in Figure 12.7; in addition to the display screen, the terminal includes function buttons B1, B2, and B3, a digit keypad with a cancel key, slots for printer receipts and ATM cards, and doors for deposits and cash withdrawals.

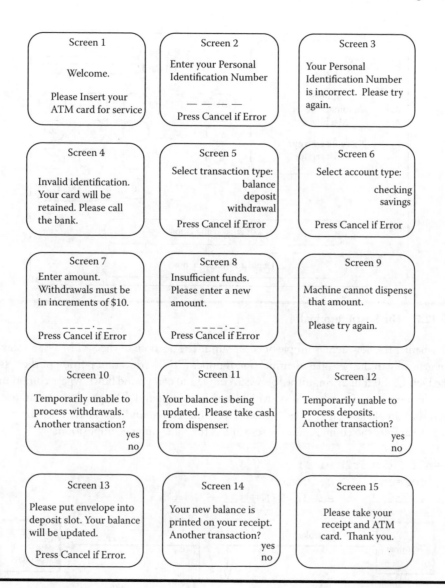

Figure 12.6 Screens for the SATM system.

The SATM system is described here with a traditional, structured analysis approach in Figure 12.8 and Figure 12.9. The models are not complete, but they contain sufficient detail to illustrate the testing techniques under discussion.

The structured analysis approach to requirements specification is still widely used. It enjoys extensive CASE tool support as well as commercial training and is described in numerous texts. The technique is based on three complementary models: function, data, and control. Here, we use dataflow diagrams for the functional model, the entity/relationship model for data, and finite state machine models for the control aspect of the SATM system. The functional and data models were drawn with the Deft CASE tool from Sybase, Inc. That tool identifies external devices (such as the terminal doors) with lowercase letters. Elements of the functional decomposition are identified with numbers (such as 1.5 for the Validate Card function). The open and filled arrowheads on flow arrows

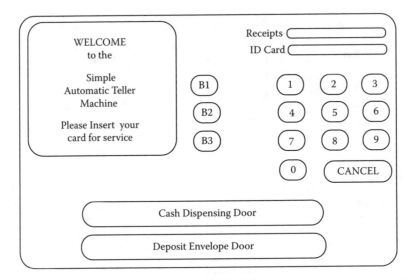

Figure 12.7   The SATM terminal.

signify whether the flow item is simple or compound. The portions of the SATM system shown here pertain generally to the personal identification number (PIN) verification portion of the system.

The Deft CASE tool distinguishes between simple and compound flows, where compound flows may be decomposed into other flows, which may be compound. The graphic appearance of this choice is that simple flows have filled arrowheads, while compound flows have open arrowheads.

As an example, the compound flow screen has the following decomposition:

```
screen is comprised of
      screen1     welcome
      screen2     enter PIN
```

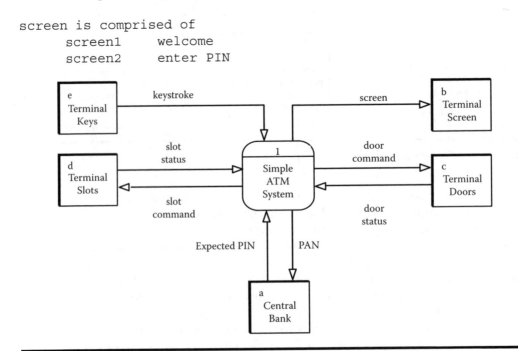

Figure 12.8   Context diagram of the SATM system.

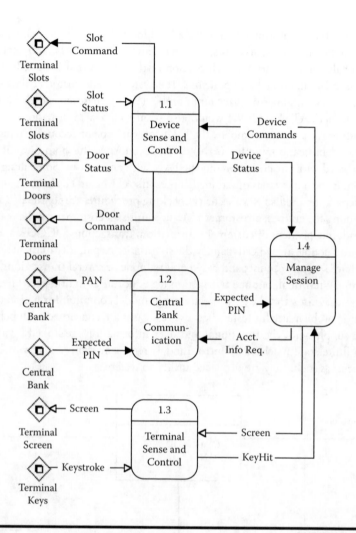

Figure 12.9 Level 1 dataflow diagram of the SATM system.

```
screen3      wrong PIN
screen4      PIN failed, card retained
screen5      select trans type
screen6      select account type
screen7      enter amount
screen8      insufficient funds
screen9      cannot dispense that amount
screen10     cannot process withdrawals
screen11     take your cash
screen12     cannot process deposits
screen13     put dep envelop in slot
screen14     another transaction?
screen15     Thanks; take card and receipt
```

Figure 12.10 is an (incomplete) entity/relationship (E/R) diagram of the major data structures in the SATM system: customers, accounts, terminals, and transactions. Good data modeling practice dictates postulating an entity for each portion of the system that is described by data that is retained (and used by functional components). The system needs customer data, including each customer's identification and personal account number (PAN); these are encoded into the magnetic strip on the customer's ATM card. We would also want to know information about a customer's accounts, including the account numbers, the balances, the type of account (savings or checking), and the personal identification number (PIN) of the account. At this point, we might ask why the PIN is not associated with the customer and the PAN with an account. Some design has crept into the specification: if the data was as questioned, a person's ATM card could be used by anyone; as it is, the present separation predisposes a security checking procedure. Part of the E/R model describes relationships among the entities: a customer HAS account(s), a customer conducts transaction(s) in a SESSION, and, independent of customer information, transactions OCCUR at an ATM terminal. The single and double arrowheads signify the singularity or plurality of these relationships: one customer may have several accounts and may conduct none or several transactions. Many transactions may occur at a terminal, but one transaction never occurs at multiple terminals.

The dataflow diagrams and the entity/relationship model contain information that is primarily structural. This is problematic for testers because test cases are concerned with behavior, not with structure. As a supplement, the functional and data information are linked by a control model; here, we use a finite state machine. Control models represent the point at which structure and behavior intersect; as such, they are of special utility to testers.

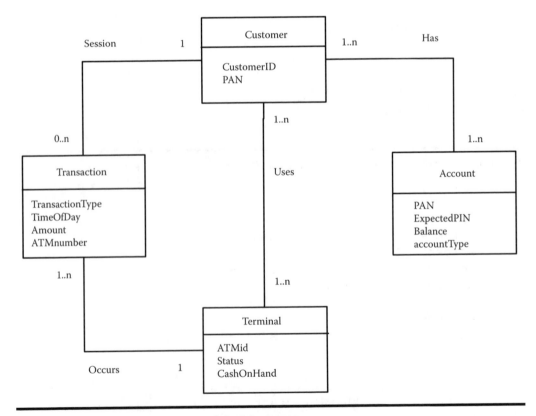

Figure 12.10   Entity/relationship model of the SATM system.

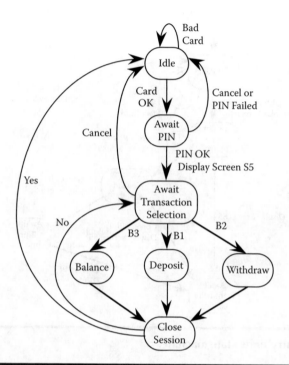

Figure 12.11   Upper-level SATM finite state machine.

The upper-level finite state machine in Figure 12.11 divides the system into states that correspond to stages of customer usage.

Other choices are possible; for instance, we might choose states to be screens displayed (this turns out to be a poor choice). Finite state machines can be hierarchically decomposed in much the same way as dataflow diagrams can. The decomposition of the Await PIN state is shown in Figure 12.12. In both figures, state transitions are caused either by events at the ATM terminal (such as a keystroke) or by data conditions (such as the recognition that a PIN is correct). When a transition occurs, a corresponding action may also occur. We choose to use screen displays as such actions; this choice will prove to be very handy when we develop system-level test cases.

The function, data, and control models are the basis for design activities in the waterfall model (and its spin-offs). During design, some of the original decisions may be revised based on additional insights and more detailed requirements (such as performance or reliability goals). The end result is a functional decomposition such as the partial one shown in the structure chart in Figure 12.13. Notice that the original first-level decomposition into eight subsystems is no longer visible: the functionality has been reallocated among four logical components. Choices such as these are the essence of design, and design is beyond the scope of this book. In practice, testers often have to live with the results of poor design choices.

If we only use a structure chart to guide integration testing, we miss the fact that some (typically lower-level) functions are used in more than one place. Here, for example, the ScreenDriver function is used by several other modules, but it only appears once in the functional decomposition. In the next chapter, we will see that a call graph is a much better basis for integration test case identification. We can develop the beginnings of such a call graph from a more detailed view of portions of the system. To support this, we need a numbered decomposition and a more detailed view of two of the components.

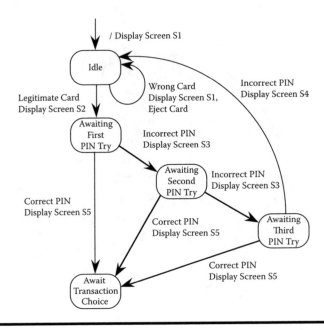

Figure 12.12 PIN entry finite state machine.

Here is the functional decomposition carried further in outline form; the numbering scheme preserves the levels of the components in Figure 12.13.

```
1       SATM System
1.1     Device Sense & Control
1.1.1 Door Sense & Control
1.1.1.1     Get Door Status
1.1.1.2     Control Door
1.1.1.3     Dispense Cash
1.1.2 Slot Sense & Control
1.1.2.1     WatchCardSlot
1.1.2.2     Get Deposit Slot Status
1.1.2.3     Control Card Roller
1.1.2.3     Control Envelope Roller
1.1.2.5     Read Card Strip
1.2     Central Bank Comm.
1.2.1 Get PIN for PAN
1.2.2 Get Account Status
1.2.3 Post Daily Transactions
1.3     Terminal Sense & Control
1.3.1 Screen Driver
1.3.2 Key Sensor
1.4     Manage Session
1.4.1 Validate Card
1.4.2 Validate PIN
```

1.4.2.1   GetPIN
1.4.3 Close Session
1.4.3.1   New Transaction Request
1.4.3.2   Print Receipt
1.4.3.3   Post Transaction Local
1.4.4 Manage Transaction
1.4.4.1   Get Transaction Type
1.4.4.2   Get Account Type
1.4.4.3   Report Balance
1.4.4.4   Process Deposit
1.4.4.5   Process Withdrawal

As part of the specification and design process, each functional component is normally expanded to show its inputs, outputs, and mechanism. We do this with pseudocode (or PDL, for program design language) for three modules. The main program description follows the finite state machine description given in Figure 12.11. States in that diagram are implemented with a CASE statement. The ValidatePIN procedure is based on the finite state machine shown in Figure 12.12, in which states refer to the number of PIN entry attempts. The GetPIN procedure is based on another finite state machine in which states refer to the number of digits received, and

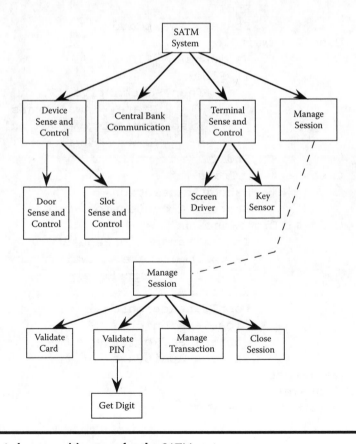

Figure 12.13   A decomposition tree for the SATM system.

in any state, either another digit key or the cancel key can be touched. Instead of another CASE statement implementation, the states are collapsed into iterations of a While loop. The pseudocode for all of this appears as numbered pseudocode in Chapter 13.

```
Main Program
      State = AwaitCard
      Do                'Main loop
      Case State
          Case 1:    AwaitCard
                     ScreenDriver(1, null)
                     WatchCardSlot(CardSlotStatus)
                     Do While CardSlotStatus is Idle
                           WatchCardSlot(CardSlotStatus)
                     End While
                     ControlCardRoller(accept)
                     ValidateCard(CardOK, PAN)
                     If CardOK
                           Then State = AwaitPIN
                           Else ControlCardRoller(eject)
                     EndIf
                     State = AwaitCard
          Case 2: AwaitPIN
                     ValidatePIN(PINok, PAN)
                     If PINok
                           Then ScreenDriver(2, null)
                                 State = AwaitTrans
                           Else  ScreenDriver(4, null)
                                 State = AwaitCard
                     EndIf
          Case 3: AwaitTrans
                     ManageTransaction
                     State = CloseSession
          Case 4: CloseSession
                     If NewTransactionRequest
                           Then State = AwaitTrans
                           Else  PrintReceipt
                     EndIf
                     PostTransactionLocal
                     CloseSession
                     ControlCardRoller(eject)
                     State = AwaitCard
      End Case (State)
      Until 'Forever
      End.   (Main program SATM)
```

```
Procedure ValidatePIN(PINok, PAN)
GetPINforPAN(PAN, ExpectedPIN)
Try = First
Case Try of
     Case 1: First
            ScreenDriver(2, null)
            GetPIN(EnteredPIN, CancelHit)
            If EnteredPIN = ExpectedPIN
                   Then PINok = True
                   Else ScreenDriver(3, null)
                   Try = Second
            EndIf
     Case 2: Second
            ScreenDriver(2, null)
            GetPIN(EnteredPIN)
            If EnteredPIN = ExpectedPIN
                   Then  PINok = True
                   Else  ScreenDriver(3, null)
                   Try = Third
            EndIf
     Case 3: Third
            ScreenDriver(2, null)
            GetPIN(EnteredPIN, CancelHit)
            If EnteredPIN = ExpectedPIN
                   Then PINok = True
                   Else  ScreenDriver(4, null)
                         PINok = False
            EndIf
EndCase (Try)
End.                (Procedure ValidatePIN)


Procedure GetPIN(EnteredPIN, CancelHit)
Local Data: DigitKeys = {0, 1, 2, 3, 4, 5, 6, 7, 8, 9}
CancelHit = False
EnteredPIN = null string
digitsRcvd=0
Do While NOT(DigitsRcvd=4 OR CancelHit)
     KeySensor(KeyHit)
     If KeyHit IN DigitKeys
           Then
                   EnteredPIN = EnteredPIN + KeyHit
                   digitsRcvd = digitsRcvd + 1
                   If digitsRcvd = 1
                         Then ScreenDirver (2, 'X---')
                   EndIf
```

```
                    If digitsRcvd = 2
                        Then ScreenDirver (2, 'XX--')
                    EndIf
                    If digitsRcvd = 3
                        Then ScreenDirver (2, 'XXX-')
                    EndIf
                    If digitsRcvd = 4
                        Then ScreenDirver (2, 'XXXX')
                    EndIf
            Else
                    CancelHit = True
        EndIf
    End While
    End.   (Procedure GetPIN)
```

If we follow the pseudocode in these three modules, we can identify the uses relationship among the modules in the functional decomposition. In Chapter 13, we shall see how this provides useful insights into integration testing.

Module	Uses Modules
SATM Main	WatchCardSlot
	ControlCardRoller
	ScreenDriver
	ValidateCard
	ValidatePIN
	ManageTransaction
ValidatePIN	GetPINforPAN
	GetPIN
	ScreenDriver
GetPIN	KeySensor
	ScreenDriver

Notice that the uses information is not readily apparent in the functional decomposition. This information is developed (and extensively revised) during the more detailed phases of the design process. We will revisit this in Chapter 13.

12.4 Separating Integration and System Testing

We are almost in a position to make a clear distinction between integration and system testing. We need this distinction to avoid gaps and redundancies across levels of testing, to clarify appropriate goals for these levels, and to understand how to identify test cases at different levels. This whole discussion is facilitated by a concept essential to all levels of testing: the notion of a thread. A thread is a construct that refers to execution time behavior. When we test a system, we use test cases to select (and execute) threads. We can speak of levels of threads: system threads describe system-level behavior, integration threads correspond to integration-level behavior, and unit threads correspond to unit-level behavior. Many authors use the term, but few define it, and of those who do, the offered definitions are not very helpful. For now, we take *thread* to be a primitive term, much like function and data. We will be very specific when we define threads in Chapter 14. In the next two chapters, we shall see that threads are most often recognized in terms of the way systems are described and developed. For example, we might think of a thread as a path through a finite state machine description of a system, or we might think of a thread as something that is determined by a data context and a sequence of port-level input events, such as those in the context diagram of the SATM system. We could also think of a thread as a sequence of source statements, or as a sequence of machine instructions. The point is, threads are a generic concept, and they exist independently of how a system is described and developed.

We have already observed the structural versus behavioral dichotomy; here, we shall find that both of these views help us separate integration and system testing. The structural view reflects both the process by which a system is built and the techniques used to build it. We certainly expect that test cases at various levels can be traced back to developmental information. Although this is necessary, it fails to be sufficient: we will finally make our desired separation in terms of behavioral constructs.

12.4.1 Structural Insights

Everyone agrees that some distinction must be made, and that integration testing is at a more detailed level than system testing. There is also general agreement that integration testing can safely assume that the units have been separately tested, and that, taken individually, the units function correctly. One common view, therefore, is that integration testing is concerned with the interfaces among the units.

One possibility is to fall back on the symmetries in the waterfall life cycle model and say that integration testing is concerned with preliminary design information, while system testing is at the level of the requirements specification. This is a popular academic view, but it begs an important question: How do we discriminate between specification and preliminary design? The pat academic answer to this is the *what* versus *how* dichotomy: the requirements specification defines what, and the preliminary design describes how. Although this sounds good at first, it does not stand up well in practice. Some scholars argue that even the choice of a requirements specification technique is a design choice.

The life cycle approach is echoed by designers who often take a "Don't tread on me" view of a requirements specification: a requirements specification should neither predispose nor preclude a design option. With this view, when information in a specification is so detailed that it "steps on the designer's toes," the specification is too detailed. This sounds good, but it still does not yield an operational way to separate integration and system testing.

The models used in the development process provide some clues. If we follow the definition of the SATM system, we could first postulate that system testing should make sure that all 15 display screens have been generated (an output domain-based, functional view of system testing). The entity/relationship model also helps: the one-to-one and one-to-many relationships help us understand how much testing must be done. The control model (in this case, a hierarchy of finite state machines) is the most helpful. We can postulate system test cases in terms of paths through the finite state machine(s); doing this yields a system-level analog of structural testing. The functional models (dataflow diagrams and structure charts) move in the direction of levels because both express a functional decomposition. Even with this, we cannot look at a structure chart and identify where system testing ends and integration testing starts. The best we can do with structural information is identify the extremes. For instance, the following threads are all clearly at the system level:

1. Insertion of an invalid card (this is probably the shortest system thread)
2. Insertion of a valid card, followed by three failed PIN entry attempts
3. Insertion of a valid card, a correct PIN entry attempt, followed by a balance inquiry
4. Insertion of a valid card, a correct PIN entry attempt, followed by a deposit
5. Insertion of a valid card, a correct PIN entry attempt, followed by a withdrawal
6. Insertion of a valid card, a correct PIN entry attempt, followed by an attempt to withdraw more cash than the account balance

We can also identify some integration-level threads. Go back to the pseudocode descriptions of ValidatePIN and GetPIN. ValidatePIN calls GetPIN, and GetPIN waits for KeySensor to report when a key is touched. If a digit is touched, GetPIN echoes an "X" to the display screen, but if the cancel key is touched, GetPIN terminates, and ValidatePIN considers another PIN entry attempt. We could push still lower and consider keystroke sequences such as two or three digits followed by cancel keystroke.

12.4.2 Behavioral Insights

Here is a pragmatic, explicit distinction that has worked well in industrial applications. Think about a system in terms of its port boundary, which is the location of system-level inputs and outputs. Every system has a port boundary; the port boundary of the SATM system includes the digit keypad, the function buttons, the screen, the deposit and withdrawal doors, the card and receipt slots, and so on. Each of these devices can be thought of as a port, and events occur at system ports. The port input and output events are visible to the customer, and the customer very often understands system behavior in terms of sequences of port events. Given this, we mandate that system port events are the "primitives" of a system test case; that is, a system test case (or equivalently, a system thread) is expressed as an interleaved sequence of port input and port output events. This fits our understanding of a test case, in which we specify preconditions, inputs, outputs, and postconditions. With this mandate, we can always recognize a level violation: if a test case (thread) ever requires an input (or an output) that is not visible at the port boundary, the test case cannot be a system-level test case (thread). Notice that this is clear, recognizable, and enforceable. We will refine this in Chapter 14 when we discuss threads of system behavior.

Threads support a highly analytical view of testing. Unit-level threads, for example, are sequences of source statements that execute (feasible paths). Integration-level threads can be thought of as sequences of unit-level threads, where we are concerned not with the internals of unit threads, but the interaction among them. Finally, system-level threads can be interpreted as sequences of integration-level threads. We will also be able to describe the interaction among system-level threads. To end on a pun, the definitions of the next two chapters will tie these threads together.

References

Agresti, W.W., *New Paradigms for Software Development*, IEEE Computer Society Press, Washington, DC, 1986.

Boehm, B.W., A spiral model for software development and enhancement, *IEEE Computer*, Vol. 21, No. 6, IEEE Computer Society Press, Washington, DC, May 1988, pp. 61–72.

Topper, A. et al., *Structured Methods: Merging Models, Techniques, and CASE*, McGraw-Hill, New York, 1993.

Chapter 13

Integration Testing

In September 1999, the Mars Climate Orbiter mission failed after successfully traveling 416 million miles in 41 weeks. It disappeared just as it was to begin orbiting Mars. The fault should have been revealed by integration testing: Lockheed Martin Astronautics used acceleration data in English units (pounds), while the Jet Propulsion Laboratory did its calculations with metric units (newtons). NASA announced a $50,000 project to discover how this could have happened (Fordahl, 1999). They should have read this chapter.

Software testing has three distinct levels — unit, integration, and system — each with its unique problems and goals. Integration testing is the least well understood of these; hence in practice, it is the phase most poorly done. This chapter examines two mainline and one less well known integration testing strategies. They are illustrated with a continuing procedural example, discussed in some detail, and then critiqued with respect to their advantages and disadvantages.

Craftspersons are recognized by two essential characteristics: they have a deep knowledge of the tools of their trade, and they have a similar knowledge of the medium in which they work so that they understand their tools in terms of how they work with the medium. In Parts II and III, we focused on the tools (techniques) available to the testing craftsperson. Our goal there was to understand testing techniques in terms of their advantages and limitations with respect to particular types of software. Here, we shift our emphasis to the medium, with the goal of improving the testing craftsperson's judgment through a better understanding of the medium. We make a deliberate separation here: this chapter and the next address testing for software that has been defined, designed, and developed with the traditional models for function, data, control, and structure. Testing for object-oriented software is deferred to Part V. Thus, we are making a conscious choice in the direction of model-driven development (MDD) and model-based testing (MBT). We continue our refinement of the simple automated teller machine (SATM) system in this chapter and use it to illustrate three distinct approaches to integration testing. For each approach, we begin with its basis and then discuss various techniques that use the base information. To continue the craftsperson metaphor, we emphasize the advantages and limitations of each integration testing technique.

Table 13.1   SATM Units and Abbreviated Names

Unit Number	Level Number	Unit Name
1	1	SATM System
A	1.1	Device Sense & Control
D	1.1.1	Door Sense & Control
2	1.1.1.1	Get Door Status
3	1.1.1.2	Control Door
4	1.1.1.3	Dispense Cash
E	1.1.2	Slot Sense & Control
5	1.1.2.1	WatchCardSlot
6	1.1.2.2	Get Deposit Slot Status
7	1.1.2.3	Control Card Roller
8	1.1.2.4	Control Envelope Roller
9	1.1.2.5	Read Card Strip
10	1.2	Central Bank Comm.
11	1.2.1	Get PIN for PAN
12	1.2.2	Get Account Status
13	1.2.3	Post Daily Transactions
B	1.3	Terminal Sense & Control
14	1.3.1	Screen Driver
15	1.3.2	Key Sensor
C	1.4	Manage Session
16	1.4.1	Validate Card
17	1.4.2	Validate PIN
18	1.4.2.1	GetPIN
F	1.4.3	Close Session
19	1.4.3.1	New Transaction Request
20	1.4.3.2	Print Receipt
21	1.4.3.3	Post Transaction Local
22	1.4.4	Manage Transaction
23	1.4.4.1	Get Transaction Type
24	1.4.4.2	Get Account Type
25	1.4.4.3	Report Balance
26	1.4.4.4	Process Deposit
27	1.4.4.5	Process Withdrawal

13.1 A Closer Look at the SATM System

In Chapter 12, we described the SATM system in terms of its output screens (Figure 12.6), the actual terminal (Figure 12.7), its context and partial dataflow diagrams (Figure 12.8 and Figure 12.9), an entity/relationship model of its data (Figure 12.10), finite state machines describing some of its behavior (Figure 12.11 and Figure 12.12), and a partial functional decomposition (Figure 12.13). We also developed a pseudocode description of the Main program and two units, ValidatePIN and GetPIN.

We begin here by expanding the functional decomposition that was started in Figure 12.13; the numbering scheme preserves the levels of the components in that figure. For easier reference, each component that appears in our analysis is given a new (shorter) number; these numbers are given in Table 13.1. (The only reason for this is to make the figures more readable.)

The decomposition in Table 13.1 is pictured as a decomposition tree in Figure 13.1. This decomposition is the basis for the usual view of integration testing. It is important to remember that such a decomposition is primarily a packaging partition of the system. As software design moves into more detail, the added information lets us refine the functional decomposition tree into a unit calling graph. The unit calling graph is the directed graph in which nodes are program units and edges correspond to program calls; that is, if unit A calls unit B, a directed edge runs from node A to node B. We began the development of the call graph for the SATM system in Chapter 12 when we examined the calls made by the Main program and the ValidatePIN and GetPIN modules. That information is captured in the adjacency matrix given in Table 13.2. This matrix was created with a spreadsheet; this turns out to be a handy tool for testers.

The SATM call graph is shown in Figure 13.2 Some of the hierarchy is obscured to reduce the confusion in the drawing.

One thing should be quite obvious: drawings of call graphs do not scale up well. Both the drawings and the adjacency matrix provide insights to the tester. Nodes with a high degree will be

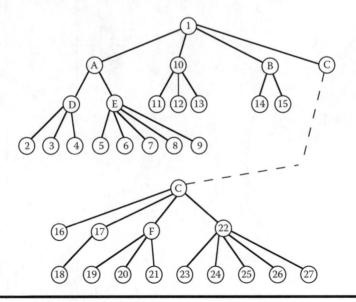

Figure 13.1 SATM functional decomposition tree.

Table 13.2 Adjacency Matrix for the SATM Call Graph

	2	3	4	5	6	7	8	9	10	11	12	13	14	15	16	17	18	19	20	21	22	23	24	25	26	27
1				X																						
2						X									X	X		X	X	X	X					
3																										
4																										
5																										
6																										
7																										
8																										
9																										
10																										
11																										
12																										
13																										
14																										
15																										
16								X	X																	
17										X	X	X	X	X			X									
18												X	X	X												
19													X	X												
20													X	X												
21																										
22													X	X								X	X	X	X	X
23													X	X												
24													X	X												
25														X												
26	X	X			X		X							X												
27	X	X	X		X		X					X		X												

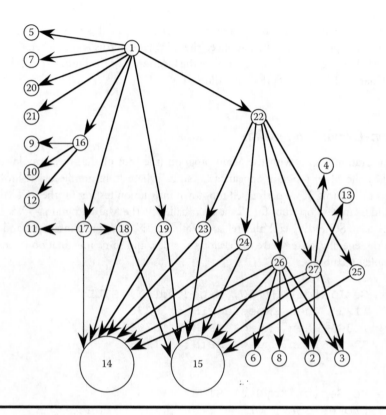

Figure 13.2   SATM call graph.

important to integration testing, and paths from the Main program (node 1) to the sink nodes can be used to identify contents of builds for an incremental development.

13.2   Decomposition-Based Integration

Mainline introductory software engineering texts (e.g., Pressman, 2005; Schach, 2005) typically present four integration strategies based on the functional decomposition tree of the procedural software: top-down, bottom-up, sandwich, and the vividly named big bang. Many classic software testing texts echo this approach: Deutsch (1982), Hetzel (1988), Kaner et al. (1993), and Mosley (1993), to name a few. Each of these strategies (except big bang) describes the order in which units are to be integrated. The functional decomposition tree is the basis for integration testing because it is the main representation, usually derived from some source code, which shows the structural relationship of the system with respect to its units. All these integration orders presume that the units have been separately tested; thus, the goal of decomposition-based integration is to test the interfaces among separately tested units. The functional decomposition tree reflects the lexical inclusion of units, in terms of the order in which they need to be compiled to ensure the correct referential scope of variables and unit names. Figure 13.1 contains the functional decomposition tree for the NextDate example. For the remainder of this chapter, the term *unit* will refer to procedures or functions.

We can dispense with the big bang approach most easily: in this view of integration, all the units are compiled together and tested at once. The drawback to this is that when (not if) a failure is observed, few clues are available to help isolate the location(s) of the fault. (Recall the distinction we made in Chapter 1 between faults and failures.)

13.2.1 Top-Down Integration

Top-down integration begins with the Main program (the root of the tree). Any lower-level unit that is called by the Main program appears as a "stub," where stubs are pieces of throwaway code that emulate a called unit. If we performed top-down integration testing for the SATM system, the first step would be to develop stubs for all the units called by the Main program — WatchCardSlot, ControlCardRoller, ScreenDriver, ValidateCard, ValidatePIN, ManageTransaction, and NewTransactionRequest. Generally, testers have to develop the stubs, and some imagination is required. Here are two examples of stubs:

```
Procedure GetPINforPAN(PAN, ExpectedPIN) STUB
If PAN = '1123' Then ExpectedPIN = '8876'
If PAN = '1234' Then ExpectedPIN = '8765'
If PAN = '8746' Then ExpectedPIN = '1253'
End

Procedure KeySensor(KeyHit) STUB
data: KeyStrokes STACK OF '8'. '8', '7', 'cancel'
KeyHit = POP (KeyStrokes)
End
```

In the stub for GetPINforPAN, the tester replicates a table lookup with just a few values that will appear in test cases. In the stub for KeySensor, the tester must devise a sequence of port events that can occur once each time the KeySensor procedure is called. (Here, we provided the keystrokes to partially enter the PIN 8876, but the user hit the cancel button before the fourth digit.) In practice, the effort to develop stubs is usually quite significant. There is good reason to consider stub code as part of the software development and maintain it under configuration management.

Once all the stubs for SATM Main have been provided, we test the Main program as if it were a stand-alone unit. We could apply any of the appropriate functional and structural techniques and look for faults. When we are convinced that the Main program logic is correct, we gradually replace stubs with the actual code. Figure 13.3 shows part of the top-down integration testing sequence for the SATM decomposition in Figure 13.1. At the uppermost level, we would have stubs for the four components in the first-level decomposition. There would be four integration sessions; in each, one component would be actual (previously unit tested) code, and the other three would be stubs. Top-down integration follows a breadth-first traversal of the functional decomposition tree. Two additional integration levels are shown in Figure 13.3.

Even this can be problematic. Would we replace all the stubs at once? If we did, we would have a "small bang" for units with a high outdegree. If we replace one stub at a time, we retest the Main program once for each replaced stub. This means that for the SATM Main program example

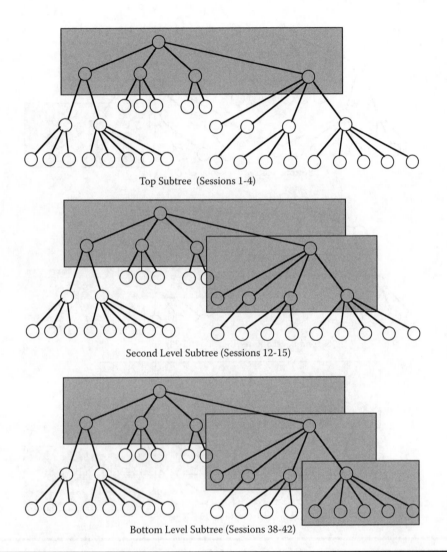

Top Subtree (Sessions 1-4)

Second Level Subtree (Sessions 12-15)

Bottom Level Subtree (Sessions 38-42)

Figure 13.3   Top-down integration.

here, we would repeat its integration test five times (once for each replaced stub, and once with all the stubs).

13.2.2 Bottom-Up Integration

Bottom-up integration is a mirror image to the top-down order, with the difference that stubs are replaced by driver modules that emulate units at the next level up in the tree (see Figure 13.4). In bottom-up integration, we start with the leaves of the decomposition tree (units like ControlDoor and DispenseCash) and test them with specially coded drivers. Less throwaway code exists in drivers than in stubs. Recall we had one stub for each child node in the decomposition tree. Most systems have a fairly high fan-out near the leaves; so in the bottom-up integration order, we will not have as many drivers. This is partially offset by the fact that the driver modules will be more complicated.

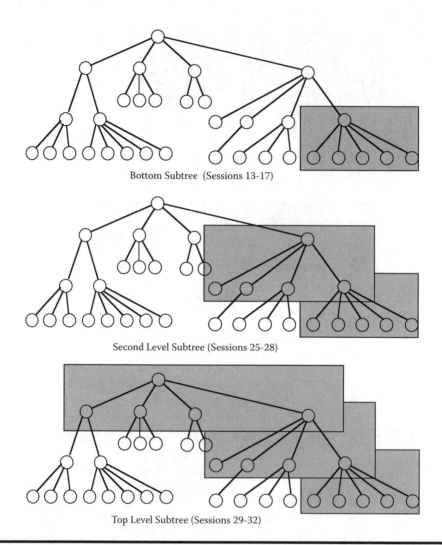

Bottom Subtree (Sessions 13-17)

Second Level Subtree (Sessions 25-28)

Top Level Subtree (Sessions 29-32)

Figure 13.4   Bottom-up integration.

13.2.3 Sandwich Integration

Sandwich integration is a combination of top-down and bottom-up integration. If we think about it in terms of the decomposition tree, we are really only doing big bang integration on a subtree (see Figure 13.5). There will be less stub and driver development effort, but this will be offset to some extent by the added difficulty of fault isolation that is a consequence of big bang integration. (We could discuss the size of a sandwich, from dainty finger sandwiches to Dagwood-style sandwiches, but we won't.)

13.2.4 Pros and Cons

With the exception of big bang integration, the decomposition-based approaches are all intuitively clear. Build with tested components. Whenever a failure is observed, the most recently added unit is suspected. Integration testing progress is easily tracked against the decomposition tree. (If the

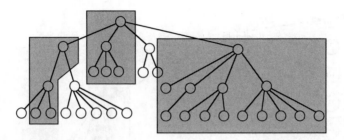

Figure 13.5 Sandwich integration.

tree is small, it is a nice touch to shade in nodes as they are successfully integrated.) The top-down and bottom-up terms suggest breadth-first traversals of the decomposition tree, but this is not mandatory. (We could use full-height sandwiches to test the tree in a depth-first manner.)

One of the most frequent objections to functional decomposition and waterfall development is that both are artificial, and both serve the needs of project management more than the needs of software developers. This holds true also for decomposition-based testing. The whole mechanism is that units are integrated with respect to structure; this presumes that correct behavior follows from individually correct units and correct interfaces. (Practitioners know better.) The development effort for stubs or drivers is another drawback to these approaches, and this is compounded by the retesting effort. Here is a formula that computes the number of integration test sessions for a given decomposition tree (a test session is one set of tests for a specific configuration of actual code and stubs):

$$\text{Sessions} = \text{nodes} - \text{leaves} + \text{edges}$$

The SATM system has 42 integration testing sessions, which means 42 separate sets of integration test cases.

For top-down integration, (nodes − 1) stubs are needed, and for bottom-up integration, (nodes − leaves) drivers are needed. For the SATM system, this is 32 stubs and 10 drivers.

13.3 Call Graph–Based Integration

One of the drawbacks of decomposition-based integration is that the basis is the functional decomposition tree. If we use the call graph instead, we mitigate this deficiency; we also move in the direction of structural testing.

We are in a position to enjoy the investment we made in the discussion of graph theory. Because the call graph is a directed graph, why not use it the way we used program graphs? This leads us to two new approaches to integration testing: we will refer to them as pairwise integration and neighborhood integration.

13.3.1 Pairwise Integration

The idea behind pairwise integration is to eliminate the stub/driver development effort. Instead of developing stubs and drivers, why not use the actual code? At first, this sounds like big bang integration, but we restrict a session to only a pair of units in the call graph. The end result is that

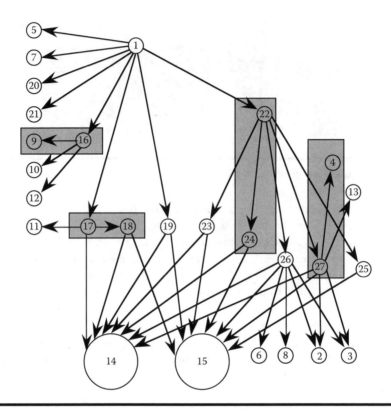

Figure 13.6   Pairwise integration.

we have one integration test session for each edge in the call graph (40 for the SATM call graph in Figure 13.2). This is not much of a reduction in sessions from either top-down or bottom-up (42 sessions), but it is a drastic reduction in stub/driver development. Four pairwise integration sessions are shown in Figure 13.6.

13.3.2 Neighborhood Integration

We can let the mathematics carry us still further by borrowing the notion of a neighborhood from topology. (This is not too much of a stretch — graph theory is a branch of topology.) The neighborhood of radius 1 of a node in a graph is the set of nodes that are one edge away from the given node. In a directed graph, this includes all the immediate predecessor nodes and all the immediate successor nodes (notice that these correspond to the set of stubs and drivers of the node). The neighborhoods for nodes 16 and 26 are shown in Figure 13.7. The 11 neighborhoods for the SATM example (based on the call graph in Figure 13.2) are listed in Table 13.3.

We can always compute the number of neighborhoods for a given call graph. Each interior node will have one neighborhood, plus one extra in case leaf nodes are connected directly to the root node. (An interior node has a nonzero indegree and a nonzero outdegree.) We have:

$$\text{Interior nodes} = \text{nodes} - (\text{source nodes} + \text{sink nodes})$$

$$\text{Neighborhoods} = \text{interior nodes} + \text{source nodes}$$

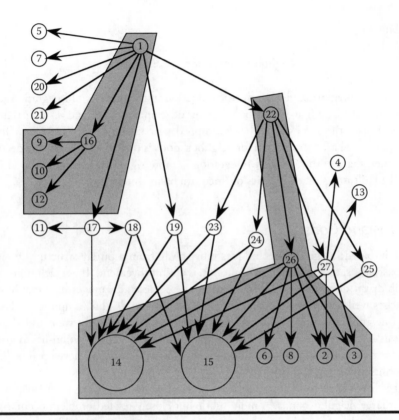

Figure 13.7   Neighborhood integration.

Table 13.3   SATM Neighborhoods

Node	Predecessors	Successors
16	1	9, 10, 12
17	1	11, 14, 18
18	17	14, 15
19	1	14, 15
23	22	14, 15
24	22	14, 15
26	22	14, 15, 6, 8, 2, 3
27	22	14, 15, 2, 3, 4, 13
25	22	15
22	1	23, 24, 26, 27, 25
1	n/a	5, 7, 2, 21, 16, 17, 19, 22

which combine to:

$$\text{Neighborhoods} = \text{nodes} - \text{sink nodes}$$

Neighborhood integration yields a drastic reduction in the number of integration test sessions (down to 11 from 40), and it avoids stub and driver development. The end result is that neighborhoods are essentially the sandwiches that we slipped past in the previous section. (It is slightly different, because the base information for neighborhoods is the call graph, not the decomposition tree.) What they share with sandwich integration is more significant: neighborhood integration testing has the fault isolation difficulties of "medium bang" integration.

13.3.3 Pros and Cons

The call graph–based integration techniques move away from a purely structural basis toward a behavioral basis; thus, the underlying assumption is an improvement. These techniques also eliminate the stub/driver development effort. In addition to these advantages, call graph–based integration matches well with developments characterized by builds and composition. For example, sequences of neighborhoods can be used to define builds. Alternatively, we could allow adjacent neighborhoods to merge (into villages?) and provide an orderly, composition-based growth path. All this supports the use of neighborhood-based integration for systems developed by life cycles in which composition dominates.

The biggest drawback to call graph–based integration testing is the fault isolation problem, especially for large neighborhoods. A more subtle but closely related problem occurs. What happens if (when) a fault is found in a node (unit) that appears in several neighborhoods? (For example, the screen driver unit appears in 7 of the 11 neighborhoods.) Obviously, we resolve the fault, but this means changing the unit's code in some way, which in turn means that all the previously tested neighborhoods that contain the changed node need to be retested.

Finally, a fundamental uncertainty exists in any structural form of testing: the presumption that units integrated with respect to structural information will exhibit correct behavior. We know where we are going: we want system-level threads of behavior to be correct. When integration testing based on call graph information is complete, we still have quite a leap to get to system-level threads. We resolve this by changing the basis from call graph information to special forms of paths.

13.4 Path–Based Integration

Much of the progress in the development of mathematics comes from an elegant pattern: have a clear idea of where you want to go, and then define the concepts that take you there. We do this here for path–based integration testing, but first we need to motivate the definitions.

We already know that the combination of structural and functional testing is highly desirable at the unit level; it would be nice to have a similar capability for integration (and system) testing. We also know that we want to express system testing in terms of behavioral threads. Lastly, we revise our goal for integration testing: instead of testing interfaces among separately developed and tested units, we focus on interactions among these units. (*Co-functioning* might be a good term.) Interfaces are structural; interaction is behavioral (Jorgensen, 1985; Jorgensen, 1994).

When a unit executes, some path of source statements is traversed. Suppose that a call goes to another unit along such a path: at that point, control is passed from the calling unit to the called unit, where some other path of source statements is traversed. We conveniently ignored this situation in Part III, because this is a better place to address the question. Two possibilities are available: abandon the single-entry, single-exit precept and treat such calls as an exit followed by an entry, or suppress the call statement because control eventually returns to the calling unit anyway. The suppression choice works well for unit testing, but it is antithetical to integration testing.

13.4.1 New and Extended Concepts

To get where we need to go, we need to refine some of the program graph concepts. As before, these refer to programs written in an imperative language. We allow statement fragments to be a complete statement, and statement fragments are nodes in the program graph.

Definition

A *source node* in a program is a statement fragment at which program execution begins or resumes.

The first executable statement in a unit is clearly a source node. Source nodes also occur immediately after nodes that transfer control to other units.

Definition

A *sink node* in a program is a statement fragment at which program execution terminates.

The final executable statement in a program is clearly a sink node; so are statements that transfer control to other units.

Definition

A *module execution path* is a sequence of statements that begins with a source node and ends with a sink node, with no intervening sink nodes.

The effect of the definitions so far is that program graphs now have multiple source and sink nodes. This would greatly increase the complexity of unit testing, but integration testing presumes unit testing is complete.

Definition

A *message* is a programming language mechanism by which one unit transfers control to another unit.

Depending on the programming language, messages can be interpreted as subroutine invocations, procedure calls, and function references. We follow the convention that the unit that receives a message (the message destination) always eventually returns control to the message source. Messages can pass data to other units. We can finally make the definitions for path–based integration testing. Our goal is to have an integration testing analog of DD-Paths.

Definition

An *MM-Path* is an interleaved sequence of module execution paths and messages.

The basic idea of an MM-Path is that we can now describe sequences of module execution paths that include transfers of control among separate units. These transfers are by messages; therefore, MM-Paths always represent feasible execution paths, and these paths cross unit boundaries.

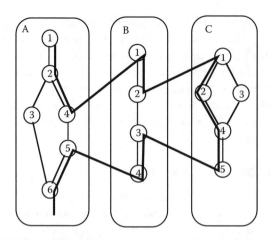

Figure 13.8 MM-Path across three units.

We can find MM-Paths in an extended program graph in which nodes are module execution paths and edges are messages. The hypothetical example in Figure 13.8 shows an MM-Path (the dark line) in which module A calls module B, which in turn calls module C. Notice that, for traditional (procedural) software, MM-Paths will always begin (and end) in the Main program.

In module A, nodes 1 and 5 are source nodes, and nodes 4 and 6 are sink nodes. Similarly, in module B, nodes 1 and 3 are source nodes, and nodes 2 and 4 are sink nodes. Module C has a single source node, 1, and a single sink node, 4. Seven module execution paths are shown in Figure 13.8:

```
MEP(A,1)  = <1, 2, 3, 6>
MEP(A,2)  = <1, 2, 4>
MEP(A,3)  = <5, 6>
MEP(B,1)  = <1, 2>
MEP(B,2)  = <3, 4>
MEP(C,1)  = <1, 2, 4, 5>
MEP(C,2)  = <1, 3, 4, 5>
```

We can now define an integration testing analog of the DD-Path graph that serves unit testing so effectively.

Definition

Given a set of units, their *MM-Path graph* is the directed graph in which nodes are module execution paths and edges correspond to messages and returns from one unit to another.

Notice that MM-Path graphs are defined with respect to a set of units. This directly supports composition of units and composition-based integration testing. We can even compose down to the level of individual module execution paths, but that is probably more detailed than necessary.

Figure 13.9 shows the MM-Path graph for the example in Figure 13.8. The solid arrows indicate messages; the corresponding returns are indicated by dotted arrows. We should consider the relationships among module execution paths, program paths, DD-Paths, and MM-Paths. A program path is a sequence of DD-Paths, and an MM-Path is a sequence of module execution paths. Unfortunately, there is no simple relationship between DD-Paths and module execution

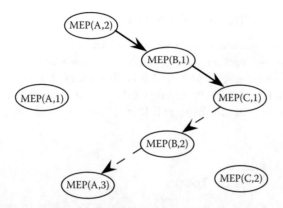

Figure 13.9   MM-Path graph derived from Figure 13.8.

paths. Either might be contained in the other, but more likely, they partially overlap. Because MM-Paths implement a function that transcends unit boundaries, we do have one relationship: consider the intersection of an MM-Path with a unit. The module execution paths in such an intersection are an analog of a slice with respect to the (MM-Path) function. Stated another way, the module execution paths in such an intersection are the restriction of the function to the unit in which they occur.

The MM-Path definition needs some practical guidelines. How long (deep might be better) is an MM-Path? Two observable behavioral criteria put endpoints on MM-Paths: message and data quiescence. Message quiescence occurs when a unit that sends no messages is reached (like module C in Figure 13.8).

Data quiescence occurs when a sequence of processing culminates in the creation of stored data that is not immediately used. In the ValidateCard unit, the account balance is obtained, but it is not used until after a successful PIN entry. Figure 13.10 shows how data quiescence appears in a traditional dataflow diagram. Points of quiescence are natural endpoints for an MM-Path.

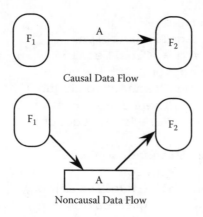

Figure 13.10   Data quiescence.

13.4.2 MM-Paths in the SATM System

The pseudocode descriptions mentioned in Chapter 12 are given here; the statement fragments are numbered as we did to construct program graphs. Also, the messages are numbered as comments. We will use these to describe selected MM-Paths. The arguments to ScreenDriver refer to the screens as numbered in Figure 12.6. Procedure GetPIN is really a stub that is designed to respond to a correct digit event sequence for ExpectedPIN = 1234.

```
1.   Main Program
2.   State = AwaitCard
3.   Do              'Main loop
4.   Case State
5.     Case 1:    AwaitCard
6.                   ScreenDriver(1, null)                    msg1
7.                   WatchCardSlot(CardSlotStatus)            msg2
8.                   Do While CardSlotStatus is Idle
9.                       WatchCardSlot(CardSlotStatus)        msg3
10.                  End While
11.                  ControlCardRoller(accept)                msg4
12.                  ValidateCard(CardOK, PAN)                msg5
13.                  If CardOK
14.                      Then State = AwaitPIN
15.                      Else ControlCardRoller(eject)        msg6
16.                  EndIf
17.                  State = AwaitCard
18.    Case 2: AwaitPIN
19.                  ValidatePIN(PINok, PAN)                  msg7
20.                  If PINok
21.                      Then ScreenDriver(2, null)           msg8
22.                          State = AwaitTrans
23.                      ElseScreenDriver(4, null)            msg9
24.                          State = AwaitCard
25.                  EndIf
26.    Case 3: AwaitTrans
27.                  ManageTransaction                        msg10
28.                  State = CloseSession
29.    Case 4: CloseSession
30.                  If NewTransactionRequest
31.                      Then State = AwaitTrans
32.                      ElsePrintReceipt                     msg11
33.                  EndIf
34.                  PostTransactionLocal                     msg12
35.                  CloseSession                             msg13
36.                  ControlCardRoller(eject)                 msg14
37.                  State = AwaitCard
38. End Case (State)
39. Until 'Forever
```

```
40.  End. (Main program SATM)
41.  Procedure ValidatePIN(PINok, PAN)
42.  GetPINforPAN(PAN, ExpectedPIN)                              msg15
43.  Try = First
44.  Case Try of
45.    Case 1: First
46.          ScreenDriver(2, null)                              msg16
47.          GetPIN(EnteredPIN, CancelHit)                      msg17
48.          If EnteredPIN = ExpectedPIN
49.                  Then PINok = True
50.                  Else ScreenDriver(3, null)                 msg18
51.                       Try = Second
52.                  EndIf
53.        Case 2: Second
54.                  ScreenDriver(2, null)                      msg19
55.                  GetPIN(EnteredPIN,CancelHit)               msg20
56.                  If EnteredPIN = ExpectedPIN
57.                       Then PINok = True
58.                       Else ScreenDriver(3, null)            msg21
59.                  EndIf
60.                       Try = Third
61.        Case 3: Third
62.                  ScreenDriver(2, null)                      msg22
63.                  GetPIN(EnteredPIN, CancelHit)              msg23
64.                  If EnteredPIN = ExpectedPIN
65.                       Then PINok = True
66.                       Else  ScreenDriver(4, null)           msg24
67.                             PINok = False
68.                  EndIf
69.    EndCase (Try)
70.    End.          (Procedure ValidatePIN)


71.    Procedure GetPIN(EnteredPIN, CancelHit)
72.    Local Data: DigitKeys = {0, 1, 2, 3, 4, 5, 6, 7, 8, 9}
73.    CancelHit = False
74.    EnteredPIN = null string
75.    digitsRcvd=0
76.    Do While NOT(DigitsRcvd=4 OR CancelHit)
77.          KeySensor(KeyHit)msg25
78.          If KeyHit IN DigitKeys
79.                  Then
80.                          EnteredPIN = EnteredPIN + KeyHit
81.                          digitsRcvd = digitsRcvd + 1
82.                          If digitsRcvd = 1
83.                            Then ScreenDirver (2, 'X---')     msg26
84.                          EndIf
```

```
85.                        If digitsRcvd = 2
86.                           Then ScreenDirver (2, 'XX--')    msg27
87.                        EndIf
88.                        If digitsRcvd = 3
89.                           Then ScreenDirver (2, 'XXX-')   msg28
90.                        EndIf
91.                        If digitsRcvd = 4
92.                           Then ScreenDirver (2, 'XXXX')    msg29
93.                        EndIf
94.                Else
95.                        CancelHit = True
96.            EndIf
97.    End While
98.    End.  (Procedure GetPIN)
```

SATM Main contains 16 source nodes. All except node 1 are where a procedure/function call returns control: 1, 7, 8, 10, 12, 13, 16, 20, 22, 24, 28, 31, 33, 35, 36, 37, and 38. SATM Main contains 16 sink nodes. As with the source nodes, most of these are at procedure/function calls: 6, 7, 9, 11, 12, 15, 18, 19, 21, 23, 27, 32, 34, 35, 36, and 39. Notice that when two sequential procedure calls are used, a statement can be both a sink and a source node. Most of the module execution paths in SATM Main are very short; this pattern is due to the high density of messages to other units.

Only one nontrivial module execution path is contained in the first 17 lines of SATM Main: <1, 2, 3, 4, 5>. Procedure calls, such as <6>, <7>, <9>, <11>, <12>, and <15>, are trivial in the sense that not much happens in SATM Main. Other very short module execution paths are associated with the control structures — for example, <10, 8>, <10, 11>, and <16, 16>.

Here is the MM-Path for a correct PIN entry on the first try. The module execution paths are described by giving the name of the unit followed by the sequence of the statement fragment numbers. Figure 13.11 illustrates the sequential nature of an MM-Path using a Unified Modeling Language (UML)-style sequence diagram.

```
Main (1, 2, 3, 18, 19)
msg 7
ValidatePIN (41, 42)
msg 15
GetPINforPAN (no pseudo-code given)
ValidatePIN (43, 44, 45, 46)
msg 16
ScreenDriver (no pseudo-code given)
ValidatePIN (47)
msg 17
GetPIN(71, 72, 73, 74, 75, 76, 77)
msg 25
KeySensor (no pseudo-code given)   'first digit
GetPIN (78, 79, 80, 81, 82, 83)
msg 26
ScreenDriver (no pseudo-code given)
GetPIN (84, 85, 87, 88, 90, 91, 93, 96, 97, 76, 77)
```

```
msg 25
KeySensor (no pseudo-code given) )        'second digit
GetPIN (78, 79, 80, 81, 82, 84, 85, 86)
msg 27
ScreenDriver (no pseudo-code given)
GetPIN (87, 88, 90, 91, 93, 96, 97, 76, 77)
msg 25
KeySensor (no pseudo-code given) )        'third digit
GetPIN (78, 79, 80, 81, 82, 84, 85, 87, 88, 89)
msg 28
ScreenDriver (no pseudo-code given)
GetPIN (90, 91, 93, 96, 97, 76, 77)
msg 25
KeySensor (no pseudo-code given) )        'fourth digit
GetPIN (78, 79, 80, 81, 82, 84, 85, 87, 88, 90, 91, 92)
msg 29
ScreenDriver (no pseudo-code given)
GetPIN (93, 96, 97, 76, 98)
ValidatePIN (48, 49, 52, 69, 70)
Main(20)
```

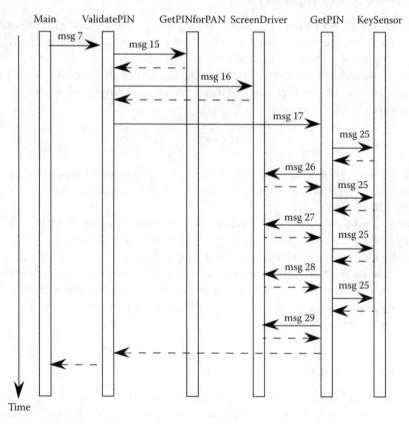

Figure 13.11   UML sequence diagram of the sample MM-Path.

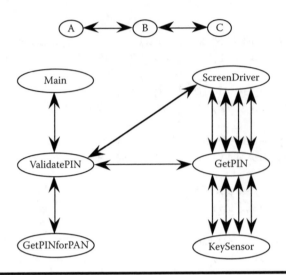

Figure 13.12 MM-Path directed graphs.

13.4.3 MM-Path Complexity

If you compare the MM-Paths in Figure 13.8 and Figure 13.11, it is intuitively clear that the latter is more complex than the former. Their directed graphs are shown together in Figure 13.12. The multiplicity of edges (e.g., between ScreenDriver and GetPIN) preserves the message connections, and the double-headed arrows capture the sending and return of a message (with less clutter). Because these are strongly connected directed graphs, we can "blindly" compute their cyclomatic complexities; recall that the formula is

$$V(G) = e - n + 2p$$

where p is the number of strongly connected regions. For structured procedural code, we will always have p = 1, so the formula reduces to $V(G) = e - n + 2$. The results, respectively, are $V(G) = 3$ and $V(G) = 20$.

This seems reasonable. The second graph is clearly more complex than the first, and if we remove some of the message traffic, say between the GetPIN and KeySensor nodes, both the intuitive and the computed complexity will be reduced. The role of 2p in the formula is annoying. It acts like an offset because it will always be exactly 2. This suggests simply dropping it. If we were to do this, the simplest MM-Path, in which unit A calls unit B and B returns, would have a complexity of 0. Worse yet, a stand-alone unit would have a negative complexity of –1. Some other possibilities are suggested in the exercises.

13.4.4 Pros and Cons

MM-Paths are a hybrid of functional and structural testing. They are functional in the sense that they represent actions with inputs and outputs. As such, all the functional testing techniques are potentially applicable. The structural side comes from how they are identified, particularly the

MM-Path graph. The net result is that the cross-check of the functional and structural approaches is consolidated into the constructs for path–based integration testing. We therefore avoid the pitfall of structural testing, and at the same time, integration testing gains a fairly seamless junction with system testing. Path–based integration testing works equally well for software developed in the traditional waterfall process or with one of the composition-based alternative life cycle models. We will revisit these concepts again in Chapter 18; there we will see that the concepts are equally applicable to object-oriented software testing.

The most important advantage of path–based integration testing is that it is closely coupled with actual system behavior, instead of the structural motivations of decomposition and call graph–based integration.

The advantages of path–based integration come at a price: more effort is needed to identify the MM-Paths. This effort is probably offset by the elimination of stub and driver development.

13.5 Case Study

Our now familiar NextDate is rewritten here as a Main program with a functional decomposition into procedures and functions. This "integration version" is a slight extension: there is (limited) added validity checking for months, days, and years. The pseudocode grows from 50 statements to 81. Figure 13.13 and Figure 13.14 show the program graphs of units in the integration version of NextDate. The functional decomposition is shown in Figure 13.15, and the Call Graph is shown in Figure 13.16.

```
1.      Main integrationNextDate
            Type          Date
                          Month As Integer
                          Day As Integer
                          Year As Integer
            EndType
            Dim today As Date
            Dim tomorrow As Date
2.          GetDate(today)                                        'msg1
3.          PrintDate(today)                                      'msg2
4.          tomorrow = IncrementDate(today)                       'msg3
5.          PrintDate(tomorrow)                                   'msg4
6.      End Main
7.      Function isLeap(year)                          Boolean
8.          If (year divisible by 4)
9.              Then
10.                     If (year is NOT divisible by 100)
11.                         Then isLeap = True
12.                         Else
13.                             If (year is divisible by 400)
14.                                 Then isLeap = True
15.                                 Else isLeap = False
16.                             EndIf
17.                     EndIf
```

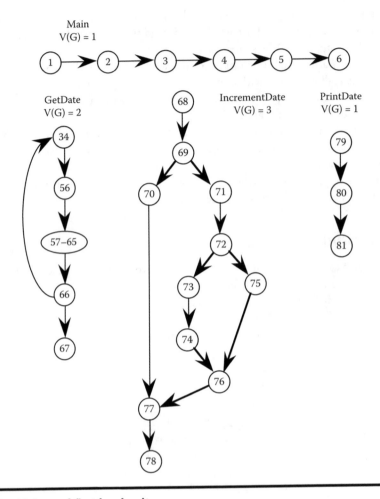

Figure 13.13   Main- and first-level units.

```
18.                 Else isLeap = False
19.         EndIf
20.     End (Function isLeap)

21.     Function lastDayOfMonth(month, year)      Integer
22.         Case month Of
23.             Case 1: 1, 3, 5, 7, 8, 10, 12
24.                 lastDayOfMonth = 31
25.             Case 2: 4, 6, 9, 11
26.                 lastDayOfMonth = 30
27.             Case 3: 2
28.                 If (isLeap(year))                        'msg5
29.                     Then lastDayOfMonth = 29
30.                     Else lastDayOfMonth = 28
31.                 EndIf
```

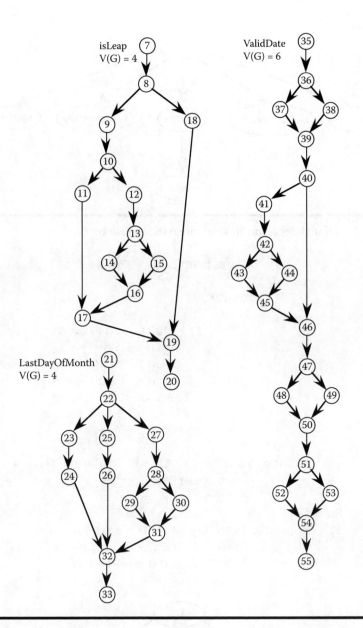

Figure 13.14 Lower-level units.

```
32.              EndCase
33.      End (Function lastDayOfMonth)
34.      Function GetDate(aDate)            Date
             dim aDate As Date
35.          Function ValidDate(aDate)      Boolean
             dim aDate As Date
                dim dayOK, monthOK, yearOK As Boolean
36.              If ((aDate.Month > 0) AND (aDate.Month <=12)
37.                  Then monthOK = True
```

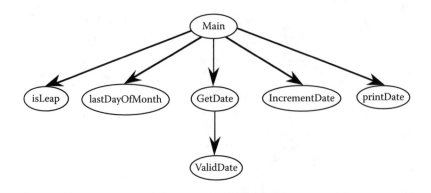

Figure 13.15 Functional decomposition of integration version.

```
38.                    Else monthOK = False
39.             EndIf
40.             If (monthOK)
41.                    Then
42.                           If ((aDate.Day > 0) AND
                                  (aDate.Day <=
                                  lastDayOfMonth(aDate.Month,
                                  aDate.Year))                    'msg6
43.                           Then dayOK = True
44.                           Else dayOK = False
45.                           EndIf
46.             EndIf
47.         If ((aDate.Year > 1811) AND (aDate.Year <= 2012))
48.                    Then yearOK = True
49.                    Else yearOK = False
50.         EndIf
51.         If (monthOK AND dayOK AND yearOK)
52.                    Then ValidDate = True
53.                    Else ValidDate = False
```

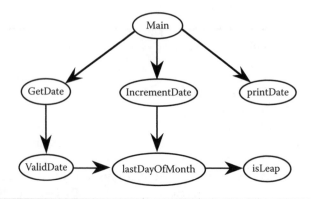

Figure 13.16 Call graph of integration version.

```
54.            EndIf
55.            End (Function ValidDate)

      ' GetDate body begins here
56.         Do
57.                Output("enter a month")
58.                Input(aDate.Month)
59.                Output("enter a day")
60.                Input(aDate.Day)
61.                Output("enter a year")
62.                Input(aDate.Year)
63.                GetDate.Month = aDate.Month
64.                GetDate.Day = aDate.Day
65.                GetDate.Year = aDate.Year
66.         Until (ValidDate(aDate))                        'msg7
67.            End (Function GetDate)
68.     Function IncrementDate(aDate)         Date
69.            If (aDate.Day < lastDayOfMonth(aDate.Month))  'msg8
70.                Then aDate.Day = aDate.Day + 1
71.                Else aDate.Day = 1
72.                    If (aDate.Month = 12)
73.                        Then aDate.Month = 1
74.                              aDate.Year = aDate.Year + 1
75.                        Else aDate.Month = aDate.Month + 1
76.                    EndIf
77.            EndIf
78.     End (IncrementDate)
79.     Procedure PrintDate(aDate)
80.            Output( "Day is ", aDate.Month, "/", aDate.Day,
               "/", aDate.Year)
81.     End (PrintDate)
```

13.5.1 Decomposition-Based Integration

The isLeap and lastDayOfMonth functions are in the first level of decomposition because they must be available to both GetDate and IncrementDate. (We could move isLeap to be contained within the scope of lastDayOfMonth.) Pairwise integration based on the decomposition in Figure 13.15 is problematic; the isLeap and lastDayOfMonth functions are never directly called by the Main program, so these integration sessions would be empty. Bottom-up pairwise integration starting with isLeap, then lastDayOfMonth, ValidDate, and GetDate, would be useful. The pairs involving Main and GetDate, IncrementDate, and PrintDate are all useful (but short) sessions. Building stubs for ValidDate and lastDayOfMonth would be easy.

13.5.2 Call Graph–Based Integration

Pairwise integration based on the call graph in Figure 13.16 is an improvement over that for the decomposition-based pairwise integration. Obviously there are no empty integration sessions because edges refer to actual unit references. There is still the problem of stubs. Sandwich integration is appropriate because this example is so small. In fact, it lends itself to a build sequence. Build 1 could contain Main and PrintDate. Build 2 could contain Main, IncrementDate, lastDayOfMonth, and IncrementDate in addition to the already present PrintDate. Finally, Build 3 would add the remaining units, GetDate and ValidDate.

Neighborhood integration based on the call graph would likely proceed with the neighborhoods of ValidDate and lastDayOfMonth. Next, we could integrate the neighborhoods of GetDate and IncrementDate. Finally, we would integrate the neighborhood of Main. Notice that these neighborhoods form a build sequence.

13.5.3 MM-Path–Based Integration

Because the program is data driven, all MM-Paths begin in and return to the Main program. Here is the first MM-Path for May 27, 2007 (there are others when the Main program calls PrintDate and IncrementDate):

```
Main (1, 2)
     msg1
     GetDate (34, 56, 57, 58, 59, 60, 61, 62, 63, 64, 65, 66)
          msg7
          ValidDate (35, 36, 37, 39, 40, 41, 42))
               msg6
               lastDayOfMonth (21, 22, 23, 24, 32, 33)
                                             'point of
               message quiescence
          ValidDate (43, 45, 46, 47, 48, 50, 51, 52, 54, 55)
     GetDate (67)
Main (3)
```

Notice that the statement fragment sequences (Figure 13.13 and Figure 13.14) identify full paths from source to sink nodes. This is at the point of message quiescence; at the other units, the pair of node sequences must be concatenated to get the full source-to-sink path. We are now in a strong position to describe how many MM-Paths are sufficient: the set of MM-Paths should cover all source-to-sink paths in the set of units. When loops are present, condensation graphs will result

Table 13.4 Comparison of Integration Testing Strategies

Strategy Basis	Ability to Test Interfaces	Ability to Test Co-Functionality	Fault Isolation Resolution
Functional decomposition	Acceptable but can be deceptive	Limited to pairs of units	Good, to faulty unit
Call graph	Acceptable	Limited to pairs of units	Good, to faulty unit
MM-Path	Excellent	Complete	Excellent, to faulty unit execution path

in directed acyclic graphs, thereby resolving the problem of a potentially infinite (or excessively large) number of paths.

Table 13.4 summarizes the observations made in the preceding discussion. The significant improvement of MM-Paths as a basis for integration testing is due to their exact representation of dynamic software behavior. MM-Paths are also the basis for present research in dataflow (define/ use) approaches to integration testing.

References

Deutsch, M.S., *Software Verification and Validation-Realistic Project Approaches*, Prentice-Hall, Englewood Cliffs, NJ, 1982.

Fordahl, M., Elementary Mistake Doomed Mars Probe, Associated Press, October 1, 1999, www.fas.org/ mars/991001/~mars01.htm.

Hetzel, B., *The Complete Guide to SOFTWARE TESTING*, 2nd ed., QED Information Sciences, Inc., Wellesley, MA, 1988.

Jorgensen, P.C., The Use of MM-Paths in Constructive Software Development, Ph.D. dissertation, Arizona State University, Tempe, 1985.

Jorgensen, P.C. and Erickson, C., Object-oriented integration testing, *Communications of the ACM*, September 1994.

Kaner, C., Falk, J., and Nguyen, H.Q., *Testing Computer Software*, 2nd ed., Van Nostrand Reinhold, New York, 1993.

Mosley, D.J., *The Handbook of MIS Application Software Testing*, Yourdon Press, Prentice-Hall, Englewood Cliffs, NJ, 1993.

Exercises

1. Find the source and sink nodes in ValidatePIN and in GetPIN.
2. Find the module execution paths in ValidatePIN.
3. Here are some other possible complexity metrics for MM-Paths:

   $V(G) = e - n$
   $V(G) = 0.5e - n + 2$
   Sum of the outdegrees of the nodes
   Sum of the nodes plus the sum of the edges
   Which of these makes the most sense to you?

4. Make up some examples, try these out, and see if they have any explanatory value.
5. Make up a few test cases, interpret them as MM-Paths, and then see what portions of the call graph in Figure 13.16 are traversed by your MM-Paths. Try to devise a coverage metric for MM-Path–based integration testing.

Chapter 14

System Testing

Of the three levels of testing, the system level is closest to everyday experience. We test many things: a used car before we buy it, an online network service before we subscribe, and so on. A common pattern in these familiar forms is that we evaluate a product in terms of our expectations — not with respect to a specification or a standard. Consequently, the goal is not to find faults, but to demonstrate correct behavior. Because of this, we tend to approach system testing from a functional standpoint instead of from a structural one. Because it is so intuitively familiar, system testing in practice tends to be less formal than it might be, and this is compounded by the reduced testing interval that usually remains before a delivery deadline.

The craftsperson metaphor continues to serve us. We need a better understanding of the medium; as we said in Chapter 12, we will view system testing in terms of threads of system-level behavior. We begin with a new construct — an atomic system function — and further elaboration on the thread concept, highlighting some of the practical problems of thread-based system testing. System testing is closely coupled with requirements specification; therefore, we will discuss how to find threads in common notations. All this leads to an orderly thread-based system testing strategy that exploits the symbiosis between functional and structural testing. We will apply the strategy to our simple automated teller machine (SATM) system.

14.1 Threads

Threads are hard to define; in fact, some published definitions are counterproductive, misleading, or wrong. It is possible to simply treat threads as a primitive concept that needs no formal definition. For now, we will use examples to develop a shared vision. Here are several views of a thread:

> A scenario of normal usage
> A system-level test case
> A stimulus–response pair
> Behavior that results from a sequence of system-level inputs
> An interleaved sequence of port input and output events
> A sequence of transitions in a state machine description of the system

An interleaved sequence of object messages and method executions
A sequence of machine instructions
A sequence of source instructions
A sequence of MM-Paths
A sequence of atomic system functions

Threads have distinct levels. A unit-level thread is usefully understood as an execution–time path of source instructions or, alternatively, as a sequence of DD-Paths. An integration-level thread is an MM-Path — that is, an alternating sequence of module executions and messages. If we continue this pattern, a system-level thread is a sequence of atomic system functions (to be defined shortly). Because atomic system functions have port events as their inputs and outputs, a sequence of atomic system functions implies an interleaved sequence of port input and output events. The end result is that threads provide a unifying view of our three levels of testing. Unit testing tests individual functions; integration testing examines interactions among units; and system testing examines interactions among atomic system functions. In this chapter, we focus on system-level threads and answer some fundamental questions, such as: How big is a thread? Where do we find them? How do we test them?

14.1.1 Thread Possibilities

Defining the endpoints of a system-level thread is a bit awkward. We motivate a tidy, graph theory-based definition by working backward from where we want to go with threads. Here are four candidate threads in our SATM system:

Entry of a digit
Entry of a personal identification number (PIN)
A simple transaction: ATM card entry, PIN entry, select transaction type (deposit, withdraw), present account details (checking or savings, amount), conduct the operation, and report the results
An ATM session containing two or more simple transactions

Digit entry is a good example of a minimal atomic system function. It begins with a port input event (the digit keystroke) and ends with a port output event (the screen digit echo), so it qualifies as a stimulus–response pair. If you go back to our example in Chapter 13, you will see that this atomic system function (ASF) is a subpath of the sample MM-Path that we listed in great detail. This level of granularity is too fine for the purposes of system testing. We saw this to be an appropriate level for integration testing.

The second candidate, PIN entry, is a good example of an upper limit to integration testing and, at the same time, a starting point of system testing. PIN entry is also a good example of an atomic system function and a family of stimulus–response pairs (system-level behavior that is initiated by a port input event, traverses some programmed logic, and terminates in one of several possible responses (port output events)). As we saw in Chapter 13, PIN entry entails a sequence of system-level inputs and outputs:

1. A screen requesting PIN digits.
2. An interleaved sequence of digit keystrokes and screen responses.

3. The possibility of cancellation by the customer before the full PIN is entered.
4. A system disposition: A customer has three chances to enter the correct PIN. Once a correct PIN has been entered, the user sees a screen requesting the transaction type; otherwise, a screen advises the customer that the ATM card will not be returned, and no access to ATM functions is provided.

This is clearly in the domain of system-level testing, and several stimulus–response pairs are evident. Other examples of ASFs include card entry, transaction selection, provision of transaction details, transaction reporting, and session termination. Each of these is maximal in an integration testing sense and minimal in a system testing sense. That is, we would not want to integration test something larger than an ASF; at the same time, we would not want to system test anything smaller.

The third candidate, the simple transaction, has a sense of end-to-end completion. A customer could never execute PIN entry alone (a card entry is needed), but the simple transaction is commonly executed. This is a good example of a system-level thread; note that it involves the interaction of several ASFs.

The last possibility (the session) is actually a sequence of threads. This is also properly a part of system testing; at this level, we are interested in the interactions among threads. Unfortunately, most system testing efforts never reach the level of thread interaction (more on this in Chapter 15).

14.1.2 Thread Definitions

We simplify our discussion by defining a new term that helps us get to our desired goal.

Definition

An *atomic system function* (ASF) is an action that is observable at the system level in terms of port input and output events.

In an event-driven system, ASFs are separated by points of event quiescence; these occur when a system is (nearly) idle, waiting for a port input event to trigger further processing. Event quiescence has an interesting Petri net insight. In a traditional Petri net, deadlock occurs when no transition is enabled. In an event-driven Petri net, event quiescence is similar to deadlock, but an input event can bring new life to the net. The SATM system exhibits event quiescence in several places: one is the tight loop at the beginning of SATM Main, where the system has displayed the welcome screen and is waiting for a card to be entered into the card slot. Event quiescence is a system-level property; there is an analog at the integration level — message quiescence.

The notion of event quiescence does for ASFs what message quiescence does for MM-Paths: it provides a natural endpoint. An ASF begins with a port input event, traverses parts of one or more MM-Paths, and terminates with a port output event. When viewed from the system level, no compelling reason exists to decompose an ASF into lower levels of detail (hence the atomicity). In the SATM system, digit entry is a good example of an ASF — so are card entry, cash dispensing, and session closing. PIN entry is probably too big; perhaps we should call it a molecular system function.

Atomic system functions represent the seam between integration and system testing. They are the largest item to be tested by integration testing and the smallest item for system testing. We can test an ASF at both levels. Again, the digit entry ASF is a good example (see the MM-Path example in Chapter 13). During system testing, the port input event is a physical key press that is detected by KeySensor and sent to GetPIN as a string variable. (Notice that KeySensor performs the physical-to-logical transition.) GetPIN determines whether the digit key or the cancel key was pressed and responds accordingly. (Notice that button presses are ignored.) The ASF terminates with either screen 2 or 4 displayed. Instead of requiring system keystrokes and visible screen displays, we could use a driver to provide these and test the digit entry ASF via integration testing.

Interesting ASFs are included in ValidatePIN. This unit controls all screen displays relevant to the PIN entry process. It begins with the display of screen 2 (which asks the customer to enter the PIN). Next, GetPIN is called, and the system is event quiescent until a keystroke occurs. These keystrokes initiate the GetDigit ASFs we just discussed. Here, we find a curious integration fault. Notice that screen 2 is displayed in two places: by the Then clauses in the While loop in GetPIN and by the first statements in each Case clause in ValidatePIN. We could fix this by removing the screen displays from GetPIN and simply returning the string (e.g., X —) to be displayed.

Referring to the pseudocode example in Chapter 13, four ASFs are included in statements 75 through 93: each begins with KeySensor observing a port input event (a keystroke) and ends with a closely knit family of port output events (the calls to ScreenDriver with different PIN echoes). We could name these four ASFs GetDigit1, GetDigit2, GetDigit3, and GetDigit4. They are slightly different because the later ones include the earlier If statements. (This module might be reworked so that the While loop repeated a single ASF.)

This portion of the SATM system also illustrates the difference between unit and integration testing. When GetPIN is unit tested, its inputs come from KeySensor (which acts like an input statement). The input space of GetPIN contains the digits 0 through 9 and the cancel key. (These would likely be treated as string or character data.) We could add inputs for the function keys B1, B2, and B3; if we did, traditional equivalence class testing would be a good choice. The function we test is whether GetDigit reconstructs the keystrokes into a digit string and whether the Boolean indication for the cancel key is correct.

Definition

Given a system defined in terms of atomic system functions, the *ASF graph* of the system is the directed graph in which nodes are ASFs and edges represent sequential flow.

Definition

A *source ASF* is an atomic system function that appears as a source node in the ASF graph of a system; similarly, a *sink ASF* is an atomic system function that appears as a sink node in the ASF graph.

In the SATM system, the card entry ASF is a source ASF, and the session termination ASF is a sink ASF. Notice that intermediary ASFs could never be tested at the system level by themselves — they need the predecessor ASFs to get there.

Definition

A *system thread* is a path from a source ASF to a sink ASF in the ASF graph of a system.

Definition

Given a system defined in terms of system threads, the *thread graph* of the system is the directed graph in which nodes are system threads and edges represent sequential execution of individual threads.

This set of definitions provides a coherent set of increasingly broader views of threads, starting with very short threads (within a unit) and ending with interactions among system-level threads.

We can use these views much like the ocular on a microscope, switching among them to see different levels of granularity. Having these concepts is only part of the problem; supporting them is another. We next take a tester's view of requirements specification to see how to identify threads.

14.2 Basis Concepts for Requirements Specification

Recall the notion of a basis of a vector space: a set of independent elements from which all the elements in the space can be generated. Instead of anticipating all the variations in scores of requirements specification methods, notations, and techniques, we will discuss system testing with respect to a basis set of requirements specification constructs: data, actions, devices, events, and threads (Jorgensen, 1989). Every system can be expressed in terms of these five fundamental concepts (and every requirements specification technique is some combination of these). We examine these fundamental concepts here to see how they support the tester's process of thread identification.

14.2.1 Data

When a system is described in terms of its data, the focus is on the information used and created by the system. We describe data in terms of variables, data structures, fields, records, data stores, and files. Entity/relationship models are the most common choice at the highest level, and some form of a regular expression (e.g., Jackson diagrams or data structure diagrams) is used at a more detailed level. The data-centered view is also the starting point for several flavors of object-oriented analysis. Data refers to information that is initialized, stored, updated, or (possibly) destroyed. In the SATM system, initial data describes the various accounts (PANs) and their PINs, and each account has a data structure with information such as the account balance. As ATM transactions occur, the results are kept as created data and used in the daily posting of terminal data to the central bank. For many systems, the data-centered view dominates. These systems are often developed in terms of CRUD actions (create, retrieve, update, delete). We could describe the transaction portion of the SATM system in this way, but it would not work well for the user interface portion.

Sometimes threads can be identified directly from the data model. Relationships between data entities can be one-to-one, many-to-one, or many-to-many; these distinctions all have implications for threads that process the data. For example, if bank customers can have several accounts, each account needs a unique PIN. If several people can access the same account, they need ATM cards with identical PANs. We can also find initial data (such as PAN, ExpectedPIN pairs) that is read but never written. Such read-only data must be part of the system initialization process. If not, there must be threads that create such data. Read-only data is therefore an indicator of source ASFs.

14.2.2 Actions

Action-centered modeling is still a common requirements specification form. This is a historical outgrowth of the action-centered nature of imperative programming languages. Actions have inputs and outputs, and these can be either data or port events. Here are some methodology-specific synonyms for actions: transform, data transform, control transform, process, activity, task, method, and service. Actions can also be decomposed into lower-level actions, as we saw with the dataflow diagrams in Chapter 12. The input/output (I/O) view of actions is exactly the basis of functional testing, and the decomposition (and eventual implementation) of actions is the basis of structural testing.

14.2.3 Devices

Every system has port devices; these are the sources and destinations of system-level inputs and outputs (port events). The slight distinction between ports and port devices is sometimes helpful to testers. Technically, a port is the point at which an I/O device is attached to a system, as in serial and parallel ports, network ports, and telephone ports. Physical actions (keystrokes and light emissions from a screen) occur on port devices, and these are translated from physical to logical (or logical to physical). In the absence of actual port devices, much of system testing can be accomplished by "moving the port boundary inward" to the logical instances of port events. From now on, we will just use the term *port* to refer to port devices. The ports in the SATM system include the digit and cancel keys, the function keys, the display screen, the deposit and withdrawal doors, the card and receipt slots, and several less obvious devices, such as the rollers that move cards and deposit envelopes into the machine, the cash dispenser, the receipt printer, and so on.

Thinking about the ports helps the tester define the input space that functional system testing needs; similarly, the output devices provide output-based functional test information. (For example, we would like to have enough threads to generate all 15 SATM screens.)

14.2.4 Events

Events are somewhat schizophrenic: they have some characteristics of data and some of actions. An event is a system-level input (or output) that occurs on a port device. Similar to data, events can be inputs to or outputs of actions. Events can be discrete (such as SATM keystrokes) or continuous (such as temperature, altitude, or pressure). Discrete events necessarily have a time duration, and this can be a critical factor in real-time systems. We might picture input events as destructive readout data, but it is a stretch to imagine output events as destructive write operations.

Events are like actions in the sense that they are the translation point between real-world physical events and internal logical manifestations of these. Port input events are physical-to-logical translations, and symmetrically, port output events are logical-to-physical translations. System testers should focus on the physical side of events, not the logical side (the focus of integration testers). Situations occur where the context of present data values changes the logical meaning of physical events. In the SATM system, for example, the port input event of depressing button B1 means "Balance" when screen 5 is displayed, "checking" when screen 6 is displayed, and "yes" when screens 10, 11, and 14 are displayed. We refer to such situations as context-sensitive port events, and we would expect to test such events in each context.

14.2.5 Threads

Unfortunately for testers, threads are the least frequently used of the five fundamental constructs. Because we test threads, it usually falls to the tester to find them in the interactions among the data, events, and actions. About the only place that threads appear per se in a requirements specification is when rapid prototyping is used in conjunction with a scenario recorder. It is easy to find threads in control models, as we will soon see. The problem with this is that control models are just that — they are models, not the reality of a system.

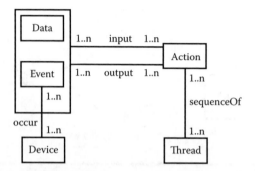

Figure 14.1   E/R model of basis concepts.

14.2.6 Relationships among Basis Concepts

Figure 14.1 is an entity/relationship (E/R) model of our basis concepts. Notice that all relationships are many-to-many: Data and Events are generalized into an entity; the two relationships to the Action entity are for inputs and outputs. The same event can occur on several ports, and typically many events occur on a single port. Finally, an action can occur in several threads, and a thread is composed of several actions. This diagram demonstrates some of the difficulty of system testing. Testers must use events and threads to ensure that all the many-to-many relationships among the five basis concepts are correct.

14.2.7 Modeling with Basis Concepts

All flavors of requirements specification develop models of a system in terms of the basis concepts. Figure 14.2 shows three fundamental forms of requirements specification models: structural, contextual, and behavioral. Structural models are used for development; these express the functional decomposition, data decomposition, and interfaces among components. Contextual models are often the starting point of structural modeling. They emphasize system devices and, to a lesser extent, actions, and threads very indirectly. The models of behavior (also called control models)

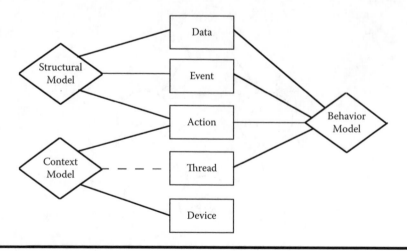

Figure 14.2   Modeling relationships among basic constructs.

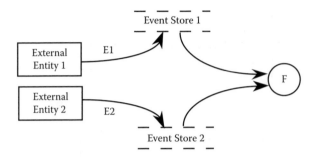

Figure 14.3   Event partitioning view of function F.

are where four of the five basis constructs come together. Selection of an appropriate control model is the essence of requirements specification: models that are too weak cannot express important system behaviors, while models that are too powerful typically obscure interesting behaviors. As a general rule, decision tables are a good choice only for computational systems; finite state machines are good for menu-driven systems; and Petri nets are the model of choice for concurrent systems. Here, we use finite state machines for the SATM system, and in Chapter 15, we will use Petri nets to analyze thread interaction.

We must make an important distinction between a system itself (reality) and models of a system. Consider a system in which some function F cannot occur until two prerequisite events E1 and E2 have occurred, and that they can occur in either order. We could use the notion of event partitioning to model this situation. The result would be a diagram like that in Figure 14.3.

In the event partitioning view, events E1 and E2 occur on their respective external devices. When they occur, they are held in their respective event stores. (An event store acts like a destructive read operation.) When both events have occurred, function F gets its prerequisite information from the event stores. Notice that we cannot tell from the model which event occurs first; we only know that both must occur.

We could also model the system as a finite state machine (FSM) in Figure 14.4, in which states record which event has occurred. The state machine view explicitly shows the two orders of the events.

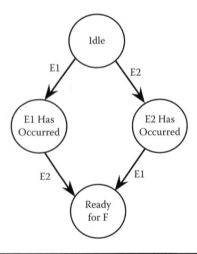

Figure 14.4   FSM for function F.

Both models express the same prerequisites for the function F, and neither is the reality of the system. Of these two models, the state machine is more useful to the tester, because paths are instantly convertible to threads.

14.3 Finding Threads

The finite state machine models of the SATM system are the best place to look for system testing threads. We will start with a hierarchy of state machines; the upper level is shown in Figure 14.5. At this level, states correspond to stages of processing, and transitions are caused by logical (instead of port) events. The card entry state, for example, would be decomposed into lower levels that deal with details like jammed cards, cards that are upside down, stuck card rollers, and checking the card against the list of cards for which service is offered. Once the details of a macro-state are tested, we use a "normal" thread to get to the next macro-state.

The PIN entry state is decomposed into the more detailed view in Figure 14.6, which is a slight revision of the version in Chapter 12.

The adjacent states are shown because they are sources and destinations of transitions from the PIN entry portion. At this level, we focus on the PIN retry mechanism; all of the output events are true port events, but the input events are still logical events. The states and edges are numbered for reference later when we discuss test coverage.

To start the thread identification process, we first list the port events shown on the state transitions; they appear in Table 14.1. We skipped the eject card event because it is not really part of the PIN entry component.

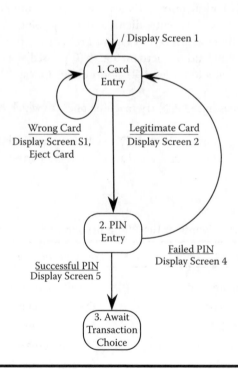

Figure 14.5   Top-level SATM state machine.

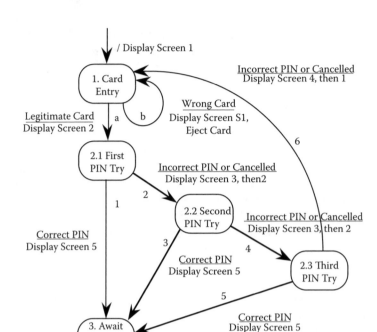

Figure 14.6 PIN entry finite state machine.

Notice that correct PIN and incorrect PIN are really compound port input events. We cannot actually enter an entire PIN — we enter digits, and at any point, we might hit the cancel key. These more detailed possibilities are shown in Figure 14.7. A truly paranoid tester might decompose the digit port input event into the actual choices (0-pressed, 1-pressed, …, 9-pressed), but this should have been tested at a lower level. The port events in the PIN try finite state machine are in Table 14.2.

The "x" in the state names in the PIN try machine refers to which try (first, second, or third) is passing through the machine.

In addition to the true port events in the PIN try finite state machine, there are three logical output events (correct pin, incorrect pin, and canceled); these correspond exactly to the higher-level events in Figure 14.6.

Table 14.1 Events in the PIN Entry Finite State Machine

Port Input Events	Port Output Events
Legitimate card	Display screen 1
Wrong card	Display screen 2
Correct PIN	Display screen 3
Incorrect PIN	Display screen 4
Canceled	Display screen 5

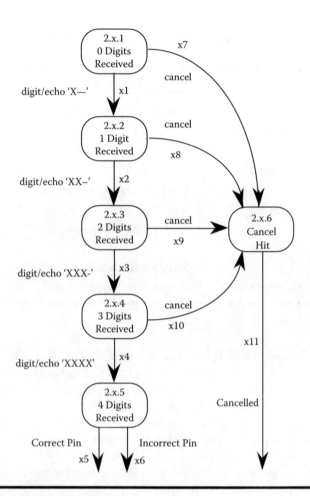

Figure 14.7 PIN try finite state machine.

The hierarchy of finite state machines multiplies the number of threads. There are 156 distinct paths from the first PIN try state to the await transaction choice or card entry states in Figure 14.6. Of these, 31 correspond to eventually correct PIN entries (1 on the first try, 5 on the second try, and 25 on the third try); the other 125 paths correspond to those with incorrect digits or with cancel keystrokes. This is a fairly typical ratio. The input portion of systems, especially interactive systems, usually has a large number of threads to deal with input errors and exceptions.

Table 14.2 Port Events in the PIN Try Finite State Machine

Port Input Events	Port Output Events
Digit	echo "X- - -"
Cancel	echo "XX- -"
	echo "XXX-"
	echo "XXXX"

Table 14.3 Port Event Sequence for Correct PIN on First Try

Port Input Event	Port Output Event
	Screen 2 displayed with "- - - -"
1 pressed	
	Screen 2 displayed with "X- - -"
2 pressed	
	Screen 2 displayed with "XX- -"
3 pressed	
	Screen 2 displayed with "XXX-"
4 pressed	
	Screen 2 displayed with "XXXX"
(Correct PIN)	Screen 5 displayed

It is good form to reach a state machine in which transitions are caused by actual port input events, and the actions on transitions are port output events. If we have such a finite state machine, generating system test cases for these threads is a mechanical process — simply follow a path of transitions and note the port inputs and outputs as they occur along the path.

This interleaved sequence is performed by the test executor (person or program). Table 14.3 and Table 14.4 follow two paths through the hierarchic state machines. Table 14.3 corresponds to a thread in which a PIN is correctly entered on the first try. Table 14.4 corresponds to a thread in which a PIN is incorrectly entered on the first try, canceled after the third digit on the second try, and correctly entered on the third try. To make the test case explicit, we assume a precondition that the expected PIN is 1234.

The event in parentheses in the last row of Table 14.3 is the logical event that "bumps up" to the parent state machine and causes a transition there to the await transaction choice state.

If you look closely at Table 14.3 and Table 14.4, you will see that the bottom third of Table 14.4 is exactly Table 14.3; thus, a thread can be a subset of another thread.

14.4 Structural Strategies for Thread Testing

Although generating thread test cases is easy, deciding which ones to actually use is more complex. (If you have an automatic test executor, this is not a problem.) We have the same path explosion problem at the system level that we had at the unit level. Just as we did there, we can use the directed graph insights to make an intelligent choice of threads to test.

14.4.1 Bottom-Up Threads

When we organize state machines in a hierarchy, we can work from the bottom up. Six paths are used in the PIN try state machine. If we traverse these six, we test for three things: correct

Table 14.4 Port Event Sequence for Correct PIN on Third Try

Port Input Event	Port Output Event
	Screen 2 displayed with "– – – –"
1 pressed	
	Screen 2 displayed with "X– – –"
2 pressed	
	Screen 2 displayed with "XX– –"
3 pressed	
	Screen 2 displayed with "XXX–"
5 pressed	
	Screen 2 displayed with "XXXX"
(Incorrect PIN)	Screen 3 displayed
(Second try)	Screen 2 displayed with "– – – –"
1 pressed	
	Screen 2 displayed with "X– – –"
2 pressed	
	Screen 2 displayed with "XX– –"
3 pressed	
	Screen 2 displayed with "XXX–"
Cancel key pressed	
(End of second try)	Screen 3 displayed
	Screen 2 displayed with "– – – –"
1 pressed	
	Screen 2 displayed with "X– – –"
2 pressed	
	Screen 2 displayed with "XX– –"
3 pressed	
	Screen 2 displayed with "XXX–"
4 pressed	
	Screen 2 displayed with "XXXX"
(Correct PIN)	Screen 5 displayed

recognition and echo of entered digits, response to the cancel keystroke, and matching expected and entered PINs. These paths are described in Table 14.5 as sequences of the transitions in Figure 14.7. A thread that traverses the path is described in terms of its input keystrokes; thus, the input sequence 1234 corresponds to the thread described in more detail in Table 14.3 (the cancel keystroke is indicated with a "C").

Table 14.5 Thread Paths in the PIN Try FSM

Input Event Sequence	Path of Transitions
1234	x1, x2, x3, x4, x5
1235	x1, x2, x3, x4, x6
C	x7, x11
1C	x1, x8, x11
12C	x1, x2, x9, x11
123C	x1, x2, x3, x10, x11

Once this portion is tested, we can go up a level to the PIN entry machine, where four paths are used. These four are concerned with the three-try mechanism and the sequence of screens presented to the user. In Table 14.6, the paths in the PIN entry state machine (Figure 14.6) are named as transition sequences.

These threads were identified with the goal of path traversal in mind. Recall from our discussion of structural testing that these goals can be misleading. The assumption is that path traversal uncovers faults, and traversing a variety of paths reduces redundancy. The last path in Table 14.6 illustrates how structural goals can be counterproductive. Hitting the cancel key three times does indeed cause the three-try mechanism to fail and returns the system to the card entry state; but it seems like a degenerate thread. A more serious flaw occurs with these threads: we could not really execute them alone because of the hierarchic state machines. What really happens with the 1235 input sequence in Table 14.5? It traverses an interesting path in the PIN try machine, and then it "returns" to the PIN entry machine where it is seen as a logical event (incorrect PIN), which causes a transition to state 2.2 (second PIN try). If no additional keystrokes occur, this machine would remain in state 2.2. We show how to overcome such situations next.

14.4.2 Node and Edge Coverage Metrics

Because the finite state machines are directed graphs, we can use the same test coverage metrics that we applied at the unit level. The hierarchic relationship means that the upper-level machine must treat the lower machine as a procedure that is entered and returned. (Actually, we need to do

Table 14.6 Thread Paths in the PIN Entry FSM

Input Event Sequence	Path of Transitions
1234	1
12351234	2, 3
1235C1234	2, 4, 5
CCC	2, 4, 6

Table 14.7   Node and Edge Traversal of a Thread

Port Input Event	Port Output Event	Nodes	Edges
	Screen 2 displayed with "– – – –"	2.1	a
1 pressed		2.1.1	
	Screen 2 displayed with "X– – –"		x1
2 pressed		2.1.2	
	Screen 2 displayed with "XX– –"		x2
3 pressed		2.1.3	
	Screen 2 displayed with "XXX–"		x3
5 pressed		2.1.4	
	Screen 2 displayed with "XXXX"		x4
(Incorrect PIN)	Screen 3 displayed	2.1.5, 3	x6, 2
(Second try)	Screen 2 displayed with "– – – –"	2.2	
1 pressed		2.2.1	
	Screen 2 displayed with "X– – –"		x1
2 pressed		2.2.2	
	Screen 2 displayed with "XX– –"		x2
3 pressed		2.2.3	
	Screen 2 displayed with "XXX–"		x3
Cancel pressed		2.2.4	x10
(End of second try)	Screen 3 displayed	2.2.6	x11
	Screen 2 displayed with "– – – –"	2.3	4
1 pressed		2.3.1	
	Screen 2 displayed with "X– – –"		x1
2 pressed		2.3.2	
	Screen 2 displayed with "XX– –"		x2
3 pressed		2.3.3	
	Screen 2 displayed with "XXX–"		x3
4 pressed		2.3.4	
	Screen 2 displayed with "XXXX"		x4
(Correct PIN)	Screen 5 displayed	2.3.5, 3	x5, 5

this for one more level to get to true threads that begin with the card entry state.) The two obvious choices are node coverage and edge coverage. Table 14.7 is extended from Table 14.4 to show the node and edge coverage of the three-try thread.

Node (state) coverage is analogous to statement coverage at the unit level — it is the bare minimum. In the PIN entry example, we can attain node coverage without ever executing a thread

Table 14.8 Thread/State Incidence

Input Events	2.1	2.x.1	2.x.2	2.x.3	2.x.4	2.x.5	2.2.6	2.2	2.3	3	1
1234	x	x	x	x	x	x				x	
12351234	x	x	x	x	x	x		x		x	
C1234	x	x	x	x	x	x	x	x		x	
1C12C1234	x	x	x	x			x	x	x	x	
123C1C1C	x	x	x	x	x		x	x	x		x

with a correct PIN. If you examine Table 14.8, you will see that two threads (initiated by C1234 and 123C1C1C) traverse all the states in both machines.

Edge (state transition) coverage is a more acceptable standard. If the state machines are well formed (transitions in terms of port events), edge coverage also guarantees port event coverage. The threads in Table 14.9 were picked in a structural way to guarantee that the less traveled edges (those caused by cancel keystrokes) are traversed.

Table 14.9 Thread/Transition Incidence

Input Events	x1	x2	x3	x4	x5	x6	x7	x8	x9	x10	x11	1	2	3	4	5	6
1234	x	x	x	x	x						x						
12351234	x	x	x	x	x	x							x	x			
C1234	x	x	x	x	x		x			x			x	x			
1C12C1234	x	x	x	x	x			x	x	x			x		x	x	
123C1C1C	x	x	x					x		x	x		x		x		x

14.5 Functional Strategies for Thread Testing

The finite state machine-based approaches to thread identification are clearly useful, but what if no behavioral model exists for a system to be tested? The testing craftsperson has two choices: develop a behavioral model or resort to the system-level analogs of functional testing. Recall that when functional test cases are identified, we use information from the input and output spaces as well as the function itself. We describe functional threads here in terms of coverage metrics that are derived from three of the basis concepts (events, ports, and data).

14.5.1 Event-Based Thread Testing

Consider the space of port input events. Five port input thread coverage metrics are of interest. Attaining these levels of system test coverage requires a set of threads such that:

PI1: Each port input event occurs

PI2: Common sequences of port input events occur

PI3: Each port input event occurs in every relevant data context

PI4: For a given context, all inappropriate input events occur

PI5: For a given context, all possible input events occur

The PI1 metric is a bare minimum and is inadequate for most systems. PI2 coverage is the most common, and it corresponds to the intuitive view of system testing because it deals with normal use. It is difficult to quantify, however. What is a common sequence of input events? What is an uncommon one?

The last three metrics are defined in terms of a context. The best view of a context is that it is a point of event quiescence. In the SATM system, screen displays occur at the points of event quiescence. The PI3 metric deals with context-sensitive port input events. These are physical input events that have logical meanings determined by the context within which they occur. In the SATM system, for example, a keystroke on the B1 function button occurs in five separate contexts (screens displayed) and has three different meanings. The key to this metric is that it is driven by an event in all of its contexts. The PI4 and PI5 metrics are converses: they start with a context and seek a variety of events. The PI4 metric is often used on an informal basis by testers who try to break a system. At a given context, they want to supply unanticipated input events just to see what happens. In the SATM system, for example, what happens if a function button is depressed during the PIN entry stage? The appropriate events are the digit and cancel keystrokes. The inappropriate input events are the keystrokes on the B1, B2, and B3 buttons.

This is partially a specification problem: we are discussing the difference between prescribed behavior (things that should happen) and proscribed behavior (things that should not happen). Most requirements specifications have a hard time only describing prescribed behavior; it is usually testers who find proscribed behavior. The designer who maintains my local ATM system told me that once someone inserted a fish sandwich in the deposit envelope slot. (Apparently they thought it was a waste receptacle.) At any rate, no one at the bank ever anticipated insertion of a fish sandwich as a port input event. The PI4 and PI5 metrics are usually very effective, but they raise one curious difficulty. How does the tester know what the expected response should be to a proscribed input? Are they simply ignored? Should there be an output warning message? Usually, this is left to the tester's intuition. If time permits, this is a powerful point of feedback to requirements specification. It is also a highly desirable focus for either rapid prototyping or executable specifications.

We can also define two coverage metrics based on port output events:

PO1: Each port output event occurs

PO2: Each port output event occurs for each cause

PO1 coverage is an acceptable minimum. It is particularly effective when a system has a rich variety of output messages for error conditions. (The SATM system does not.) PO2 coverage is a good goal, but it is hard to quantify; we will revisit this in Chapter 15 when we examine thread interaction. For now, note that PO2 coverage refers to threads that interact with respect to a port output event. Usually, a given output event only has a small number of causes. In the SATM system, screen 10 might be displayed for three reasons: the terminal might be out of cash, it may be impossible to make a connection with the central bank to get the account balance, or the withdrawal door might be jammed. In practice, some of the most difficult faults found in field trouble reports are those in which an output occurs for an unsuspected cause. Here is one example: My local ATM system (not the SATM) has a screen that informs me "Your daily withdrawal limit has been reached." This screen should occur when I attempt to withdraw more than $300 in one day. Upon seeing this screen, I used to assume that my wife had made a major withdrawal (thread interaction), so I requested a lesser amount. I found out that the ATM also produces this screen when the amount of cash in the dispenser is low. Instead of providing a lot of cash to the first users, the central bank prefers to provide less cash to more users.

14.5.2 Port-Based Thread Testing

Port-based testing is a useful complement to event-based testing. With port-based testing, we ask, for each port, what events can occur at that port. We then seek threads that exercise input ports and output ports with respect to the event lists for each port. (This presumes such event lists have been specified; some requirements specification techniques mandate such lists.) Port-based testing is particularly useful for systems in which the port devices come from external suppliers. The main reason for port-based testing can be seen in the E/R model of the basis constructs (Figure 14.1). The many-to-many relationship between devices and events should be exercised in both directions. Event-based testing covers the one-to-many relationship from events to ports, and conversely, port-based testing covers the one-to-many relationship from ports to events. The SATM system fails us at this point — no SATM event occurs at more than one port.

14.5.3 Data-Based Thread Testing

Port- and event-based testing work well for systems that are primarily event driven. Such systems are sometimes called reactive systems because they react to stimuli (port input events), and often the reaction is in the form of port output events. Reactive systems have two important characteristics: they are long running (as opposed to the short burst of computation we see in a payroll program) and they maintain a relationship with their environment. Typically, event-driven, reactive systems do not have a very interesting data model (as we see with the SATM system), so data model-based threads are not particularly useful. So, what about conventional systems that are data driven? These systems, described as "static" in Topper (1993), are transformational (instead of reactive); they support transactions on a database. When these systems are specified, the E/R model is dominant and is therefore a fertile source of system testing threads. To attach our discussion to something familiar, we use the E/R model of a simple library system. See Figure 14.8 from Topper (1993).

Here are some typical transactions in the library system:

1. Add a book to the library.
2. Delete a book from the library.
3. Add a borrower to the library.
4. Delete a borrower from the library.
5. Loan a book to a borrower.
6. Process the return of a book from a borrower.

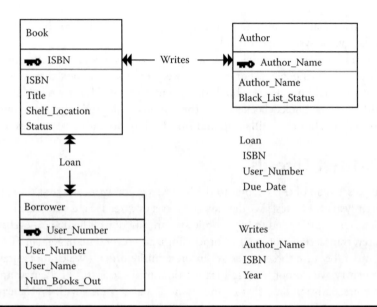

Figure 14.8   E/R model of a library.

These transactions are all mainline threads; in fact, they represent families of threads. For example, suppose the book loan transaction is attempted for a borrower whose current number of checked-out books is at the lending limit (a nice boundary value example). We might also try to return a book that was never owned by the library. Here is one more: suppose we delete a borrower that has some unreturned books. All are interesting threads to test, and all are at the system level.

We can identify each of these examples, and many more, by close attention to the information in the entity/relationship model. As we did with event-based testing, we describe sets of threads in terms of data-based coverage metrics. These refer to relationships for an important reason. Information in relationships is generally populated by system-level threads, whereas that in the entities is usually handled at the unit level. (When E/R modeling is the starting point of object-oriented analysis, this is enforced by encapsulation.)

> DM1: Exercise the cardinality of every relationship
> DM2: Exercise the participation of every relationship
> DM3: Exercise the functional dependencies among relationships

Cardinality refers to the four possibilities of relationship that we discussed in Chapter 3: one-to-one, one-to-many, many-to-one, and many-to-many. In the library example, both the loan and the writes relationships are many-to-many, meaning that one author can write many books, and one book can have many authors; and that one book can be loaned to many borrowers (in sequence), and one borrower can borrow many books. Each of these possibilities results in a useful system testing thread.

Participation refers to whether every instance of an entity participates in a relationship. In the writes relationship, both the book and the author entities have mandatory participation (we cannot have a book with no authors, or an author of no books). In some modeling techniques, participation is expressed in terms of numerical limits; the author entity, for example, might be expressed as "at least 1 and at most 12." When such information is available, it leads directly to obvious boundary value system test threads.

Sometimes, transactions determine explicit logical connections among relationships; these are known as functional dependencies. For example, we cannot loan a book that is not possessed by the library, and we would not delete a book that is out on loan. Also, we would not delete a borrower who still has some books checked out. These kinds of dependencies are reduced when the database is normalized, but they still exist, and they lead to interesting system test threads.

14.6 SATM Test Threads

If we apply the discussion of this chapter to the SATM system, we get a set of threads that constitutes a thorough system-level test. We develop such a set of threads here in terms of an overall state model in which states correspond to key atomic system functions. The macro-level states are card entry, PIN entry, transaction request (and processing), and session management. The stated order is the testing order, because these stages are in prerequisite order. (We cannot enter a PIN until successful card entry, we cannot request a transaction until successful PIN entry, and so on.) We also need some precondition data that defines some actual accounts with PANs, expected PINs, and account balances. These are given in Table 14.10. Two less obvious preconditions are that the ATM terminal is initially displaying screen 1 and the total cash available to the withdrawal dispenser is $500 (in $10 notes).

Table 14.10   SATM Test Data

PAN	Expected PIN	Checking Balance	Savings Balance
100	1234	$1000.00	$800.00
200	4567	$100.00	$90.00
300	6789	$25.00	$20.00

We will express threads in tables in which pairs of rows correspond to port inputs and expected port outputs at each of the four major stages. We start with three basic threads, one for each transaction type (balance inquiry, deposit, and withdrawal).

	Card Entry (PAN)	PIN Entry	Transaction Request	Session Management
Thread 1 (Balance)				
Port inputs	100	1234	B1, B1	B2
Port outputs	Screen 2	Screen 5	Screen 6, screen 14, $1000.00	Screen 15, eject card, screen 1

In thread 1, a valid card with PAN = 100 is entered, which causes screen 2 to be displayed. The PIN digits 1234 are entered, and because they match the expected PIN for the PAN, screen 5 inviting a transaction selection is displayed. When button B1 is touched the first time (requesting a balance inquiry), screen 6 asks which account is displayed. When B1 is pressed the second time (checking), screen 14 is displayed and the checking account balance ($1000.00) is printed on the receipt. When B2 is pushed, screen 15 is displayed, the receipt is printed, the ATM card is ejected, and then screen 1 is displayed.

Thread 2 is a deposit to checking — same PAN and PIN, but B2 is touched when screen 5 is displayed and B1 is touched when screen 6 is displayed. The amount 25.00 is entered when screen 7 is displayed, and then screen 13 is displayed. The deposit door opens and the deposit envelope is placed in the deposit slot. Screen 14 is displayed, and when B2 is pushed, screen 15 is displayed, the receipt showing the new checking account balance of $1025.00 is printed, the ATM card is ejected, and then screen 1 is displayed.

	Card Entry (PAN)	PIN Entry	Transaction Request	Session Management
Thread 2 (Deposit)				
Port inputs	100	1234	B2, B1, 25.00	B2
			Insert envelope	
Port outputs	Screen 2	Screen 5	Screen 6, screen 7, screen 13	Screen 15, eject card, screen 1
			Deposit door opens	
			Screen 14	
			$1025.00	

Thread 3 is a withdrawal from savings — again the same PAN and PIN, but B3 is touched when screen 5 is displayed, and B2 is touched when screen 6 is displayed. The amount $30.00 is entered when screen 7 is displayed, and then screen 11 is displayed. The withdrawal door opens and three $10 notes are dispensed. Screen 14 is displayed, and when B2 is pushed, screen 15 is displayed, the receipt showing the new savings account balance of $770.00 is printed, the ATM card is ejected, and then screen 1 is displayed.

	Card Entry (PAN)	PIN Entry	Transaction Request	Session Management
Thread 3 (Withdrawal)				
Port inputs	100	1234	B3, B2, 30.00	B2
Port outputs	Screen 2	Screen 5	Screen 6, screen 7, screen 11, withdrawal	Screen 15, eject card, screen 1
			Door opens, three $10 notes Screen 14	
			$770.00	

A few of these detailed descriptions are needed to show the pattern; the remaining threads are described in terms of input and output events that are the objective of the test thread.

Thread 4 is the shortest thread in the SATM system; it consists of an invalid card, which is immediately rejected.

Thread 4	Card Entry (PAN)	PIN Entry	Transaction Request	Session Management
Port inputs	400			
Port outputs	Eject card			
	Screen 1			

Following the macro-states along thread 1, we next perform variations on PIN entry. We get four new threads from Table 14.9, which yield edge coverage in the PIN entry finite state machines.

	Card Entry (PAN)	PIN Entry	Transaction Request	Session Management
Thread 5 (Balance)				
Port inputs	100	12351234	As in thread 1	
Port outputs	Screen 2	Screens 3, 2, 5		
Thread 6 (Balance)				
Port inputs	100	C1234	As in thread 1	
Port outputs	Screen 2	Screens 3, 2, 5		
Thread 7 (Balance)				
Port inputs	100	1C12C1234	As in thread 1	
Port outputs	Screen 2	Screens 3, 2, 3, 2, 5		
Thread 8 (Balance)				
Port inputs	100	123C1C1C		
Port outputs	Screen 2	Screens 3, 2, 3, 2, 4, 1		

Moving to the transaction request stage, variations exist with respect to the type of transaction (balance, deposit, or withdraw), the account (checking or savings), and the amount requested. Threads 1, 2, and 3 cover the type and account variations, so we focus on the amount-driven threads. Thread 9 rejects the attempt to withdraw an amount not in $10 increments, thread 10 rejects the attempt to withdraw more than the account balance, and thread 11 rejects the attempt to withdraw more cash than the dispenser contains.

	Card Entry (PAN)	PIN Entry	Transaction Request	Session Management
Thread 9 (Withdrawal)				
Port inputs	100	1234	B3, B2, 15.00 Cancel	B2
Port outputs	Screen 2	Screen 5	Screens 6, 7, 9, 7	Screen 15, eject card, screen 1
Thread 10 (Withdrawal)				
Port inputs	300	6789	B3, B2, 50.00 Cancel	B2
Port outputs	Screen 2	Screen 5	Screens 6, 7, 8	Screen 15, eject card, screen 1
Thread 11 (Withdrawal)				
Port inputs	100	1234	B3, B2, 510.00 Cancel	B2
Port outputs	Screen 2	Screen 5	Screens 6, 7, 10	Screen 15, eject card, screen 1

Having exercised the transaction processing portion, we proceed to the session management stage, where we test the multiple transaction option.

Thread 12 (Balance)	Card Entry (PAN)	PIN Entry	Transaction Request	Session Management
Port inputs	100	1234	B1, B1	B1, cancel
Port outputs	Screen 2	Screen 5	Screen 6, screen 14 $1000.00	Screen 15, screen 5 screen 15, eject card, screen 1

At this point, the threads provide coverage of all output screens except for screen 12, which informs the user that deposits cannot be processed. Causing this condition is problematic (perhaps we should place a fish sandwich in the deposit envelope slot). This is an example of a thread selected by a precondition that is a hardware failure. We simply give it a thread name here: thread 13. Next, we develop threads 14 through 22 to exercise context-sensitive input events. They are shown in Table 14.11; notice that some of the first 13 threads exercise context sensitivity.

These 22 threads comprise a reasonable test of the portion of the SATM system that we have specified. Of course, certain aspects are untested; one good example involves the balance of an account. Consider two threads — one that deposits $40 to an account and a second that withdraws $80 — and suppose that the balance obtained from the central bank at the card entry stage

Table 14.11 Threads for Context-Sensitive Input Events

Thread	Keystroke	Screen	Logical Meaning
6	Cancel	2	PIN entry error
14	Cancel	5	Transaction selection error
15	Cancel	6	Account selection error
16	Cancel	7	Amount selection error
17	Cancel	8	Amount selection error
18	Cancel	13	Deposit envelope not ready
1	B1	5	Balance
1	B1	6	Checking
19	B1	10	Yes (a nonwithdrawal transaction)
20	B1	12	Yes (a nondeposit transaction)
12	B1	14	Yes (another transaction)
2	B2	5	Deposit
3	B2	6	Savings
21	B2	10	No (no additional transaction)
22	B2	12	No (no additional transaction)
1	B2	14	No (no additional transaction)

is $50. Two possibilities exist: one is to use the central bank balance, record all transactions, and then resolve these when the daily posting occurs. The other is to maintain a running local balance, which is what would be shown on a balance inquiry transaction. If the central bank balance is used, the withdrawal transaction is rejected, but if the local balance is used, it is processed. This detail was not addressed in our specification; we will revisit this when we discuss thread interaction in Chapter 15.

Another prominent untested portion of the SATM system is the amount entry process that occurs in screens 7 and 8. The possibility of a cancel keystroke at any point during amount entry produces a multiplicity greater than that of PIN entry. A more subtle (and therefore more interesting) test for amount entry can be used. What actually happens when we enter an amount? To be specific, suppose we wish to enter $40.00. We expect an echo after each digit keystroke, but in which position does the echo occur? Two obvious solutions are available: always require six digits to be entered (so we would enter "004000") or use the high-order digits first and shift left as successive digits are entered, as shown in Figure 14.9.

Most ATM systems use the shift approach, and this raises a subtle point: How does the ATM system know when all amount digits have been entered? The ATM system clearly cannot predict that the deposit amount is $40.00 instead of $400.00 or $4000.00 because no "enter" key is used to signify when the last digit has been entered. The reason for this digression is that this is a good example of the kind of detail discovered by testers that is often missing from a requirements specification. (Such details would likely be found with either rapid prototyping or using an executable specification.)

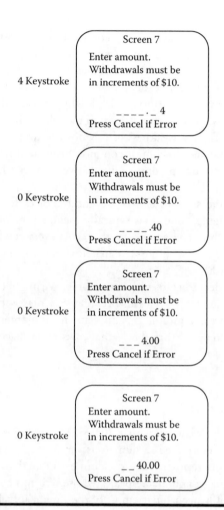

Figure 14.9 Digit echoes with left shifts.

14.7 System Testing Guidelines

If we disallow compound sessions (more than one transaction) and if we disregard the multiplicity due to amount entry possibilities, there are 435 distinct threads per valid account in the SATM system. Factor in the effects of compound sessions and the amount entry possibilities, and tens of thousands of threads are possible for the SATM system. We end this chapter with three strategies to deal with the thread explosion problem.

14.7.1 Pseudostructural System Testing

When we studied unit testing, we saw that the combination of functional and structural testing yields a desirable cross-check. We have something similar with system-level threads: we defined 10 system-level, functional coverage metrics in Section 14.5 and two graph–based metrics (node and edge coverage) in Section 14.4. We can use the graph–based metrics as a cross-check on the functional threads in much the same way that we used DD-Paths at the unit level to identify gaps and redundancies in functional test cases. We can only claim pseudostructural testing (Jorgensen, 1994) because the node and edge coverage metrics are defined in terms of a control model of a system and are not derived directly from the system implementation. (Recall that we started out with a concern over the distinction between reality and models of reality.) In general, behavioral models are only approximations of a system's reality, which is why we could decompose our models down to several levels of detail. If we made a true structural model, its size and complexity would make it too cumbersome to use. The big weakness of pseudostructural metrics is that the underlying model may be a poor choice. The three most common behavioral models (decision tables, finite state machines, and Petri nets) are appropriate, respectively, to transformational, interactive, and concurrent systems.

Decision tables and finite state machines are good choices for ASF testing. If an ASF is described using a decision table, conditions typically include port input events, and actions are port output events. We can then devise test cases that cover every condition, every action, or, most completely, every rule. As we saw for finite state machine models, test cases can cover every state, every transition, or every path.

Thread testing based on decision tables is cumbersome. We might describe threads as sequences of rules from different decision tables, but this becomes very messy to track in terms of coverage. We need finite state machines as a minimum, and if any form of interaction occurs, Petri nets are a better choice. There, we can devise thread tests that cover every place, every transition, and every sequence of transitions.

14.7.2 Operational Profiles

In its most general form, Zipf's law holds that 80% of the activities occur in 20% of the space. Activities and space can be interpreted in numerous ways: people with messy desks hardly ever use most of their desktop clutter; programmers seldom use more than 20% of the features of their favorite programming language; and Shakespeare (whose writings contain an enormous vocabulary) uses a small fraction of his vocabulary most of the time. Zipf's law applies to software (and testing) in several ways. The most useful interpretation for testers is that the space consists of all possible threads, and activities are thread executions (or traversals). Thus, for a system with many threads, 80% of the execution traverses only 20% of the threads.

Recall that a failure occurs when a fault is executed. The whole idea of testing is to execute test cases such that when a failure occurs, the presence of a fault is revealed. We can make an important distinction: the distribution of faults in a system is only indirectly related to the reliability of the system. The simplest view of system reliability is the probability that no failure occurs during a specific time interval. (Notice that no mention is even made of faults, the number of faults, or fault density.) If the only faults are "in the corners" on threads that are seldom traversed, the overall reliability is higher than if the same number of faults were on "high-traffic" threads. The idea of operational profiles is to determine the execution frequencies of various threads and to use this information to select threads for system testing. Particularly when test time is limited (usually), operational profiles maximize the probability of finding faults by inducing failures in the most frequently traversed threads.

One way to determine the operational profile of a system is to use a decision tree. This works particularly well when system behavior is modeled in hierarchic state machines, as we did with the SATM system. For any state, we find (or estimate) the probability of each outgoing transition (the sum of these must be 1). When a state is decomposed into a lower level, the probabilities at

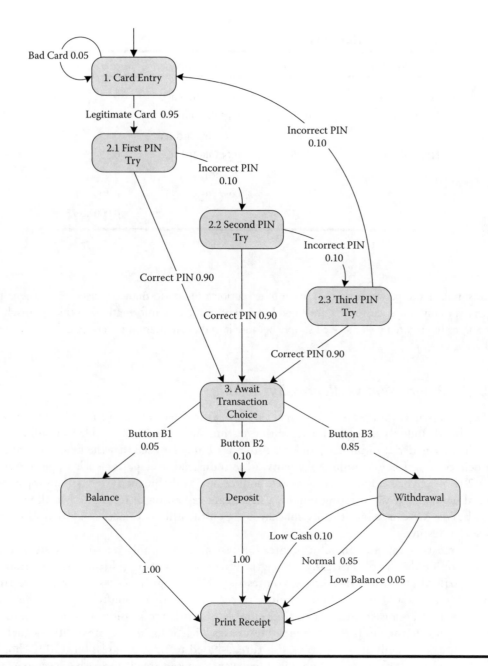

Figure 14.10 Transition probabilities for the SATM system.

the lower level become "split edges" at the upper level. Figure 14.10 shows the result of this with hypothetical transition probabilities. Given the transition probabilities, the overall probability of a thread is simply the product of the transition probabilities along the thread. Table 14.12 shows this calculation for the most and least frequent threads.

Operational profiles provide a feeling for the traffic mix of a delivered system. This is helpful for reasons other than only optimizing system testing. These profiles can also be used in conjunction

Table 14.12   Thread Probabilities

Common Thread	Probabilities	Rare Thread	Probabilities
Legitimate card	0.95	Legitimate card	0.95
PIN OK 1st try	0.90	Bad PIN 1st try	0.10
Withdraw	0.85	Bad PIN 2nd try	0.10
Normal	0.85	PIN OK 3rd try	0.90
		Withdraw	0.85
		Low cash	0.10
	0.6177375		0.00072675

with simulators to get an early indication of execution time performance and system transaction capacity. Many times, customers are a good source of traffic mix information, so this approach to system testing is often well received simply because it makes an attempt to replicate the reality of a delivered system.

14.7.3   Progression vs. Regression Testing

When we discussed software development life cycles in Chapter 12, we mentioned that the use of builds induces the need for regression testing. When build 2 is added to build 1, we test the new material in build 2, and we also retest build 1 to see that the new material has no deleterious effect on build 1 contents. (The industrial average for such ripple effect is that 20% of changes to an existing system induce new faults in the system.) If a project has several builds, regression testing implies a significant repetition of testing, especially for the early builds. We can reduce this by concentrating on the difference between progression and regression testing.

The most common approach to regression testing is to simply repeat the system tests. We can refine this (and drastically reduce the effort) by choosing test threads with respect to the goals of regression and progression testing. With progression testing, we are testing new territory, so we expect a higher failure rate than with regression testing. Another difference is that because we expect to find more faults with progression testing, we need to be able to locate the faults. This requires test cases with a diagnostic capability — that is, tests that can fail only in a few ways. For thread-based testing, progression testing should use shorter threads that can fail only in a few ways. These threads might be ordered as we did with the SATM thread test set, such that longer threads are built up from shorter (and previously tested) threads.

We have lower expectations of failure with regression testing, and we are less concerned with fault isolation. Taken together, this means regression testing should use longer threads, ones that can fail in several ways. If we think in terms of coverage, both progression and regression testing will have thorough coverage, but the density is different. State and transition coverage matrices (like Table 14.8 and Table 14.9) will be sparse for progression testing threads and dense for regression testing threads. This is somewhat antithetical to the use of operational profiles. As a rule, "good" regression testing threads will have low operational frequencies, and progression testing threads will have high operational frequencies.

14.8 ASF Testing Example

Please refer to the integration testing version of NextDate pseudocode in Chapter 13. The first step in ASF testing is to identify the system level input and output events; these are shown in Table 14.13 and Table 14.14.

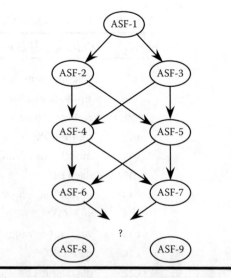

Figure 14.11   ASF Sequences in NextDate.

The next step is to identify a trial set of atomic system functions (ASFs). Table 14.15 contains a trial set.

At first these seem reasonable, but remember we would like to concatenate ASFs into longer threads. This set does not lend itself to convenient concatenation. The awkward nature of this set of ASFs is shown in Figure 14.11. The ASF graph shows all the ways valid months, days, and years can be entered, but the transition to ASF-8 (or to ASF-9) depends on the history of previous ASFs. Because FSMs have no memory, these transitions are necessarily undefined.

Table 14.16 contains a second set of ASFs. Now each ASF is the entry of a triple (month, day, year). The first few make one mistake at a time. Would we really need the last four (two or three mistakes at a time)? Probably not. That kind of testing should have been done at the unit level.

Table 14.13   NextDate Input Events

Event	Input Event Description	Statement Numbers
e0	Start program event	1
e1	Enter a valid month	67
e2	Enter an invalid month	67
e3	Enter a valid day	69
e4	Enter an invalid day	69
e5	Enter a valid year	71
e6	Enter an invalid year	71

Table 14.14   NextDate Output Events

Event	Output Event Description	Statement Numbers
e7	Welcome message	2
e8	Print today's date	4
e9	Print tomorrow's date	6
e10	"month OK"	39
e11	"month out of range"	41
e12	"day OK"	47
e13	"day out of range"	49
e14	"year OK"	54
e15	"year out of range"	56
e16	"date OK"	60
e17	"please enter a valid date"	62
e18	"enter a month"	66
e19	"enter a day"	68
e20	"enter a year"	70
e21	"Day is month, day, year"	89

Table 14.15   First Attempt at ASFs for NextDate

Atomic System Function	Inputs	Outputs
ASF-1 start program	e0	e7
ASF-2 enter a valid month	e1	e10
ASF-3 enter an invalid month	e2	e11
ASF-4 enter a valid day	e3	e12
ASF-5 enter an invalid day	e4	e13
ASF-6 enter a valid year	e5	e14
ASF-7 enter an invalid year	e6	e15
ASF-8 print for valid input		
ASF-9 print for invalid input		

Table 14.16 Second Attempt at ASFs for NextDate

Atomic System Function	Inputs	Outputs
ASF-1 start program	e0	e7
ASF-2 enter a date with an invalid month, rest OK	e2, e3, e5	e11, e12, e14, e17
ASF-3 enter a date with an invalid day, rest OK	e1, e4, e5	e10, e13, e14, e17
ASF-4 enter a date with an invalid year, rest OK	e1, e3, e6	e10, e12, e15, e17
ASF-5 enter a date with valid month, day, and year	e1, e3, e5	e10, e12, e14, e16, e21
ASF-6 enter a date with valid month, rest invalid		
ASF-7 enter a date with valid day, rest invalid		
ASF-8 enter a date with valid year, rest invalid		
ASF-9 enter a date with invalid month, day, year		

References

Jorgensen, P.C., An operational common denominator to the structured real-time methods, *Proceedings of the Fifth Structured Techniques Association (STA-5) Conference*, Chicago, May 11, 1989.

Jorgensen, P.C., System testing with pseudo-structures, *American Programmer*, Vol. 7, No. 4, April 1994, pp. 29–34.

Topper, A. et al., *Structured Methods: Merging Models, Techniques, and CASE*, McGraw-Hill, New York, 1993.

Exercises

1. One of the problems of system testing, particularly interactive systems, is to anticipate all the strange things the user might do. What happens in the SATM system if a customer enters three digits of a PIN and then leaves?

2. To remain "in control" of abnormal user behavior (the behavior is abnormal, not the user), the SATM system might introduce a timer with a 30-second time-out. When no port input event occurs for 30 seconds, the SATM system asks if the user needs more time. The user can answer yes or no. Devise a new screen and identify port events that would implement such a time-out event.

3. Suppose you add the time-out feature described in exercise 2 to the SATM system. What regression testing would you perform?

4. Make an additional refinement to the PIN try finite state machine (Figure 14.6) to implement your time-out mechanism from exercise 2, then revise the thread test case in Table 14.3.

5. The text asserts that "the B1 function button occurs in five separate contexts (screens displayed) and has three different meanings." Examine the 15 screens (points of event quiescence) and decide whether a B1 keystroke has three or five different logical meanings.

6. Does it make sense to use test coverage metrics in conjunction with operational profiles? Discuss.

7. Fill in the input and output events for the last four ASFs in Table 14.16.

8. If we can add a cost penalty to the threads in operational profiles, we have the basis for risk-based testing. Make up cost penalties for the threads in Figure 14.10, then see which threads are high risk. (Use a spreadsheet!)

Chapter 15

Interaction Testing

Faults and failures due to interaction are the bane of testers. Their subtleties make them difficult to recognize and even more difficult to reveal by testing. These are deep faults, ones that remain in a system even after extensive thread testing. Unfortunately, faults of interaction most frequently occur as failures in delivered systems that have been in use for some time. Typically, they have a very low probability of execution, and they occur only after a large number of threads has been executed. Most of this chapter is devoted to describing forms of interaction, not to testing them. As such, it is really more concerned with requirements specification than with testing. The connection is important: knowing how to specify interactions is the first step in detecting and testing for them. This chapter is also a somewhat philosophical and mildly mathematical discussion of faults and failures of interaction; we cannot hope to test something if we do not understand it. We begin with an important addition to our five basic constructs and use this to develop a taxonomy of types of interaction. Next we develop a simple extension to conventional Petri nets that reflects the basic constructs, and then we illustrate the whole discussion with the simple automated teller machine (SATM) and Saturn windshield wiper systems, and sometimes with examples from telephone systems. We conclude by applying the taxonomy to an important application type: client/server systems.

15.1 Context of Interaction

Part of the difficulty of specifying and testing interactions is that they are so common. Think of all the things that interact in everyday life: people, automobile drivers, regulations, chemical compounds, and abstractions, to name just a few. We are concerned with interactions in software-controlled systems (particularly the unexpected ones), so we start by restricting our discussion to interactions among our basic system constructs: actions, data, events, ports, and threads.

One way to establish a context for interaction is to view it as a relationship among the five constructs. If we did this, we would find that the relation InteractsWith is a reflexive relationship on each entity (data interact with data, actions with other actions, and so on). It also is a binary relationship between data and events, data and threads, and events and threads. The data modeling approach is not a dead end, however. Whenever a data model contains such pervasive relationships, that is a clue that an important entity is missing. If we add some tangible reality to our fairly abstract constructs, we get a more useful framework for our study of interaction. The missing element is location, and location has two components: time and position. Data modeling provides another choice: we can treat location as a sixth basic entity or as an attribute of the other five. We choose the attribute approach here.

What does it mean for location (time and position) to be an attribute of any of the five basic constructs? This is really a shortcoming of nearly all requirements, specification notations, and techniques. (This is probably also the reason that interactions are seldom recognized and tested.) Information about location is usually created when a system is implemented. Sometimes location is mandated as a requirement — when this happens, the requirement is actually a forced implementation choice. We first clarify the meaning of the attributes of location: time and position.

We can take two views of time: as an instant or as an interval. The instantaneous view lets us describe when something happens — it is a point on the time axis. The duration view is an interval on the time axis. When we think about durations, we usually are interested in the length of the time interval, not the endpoints (the start and finish times). Both views are useful. Because threads execute, they have duration, and they also have points in time when they execute. Similar observations apply to events. Often, events have very short durations, and this is problematic if the duration is so short that the event is not recognized by the system.

The position aspect is easier. We could take a very tangible, physical view of position and describe it in terms of some coordinate system. Position can be a three-dimensional Cartesian coordinate system with respect to some origin, or it could be a longitude-latitude-elevation geographic point. For most systems, it is more helpful to slightly abstract position into processor residence. Taken together, time and position tell the tester when and where something happens, and this is essential to understanding interactions.

Before we develop our taxonomy, we need some ground rules about threads and processors. For now, a processor is something that executes threads or a device where events occur.

1. Because threads execute, they have a strictly positive time duration. We usually speak of the execution time of a thread, but we might also be interested in when thread execution begins. Actions are degenerate cases of threads; therefore, actions also have durations.
2. In a single processor, two threads cannot execute simultaneously. This resembles a fundamental precept of physics: no two bodies may occupy the same space at the same time. Sometimes threads appear to be simultaneous, as in time-sharing on a single processor; in fact, time-shared threads are interleaved. Even though threads cannot execute simultaneously on a single processor, events can be simultaneous. (This is really problematic for testers.)
3. Events have a strictly positive time duration. When we consider events to be actions that execute on port devices, this reduces to the first ground rule.
4. Two (or more) input events can occur simultaneously, but an event cannot occur simultaneously in two (or more) processors. This is immediately clear if we consider port devices to be separate processors.
5. In a single processor, two output events cannot begin simultaneously. This is a direct consequence of output events being caused by thread executions. We need both the instantaneous and duration views of time to fully explain this ground rule. Suppose two output events are such that the duration of one is much greater than the duration of the other. The durations may overlap (because they occur on separate devices), but the start times cannot be identical, as shown in Figure 15.1. An example of this occurs in the SATM system,

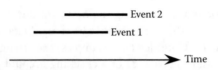

Figure 15.1 Overlapping events.

when a thread causes screen 15 to be displayed and then ejects the ATM card. The screen is still displayed when the card eject event occurs. (This may be a fine distinction; we could also say that port devices are separate processors, and that port output events are really a form of interprocessor communication.)

6. A thread cannot span more than one processor. This convention helps in the definition of threads. By confining a thread to a single processor, we create a natural endpoint for threads; this also results in more simple threads instead of fewer complex threads. In a multiprocessing setting, this choice also results in another form of quiescence — transprocessor quiescence.

Taken together, these six ground rules force what we might call sane behavior onto the interactions in the taxonomy we define in Section 15.2.

15.2 A Taxonomy of Interactions

The two aspects of location, time and position, form the starting point of a useful taxonomy of interaction. Certain interactions are completely independent of time; for example, two data items that interact exhibit their interaction regardless of time. Certain time-dependent interactions also occur, such as when something is a prerequisite for something else. We will refer to time-independent interactions as static and time-dependent interactions as dynamic. We can refine the static/dynamic dichotomy with the distinction between single and multiple processors. These two considerations yield a two-dimensional plane (as shown in Figure 15.2) with four basic types of interactions:

Static interactions in a single processor
Static interactions in multiple processors
Dynamic interactions in a single processor
Dynamic interactions in multiple processors

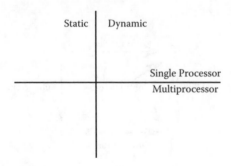

Figure 15.2 Types of interactions.

We next refine these basic four types using the notion of duration. Threads and events have durations (because they execute); thus, they cannot be static. Data, on the other hand, is static, but we need to be careful here. Consider two examples, the triangle type that corresponds to the triplet (5, 5, 5) of sides, and the balance of a checking account. The triangle type is always equilateral — time will never change geometry — but the balance of a bank account is likely to change in time. If it does, the change is due to the execution of some thread, and this will be a key consideration.

15.2.1 Static Interactions in a Single Processor

Of the five basic constructs, only two have no duration — ports and data. Ports are physical devices; therefore, we can view them as separate processors and thereby simplify our discussion. Port devices interact in physical ways, such as space and power consumption, but this is usually not important to testers. Data items interact in logical ways (as opposed to physical), and this is important to testers. In an informal way, we often speak of corrupt data and of maintaining the integrity of a database. We sometimes get a bit more precise and speak of incompatible or even inconsistent data. We can be very specific if we borrow some terms from Aristotle. (We finally have a chance to use the propositional logic discussed in Chapter 3.) In the following definitions, let p and q be propositions about data items. As examples, we might take p and q to be:

p: AccountBalance = $10.00
q: Sales < $1800.00

Definition
Propositions p and q are:

Contraries if they cannot both be true
Subcontraries if they cannot both be false
Contradictories if exactly one is true
q is a *subaltern* of p if the truth of p guarantees the truth of q

These relationships are known to logicians as the square of opposition, which is shown in Figure 15.3, where p, q, r, and s are all propositions.

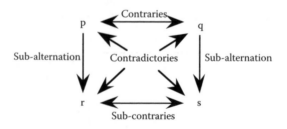

Figure 15.3 The square of opposition.

Aristotelian logic seems arcane for software testers, but here are some situations that are exactly characterized by data interactions in the square of opposition:

> When the precondition for a thread is a conjunction of data propositions, contrary or contradictory data values will prevent thread execution.
> Context-sensitive port input events usually involve contradictory (or at least contrary) data.
> Case statement clauses are (or should be) contradictories.
> Rules in a decision table are (or should be) contradictories.

Static interactions in a single processor are exactly analogous to combinatorial circuits; they are also well represented by decision tables and unmarked event-driven Petri nets (EDPNs). Features in telephone systems are good examples of interaction (Zave, 1993). One example is the logical conflict between calling party identification service and unlisted directory numbers. With calling party identification, the directory number of the source of a telephone call is provided to the called party. A conflict occurs when a party with an unlisted directory number makes a call to a party with calling party identification. Which takes precedence — the calling party's desire for privacy or the called party's right to know who is placing an incoming call? These two features are contraries: they cannot both be satisfied, but they could both be waived.

15.2.2 *Static Interactions in Multiple Processors*

The location of data helps resolve the contraries in the telephone system examples. We would expect that the data for call waiting and data line conditioning are located in the same processor because both refer to the same subscriber line. Thus, the software that controls calls for that line could check for contrary line data. This is an unreasonable expectation for the calling party identification problem, however. Suppose the calling party is a line in an office remote from the office that serves the line with calling party identification. Because these data are in separate locations (processors), neither knows about the other; so their contrary nature can only be detected when they are connected by a thread. To be very precise, we can say that the contrary relationship exists as a static interaction across multiple processors, and it becomes a failure when executing threads in the two telephone offices (processors) interact.

Call forwarding provides a better example of a static, distributed interaction. Suppose we have three telephone subscribers in separate cities:

> Subscriber A is in Grand Rapids, Michigan.
> Subscriber B is in Phoenix, Arizona.
> Subscriber C is in Baltimore, Maryland.

We further suppose that each subscriber has call forwarding service, and that calls are forwarded as follows: calls to A are forwarded to B, calls to B are forwarded to C, and calls to C are forwarded to A.

These call forwarding data are contrary — they cannot all be true. Call forwarding data is local to the telephone office that provides the service; it is set by a thread when a subscriber defines a new forwarding destination. This means that none of the offices knows of call forwarding data in the other offices; we have distributed contraries. This is a fault, but it does not become a failure until someone (other than A, B, or C) places a call to any phone in this call forwarding loop.

Such a call, say to subscriber B, generates a call forwarding thread in B's local telephone office, which results in a call to C's directory number. This generates another thread in C's telephone office, and so on. For now, please note that the existence of the connecting threads moves us out of the static quadrants and into dynamic interactions. The potential failure still exists; it is just in a different part of our taxonomy. (Telephone system avoid this by refusing to forward a call a second time.)

The bottom line is that static interactions are essentially the same, whether they are centralized into a single processor or distributed among multiple processors. (They are harder to detect when they are distributed, however.) Another common form of static interactions occurs with weak relationships and functional dependencies in a database (centralized or distributed). Both of these interactions are forms of subalternation.

15.2.3 Dynamic Interactions in a Single Processor

Interactions in the dynamic quadrants force consideration of the implications of time. Among other things, this means we must expand from the data-only interactions to interactions among data, events, and threads. We also must shift from the strictly declarative relationships in the square of opposition to a more imperative view. The notion of n-connectedness in a directed graph (see Chapter 4) serves perfectly. Figure 15.4 shows the four forms of n-connectedness in a directed graph.

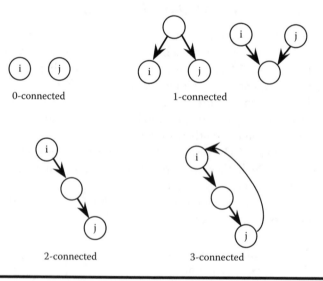

Figure 15.4   Forms of n-connectedness.

Even the data–data interactions exhibit forms of n-connectedness. Data that are logically independent are 0-connected, and subalternates are 2-connected. The other three relationships, contraries, contradictories, and subcontraries, all pertain to 3-connected data, because each of these is a bidirectional relationship.

Six potential pairs of concepts can interact: data–data, data–events, data–threads, events–events, events–threads, and threads–threads. Each of these is further qualified by four degrees of n-connectedness, resulting in 24 elements to our taxonomy for this quadrant. Take some time to think through these interactions. Here are four examples:

1-connected data with data: Occurs when two or more data items are inputs to the same action

2-connected data with data: Occurs when a data item is used in a computation (as in dataflow testing)

3-connected data with data: Occurs when data are deeply related, as in repetition and semaphores

1-connected data with events: Context-sensitive port input events

We do not need to analyze all 24 possibilities because faults of interaction only become failures when threads establish some connection. The faults are latent, and when a thread makes a connection, the latent fault becomes a failure. Threads can only interact in two ways, via events or via data. We will see this more clearly using EDPNs after we make another definition.

Definition

In an EDPN, the *external inputs* are the places with indegree = 0, and the *external outputs* are the places with outdegree = 0.

In the EDPN in Figure 15.5, p1 and p2 are the only external inputs, and p5, p9, and p10 are the only external outputs. Although not shown here, data places that are preconditions and

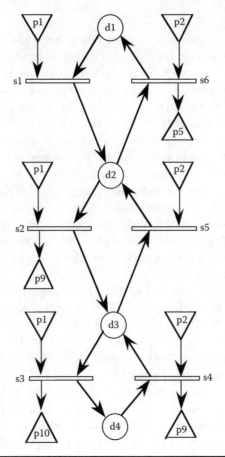

Figure 15.5   External inputs and outputs in an EDPN.

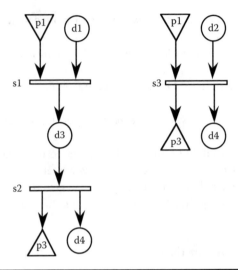

Figure 15.6   Two EDPN threads.

postconditions are external inputs and outputs, respectively. The best description is that the indegrees of external inputs and the outdegrees of external outputs are always 0.

Now we are at a key point: we can represent the interaction among threads by the composition of their EDPNs. We do this as follows: each thread has its own (unique) EDPN, and within each EDPN, the places and transitions have symbolic names. In one sense, these names are local to the thread, but in a larger sense (when they are composed), local names must be resolved into global synonyms. Suppose, for example, that in one SATM thread, a keystroke on the Cancel key is named as port input event p2, and in another thread the same event is called p6. When these two threads are composed, the synonyms must be collapsed onto a single name. (Earlier, we noted that it was good practice to use physical names for port events instead of their logical names; synonym resolution is the reason for this recommendation.) Once synonyms are resolved, the individual threads are drawn as EDPNs. Because threads interact only with respect to their external inputs and outputs, we next identify the sets of external inputs and outputs of each thread. The intersection of these sets contains the events and places at which the composed threads can interact. This process is illustrated in Figure 15.6 and Figure 15.7.

Thread 1 is the sequence <s1, s2>, and thread 2 is the sequence <s3>. The external inputs of these threads are the sets EI1 = {p1, d1} and EI2 = {p1, d2}, and the external outputs of these threads are the sets EO1 = {p3, d4} and EO2 = {p3, d4}. Intersecting these, we get the sets EI = EI1 ∩ EI2 = {p1} and EO = EO1 ∩ EO2 = {p3, d4}. The sets EI and EO contain the external inputs and outputs at which threads 1 and 2 may possibly interact. Notice that the external inputs and outputs of the composed threads are the sets EI1 ∪ EI2 and EO1 ∪ EO2. External events will always be preserved as external, but external data may not be. It is possible for output data of one thread to be input data to another thread. (This happens in the call forwarding loop.)

We can formalize this process into another definition. Let T1 and T2 be two EDPN threads in which synonym places have been resolved, and with external input and output sets EI1, EI2, EO1,

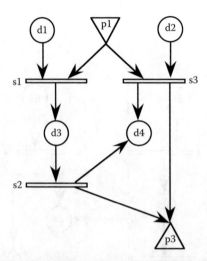

Figure 15.7   Composition of EDPN threads.

and EO2. Furthermore, let T be the composition of threads T1 and T2, where EI = EI1 ∩ EI2 and EO = EO1 ∩ EO2 are the external input and output sets of the composed thread T.

Definition
The threads *T1 and T2* are:

> *0-connected* if EI1 ∩ EI2 = ∅, EO1 ∩ EO2 = ∅, EI1 ∩ EO2 = ∅, and EO1 ∩ EI2 = ∅
> *1-connected* if either EI ≠ ∅ or EO ≠ ∅
> *2-connected* if either EI1 ∩ EO2 ≠ ∅ or EI2 ∩ EO1 ≠ ∅
> *3-connected* if both EI1 ∩ EO2 ≠ ∅ and EI2 ∩ EO1 ≠ ∅

Compare this with the definition of n-connectedness in Chapter 4. There we were concerned with relationships among pairs of nodes; here we are concerned with a relationship among threads. We can eliminate these somewhat overlapping definitions by constructing a rather elaborate directed graph in which nodes are threads from which the external inputs and outputs have been deleted, and edges connect threads according to the deleted external input and output places. Figure 15.8 shows such a graph for the composition in Figure 15.7. Notice how we see directly that the threads are 1-connected via the input place p1 and via the output places p3 and d4.

The definition of n-connectedness exactly addresses the ways in which threads can interact in the dynamic, single-processor quadrant. Only one thing is missing: just as with n-connectedness in an ordinary directed graph, the connectivity can be established by chains of threads instead of by adjacent threads, as we have done here. (Imagine a call forwarding loop that involves a dozen phone subscribers in as many states.) In my personal testing experience, many of the problems described in field trouble reports were unexpected instances of 1-, 2-, or 3-connectedness among threads that were thought to be 0-connected.

The two forms of 1-connectedness among threads deserve special comment. When two threads are connected via a common input (event or data), the interaction is the classical form of Petri net

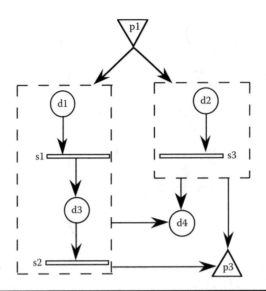

Figure 15.8   n-connected threads.

conflict. (In Figure 15.7, threads 1 and 2 are 1-connected via the port input event p1; this is also an example of a context-sensitive port input event.) If we imagine a marking in which the first transitions in each thread are both enabled, then firing one of them consumes the token from the common input place, and this disables the other. When two threads are 1-connected by an output place (again either an event or data), no conflict occurs, but there is an interesting ambiguity. The common output place is marked when one of the threads executes, but we usually do not know which one. This can happen in the SATM system when screen 10 (temporarily unable to process withdrawals) is displayed. It could be displayed because the ATM has no more cash or because there is a malfunction in the withdrawal door. This form of output-caused ambiguity is very common in field trouble reports. Many times, it is due to an unexpected interaction among threads, some of which may have executed long before others.

Port events cannot be both inputs and outputs; therefore, the only way threads can be 2-connected is via data places, and because 3-connectedness is bidirectional 2-connectedness, threads can only be 3-connected via data places. In a sense, this simplifies interactions because the number of possibilities is reduced. The real problem with interaction via data is that long intervals of time can be involved. We can add a small refinement here: the difference between read-only data and read-write data. Read-only data never changes, so we could say it has an infinite (or indefinite) duration. Read-write data obviously changes upon a write, so it has a duration — the interval between successive writes. The real problem with this is that seldom used (written) data may be the connection that causes two threads to be 2- or 3-connected, and the long time separation between the first and second threads can be very difficult to diagnose and difficult to cause with a test case.

Several dynamic interactions occur in the SATM system. First, notice that we are dealing with one ATM terminal, so we are concerned with dynamic interactions in a single processor. Technically two processors are used, because the SATM system gets the account information from the central bank, but we can treat this interaction as though the bank is a port device. Several context-sensitive port input events take place in the SATM system; because we discussed these at length in Chapter 14, we move on to 1- and 2-connected interactions among threads.

It is easy to devise threads that make deposits to and withdrawals from a given bank account. These are 1- and 2-connected via the data place for the account balance. Withdrawal threads that attempt to withdraw more than, and less than, the existing balance are 1-connected to the balance place. A successful withdrawal (in which the requested amount is less than the balance) clearly changes the balance, so the before and after instances of the balance place are 2-connected via the withdrawal thread. If we add a deposit thread, we obtain even richer interactions, and the key to all of this is the time order in which they execute.

Another subtlety exists in the foregoing discussion that has to do with how we describe such interacting threads. One possibility is to rely on specific values, both for preconditions and for amounts entered in the input portion of the threads. With the explicit approach, we might postulate, as a precondition, a balance of $50.00; define thread T1 as a withdrawal of $40.00; and define thread T2 as a withdrawal of $60.00. Superficially, this is easy — thread T2 will not execute and thread T1 will. We could be more precise by defining two port inputs for the withdrawal amount: p1 is withdrawal amount = $40.00 and p2 is withdrawal amount = $60.00. With these, thread T1 will contain a port event to display screen 11 (take cash), and T2 will contain a port event to display screen 8 (insufficient funds). Here is where the subtlety comes into play. Through greater precision, we also remove the conflict because we have stated in advance which port output will occur. When do these values exist — when the thread is described (specified) or when it actually executes? The explicit approach is commonly used by testers, but it does not work well for requirements specification because of the predisposition. Alternatively, we could be more general and say that thread T1 is a withdrawal of an amount less than the balance and thread T2 is a withdrawal of an amount greater than the balance, and not state the balance until execution time. (This is a good choice when executable specifications are used as a rapid prototype.) The problem with the latter choice is that testers cannot provide the expected output portions of a test case. The subtlety hinges on when the path of a thread is determined: before it begins to execute, as in a test case, or as it executes, as in a rapid prototype. We will revisit this discussion in Section 15.3 when we discuss the connections among interaction, composition, and determinism. For now, testers might relish the idea that they can control the destiny of threads, but specifiers cannot.

15.2.4 Dynamic Interactions in Multiple Processors

Dynamic interactions among multiple processors are the most complex in our taxonomy. Because threads and events can execute simultaneously, strictly sequential, deterministic behavior is replaced by concurrent behavior. In the words of Robin Milner, "Concurrency inflicts nondeterminism" (Milner, 1993). The added complexity is also seen in the models mandated by each quadrant: decision tables suffice for static interactions, and finite state machines express dynamic interactions on a single processor. Dynamic interactions on multiple processors need the expressive power of communicating finite state machines or some form of Petri nets. We will see these interactions in the Saturn windshield wiper system.

The windshield wiper on the Saturn automobile is controlled by a lever and a dial. The lever has four positions, OFF, INT (for intermittent), LOW, and HIGH; and the dial has three positions, numbered simply 1, 2, and 3. The dial positions indicate three intermittent speeds, and the dial position is relevant only when the lever is at the INT position. The following decision table shows the windshield wiper speeds (in wipes per minute) for the lever and dial positions.

Conditions						
Lever	OFF	INT	INT	INT	LOW	HIGH
Dial	n/a	1	2	3	n/a	n/a
Wiper	0	4	6	12	30	60

If we think about the Saturn windshield wiper system, we find three natural, interacting devices: the lever, the dial, and the wiper. Two events occur on the lever: it can be moved up one position or it can be moved down one position. Similarly, two events occur on the dial: it can be moved clockwise or counterclockwise. We can decompose these into the finer granularity shown in Table 15.1.

The wiper device produces six port output events — the six different wiper speeds (expressed in wipes per minute). These are shown in Table 15.2.

The finite state machines for the lever and dial are given in Figure 15.9. Notice we can easily show the events that cause the state transitions, but some of the associated outputs (indicated by question marks) are indeterminate. For example, when we move the lever from OFF to INT, we cannot assert a specific port output event because we do not know the state of the dial machine. We can assert no output events in the dial machine, because we do not know if the lever is in the INT position. The lever and the dial, acting concurrently, drive the wiper.

We will use EDPNs to compose the lever and dial finite state machines, and this composition will exactly describe the interaction. Figure 15.5 is the EDPN equivalent of the lever finite state machine; the EDPN of the dial finite state machine is shown in Figure 15.10. The EDPN transitions, places, and events used in Figure 15.11 are summarized in Table 15.4.

To cast a finite state machine into an EDPN, states become data places and state transitions become EDPN transitions. The events that cause state transitions become port input events, and

Table 15.1   Port Input Events in the Saturn Windshield Wiper

Port Input Event	Description
ie1	Lever from OFF to INT
ie2	Lever from INT to LOW
ie3	Lever from LOW to HIGH
ie4	Lever from HIGH to LOW
ie5	Lever from LOW to INT
ie6	Lever from INT to OFF
ie7	Dial from 1 to 2
ie8	Dial from 2 to 3
ie9	Dial from 3 to 2
ie10	Dial from 2 to 1

Table 15.2   Port Output Events in the Saturn Windshield Wiper

Port Output Event	Description
oe1	0 wpm
oe2	4 wpm
oe3	6 wpm
oe4	12 wpm
oe5	30 wpm
oe6	60 wpm

the outputs associated with a state transition become port output events. In the lever EDPN (Figure 15.5), transitions to the OFF, LO, and HI states require no interaction with the dial EDPN to determine the associated port output events (p5, p9, and p10). Also, transitions to the INT state (s1 and s5) have no port output events. In the dial EDPN (Figure 15.10), the three dial positions are the three data places, and the dial events (p3 and p4) are inputs that cause transitions. The dial EDPN has no port output events, because these are never outputs of transitions in the dial EDPN.

The interaction between the lever and the dial EDPNs is shown in Figure 15.11. It entails places d2, d5, d6, and d7, transitions s11, s12, and s13, and port events p6, p7, and p8, which are the INT state, the dial position states, and the three intermittent wiper speeds. The edges with arrowheads at each end (e.g., between d2 and s11) indicate that the places are inputs to and outputs of the associated transitions. This seems a little artificial, but it makes the markings work smoothly.

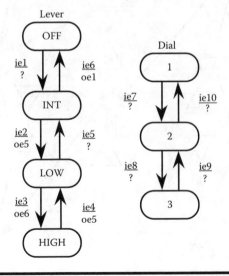

Figure 15.9   Lever and dial finite state machines.

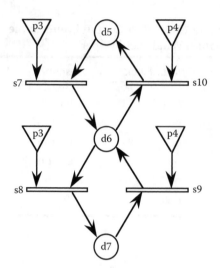

Figure 15.10 Dial EDPN.

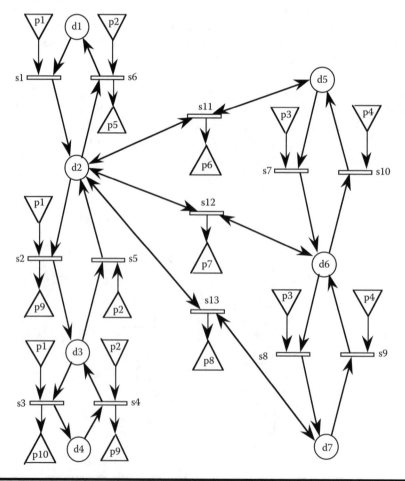

Figure 15.11 EDPN for the windshield wiper system.

Table 15.3

User Input	Expected Output
Lever up one position	6 strokes per minute
Lever up one position	30 strokes per minute
Dial up one position	30 strokes per minute
Lever down one position	12 strokes per minute
Lever down one position	0 strokes per minute

We can execute the EDPN in Figure 15.11, but we need to devise (or rationalize) an initial marking. Notice that none of the places are external inputs. This means we must arbitrarily determine some starting position for the dial and lever. The physical reality is that both devices can be in exactly one position at a time (a form of contraries); thus, exactly one of d1, d2, d3, and d4 is always marked, and similarly for d5, d6, and d7. We will assume that the car is shipped with the lever in the off position and the dial at position 1. Table 15.5 shows the marking sequence for the following scenario of events in Table 15.3.

The EDPN of the full Saturn windshield wiper system in Figure 15.11 merely begins to show the complexity of dynamic interactions among multiple processors. For starters, consider cyclomatic complexity: it is 3 for the lever EDPN, 2 for the dial EDPN, and 20 for the full EDPN. The jump in complexity is directly attributable to the interactions. Now, consider the complexities that result from the various strictly sequential markings of this net, and then the contribution to complexity when concurrent execution is allowed.

Some of this becomes clear if you carefully follow the marking sequence in Table 15.5 for the EDPN in Figure 15.11. First notice that several points of event quiescence occur, such as at marking steps m0 and m2. The net at steps m3 and m5 requires some explanation. Basically, we need to clarify the nature of the port output events (the wiper speeds). When a port output occurs, what is its duration? Does it continue to provide wiper strokes, or must it be executed periodically? Both of these styles are shown in Figure 15.11. At step m3, when transition s11 fires, it remarks its input places (d2 and d5) and executes p6 (six strokes per minute). Because no other transition is enabled, we can picture s11 as continuously firing until something else (an event) happens. This is a strange form of event quiescence, but it is clearly a steady state of the system. The other form is shown at marking step m5, where transition s2 has fired, resulting in port output p9 (30 strokes per minute). Here, we picture p9 as having a duration that lasts as long as d3 is marked. While p9 is operating, the user can cause dial port events (steps 6 and 7) with no effect on the wiper strokes. The possible markings, then, give us additional insight into the complexity of these interactions.

The role of time adds the last increment of complexity. Consider the time interval between port input events and what we might call the reaction time of the system. The highest wiper speed is 60 strokes per minute, and a driver can easily move the lever from the OFF position to the HI position in less than one second. What happened to the intervening port events (p9 and one of p6, p7, and p8)? The model is incomplete on this detail. Markings let us deal with simultaneity: if two events (or transitions) occur at exactly the same point in time, we can easily show this by marking their corresponding positions in the marking vector. We can also amend the firing rules

Table 15.4   EDPN Windshield Wiper Elements

Element	Description
s1	Transition OFF to INT
s2	Transition INT to LO
s3	Transition LO to HI
s4	Transition HI to LO
s5	Transition LO to INT
s6	Transition INT to OFF
s7	Transition 1 to 2
s8	Transition 2 to 3
s9	Transition 3 to 2
s10	Transition 2 to 1
s11	Provide 6 strokes per minute
s12	Provide 12 strokes per minute
s13	Provide 20 strokes per minute
d1	Lever at OFF
d2	Lever at INT
d3	Lever at LO
d4	Lever at HI
d5	Dial at 1
d6	Dial at 2
d7	Dial at 3
p1	Move lever up one position
p2	Move lever down one position
p3	Move dial up one position
p4	Move dial down one position
p5	Provide 0 strokes per minute
p6	Provide 6 strokes per minute
p7	Provide 12 strokes per minute
p8	Provide 20 strokes per minute
p9	Provide 30 strokes per minute
p10	Provide 60 strokes per minute

to allow simultaneous transition firings as long as the transitions are in different processors. We can represent all of this with diagrams similar to the timing diagrams used to describe electronic circuits. (They are also similar to music notation, in which each voice has its own clef. Music also has a notion of time steps, the measures of equal time duration.) Table 15.6 and Table 15.7 show two possible ways to present the concurrent behavior of the marking in Table 15.5.

Table 15.5 Marking for Sample Scenario

m	d1	d2	d3	d4	d5	d6	d7	p1	p2	p3	p4	p5	p6	p7	p8	p9	p10	Description
0	1				1													Off, 1
1	1				1		1											Lever up, s1 enabled
2		1			1													s1 fired, s11 enabled
3		1			1							1						s11 fired, s11 enabled
4		1			1		1											Lever up, s2 and s11 enabled
5			1		1										1			s2 fired
6			1		1				1									Dial up, s7 enabled
7			1			1												s7 fired
8			1			1		1										Lever down, s5 enabled
9	1					1												s5 fired, s12 enabled
10	1					1							1					s12 fired
11	1					1		1										Lever down, s6 enabled
12	1					1					1							s6 fired

15.3 Interaction, Composition, and Determinism

The question of nondeterminism looms as a backdrop to deep questions in science and philosophy. Einstein did not believe in nondeterminism; he once commented that he doubted that God would play dice with the universe. Nondeterminism generally refers to consequences of random events, asking, in effect, if there are truly random events (inputs), can we ever predict their consequences? The logical extreme of this debate ends in the philosophical/theological question of free will versus predestination. Fortunately for testers, the software version of nondeterminism is less severe. You might want to consider this section to be a technical editorial. It is based on my experience and analysis using the EDPN framework. I find it yields reasonable answers to the problem of nondeterminism; you may too.

Let us start with a working definition of determinism; here are two possibilities:

1. A system is deterministic if, given its inputs, we can always predict its outputs.
2. A system is deterministic if it always produces the same outputs for a given set of inputs.

The second view (repeatable outputs) is less stringent than the first (predictable outputs); therefore, we will use it as our working definition. Then a nondeterministic system is one in which there is at least one set of inputs that results in two distinct sets of outputs. It is easy to devise a nondeterministic finite state machine; Figure 15.12 is one example.

When the machine in Figure 15.12 is in state d1, if event e1 occurs, a transition takes place either to state d2 or to d3.

Table 15.6   Concurrent Behavior of the Sample Scenario

Time	0	1	2	3	4	5	6	7	8	9	10	11	12
Lever													
d1	1	1											
d2				1	1								1
d3							1	1	1	1	1		
d4													
s1				1									
s2						1							
s3													
s4													
s5													
s6												1	
p1		1			1								
p2											1		
Dial													
d5	1	1	1	1	1	1	1	1					
d6										1	1	1	1
d7													
s7									1				
s8													
s9													
s10													
p3								1					
p4													
Wiper													
s11													
s12													
s13													
p5													
p6				1	1	1							
p7													1
p8													
p9							1	1	1	1	1	1	
p10													
Time	0	1	2	3	4	5	6	7	8	9	10	11	12

Table 15.7 Condensed Version of Table 15.6

		0	1	2	3	4	5	6	7	8	9	10	11	12
	Time	0	1	2	3	4	5	6	7	8	9	10	11	12
Lever	Data	d1	d1		d2	d2		d3	d3	d3	d3	d3		d2
	Transition			s1			s2						s5	
	Input		p1			p1						p2		
	Output							p9	p9	p9	p9	p9	p9	
Dial	Data	d5	d5	d5	d5	d5	d5	d5	d5		d6	d6	d6	d6
	Transition									s7				
	Input							p3						
	Output													
Wiper	Data													
	Transition													
	Input													
	Output					p6	p6	p6						p7

If it is so easy to create a nondeterministic finite state machine, why all the fuss about determinism in the first place? Recall that in Chapter 12 we took great pains to separate the reality of a system from models of the system's behavior. Finite state machines are models of reality; they only approximate the behavior of a real system. This is why it is so important to choose an appropriate model — we would like to use the best approximation. Roughly speaking, decision tables are the model of choice for static interactions, finite state machines suffice for dynamic interactions in a single processor, and some form of Petri nets is needed for dynamic interactions in multiple processors. Before going on, we should indicate instances of nondeterminism in the other two models. A multiple-hit decision table is one in which the inputs (variables in the condition stub) are such that more than one rule is selected. In Petri nets, nondeterminism occurs when more than one transition is enabled. The choice of which rule executes or which transition fires is made by an external agent. (Notice that the choice is actually an input.)

Our question of nondeterminism reduces to threads in an EDPN, and this is where interactions, composition, and determinism come together. To ground our discussion in something real, consider the SATM threads we used earlier:

> T1: Withdraw $40.00
> T2: Withdraw $60.00
> T3: Deposit $30.00

Threads T1, T2, and T3 interact via a data place for the account balance, and they may be executed in different processors. The initial balance is $50.00.

Begin with thread T1; if no other thread executes, it will execute correctly, leaving a balance of $10.00. Suppose we began with thread

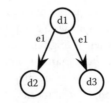

Figure 15.12 A nondeterministic finite state machine.

T2; we should really call it "attempt to withdraw $60.00," because if no other thread executes, it will result in the insufficient funds screen. We should really separate T2 into two threads: T2.1, which is a successful withdrawal that ends with the display of screen 11 (take cash), and T2.2, which is a failed withdrawal that ends with the display of screen 8 (insufficient funds). Now let us add some interaction with thread T3. Threads T2 and T3 are 2-connected via the balance data place. If T3 executes before T2 reads the balance data, then T2.1 occurs; otherwise, T2.2 occurs. The difference between the two views of determinism is visible here: when the EDPN of T2 begins to execute, we cannot predict the outcome (T2.1 or T2.2); so by the first definition, this is nondeterministic. By the second definition, however, we can recreate the interaction (including times) between T2 and T3. If we do, and we capture the behavior as a marking of the composite EDPN, we will satisfy the repeatable definition of determinism.

We now have a mild resolution to the question of determinism, at least as it applies to testing threads that are expressed as EDPNs. We can go so far as to say that a thread is locally nondeterministic, in the sense that its outcome cannot be predicted with information local to the thread. We also saw this in the windshield wiper system. If we are confined to the lever finite state machine, we cannot determine the output when the lever moves to the intermittent position, because we do not know the dial position. In a global sense, however, nondeterminism vanishes, because all the inputs are known. The implication for testers is that when testing threads with external inputs (particularly data places), it is important to test the interaction with all other threads that can be n-connected via external inputs.

15.4 Client/Server Testing

Client/server (CS) systems are difficult to test because they exhibit the most problematical form of interactions, the dynamic ones across multiple processors. Here, we can enjoy the benefits of our strong theoretical development. Client/server systems always entail at least two processors — one where the server software exists and executes, and one (usually several) where the client software executes. The main components are usually a database management system, application programs that use the database, and presentation programs that produce user-defined output. The position of these components results in the fat server versus fat client distinction (Lewis, 1994) (see Figure 15.13).

Client/server systems also include a network to connect the clients with the server, the network software, and a graphical user interface (GUI) for the clients. To make matters worse, we can differentiate homogeneous and heterogeneous CS systems in terms of client processors that are identically diverse. The multiple terminal version of the SATM system would be a fat client system, because the central bank does very little of the transaction processing.

In our formulation of EDPN threads, we confined a thread to a processor. With CS systems, we need a term for a sequence of threads that cross the CS boundary; call it a CS transaction. A typical CS transaction begins with a request (or query) at a client processor. The request is transmitted over the network (where it might be scheduled) to the server, where some application program processes it using the database management system (DBMS). The results are transmitted over the network to the client, where they are mapped to a user-defined output format. If something goes wrong in a CS transaction, a lot of room for finger pointing happens: clients blame the server, servers blame the clients, and both blame the network.

The threads in the DBMS portion of CS transactions are all of the static sequential type, and because this is likely to be either a commercial product or a very stable application, testing is not

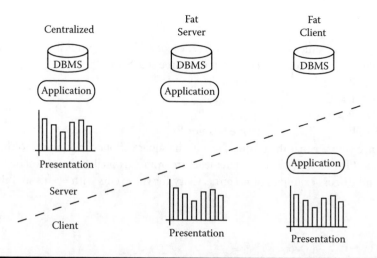

Figure 15.13   Fat clients and servers.

necessarily required. Should testing be necessary, it is almost always strictly functional, because we rarely have the source code of commercial applications. Threads in the server applications also exhibit primarily static sequential interactions, and these too are likely to be in stable, existing applications. The applications will probably be more error-prone (failure-prone is better) than the DBMS. The network software portion of a CS transaction is also likely to be a commercial application; thus, most CS transaction testing will occur on the client processor(s). The most interesting (from a testing standpoint) is the GUI portion. The user portion of a CS transaction is typically built within a commercial application program that allows the user to develop in terms of a WIMP interface (windows, icons, menus, and pull-downs), and this is where the fun begins. Clients are free to move in arbitrary ways across multiple windows, yet the results must be compatible. In our terminology, we can view a window as a finite state machine, and interwindow moves will correspond to communicating finite state machines. All the actions available to a user in a window are port input events, and the results of these actions are port output events. The client portions of a CS transaction are therefore threads that exhibit dynamic interactions across multiple processors (the windows), which we know to be the most complex.

This framework at least gives the CS tester a rigorous approach that supports testing strategies that can be measured in terms of coverage metrics. The notion of operational profiles (see Chapter 14) is very appropriate, because testing all possible interactions could be very time-consuming. Another advantage to this framework is that once a client thread is satisfactorily tested, the only further concern is its interaction with other threads. This should be an important step, because there is a lot of potential for n-connectivity among the threads of separate clients, very much like the SATM scenario in which several people conducted deposits and withdrawals on the same account.

References

Lewis, T. and Evangelist, M., Fat servers vs. fat clients: the transition from client–server to distributed computing, *American Programmer*, Vol. 7 No. 11, November 1994, pp. 2–9.

Milner, R., Elements of interaction (1993 Turing Award Lecture), *Communications of the ACM*, Vol. 36, No. 1, January 1993.

Zave, P., Feature interactions and formal specifications in telecommunications, *IEEE Computer*, August 1993.

Exercises

1. Figure 15.3 has a nice connection with set theory. Take the propositions p, q, r, and s to be the following set theory statements about some sets S and P:

   p: $S \subseteq P$ (all S is P)
   q: $S \cap P = \varnothing$ (no S is P)
   r: $S \cap P \neq \varnothing$ (some S is P)
   s: $S \not\subseteq P$ (some S is not P)

   Convince yourself that the relationships in the square of opposition apply to these set theory propositions. (The natural language statements are from Aristotelian categorical deduction.)

2. Find and discuss examples of n-connectivity for the events with events in Table 15.4.

OBJECT-ORIENTED TESTING

Chapter 16

Issues in Object-Oriented Testing

Both theoretical and practical work on the testing of object-oriented software flourished since the second half of the 1990s. The conference on Object-Oriented Programming, Systems, Languages, and Applications (OOPSLA) and vendor-sponsored testing conferences have consistently featured both papers and tutorials on object-oriented testing. One Web site boasts over 18,000 links to object-oriented testing literature (www.cetus-links.org/oo_testing.html). The beginning of the 21st century is marked, among other things, by increased consensus on questions such as: What is an object-oriented unit? How are object-oriented applications best modeled? One of the original hopes for object-oriented software was that objects could be reused without modification or additional testing. This was based on the assumption that well-conceived objects encapsulate functions and data "that belong together," and once such objects are developed and tested, they become reusable components. The interest in aspect-oriented programming (Kiczales, 1997) is one response to some of the limitations of the object-oriented paradigm. The new consensus is that there is little reason for this optimism — object-oriented software has potentially more severe testing problems than does traditional software. On the positive side, the Unified Modeling Language (UML) has emerged as a strong unifying (and driving) force for several aspects of object-oriented technology.

Our goal in this chapter is to identify the testing issues raised by object-oriented software. First, we have the question of levels of testing; this, in turn, requires clarification of object-oriented units. Next, we consider some of the implications of the strategy of composition (as opposed to functional decomposition). Object-oriented software is characterized by inheritance, encapsulation, and polymorphism; therefore, we look at ways that traditional testing can be extended to address the implications of these issues. In the remaining chapters of Part V, we examine class testing, graphical user interface (GUI) testing, integration and system testing, UML-based testing, and the application of dataflow testing to object-oriented software. We will do this using the object-oriented calendar and currency converter examples.

16.1 Units for Object-Oriented Testing

Traditional software has a variety of definitions for *unit*. Two that pertain to object-oriented testing are:

A unit is the smallest software component that can be compiled and executed.
A unit is a software component that would never be assigned to more than one designer to develop.

These definitions can be contradictory. Certain industrial applications have huge classes; these clearly violate the one-designer, one-class definition. In such applications, it seems better to define an object-oriented unit as the work of one person, which likely ends up as a subset of the class operations. In an extreme case, an object-oriented unit might be a subclass of a class that contains only the attributes needed by a single operation or method. (In Part V, we will use *operation* to refer to the definition of a class function and *method* to refer to its implementation.) For such units, object-oriented unit testing reduces to traditional testing. This is a nice simplification but somewhat problematic, because it shifts much of the object-oriented testing burden onto integration testing. Also, it throws out the gains made by encapsulation.

The class-as-unit choice has several advantages. In a UML context, a class has an associated StateChart that describes its behavior. Later, we shall see that this is extremely helpful in test case identification. A second advantage is that object-oriented integration testing has clearer goals, namely, to check the cooperation of separately tested classes, which echoes traditional software testing.

16.2 Implications of Composition and Encapsulation

Composition (as opposed to decomposition) is the central design strategy in object-oriented software development. Together with the goal of reuse, composition creates the need for very strong unit testing. Because a unit (class) may be composed with previously unknown other units, the traditional notions of coupling and cohesion are applicable. Encapsulation has the potential to resolve this concern, but only if the units (classes) are highly cohesive and very loosely coupled. The main implication of composition is that, even presuming very good unit-level testing, the real burden is at the integration testing level.

Some of this is clarified by example. Suppose we revisit the Saturn windshield wiper system from an object-oriented viewpoint. We would most likely identify three classes — lever, wiper, and dial; their behavior is shown in Figure 16.1.

One choice of pseudocode for the interfaces of these classes is as follows:

```
Class lever(leverPosition;
          private senseLeverUp(),
          private senseLeverDown() )
Class dial(dialPosition;
          private senseDialUp(),
          private senseDialDown() )
Class wiper(wiperSpeed;
          setWiperSpeed(newSpeed) )
```

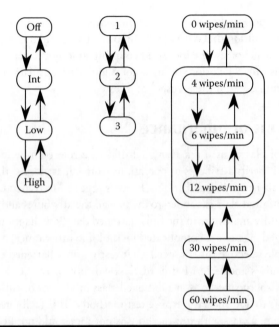

Figure 16.1   Behavior of windshield wiper classes.

The lever and dial classes have operations that sense physical events on their respective devices. When these methods (corresponding to the operations) execute, they report their respective device positions to the wiper class. The interesting part of the windshield wiper example is that the lever and the dial are independent devices, and they interact when the lever is in the INT (intermittent) position. The question raised by encapsulation is: Where should this interaction be controlled?

The precept of encapsulation requires that classes only know about themselves and operate on their own. Thus, the lever does not know the dial position, and the dial does not know the lever position. The problem is that the wiper needs to know both positions. One possibility, as shown in the previous interface, is that the lever and dial always report their positions, and the wiper figures out what it must do. With this choice, the wiper class becomes the "main program" and contains the basic logic of the whole system.

Another choice might be to make the lever class the "smart" object because it knows when it is in the intermittent (INT) state. With this choice, when the response to a lever event puts the lever in the INT state, a method gets the dial status (with a getDialPosition message) and simply tells the wiper what speed is needed. With this choice, the three classes are more tightly coupled and, as a result, less reusable. Another problem occurs with this choice. What happens if the lever is in the INT position and a subsequent dial event occurs? There would be no reason for the lever to get the new dial position, and no message would be sent to the wiper class.

A third choice might be to make the wiper the main program (as in the first choice), but use a Has relation to the lever and dial classes. With this choice, the wiper class uses the sense operations of the lever and dial classes to detect physical events. This forces the wiper class to be continuously active, in a polling sense, so that asynchronous events at the lever and dial can be observed.

Consider these three choices from the standpoint of composition and encapsulation. The first choice (cleverly named because it is the best) has very little coupling among the classes. This maximizes the potential of the classes to be reused (i.e., composed in unforeseen ways). For example, a cheaper windshield wiper might omit the dial altogether, and an expensive windshield wiper might replace the three-position dial with a "continuous" dial. Similar changes might be made to the lever. In the other two choices, the increased coupling among the classes reduces their ability to be composed. This is our conclusion: doing a good job at encapsulation results in classes that can more easily be composed (and thus reused) and tested.

16.3 Implications of Inheritance

Although the choice of classes as units seems natural, the role of inheritance complicates this choice. If a given class inherits attributes or operations from super classes, the stand-alone compilation criterion of a unit is sacrificed. Binder (1996) suggests "flattened classes" as an answer. A flattened class is an original class expanded to include all the attributes and operations it inherits. Flattened classes are mildly analogous to the fully flattened dataflow diagrams of structured analysis. (Notice that flattened classes are complicated by multiple inheritance, and really complicated by selective and multiple selective inheritance.) Unit testing on a flattened class solves the inheritance problem, but it raises another. A flattened class will not be part of a final system, so some uncertainty remains. Also, the methods in a flattened class might not be sufficient to test the class. The next workaround is to add special-purpose test methods. This facilitates class-as-unit testing but raises a final problem: a class with test methods is not (or should not be) part of the delivered system. This is perfectly analogous to the question of testing original or instrumented code in traditional software. Some ambiguity is also introduced: the test methods can also be faulty. What if a test method falsely reports a fault, or worse, incorrectly reports success? Test methods are subject to the same false-positive and false-negative outcomes as medical experiments. This leads to an unending chain of methods testing other methods, very much like the attempt to provide external proofs of consistency of a formal system.

Figure 16.2 shows a UML inheritance diagram of a part of our earlier simple automated teller machine (SATM) system; some functionality has been added to make this a better example. Both checking and savings accounts have account numbers and balances, and these can be accessed

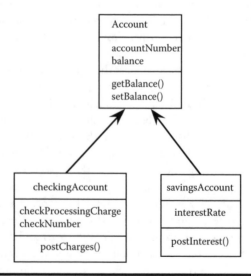

Figure 16.2   Class inheritance.

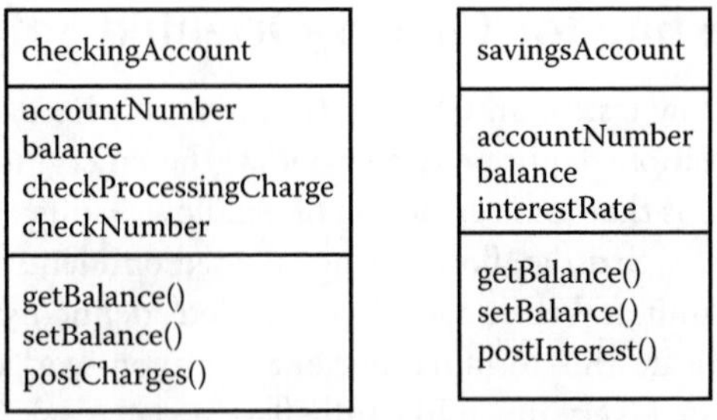

checkingAccount
accountNumber balance checkProcessingCharge checkNumber
getBalance() setBalance() postCharges()

savingsAccount
accountNumber balance interestRate
getBalance() setBalance() postInterest()

Figure 16.3   Flattened checkingAccount and savingsAccount classes.

and changed. Checking accounts have a per-check processing charge that must be deducted from the account balance. Savings accounts draw interest that must be calculated and posted on some periodic basis.

If we did not "flatten" the checkingAccount and savingsAccount classes, we would not have access to the balance attributes, and we would not be able to access or change the balances. This is clearly unacceptable for unit testing. Figure 16.3 shows the flattened checkingAccount and savingsAccount classes. These are clearly stand-alone units that are sensible to test. Solving one problem raises another: with this formulation, we would test the getBalance and setBalance operations twice, thereby losing some of the hoped-for economies of object orientation.

16.4   Implications of Polymorphism

The essence of polymorphism is that the same method applies to different objects. Considering classes as units implies that any issues of polymorphism will be covered by the class/unit testing. Again, the redundancy of testing polymorphic operations sacrifices hoped-for economies.

16.5   Levels of Object-Oriented Testing

Three or four levels of object-oriented testing are used, depending on the choice of what constitutes a unit. If individual operations or methods are considered to be units, we have four levels: operation/method, class, integration, and system testing. With this choice, operation/method testing is identical to unit testing of procedural software. Class and integration testing can be well renamed intraclass and interclass testing. The second level, then, consists of testing interactions among previously tested operations/methods. Integration testing, which we will see is the major issue of object-oriented testing, must be concerned with testing interactions among previously tested classes. Finally, system testing is conducted at the port event level and is (or should be) identical to system testing of traditional software. The only difference is where system-level test cases originate.

16.6   GUI Testing

Because graphical user interfaces have become so closely associated with object-oriented software, we will devote a separate chapter to those testing issues. GUIs are a special case of event-driven systems, and event-driven systems are vulnerable to the problem of an infinite number of event sequences. We will see that a reasonable notion of coverage is very dependent on the notation by which we represent the behavior of these systems.

16.7 Dataflow Testing for Object-Oriented Software

When we considered dataflow testing in Chapter 10, it was restricted to a single unit. The issues of inheritance and composition require a deeper view. The emerging consensus in the object-oriented testing community is that some extension of dataflow testing should address these special needs. In Chapter 10, we saw that dataflow testing is based on identifying define and use nodes in the program graph of a unit and then considering various define/use paths. Procedure calls in traditional software complicate this formulation; one common workaround is to embed called procedures into the unit tested (very much like fully flattened classes). Chapter 18 presents a revision of event-driven Petri nets that exactly describes dataflow among object-oriented operations. Within this formulation, we can express the object-oriented extension of dataflow testing.

16.8 Examples for Part V

We will use two primary examples for our discussion of object-oriented testing. The first is an object-oriented implementation of our now-familiar NextDate problem; the second is typical of GUI applications — a currency conversion application.

16.8.1 The Object-Oriented Calendar

The o-oCalendar program is an object-oriented implementation of the NextDate example given in Chapter 2. Figure 16.4 and Figure 16.5 show the UML class diagrams and the inheritance and

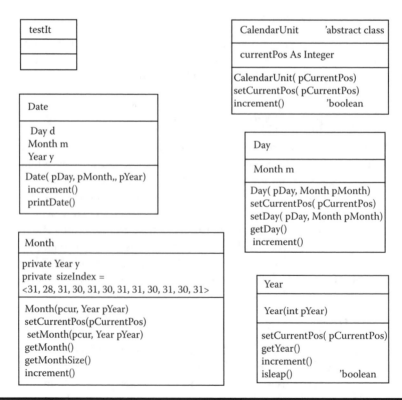

Figure 16.4   Classes in o-oCalendar.

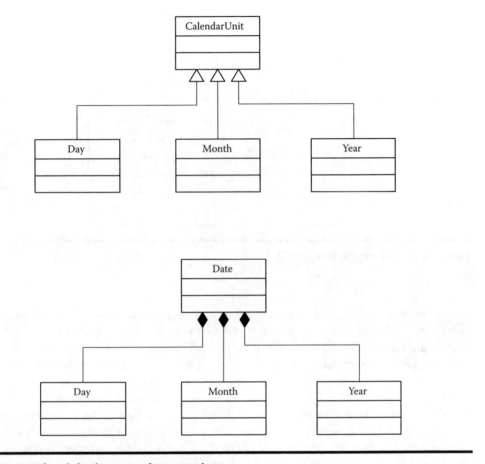

Figure 16.5   Class inheritance and aggregation.

aggregation of classes in the o-oCalendar problem. The letters and numbers on statement lines in the pseudocode will be used in Chapter 17 when we discuss structural testing for o-o software.

Object instances of the day, month, and year classes inherit their set and increment methods from the abstract CalendarUnit class. Each of these classes encapsulates exactly the information it needs; any information from other classes is obtained via messages. The testIt class instantiates a test date and then increments it and prints the resulting date. Because date objects are composed of month, day, and year instances, these are instantiated. The Date.increment method sends a message to the day object to see if it can be incremented (end-of-month question). The Day.increment method sends a message to the month object to see how many days are in the month. Next, the Date.increment method sends a message to the month object to see if it can be incremented (end-of-year question). The pseudocode for the o-oCalendar is in Chapter 17.

16.8.2 The Currency Conversion Application

The currency conversion program is an event-driven program that emphasizes code associated with a graphical user interface. A sample GUI built with Visual Basic is shown in Figure 16.6 (repeated from Chapter 2).

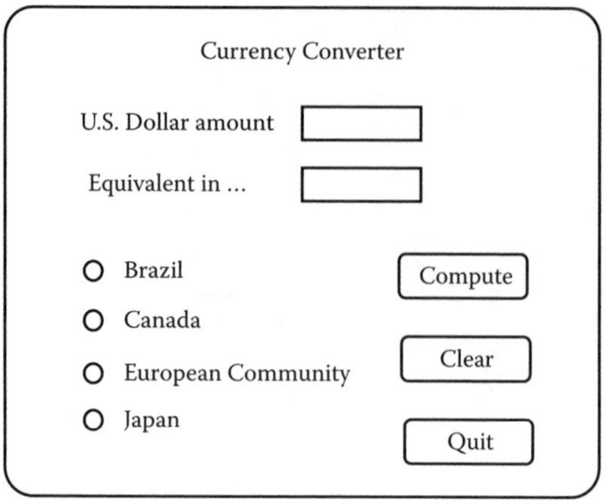

Figure 16.6 Currency converter GUI.

The application converts U.S. dollars to any of four currencies: Brazilian real, Canadian dollars, European Union euros, and Japanese yen. Currency selection is governed by the radio buttons (Visual Basic option buttons), which are mutually exclusive. When a country is selected, the system responds by completing the label; for example, "Equivalent in ..." becomes "Equivalent in Canadian dollars" when the Canada button is clicked. Also, a small Canadian flag appears next to the output position for the equivalent currency amount. Either before or after currency selection, the user inputs an amount in U.S. dollars. Once both tasks are accomplished, the user can click on the Compute button, the Clear button, or the Quit button. Clicking on the Compute button results in the conversion of the U.S. dollar amount to the equivalent amount in the selected currency. Clicking on the Clear button resets the currency selection, the U.S. dollar amount, the equivalent currency amount, and the associated label. Clicking on the Quit button ends the application.

To test a GUI application, begin by identifying all the user input events and all the system output events (these must be externally visible and observable). These are listed in Table 16.1a and b for the currency conversion program.

Table 16.1a Input Events for the Currency Conversion Program

	Input Events		*Input Events*
ip1	Enter U.S. dollar amount	ip2.4	Click on Japan
ip2	Click on a country button	ip3	Click on Compute button
ip2.1	Click on Brazil	ip4	Click on Clear button
ip2.2	Click on Canada	ip5	Click on Quit button
ip2.3	Click on European Community	ip6	Click on OK in error message

Table 16.1b   Output Events for the Currency Conversion Program

	Output Events			*Output Events*
op1	Display U.S. dollar amount		op4	Reset selected country
op2	Display currency name		op4.1	Reset Brazil
op2.1	Display Brazilian reals		op4.2	Reset Canada
op2.2	Display Canadian dollars		op4.3	Reset European Community
op2.3	Display European Community euros		op4.4	Reset Japan
op2.4	Display Japanese yen		op5	Display foreign currency value
op2.5	Display ellipsis		op6	Error message: Must select a country
op3	Indicate selected country		op7	Error message: Must enter U.S. dollar amount
op3.1	Indicate Brazil		op8	Error message: Must select a country and enter U.S. dollar amount
op3.2	Indicate Canada		op9	Reset U.S. dollar amount
op3.3	Indicate European Community	op10	Reset equivalent currency amount
op3.4	Indicate Japan			

Figure 16.7 contains a high-level, mostly complete view of the application. States are externally visible appearances of the GUI. The idle state, for example, occurs when the application is started and no user input has occurred (see Figure 16.6). It also occurs after a click event on the Clear button. The U.S. dollar amount entered state occurs when the user has entered a dollar amount and has done nothing else. The other states are similarly named. Notice that the country selected state is really a macro-state that refers to one of the four countries selected. This state is shown in more detail in Figure 16.8. The annotations on the transitions refer to the abbreviations of the input and output events listed in Tables 16.1a and b. Even this little GUI is surprisingly complex. We can suppress some of the complexity by using artificial input events such as ip2: click on a country button. Notice that the artificial input event ip2 and the artificial output events op2, op3, and op4 greatly simplify the high-level finite state machine (FSM) in Figure 16.7. Several events are missing, particularly click events on the Clear and Quit buttons. These can occur in any state; showing them results in a very cluttered diagram.

Figure 16.8 contains a detailed view of the internal behavior of the select country state, in which an exclusive-or relationship among the country buttons is maintained. The more detailed view in Figure 16.8 replaces the artificial input and output events with the corresponding multiple actual events; however, Figure 16.8 is incomplete.

The annotations for the transitions between Brazil and Japan, and the transitions between Canada and European Community, are not shown. Also, neither Figure 16.7 nor Figure 16.8 shows all the events that might occur in each state, especially clicking on either the Clear or Quit buttons.

Readers familiar with the StateChart notation will recognize the elegant way such repetitive complexity can be represented. Figure 16.9 expresses the high-level view of Figure 16.7 more

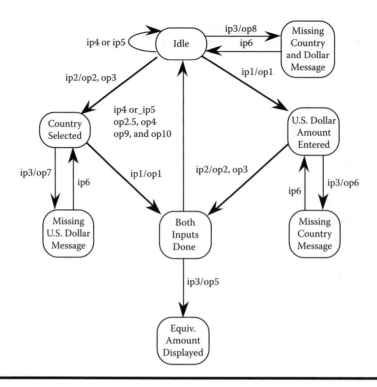

Figure 16.7   High-level FSM.

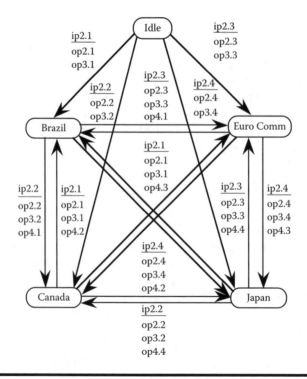

Figure 16.8   Detailed view of select country state.

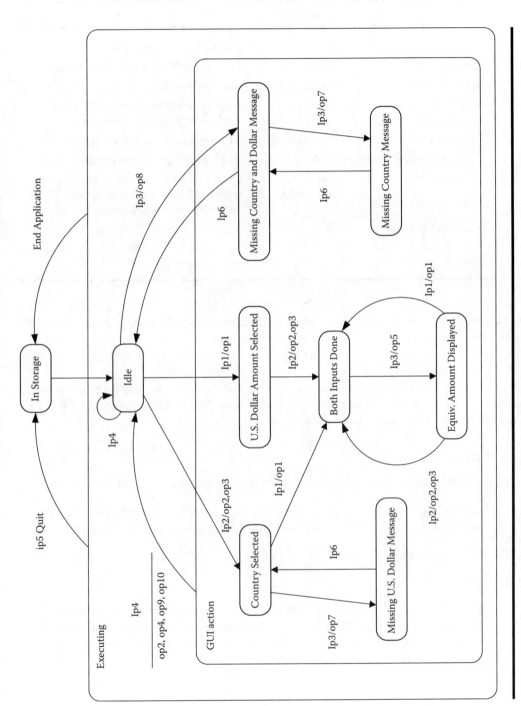

Figure 16.9 StateChart of the currency controller application.

Table 16.2   Event Table for the Both Inputs Done State

Input Events		*Output Events*	
ip1	Enter U.S. dollar amount	op1	Display U.S. dollar amount
ip2.1	Click on Brazil	op2.1 op3.1	Display Brazilian reals Indicate Brazil
ip2.2	Click on Canada	op2.2 op3.2	Display Canadian dollars Indicate Canada
ip2.3	Click on European Community	op2.3 op3.3	Display European Community euros Indicate European Community
ip2.4	Click on Japan	op2.4 op3.4	Display Japanese yen Indicate Japan
ip3	Click on Compute button	op5	Display foreign currency value
ip4	Click on Clear button	op2.5 op4 op9 op10	Display ellipsis, Reset selected country, Reset U.S. dollar amount, Reset equivalent currency amount
ip5	Click on Quit button		Application ends
ip6	Click on OK in error message		Ignored (error message not visible in this state)

completely. Notice that the transitions from the executing state to the in-storage state show that the user input ip6 to quit the application, and the operating system "End Application" event can occur in any state internal to the executing state. Similarly, the clear input event (ip4) can occur from any state inside the unnamed state.

One way to deal with the suppressed events is to make individual, state-level diagrams, showing the response to each possible input event. This is also nicely done with an event table; Table 16.2 shows this for the "both inputs done" state.

References

Binder, R.V., The free approach for testing use cases, threads, and relations, *Object*, Vol. 6, No. 2, February 1996.

Kiczales, G. et al., Aspect-oriented programming, in *Proceedings of the European Conference on Object-Oriented Programming (ECOOP)*, Finland, LNCS1241, Springer-Verlag, June 1997.

Exercises

1. The o-oCalendar problem can be extended is several ways. One extension is to add an astrological content: each zodiac sign has a name and a beginning date (usually the 21st of a month). Add attributes and methods to the month class so that testIt can find the zodiac sign for a given date.

Chapter 17

Class Testing

The main question for class testing is whether a class or a method is a unit. Most of the o-o litera-ture leans toward the class-as-unit side, but this definition has problems. In traditional software (where it is also hard to find a definition of a unit), the common guidelines are that a unit is:

> The smallest chunk that can be compiled by itself
> A single procedure/function (stand-alone)
> Something so small it would be developed by one person

These guidelines also make sense for o-o software, but they do not resolve whether classes or methods should be considered as units. A method implements a single function, and it would not be assigned to more than one person, so methods might legitimately be considered units. The smallest compilation requirement is problematic. Technically, we could compile a single-method class by ignoring the other methods in the class (probably by commenting them out), but this cre-ates an organizational mess. We will present both views of o-o unit testing; you can let particular circumstances decide which is more appropriate.

17.1 Methods as Units

Superficially, this choice reduces o-o unit testing to traditional (procedural) unit testing. A method is nearly equivalent to a procedure, so all the traditional functional and structural testing tech-niques should apply. Unit testing of procedural code requires stubs and a driver test program to supply test cases and record results. Similarly, if we consider methods as o-o units, we must provide stub classes that can be instantiated, and a "main program" class that acts as a driver to provide and analyze test cases.

When we look more closely at individual methods, we see the happy consequence of encap-sulation: they are generally simple. In the next subsection, please find the pseudocode and cor-responding program graphs for the classes that make up the o-oCalendar application. Notice that

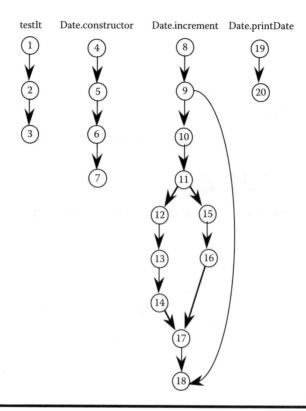

Figure 17.1 Program graphs for the testIt and Date classes.

the cyclomatic complexity is uniformly low; the increment method of the Date class has the highest cyclomatic complexity, and it is only V(G) = 3. To be fair, this implementation is intentionally simple — no checking is necessary for valid inputs. If there were, the cyclomatic complexity would increase.

Even though the cyclomatic complexity is low, the interface complexity is quite high. Looking at Date.increment again, notice the intense messaging: messages are sent to two methods in the Day class, to one method in the Year class, and to two methods in the Month class. This means that nearly as much effort will be made to create the proper stubs as in identifying test cases. Another more important consequence is that much of the burden is shifted to integration testing. In fact, we can identify two levels of integration testing: intraclass and interclass.

17.1.1 Pseudocode for o-oCalendar

Very little documentation is required by Unified Modeling Language (UML) at the unit/class level. Here, we add the class responsibility collaboration (CRC) cards for each class, followed by the class pseudocode, and then the program graphs for the class operations (see Figure 17.1 to Figure 17.4). CRC cards are not formally part of UML.

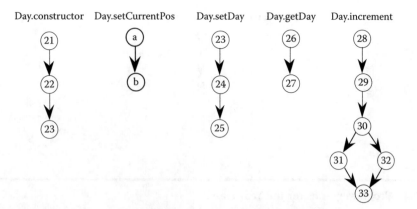

Figure 17.2   Program graphs for the Day class.

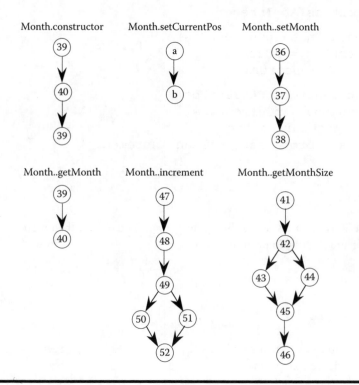

Figure 17.3   Program graphs for the Month class.

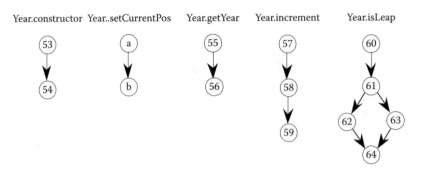

Figure 17.4   Program graphs for the Year class.

17.1.1.1 Class: CalendarUnit

Responsibility: Provides an operation to set its value in inherited classes and provides a Boolean operation that tells whether an attribute in an inherited class can be incremented.

```
Collaborates with: Day, Month, and Year

        class CalendarUnit 'abstract class
        currentPos As Integer

        CalendarUnit (pCurrentPos)
        currentPos = pCurrentPos
        End    'CalendarUnit
a.      setCurrentPos(pCurrentPos)
b.      currentPos = pCurrentPos
        End    'setCurrentPos
        abstract protected boolean increment()
```

17.1.1.2 Class: testIt

Responsibility: Serves as a test driver by creating a test date object, then requesting the object to increment itself and, finally, to print its new value.

```
Collaborates with:    Date

    class testIt
    main()
1       testdate = instantiate Date(testMonth, testDay, testYear)
2       testdate.increment()
3       testdate.printDate()

    End        'testIt
```

17.1.1.3   Class: Date

Responsibility: A Date object is composed of day, month, and year objects. A Date object increments itself using the inherited Boolean increment methods in day and month objects. If the day and month objects cannot be incremented (e.g., last day of the month or year), Date's increment method resets day and month as needed. In the case of December 31, it also increments the year. The printDate operation uses the get() methods in day, month, and year objects and prints a date value in mm/dd/yyyy format.

```
Collaborates with:    testIt, Day, Month, and Year

        class Date
        private Day d
        private Month m
        private Year y

4       Date(pMonth, pDay, pYear)
5            y = instantiate Year(pYear)
6            m = instantiate Month(pMonth, y)
7            d = instantiate Day(pDay, m)
        End    'Date constructor

8        increment ()
9        if (NOT(d.increment()))
10           Then
11                   if (NOT(m.increment()))
12                       Then
13                               y.increment()
14                               m.setMonth(1,y)
15                           Else
16                               d.setDay(1, m)
17                   EndIf
18           EndIf
        End    'increment

19      printDate ()
20           Output (m.getMonth() + "/" + d.getDay() + "/" +
             y.getYear())
        End 'printDate
```

17.1.1.4   Class: Day

Responsibility: A day object has a private month attribute that the increment method uses to see if a day value can be incremented or reset to 1. Day objects also provide get() and set() methods.

```
Collaborates with:    Month


      class Day isA CalendarUnit
      private Month m

21    Day(pDay, Month pMonth)
22          setDay(pDay, pMonth)
      End           'Day constructor

23    setDay(pDay, Month pMonth)
24          setCurrentPos(pDay)
25          m = pMonth
      End   '     setDay

26    getDay()
27          return currentPos
      End           'getDay

28    boolean increment()
29          currentPos = currentPos + 1
30          if (currentPos <= m.getMonthSize())
31                Then  return true
32                Else        return false
33          EndIf
      End           'increment
```

17.1.1.5   Class: Month

Responsibility: Month objects have a value attribute that is used as a subscript to an array of values of last month days (e.g., the last day of January is 31, the last day of February is 28, and so on). Month objects provide get() and set() services, and the inherited Boolean increment method. The possibility of February 29 is determined with the isLeap message to a year object.

```
Collaborates with:    Year


      class Month isA CalendarUnit
            private Year y
            private sizeIndex = <31, 28, 31, 30, 31, 30, 31,
            31, 30, 31, 30, 31>

34    Month( pcur, Year pYear)
35          setMonth(pCurrentPos, Year pyear)
      End           'Month constructor

36     setMonth( pcur, Year pYear)
37          setCurrentPos(pcur)
```

```
38              y = pYear
        End             'setMonth

39      getMonth()
40              return currentPos
        End             'getMonth

41      getMonthSize()
42              if (y.isleap())
43                      Then  sizeIndex[2] = 29
44                      Else        sizeIndex[2] = 28
45              EndIf
46              return sizeIndex[currentPos -1]
        End               'getMonthSize

47      boolean increment()
48              currentPos = currentPos + 1
49              if (currentPos > 12)
50                      Then  return false
51                      Else        return true
52              EndIf

        End               'increment
```

17.1.1.6 Class: Year

Responsibility: In addition to the usual get() and set() methods, a year object increments itself when the test date is December 31 of any year. Year objects provide a Boolean service that tells whether the current value corresponds to a leap year.

```
Collaborates with:      (no external messages sent)

        class Year isA CalendarUnit
53      Year( pYear)
54              setCurrentPos(pYear)
        End               'Year constructor

55      getYear()
56              return currentPos
        End             'getYear

57      boolean increment()
58              currentPos = currentPos + 1
59              return true
        End             'increment
```

```
60      boolean isleap()
61           if (((currentPos MOD 4 = 0) AND NOT(currentPos MOD
             400 = 0)) OR (currentPos MOD 400 = 0))
62                Then  return true
63                Else  return false
64           EndIf
        End        'isleap
```

17.1.2   Unit Testing for Date.increment

As we saw in Chapter 6, equivalence class testing is a good choice for logic-intensive units. The Date.increment operation treats the three equivalence classes of days:

> D1 = {day: 1 ≤ day < last day of the month}
> D2 = {day: day is the last day of a non-December month}
> D3 = {day: day is December 31}

At first, these equivalence classes appear to be loosely defined, especially D1, with its reference to the unspecified last day of the month and no reference to which month. Thanks to encapsulation, we can ignore these questions. (Actually, the questions are transferred to the testing of the Month.increment operation.)

17.2   Classes as Units

Treating a class as a unit solves the intraclass integration problem, but it creates other problems. One has to do with various views of a class. In the static view, a class exists as source code. This is fine if all we do is code reading. The problem with the static view is that inheritance is ignored, but we can fix this by using fully flattened classes. We might call the second view the compile time view, because this is when the inheritance actually occurs. The third view is the execution time view, when objects of classes are instantiated. Testing really occurs with the third view, but we still have some problems. For example, we cannot test abstract classes because they cannot be instantiated. Also, if we are using fully flattened classes, we will need to "unflatten" them to their original form when our unit testing is complete. If we do not use fully flattened classes, to compile a class, we will need all the other classes above it in the inheritance tree. One can imagine the software configuration management implications of this requirement.

The class-as-unit choice makes the most sense when little inheritance occurs, and classes have what we might call internal control complexity. The class itself should have an interesting (as opposed to simple or boring) StateChart, and there should be a fair amount of internal messaging. To explore class-as-unit testing, we will revisit the windshield wiper example with a more complex version.

17.2.1   Pseudocode for the windshieldWiper Class

The three classes discussed in Chapter 16 are merged into one class here. With this formulation, methods sense lever and dial events and maintain the state of the lever and dial in the lever-Position and dialPosition state variables. When a dial or lever event occurs, the corresponding sense method sends a (internal) message to the setWiperSpeed method, which in turn sets its corresponding state variable wiperSpeed. Our revised windshieldWiper class has three attributes, get and set operations for each variable, and methods that sense the four physical events on the lever and dial devices.

```
class windshieldWiper
      private wiperSpeed
      private leverPosition
      private dialPosition

      windshieldWiper(wiperSpeed, leverPosition, dialPosition)

      getWiperSpeed()
      setWiperSpeed()

      getLeverPosition()
      setLeverPosition()

      getDialPosition()
      setDialPosition()

      senseLeverUp()
      senseLeverDown()

      senseDialUp()
      senseDialDown()
End class windshieldWiper
```

The class behavior is shown in the StateChart in Figure 17.5, where the three devices appear in the orthogonal components. In the Dial and Lever components, transitions are caused by events, whereas the transitions in the wiper component are all caused by propositions that refer to what state is active in the dial or lever orthogonal component. (Such propositions are part of the rich syntax of transition annotations permitted in the StateMate product.)

17.2.2 Unit Testing for the windshieldWiper Class

Part of the difficulty with the class-as-unit choice is that there are levels of unit testing. In our example, it makes sense to proceed in a bottom-up order beginning with the get/set methods for the state variables (these are only present in case another class needs them). The dial and lever sense methods are all quite similar; pseudocode for the senseLeverUp method is given next.

```
senseLeverUp()
      Case leverPosition Of
            Case 1: Off
                  leverPosition = Int
                  Case dialPosition Of
                        Case 1:1
                              wiperSpeed = 4
                        Case 2:2
                              wiperSpeed = 6
```

```
                    Case 3:3
                            wiperSpeed = 12
        EndCase      'dialPosition
Case 2:Int
        leverPosition = Low
        wiperSpeed = 30
Case 3: Low
        leverPosition = High
        wiperSpeed = 60
Case 4: High
        (impossible; error condition)
EndCase       'leverPosition
```

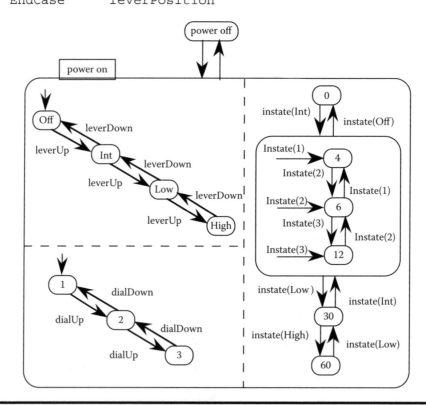

Figure 17.5   StateChart for the windshieldWiper class.

Testing the senseLeverUp method will require checking each of the alternatives in the case and nested case statements. The tests for the outer case statement cover the corresponding leverUp transitions in the statechart. In a similar way, we must test the leverDown, dialUp, and dialDown methods. Once we know that the dial and lever components are correct, we can test the wiper component.

Pseudocode for the test driver class will look something like this:

```
class testSenseLeverUp
     wiperSpeed
     leverPos
```

```
      dialPos
      testResult  'boolean
main()
      testCase = instantiate windshieldWiper(0, Off, 1)
      windshieldWiper.senseLeverUp()
      leverPos = windshieldWiper.getLeverPosition()
      If leverPos = Int
           Then testResult = Pass
           Else testResult = Fail
      EndIf
End     'main
```

There would be two other test cases, testing the transitions from INT to LOW, and LOW to HIGH. Next, we test the rest of the windshieldWiper class with the following pseudocode.

```
class test WindshieldWiper
      wiperSpeed
      leverPos
      dialPos
      testResult  'boolean
main()
      testCase = instantiate windshieldWiper(0, Off, 1)
      windshieldWiper.senseLeverUp()
      wiperSpeed = windshieldWiper.getWiperSpeed()
      If wiperSpeed = 4
           Then testResult = Pass
           Else testResult = Fail
      EndIf
End     'main
```

Two subtleties occur here. The easy one is that the instantiate windshieldWiper statement establishes the preconditions of the test case. The test case in the pseudocode happens to correspond to the default entry states of the Dial and Lever components of the StateChart in Figure 17.5. Notice it is easy to force other preconditions. The second subtlety is more obscure. The wiper component of the StateChart has what we might call the tester's (or external) view of the class. In this view, the wiper default entries and transitions are caused by various "inState" propositions. The implementation, however, causes these transitions by using the set methods to change the values of the state variables.

We have the StateChart definition of the class behavior; therefore, we can use it to define our test cases in much the same way that we used finite state machines to identify system-level test cases. StateChart-based class testing supports reasonable test coverage metrics. Some obvious ones are:

> Every event
> Every state in a component
> Every transition in a component
> All pairs of interacting states (in different components)
> Scenarios corresponding to customer-defined use cases

Table 17.1 contains test cases with the instantiate statements (to establish preconditions) and expected outputs for the "every transition in a component" coverage level for the lever component.

Table 17.1   Test Cases for the Lever Component

Test Case	Preconditions (Instantiate Statement)	windshieldWiper Event (Method)	Expected Value of leverPos
1	windshieldWiper(0, Off, 1)	senseLeverUp()	INT
2	windshieldWiper(0, Int, 1)	senseLeverUp()	LOW
3	windshieldWiper(0, Low, 1)	senseLeverUp()	HIGH
4	windshieldWiper(0, High, 1)	senseLeverDown()	LOW
5	windshieldWiper(0, Low, 1)	senseLeverDown()	INT
6	windshieldWiper(0, Int, 1)	senseLeverDown()	OFF

Notice that the higher levels of coverage actually imply an intraclass integration of methods, which seems to contradict the idea of class as unit. The scenario coverage criterion is nearly identical to that of system-level testing. Here is a use case and the corresponding message sequences needed in a test class:

UC 1	Normal Usage
Description	The windshield wiper is in the OFF position, and the Dial is at the 1 position; the user moves the lever to INT, and then moves the dial first to 2 and then to 3; the user then moves the lever to LOW; the user moves the lever to INT, and then to OFF
Preconditions	The windshield wiper is in the OFF position, and the Dial is at the 1 position; wiper speed is 0

Event Sequence	User Action	System Response
1	Move lever to INT	Wiper speed is 4
2	Move dial to 2	Wiper speed is 6
3	Move dial to 3	Wiper speed is 12
4	Move lever to LOW	Wiper speed is 20
5	Move lever to INT	Wiper speed is 12
6	Move lever to OFF	Wiper speed is 0

```
class testScenario
     wiperSpeed
     leverPos
     dialPos
     step1OK        'boolean
```

```
      step2OK       'boolean
      step3OK       'boolean
      step4OK       'boolean
      step5OK       'boolean
      step6OK       'boolean
main()
      testCase = instantiate windshieldWiper(0, Off, 1)
      windshieldWiper.senseLeverUp()
      wiperSpeed = windshieldWiper.getWiperSpeed()
      If wiperSpeed = 4
            Then step1OK = Pass
            Else step1OK = Fail
      EndIf

      windshieldWiper.senseDialUp()
      wiperSpeed = windshieldWiper.getWiperSpeed()
      If wiperSpeed = 6
            Then step2OK = Pass
            Else step2OK = Fail
      EndIf

      windshieldWiper.senseDialUp()
      wiperSpeed = windshieldWiper.getWiperSpeed()
      If wiperSpeed = 12
            Then step3OK = Pass
            Else step3OK = Fail
      EndIf

      windshieldWiper.senseLeverUp()
      wiperSpeed = windshieldWiper.getWiperSpeed()
      If wiperSpeed = 20
            Then step4OK = Pass
            Else step4OK = Fail
      EndIf

      windshieldWiper.senseLeverDown()
      wiperSpeed = windshieldWiper.getWiperSpeed()
      If wiperSpeed = 12
            Then step5OK = Pass
            Else step5OK = Fail
      EndIf

      windshieldWiper.senseLeverDown()
      wiperSpeed = windshieldWiper.getWiperSpeed()
      If wiperSpeed = 0
            Then step6OK = Pass
            Else step6OK = Fail
      EndIf
End   'main
```

Chapter 18

Object-Oriented Integration Testing

Of the three main levels of software testing, integration testing is the least understood; this is true for both traditional and object-oriented software. As with traditional procedural software, object-oriented integration testing presumes complete unit-level testing. Both unit choices have implications for object-oriented integration testing. If the operation/method choice is taken, two levels of integration are required: one to integrate operations into a full class and one to integrate the class with other classes. This should not be dismissed. The whole reason for the operation-as-unit choice is that the classes are very large, and several designers were involved.

Turning to the more common class-as-unit choice, once the unit testing is complete, two steps must occur: (1) if flattened classes were used, the original class hierarchy must be restored, and (2) if test methods were added, they must be removed.

Once we have our "integration test bed," we need to identify what needs to be tested. As we saw with traditional software integration, static and dynamic choices can be made. We can address the complexities introduced by polymorphism in a purely static way: test messages with respect to each polymorphic context. The dynamic view of object-oriented integration testing is more interesting.

18.1 UML Support for Integration Testing

In this chapter and the next, we will use the Unified Modeling Language (UML) to describe our examples. In UML-defined, object-oriented software, collaboration and sequence diagrams are the basis for integration testing. At the system level, UML description is comprised of various levels of use cases, a use case diagram, class definitions, and class diagrams (see Figure 16.4 and Figure 16.5). Once this level is defined, integration-level details are added. A collaboration diagram shows some of the message traffic among classes. Figure 18.1 is a collaboration diagram for the o-oCalendar application. A collaboration diagram is very analogous to the unit call graph we used in Chapter 13 (for example, see Figure 13.2). As such, a collaboration diagram supports both the pairwise and neighborhood approaches to integration testing.

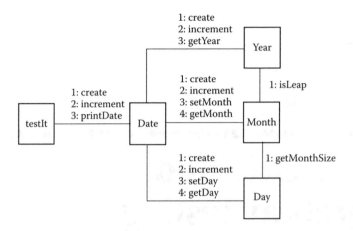

Figure 18.1 Collaboration diagram for o-oCalendar.

With pairwise integration, a unit (class) is tested in terms of separate adjacent classes that either send messages to or receive messages from the class being integrated. To the extent that the class sends/receives messages from other classes, the other classes must be expressed as stubs. All this extra effort makes pairwise integration of classes as undesirable as pairwise integration of procedural units. Based on the collaboration diagram in Figure 18.1, we would have the following pairs of classes to integrate:

> testIt and Date, with stubs for Year, Month, and Day
> Date and Year, with stubs for testIt, Month, and Day
> Date and Month, with stubs for testIt, Year, and Day
> Date and Day, with stubs for testIt, Month, and Year
> Year and Month, with stubs for Date and Day
> Month and Day, with stubs for Date and Year

One drawback to basing object-oriented integration testing on collaboration diagrams is that at the class level, the behavior model of choice in UML is the StateChart. For class-level behavior, StateCharts are an excellent basis of test cases, and this is particularly appropriate for the class-as-unit choice. The problem, however, is that in general it is difficult to combine StateCharts to see behavior at a higher level (Regmi, 1999).

Neighborhood integration raises some very interesting questions from graph theory. Using the (undirected) graph in Figure 18.1, the neighborhood of Date is the entire graph, while the neighborhood of testIt is just Date. It turns out that the mathematicians have identified various "centers" of a linear graph. One of them, for example, is the ultra-center, which minimizes the maximum distances to the other nodes in the graph. In terms of an integration order, we might picture the circular ripples caused by tossing a stone in calm water. We start with the ultra-center and the neighborhood of nodes one edge away, then add the nodes two edges away, and so on. Neighborhood integration of classes will certainly reduce the stub effort, but this will be at the expense of diagnostic precision. If a test case fails, we will have to look at more classes to find the fault.

A sequence diagram traces an execution time path through a collaboration diagram. (In UML, a sequence diagram has two levels: the system/use case level and the class interaction level). Thick, vertical lines represent either a class or an instance of a class, and the arrows are labeled with the

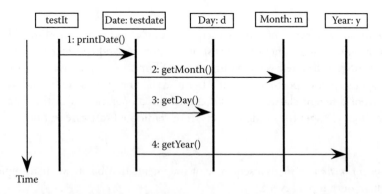

Figure 18.2   Sequence diagram for printDate.

messages sent by (instances of) the classes in their time order. The portion of the o-oCalendar application that prints out the new date is shown as a sequence diagram in Figure 18.2.

To the extent that sequence diagrams are created, they are an excellent basis for object-oriented integration testing. They are nearly equivalent to the object-oriented version of MM-Paths (which we define in the next subsection). An actual test for this sequence diagram would have pseudocode similar to this:

```
1. testDriver
2.      m.setMonth(1)
3.      d.setDay(15)
4.      y.setYear(2002)
5.      Output ("expected value is 1/15/2002"
6.      Output ("actual output is ")
7.      testIt.printDate()
8.      End testDriver
```

Statements 2 to 4 use the previously unit-tested methods to set the expected output in the classes to which messages are sent. As it stands, this test driver depends on a person to make a pass/fail judgment based on the printed output. We could put comparison logic into the testDriver class to make an internal comparison. This might be problematic in the sense that if we made a mistake in the code tested, we might make the same mistake in the comparison logic.

18.2 MM-Paths for Object-Oriented Software

When we spoke of MM-Paths in traditional software, we used *message* to refer to the invocation among separate units (modules), and we spoke of module execution paths (module-level threads) instead of full modules. Here, we use the same acronym to refer to an alternating sequence of method executions separated by messages — method-to-message path. Just as in traditional software, methods may have several internal execution paths. We choose not to operate at that level of detail for object-oriented integration testing. An MM-Path starts with a method and ends when it reaches a method that does not issue any messages of its own; this is the point of message quiescence.

Definition

An *MM-Path in object-oriented software* is a sequence of method executions linked by messages.

Recall the atomic system functions (ASFs) of Chapter 14, and consider the set of classes that support a given ASF. The system-level nature of an ASF means that, as a minimum, it represents a stimulus–response pair of port-level events. Because the port events are (most likely) associated with operations of different classes, this level entails the cooperation of distinct classes. We only need to make slight changes to two definitions from traditional software testing.

Definition

An *atomic system function* (*ASF*) is a sequence of statements that begins with an input port event and ends with an output port event.

The ASF construct addresses the event-driven nature of object-oriented software. Because ASFs commonly begin with a port input event and end with a port output event, they constitute what traditional models call a stimulus–response path. This system-level input triggers the method–message sequence of an MM-Path, which may trigger other MM-Paths until, finally, the sequence of MM-Paths ends with a port output event. When such a sequence ends, the system is event quiescent; that is, the system is waiting for another port input event that initiates another ASF. Just as we had with traditional software, this formulation places ASF testing at the point where integration- and system-level testing overlap.

18.2.1 Pseudocode for o-oCalendar

To see the complexity of object-oriented integration testing, we examine the o-oCalendar application in detail. The pseudocode is given next, with comments numbering the messages. The message traffic is shown in Figure 18.3 (just the message numbers are shown to reduce congestion).

```
class CalendarUnit    'abstract class
      currentPos As Integer

      CalendarUnit(pCurrentPos)
            currentPos = pCurrentPos
      End   'CalendarUnit

a     setCurrentPos(pCurrentPos)
b           currentPos = pCurrentPos
      End   'setCurrentPos

      abstract protected boolean increment()

class testIt
      main()
1           testdate = instantiate Date(testMonth, testDay,
            testYear)                                        msg1
2           testdate.increment()                            msg2
3           testdate.printDate()                            msg3
      End         'testIt
```

```
class Date
      private Day d
      private Month m
      private Year y

4     Date(pMonth, pDay, pYear)
5           y = instantiate Year(pYear)                      msg4
6           m = instantiate Month(pMonth, y)                 msg5
7           d = instantiate Day(pDay, m)                     msg6
      End 'Date constructor

8     increment ()
9           if (NOT(d.increment()))                          msg7
10    Then
11          if (NOT(m.increment()))                          msg8
12              Then
13                      y.increment()                        msg9
14                      m.setMonth(1,y)                       msg10
15              Else
16                      d.setDay(1, m)                        msg11
17          EndIf
18      EndIf
      End 'increment

19    printDate ()
20          Output (m.getMonth() + "/" + d.getDay() + "/" +
            y.getYear())
                                            msg12, msg13, msg14
      End             'printDate

class Day isA CalendarUnit
      private Month m

21    Day(pDay, Month pMonth)
22          setDay(pDay, pMonth)                             msg15
      End             'Day constructor

23    setDay(pDay, Month pMonth)
24          setCurrentPos(pDay)                              msg16
25          m = pMonth
      End         'setDay

26    getDay()
27          return currentPos
      End           'getDay

28    boolean increment()
29          currentPos = currentPos + 1
```

```
30            if (currentPos <= m.getMonthSize())            msg17
31                 Then   return true
32                 Else   return false
33            EndIf
        End            'increment


    class Month isA CalendarUnit
            private Year y
            private sizeIndex = <31, 28, 31, 30, 31, 30, 31,
            31, 30, 31, 30, 31>

34     Month( pcur, Year pYear)
35            setMonth(pCurrentPos, Year pyear)            msg18
        End            'Month constructor

36      setMonth( pcur, Year pYear)
37            setCurrentPos(pcur)                            msg19
38            y = pYear
        End            'setMonth

39     getMonth()
40            return currentPos
        End            'getMonth

41     getMonthSize()
42            if (y.isleap())                                msg20
43                 Then   sizeIndex[1] = 29
44                 Else   sizeIndex[1] = 28
45            EndIf
46            return sizeIndex[currentPos -1]
        End            'getMonthSize

47     boolean increment()
48            currentPos = currentPos + 1
49            if (currentPos > 12)
50                 Then   return false
51                 Else   return true
52            EndIf
        End            'increment


    class Year isA CalendarUnit

53     Year( pYear)
54            setCurrentPos(pYear)                           msg21
        End            'Year constructor

55     getYear()
```

```
56            return currentPos
      End            'getYear

57    boolean increment()
58            currentPos = currentPos + 1
59            return true
      End            'increment

60    boolean isleap()
61            if (((currentPos MOD 4 = 0) AND NOT(currentPos MOD
              100 = 0)) OR(currentPos MOD 400 = 0))
62                  Then  return true
63                  Else  return false
64            EndIf
      End            'isleap
```

Figure 18.3 is a more detailed view of the collaboration diagram in Figure 18.1. The difference is that the source and destination methods of each method are shown, instead of just the classes. With this formulation, we can view object-oriented integration testing independently of whether the units were chosen as methods or classes.

Here is a partial MM-Path to instantiate January 15, 2007. As we did in Chapter 13, we simply use the statement and message numbers from the pseudocode. This MM-Path is shown in Figure 18.4.

```
testIt<1>
      msg1
Date:testdate<4, 5>
      msg4
Year:y<53, 54>
      msg21
Year:y.setCurrentPos<a, b>
      (return to Year.y)
      (return to Date:testdate)
Date:testdate<6>
      msg5
Month:m<34, 35>
      msg18
Month:m.setMonth<36, 37>
      msg19
Month:m.setCurrentPos<a, b>
      (return to Month:m.setMonth)
      (return to Month:m)
      (return to Date:testdate)
Date:testdate<7>
      msg6
Day:d<21, 22>
      msg15
```

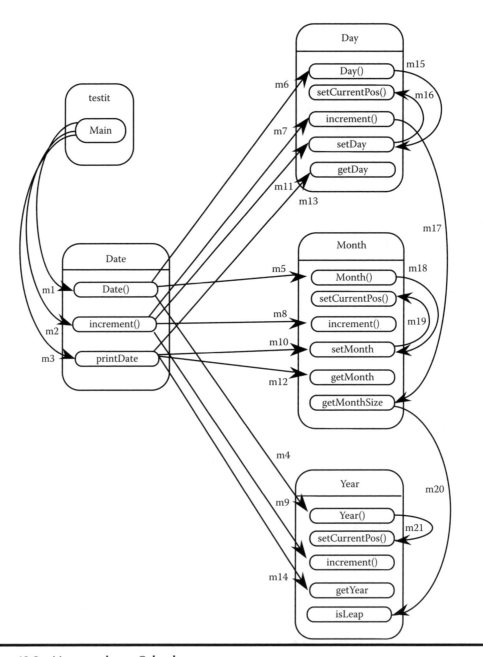

Figure 18.3   Messages in o-oCalendar.

```
Day:d.setDay<23, 24>
     msg16
Day:d.setCurrentPos<a, b>
     (return to Day:d.setDay)
Day:d.setDay<25>
     (return to Day:d)
     (return to Date:testdate)
```

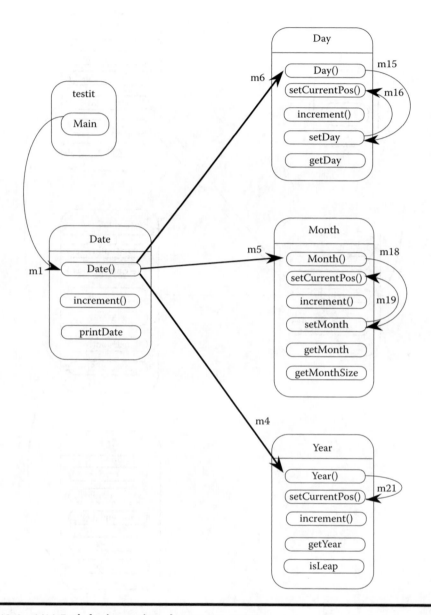

Figure 18.4   MM-Path for instantiate date (1, 15, 2007).

Here is a more interesting MM-Path, for the instantiated date April 30, 2007 (see Figure 18.5).

```
testIt<2>
      msg2
Date:testdate.increment<8, 9>
      msg7
Day:d.increment<28, 29>'now Day.d.currentPos = 31
      msg17
```

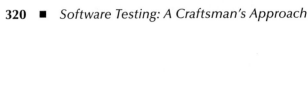

Figure 18.5 MM-Path for Date.increment (4, 30, 2007).

```
Month:m.getMonthSize<41, 42>
      msg20
Year:y.isleap<60, 61, 63, 64>        'not a leap year
      (return to Month:m.getMonthSize)
Month:m.getMonthSize<44, 45, 46>  'returns month size = 30
      (return to Day:d.increment)
Day:d.increment<32, 33>          'returns false
      (return to Date:testdate.increment)
```

```
Date:testdate.increment<10,11>
     msg8
Month:m.increment<47, 48, 49, 51, 52>    'returns true
     (return to Date:testdate.increment)
Date:testdate.increment<15, 16>
     msg11
Day:d.setDay<23, 24, 25>       'now day is 1, month is 5
     (return to Date:testdate.increment)
Date:testdate.increment<17, 18>
     return to testIt>
```

Having a directed graph formulation puts us in a position to be analytical about choosing MM-Path–based integration test cases. First, we might ask how many test cases will be needed. The directed graph in Figure 18.3 has a cyclomatic complexity of 23 (the return edges of each message are not shown, but they must be counted). Although we could certainly find the same number of basis paths, it is not necessary to do this because a single MM-Path will cover many of these paths, and many more are logically infeasible. A lower limit would be three test cases: the MM-Paths beginning with statements 1, 2, and 3 in the testIt pseudocode. This might not be sufficient because, for example, if we choose an "easy" date (such as January 15, 2007), the messages involving isLeap and setMonth will not occur. Just as we saw with unit-level testing of procedural code, as a minimum, we need a set of MM-Paths that cover every message. The 13 decision table–based functional test cases we identified for NextDate in Chapter 7 (see Table 7.16) constitute a thorough set of integration test cases for the o-oCalendar application. This is a point where the structural view of object-oriented integration testing gives insights that we cannot get from the functional view. We can look for MM-Paths to make sure that every message (edge) in the graph of Figure 18.3 is traversed.

18.3 A Framework for Object-Oriented Dataflow Integration Testing

MM-Paths were defined to serve as integration testing analogs of DD-Paths. As we saw for procedural software, DD-Path testing is often insufficient, and in such cases, dataflow testing is more appropriate. The same holds for integration testing of object-oriented software; if anything, the need is greater for two reasons: (1) data can get values from the inheritance tree, and (2) data can be defined at various stages of message passing.

Program graphs formed the basis for describing and analyzing dataflow testing for procedural code. The complexities of object-oriented software exceed the expressive capabilities of directed (program) graphs. This subsection presents an expressive framework within which dataflow testing questions for object-oriented software can be described and analyzed.

18.3.1 Event- and Message-Driven Petri Nets

Event-driven Petri nets were defined in Chapter 4; we extend them here to express the message communication among objects. Figure 18.6 shows the notational symbols used in an event- and message-driven Petri net (EMDPN).

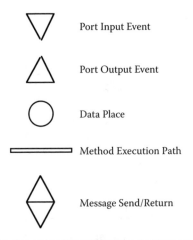

Figure 18.6 Symbols for EMDPNs.

Definition

An *Event- and message-driven petri net* (EMDPN) is a quadripartite directed graph (P, D, M, S, In, Out) composed of four sets of nodes, P, D, M, and S, and two mappings, In and Out, where:

P is a set of port events
D is a set of data places
M is a set of message places
S is a set of transitions
In is a set of ordered pairs from $(P \cup D \cup M) \times S$
Out is a set of ordered pairs from $S \times (P \cup D \cup M)$

We retain the port input and output events because these will certainly occur in event-driven, object-oriented applications. Obviously, we still need data places, and we will interpret Petri net transitions as method execution paths. The new symbol is intended to capture the essence of interobject messages:

They are an output of a method execution path in the sending object.
They are an input to a method execution path in the receiving object.
The return is a very subtle output of a method execution path in the receiving object.
The return is an input to a method execution path in the sending object.

Figure 18.7 shows the only way that the new message place can appear in an EMDPN.

The EMDPN structure, because it is a directed graph, provides the needed framework for dataflow analysis of object-oriented software. Recall that dataflow analysis for procedural code centers on nodes where values are defined and used. In the EMDPN framework, data is represented by a data place, and values are defined and used in method execution paths. A data place can be either an input to or an output of a method execution path; therefore, we can now represent the define/use paths (du-path) in a way very similar to that for procedural code. Even though four types of nodes exist, we still have paths among them; so we simply ignore the types of nodes in a du-path and focus only on the connectivity.

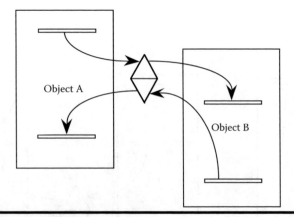

Figure 18.7   Message connections between objects.

18.3.2 Inheritance-Induced Dataflow

Consider an inheritance tree in which the value of a data item is defined, and in that tree, consider a chain that begins with a data place where the value is defined and ends at the bottom of the tree. That chain will be an alternating sequence of data places and degenerate method execution paths, in which the method execution paths implement the inheritance mechanism of the object-oriented language. This framework therefore supports several forms of inheritance: single, multiple, and selective multiple. The EMDPN that expresses inheritance is comprised only of data places and method execution paths, as shown in Figure 18.8.

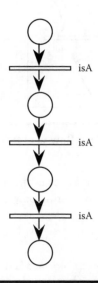

18.3.3 Message-Induced Dataflow

The EMDPN in Figure 18.9 shows the message communication among three objects. As

Figure 18.8   Dataflow with inheritance.

an example of a du-path, suppose mep3 is a define node for a data item that is passed on by mep5, modified in mep6, and finally used in the use node mep2. We can identify these two du-paths:

```
du1 = <mep3, msg2, mep5, d6, mep6, return(msg2), mep4,
       return(msg1), mep2>
du2 = <mep6, return(msg2), mep4, return(msg1), mep2>
```

In this example, du2 is definition-clear, du1 is not.

18.3.4 Slices?

It is tempting to assert that this formulation also supports slices in object-oriented software. The fundamentals are there, so we could go through the graph theory motions. Recall that the more

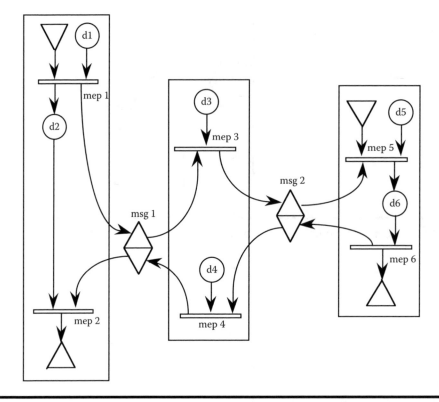

Figure 18.9 Dataflow via message communication.

desirable form of a slice is one that is executable. This appears to be a real stretch, and without it, such slices are interesting only as a desk-checking approach to fault location.

Reference

Regmi, D.R., Object-Oriented Software Construction Based on State Charts, Grand Valley State University master's project, Allendale, MI, 1999.

Exercises

Here is a real change of pace. It is an excerpt from a play that my wife's sixth-grade classes sometimes perform. It is also a sustained analogy with object-oriented integration testing. Using this analogy, apply the integration testing concepts we studied to play rehearsals. To start, consider a character in a play to be a class. Because characters communicate by cues, we can consider a character's line as a message to another character.

First, the "source code" (excerpted from *The Phantom Tollbooth*, by Susan Janus (based on the book by Norton Juster), Act I, Scene 2):

1. **WATCHDOG.** Dictionopolis, here we come.
2. **MILO.** Hey, Watchdog, are you coming along?
3. **TOCK.** You can call me Tock, and keep your eyes on the road.

4. **MILO.**   What kind of place is Dictionopolis, anyway?
5. **TOCK.**   It's where all the words in the world come from. It used to be a marvelous place, but ever since Rhyme and Reason left, it hasn't been the same.
6. **MILO.**   Rhyme and Reason?
7. **TOCK.**   The two princesses. They used to settle all the arguments between their two brothers who rule over the Land of Wisdom. You see, Azaz is the king of Dictionopolis and the Mathemagician is the king of Digitopolis and they almost never see eye to eye on anything. It was the job of the Princesses Sweet Rhyme and Pure Reason to solve the differences between the two kings, and they always did so well that both sides usually went home satisfied. But then, one day, the kings had an argument to end all arguments…

   [The lights dim on Tock and Milo and come up on King Azaz of Dictionopolis on another part of the stage. Azaz has a great stomach, a gray beard reaching to his waist, a small crown, and a long robe with the letters of the alphabet written all over it.]
8. **Azaz.**   Of course, I'll abide by the decision of Rhyme and Reason, though I have no doubt as to what it will be. They will choose words, of course. Everyone knows that words are more important than numbers any day of the week.

   [The Mathemagician appears opposite Azaz. The Mathemagician wears a long, flowing robe covered entirely with complex mathematical equations, and a tall, pointed hat. He carries a long staff with a pencil point at one end and a large rubber eraser at the other.]
9. **Mathemagician.**   That's what you think, Azaz. People wouldn't even know what day of the week it is without numbers. Haven't you ever looked at a calendar? Face it, Azaz, It's numbers that count.
10. **Azaz.**   Don't be ridiculous. [To audience, as if leading a cheer.] Let's hear it for WORDS!
11. **Mathemagician.**   [To audience, in the same manner.] Cast your vote for NUMBERS!
12. **Azaz.**   A, B, C's!
13. **Mathemagician.**   1, 2, 3's!
14. **Azaz and Mathemagician.**   [To each other.] Quiet! Rhyme and Reason are about to announce their decision.
15. **Rhyme.**   Ladies and gentlemen, letters and numerals, fractions and punctuation marks — may we have your attention please. After careful consideration of the problem set before us by King Azaz of Dictionopolis [Azaz bows.] and the Mathemagician of Digitopolis [Mathemagician raises his hands in a victory salute.] we have come to the following conclusion.
16. **Reason.**   Words and numbers are of equal value, for in the cloak of knowledge, one is the warp and the other is the woof.
17. **Rhyme.**   It is no more important to count the sands than it is to name the stars.
18. **Rhyme and Reason.**   Therefore, let both kingdoms, Dictionopolis and Digitopolis, live in peace.

   [The sound of cheering is heard.]
19. **Azaz.**   Boo! is what I say. Boo and Bah and Hiss!
20. **Mathemagician.**   What good are these girls if they can't even settle an argument in anyone's favor? I think I have come to a decision of my own.
21. **Azaz.**   So have I.
22. **Azaz and Mathemagician.**   [To the princesses.] You are hereby banished from this land to the Castle-in-the-Air. [To each other.] And as for you, KEEP OUT OF MY WAY! [They stalk off in opposite directions.]

[During this time, the set is changed to the Market Square of Dictionopolis. The lights come up on the deserted square.]

23. **TOCK.**   And ever since then, there has been neither Rhyme nor Reason in this kingdom. Words are misused and numbers are mismanaged. The argument between the two kings has divided everyone and the real value of both words and numbers has been forgotten. What a waste!

24. **MILO.**   Why doesn't somebody rescue the princesses and set everything straight again?

25. **TOCK.**   That is easier said than done. The Castle-in-the-Air is very far from here, and the one path that leads to it is guarded by ferocious demons. But hold on, here we are. [A man appears, carrying a gate and a small tollbooth.]

26. **Gatekeeper.**   AHHHHREMMMM! This is Dictionopolis, a happy kingdom, advantageously located in the foothills of confusion and caressed by gentle breezes from the Sea of Knowledge. Today, by royal proclamation, is Market Day. Have you come to buy or sell?

27. **MILO.**   I beg your pardon?

28. **Gatekeeper.**   Buy or sell, buy or sell. Which is it? You must have come here for a reason.

29. **MILO.**   Well, I …

30. **Gatekeeper.**   Come now, if you don't have a reason, you must at least have an explanation or certainly an excuse.

31. **MILO.**   [Meekly.] Uh … no.

32. **Gatekeeper.**   [Shaking his head.] Very serious. You can't get in without a reason. [Thoughtfully.] Wait a minute. Maybe I have an old one you can use. [Pulls out an old suitcase from the tollbooth and rummages through it.] No … no … no … this won't do … hmmmm …

33. **MILO.**   [To Tock.] What's he looking for? [Tock shrugs.]

34. **Gatekeeper.**   Ah! This is fine. [Pulls out a medallion on a chain. Engraved in the medallion is "WHY NOT?"] Why not. That's a good reason for almost anything … a bit used perhaps, but still quite serviceable. There you are, sir. Now I can truly say: Welcome to Dictionopolis.

Finally, the exercises:

1. Develop the analog of a call graph (or collaboration diagram) for the characters in this excerpt.

2. What is the analog of pairwise integration? How effective is this as a rehearsal technique? List several likely pairs of characters that would rehearse.

3. What is the analog of neighborhood integration? How effective is this as a rehearsal technique? Describe at least two neighborhoods of characters.

4. Can you find something that corresponds to an ASF?

5. A play director might schedule rehearsals in much the same way that a software development project would develop builds for integration testing. What builds do you find?

6. In what ways does the difference between ordinary and dress rehearsals correspond to the difference between integration and system testing?

7. What happens to this analogy if we take characters to be objects and cues to be messages? Take lines 1 to 7 as scene 1, lines 8 to 22 as scene 2, and lines 23 to 34 as scene 3, and then develop sequence diagrams for these three scenes.

Chapter 19

GUI Testing

The main characteristic of any graphical user interface (GUI) application is that it is event driven. Users can cause any of several events in any order. Although it is possible to create GUI applications in which the event sequence is "guided," many GUIs are deficient in this respect. GUI applications offer one small benefit to testers: there is little need for integration testing. Unit testing is typically at the button level; that is, buttons have functions, and these can be tested in the usual unit-level sense. The essence of system-level testing for GUI applications is to exercise the event-driven nature of the application. Unfortunately, most of the models in the Unified Modeling Language (UML) are of little help with event-driven systems. The main exception is behavioral models, specifically StateCharts and their simpler case, finite state machines.

19.1 The Currency Conversion Program

The currency conversion program is an event-driven program that emphasizes code associated with a GUI. A sample GUI built with Visual Basic is shown in Figure 19.1 (repeated from Chapters 2 and 16). The full description of the currency conversion program is in Section 16.8.2. Those pages are not repeated here, but they are necessary to the following discussion.

19.2 Unit Testing for the Currency Conversion Program

The functional buttons (Compute, Clear, and Quit) have user-supplied code; hence, they are sensible places to perform unit-level testing. Some of the output events indicate functions that should occur in the Compute click event, namely, error messages when missing inputs occur. Unit testing of the Compute button should also consider invalid U.S. dollar amount entries, such as nonnumerical inputs, negative inputs, and very large inputs. Both functional and structural testing should occur at this level, and our earlier discussion (Part II) on traditional software still applies.

The best methods for performing unit-level testing are open for discussion. One possibility is to run test cases from a specially coded driver that would provide values for input data and check output values against expected values. A second method is to use the GUI as a test bed. This looks

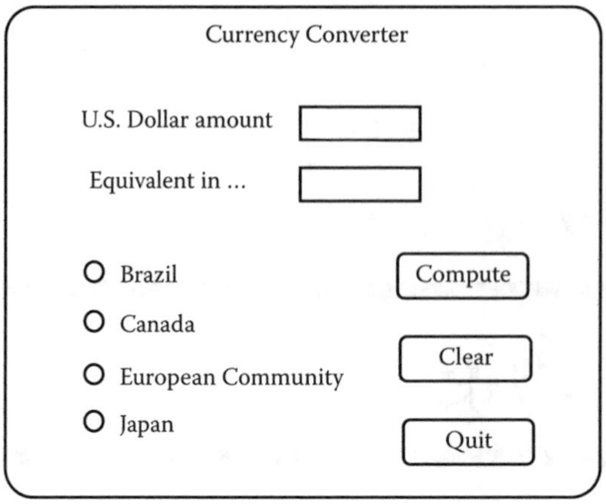

Figure 19.1 Currency converter GUI.

like system-level unit testing, which seems oxymoronic, but it is workable. It is system level in the sense that test case inputs are provided via system-level user input events, and test case result comparisons are based on system-level output events. This is okay for small applications, but it does beg some serious questions. For example, suppose the computation is correct, but a fault occurs in the output software. Another problem is that it will be harder to capture test execution results. Some other problems:

> There will be a real tendency for ad hoc testing.
> A greater potential exists for user input and observation errors.
> Repeating a set of test cases is time-consuming.

On balance, unit testing with a test driver looks preferable.

Other, more subtle unit-level tests are associated with the U.S. dollar amount text box, and these are language dependent. If implemented in Visual Basic, for example, there is little need to unit test the text box. If we have a truly object-oriented implementation, we would need to verify that the inputs observed by the keyboard handler are correctly displayed on the GUI and correctly stored in the object's attributes.

19.3 Integration Testing for the Currency Conversion Program

Whether integration testing is appropriate for this example depends on how it is implemented. Three main choices are available for the Compute button. The first concentrates all logic in one place and simply uses the status of the option buttons as conditions in IF tests, as in the following pseudocode:

```
procedure Compute ( USDollarAmount, EquivCurrencyAmount)
dim brazilRate, canadaRate, euroRate, japanRate, USDollarAmount
As Single
If (optionBrazil)
   Then EquivCurrencyAmount = brazilRate * USDollarAmount
   Else
```

```
        If (optionCanada)
            Then EquivCurrencyAmount = canadaRate *
            USDollarAmount
            Else
                If (optionEuropeanUnion)
                    Then EquivCurrencyAmount = euroRate *
                    USDollarAmount
                    Else
                        If (optionJapan)
                            Then EquivCurrencyAmount =
                            japanRate * USDollarAmount
                            Else Output ("No country selected")
                        EndIF
                EndIF
        EndIF
EndIF
End procedure Compute
```

Because this would be thoroughly tested at the unit level, there is little need for integration testing.

A second and more object oriented choice would have methods in each option button object that send the exchange rate value for the corresponding country in response to a click event. (How the exchange rate values are set is a separate question; for now, we assume they are defined when the objects are instantiated.) Pseudocode for the instantiated objects and the revised command button procedure is as follows:

```
object optionBrazil (USDollarExchangeRate)
      private procedure senseClick
            commandCompute(USDollarExchangeRate)
      End senseClick

object optionCanada(USDollarExchangeRate)
      private procedure senseClick
            commandCompute(USDollarExchangeRate)
      End senseClick

object optionEuropeanUnion (USDollarExchangeRate)
      private procedure senseClick
            commandCompute(USDollarExchangeRate)
      End senseClick

object optionJapan (USDollarExchangeRate)
      private procedure senseClick
            commandCompute(USDollarExchangeRate)
      End senseClick
procedure Compute ( exchangeRate, USDollarAmount)
```

```
dim exchangeRate, USDollarAmount As Single
        EquivCurrencyAmount = exchangeRate * USDollarAmount
End procedure Compute
```

Notice that, as units, there is very little to test. (This is why the choice of methods as units depends on size.) Everything of interest is at the integration level, and at that level, we have two concerns: Are the option/radio buttons sending the right exchange rate values, and is the equivalent amount calculation correct?

The third implementation is in the Visual Basic® style. Visual Basic is now so widespread that it warrants consideration here. The pseudocode for a Visual Basic implementation includes a global (actually a form-level) variable for the exchange rate. The event procedures for each option button give a predefined value to the exchange rate variable. The result is very similar to the pure object-oriented version. Unit testing could be replaced by simple code reading for the option button event procedures, and the testing of the commandCompute procedure is similarly trivial. Notice that in all three variations, there is little need for integration testing. This is true for small GUI applications, where a good definition of "small" is an application implemented by one person.

```
Public exchangeRate As Single

Private Sub optBrazil_Click()
        exchangeRate = 1.56
End Sub

Private Sub optCanada_Click()
        exchangeRate = 1.35
End Sub

Private Sub optEuropeanUnion_Click()
        exchangeRate = 0.93
End Sub

Private Sub optJapan_Click()
        exchangeRate = 2.04
End Sub

Private Sub cmdCompute ()
        EquivCurrencyAmount = exchangeRate *
        Val(txtUSDollarAmount.text)
End Sub
```

19.4 System Testing for the Currency Conversion Program

As we have seen, unit and integration testing, at least for small GUI applications, are minimally needed. The onus therefore shifts to system testing. Because GUI applications are event driven, we can use event-driven Petri nets (EDPNs) to describe threads to be tested. Table 19.1 and Table 19.2

Table 19.1   Port Input Events

	Input Events		Input Events
p1	Enter U.S. dollar amount	p5	Click on Japan
p2	Click on Brazil	p6	Click on Compute button
p3	Click on Canada	p7	Click on Clear button
p4	Click on European Union	p8	Click on Quit button

list the port input and output events in the currency conversion GUI; they are nearly identical to the Visual Basic events in Table 16.1a and b. Table 19.3 lists the atomic system functions (ASFs), and Table 19.4 lists the data places that we need to make the EDPN of the GUI. The events relating to the country flags are deleted to simplify both the discussion and figures.

There is a subtle change in Table 19.4: the data place d2 is named "Country selected." It is more precise to have a data place for each country, but this really complicates the subsequent drawings. As it stands, it still represents a workable implementation.

The next step in building an EDPN description of the currency conversion GUI is to develop the EDPNs for the individual atomic system functions. These are shown in Figure 19.2. As we saw in Chapter 14, system-level threads are built up by composing atomic system functions into sequences. One such thread is shown in Figure 19.3.

We are finally in a position to describe various sets of system-level test cases for the currency conversion GUI. The lowest level is to simply exercise every atomic system function. This is a little artificial, because many atomic system functions have data outputs that are not visible system-level outputs. Even worse, the possibility always exists that an atomic system function has no port outputs, as with s1: store U.S. dollar amount. At the system testing level, we cannot tell if an amount is correctly stored, although we can look at the screen and see that the correct amount has been entered.

Table 19.2   Port Output Events

	Output Events		Output Events
p9	Display U.S. dollar amount	p18	Indicate Japan
p10	Display Brazilian reals	p19	Reset Canada, EU, and Japan
p11	Display Canadian dollars	p20	Reset Brazil, EU, and Japan
p12	Display EU euros	p21	Reset Brazil, Canada, and Japan
p13	Display Japanese yen	p22	Reset Brazil, Canada, and EU
p14	Display ellipses	p23	Reset U.S. dollar amount
p15	Indicate Brazil	p24	Reset equivalent currency amount
p16	Indicate Canada	p25	End application
p17	Indicate European Union		

Table 19.3 Atomic System Functions

	Atomic System Functions		*Atomic System Functions*
s1	Store U.S. dollar amount	s5	Sense click on Japan
s2	Sense click on Brazil	s6	Sense click on Compute button
s3	Sense click on Canada	s7	Sense click on Clear button
s4	Sense click on EU	s8	Sense click on Quit button

The next level of system testing is to exercise a suitable set of threads. This begs the question of what constitutes suitable. Here are some easy possibilities; exercise a set of threads that:

Use every atomic system function
Use every port input
Use every port output

Beyond this, we can look at a directed graph of atomic system functions, as shown in Figure 19.4. This is only a partial graph; it shows mainline behavior. The thread <s1, s4, s6, s7> (the one in Figure 19.3) is one of 12 paths. Four of these end with the Clear button clicked; the other eight end with the Quit button. Consider the set T of threads {T1, T2, T3, T4}, where their ASF sequences are listed next:

T1 = <s1, s4, s6, s7>
T2 = <s1, s2, s6, s7>
T3 = <s3, s1, s6, s8>
T4 = <s5, s1, s7, s8>

The threads in set T have the following coverages:

Every atomic system function
Every port input
Every port output

As such, set T constitutes a reasonable minimum level of system testing for the currency conversion GUI. We could go into more detail by exploring some next-level user behavior. The thread T5 = <s1, s2, s6, s3, s6, s4, s6, s5, s6, s7, s8> is a good example, where the user converts a U.S. dollar amount to each of the four currencies, then clears the screen and quits. We could also explore some of the many abnormal user behavior sequences (the sequences are abnormal, not the users), such as T6 = <s1, s2, s3, s4, s5, s6, s7, s8>. In T6, the user changes his or her mind about which currency

Table 19.4 Data Places

	Data Places		*Data Places*
d1	U.S. dollar amount entered	d2	Country selected

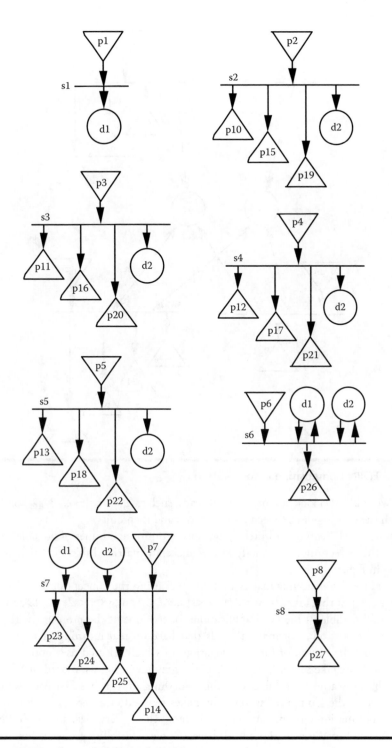

Figure 19.2 EDPNs of atomic system functions.

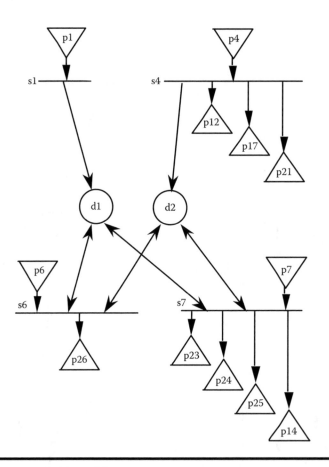

Figure 19.3 EDPN Composition of four ASFs.

to convert. We could also look at almost silly threads, such as T7 = <s1, s2, s3, s2, s3, s2, s3, s2, s3, s8>, in which the user toggles between two countries and then quits.

Threads such as T7 can be infinitely long; thus, an infinite number of possible threads occur in this GUI. This is seen more abstractly in the adjacency matrix (Table 19.5) that completes the partial graph in Figure 19.4.

We can reduce the adjacency matrix in Table 19.5 using the concept of forced navigation. It makes no sense to test threads such as <s1, s7>, <s1, s8>, <s1, s6, s8>, <s2, s6, s8>, and many others. These are all feasible in the GUI application; indeed, one of the problems with GUI design and testing is the possibility of many threads that have no real meaning or utility. Most GUI languages support the notion of forced navigation, in which selected user options only become available when they make sense. One example: the gray menu item standard in Windows applications, which, for example, prohibits copying something until it has first been selected. In the currency converter, the Compute button only makes sense after a U.S. dollar amount has been entered and a destination currency has been selected. (This is very clear in the EDPN of atomic system function s6.) In Visual Basic controls have a Boolean visibility property. Forced navigation in the currency converter could be implemented by making the Compute button invisible until its prerequisite events have occurred. Although forced navigation eliminates many curious threads, it comes at a price — additional output events and program logic. Table 19.6 contains an adjacency matrix of a highly prescriptive forced navigation currency converter.

Table 19.5   Adjacency Matrix of GUI Atomic System Functions

	s1	s2	s3	s4	s5	s6	s7	s8
s1	1	1	1	1	1	1	1	1
s2	1	0	1	1	1	1	1	1
s3	1	1	0	1	1	1	1	1
s4	1	1	1	0	1	1	1	1
s5	1	1	1	1	0	1	1	1
s6	1	1	1	1	1	1	1	1
s7	1	1	1	1	1	1	1	1
s8	0	0	0	0	0	0	0	0

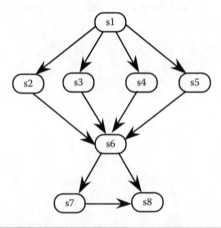

Figure 19.4   Directed graph of intended atomic system function sequences.

Table 19.6   Adjacency Matrix with Forced Navigation

	s1	s2	s3	s4	s5	s6	s7	s8
s1	1	1	1	1	1	0	0	0
s2	0	0	1	1	1	1	0	0
s3	0	1	0	1	1	1	0	0
s4	0	1	1	0	1	1	0	0
s5	0	1	1	1	0	1	0	0
s6	1	1	1	1	1	0	1	1
s7	1	1	1	1	1	0	0	1
s8	0	0	0	0	0	0	0	0

Column *s1* forces the entry of a U.S. dollar amount before a destination currency can be selected. The rows *s2*, *s3*, *s4*, *s5*, and *s6* show that the Compute button can be selected only after a destination currency has been selected. Just these few changes greatly reduce the number of feasible paths. Mathematically, the presence of loops means that there is an infinite number of possible paths, but a tester would not test the infinite number of duplications anyway.

Exercises

1. Part of the art of GUI design is to prevent user input errors. Event-driven applications are particularly vulnerable to input errors because events can occur in any order. As the given pseudocode definition stands, a user could enter a U.S. dollar amount and then click on the Compute button without selecting a country. Similarly, the user could select a country and then click on the Compute button without inputting a dollar amount. In an object-oriented application, we can control this by being careful about when we instantiate objects. Revise the GUI class pseudocode to prevent these two errors.
2. Does it make sense to test threads such as <s1, s7>, <s1, s8>, <s1, s6, s8>, and <s2, s6, s8> in the currency converter?

Chapter 20

Object-Oriented
System Testing

System testing is (or should be) independent of system implementation. A system tester does not really need to know if the implementation is in procedural or object-oriented code. As we saw in Chapter 14, the primitives of system testing are port input and output events, and we know how to express system-level threads as event-driven Petri nets (EDPNs). The issue is how to identify threads to be used as test cases. In Chapter 14, we used the requirements specification models, particularly the behavioral models, as the basis of thread test case identification. We also discussed pseudostructural coverage metrics in terms of the underlying behavioral models. In a sense, this chapter is very object oriented: we inherit many ideas from system testing of traditional software. The only real difference in this chapter is that we presume the system has been defined and refined with the Unified Modeling Language (UML). One emphasis, then, is finding system-level thread test cases from standard UML models.

20.1 Currency Converter UML Description

We will use the currency converter application as an example for system testing. Because the Unified Modeling Language from the Object Management Group is now widely accepted, we will use a rather complete UML description, in the style of Larman (1998). The terminology and UML content generally follow the Larman UML style, with the addition of pre- and postconditions in expanded essential use cases.

20.1.1 Problem Statement

The currency converter application converts U.S. dollars to any of four currencies: Brazilian real, Canadian dollars, European Union euros, and Japanese yen. The user can revise inputs and perform repeated currency conversion.

Table 20.1   System Functions for the Currency Converter Application

Reference No.	Function	Category
R1	Start application	Evident
R2	End application	Evident
R3	Input U.S. dollar amount	Evident
R4	Select country	Evident
R5	Perform conversion calculation	Evident
R6	Clear user inputs and program outputs	Evident
R7	Maintain exclusive-or relationship among countries	Hidden
R8	Display country flag images	Frill

20.1.2 System Functions

In the first step, sometimes called project inception, the customer/user describes the application in very general terms. This might take the form of user stories, which are precursors to use cases. From these, three types of system functions are identified: evident, hidden, and frill. Evident functions are the obvious ones. Hidden functions might not be discovered immediately, and frills are the "bells and whistles" that so often occur. Table 20.1 lists the system functions for the currency converter application.

20.1.3 Presentation Layer

Pictures are still worth a thousand words. The third step in Larman's approach is to sketch the user interface; our version is in Figure 20.1. This much information can support a customer walkthrough to demonstrate that the system functions identified can be supported by the interface.

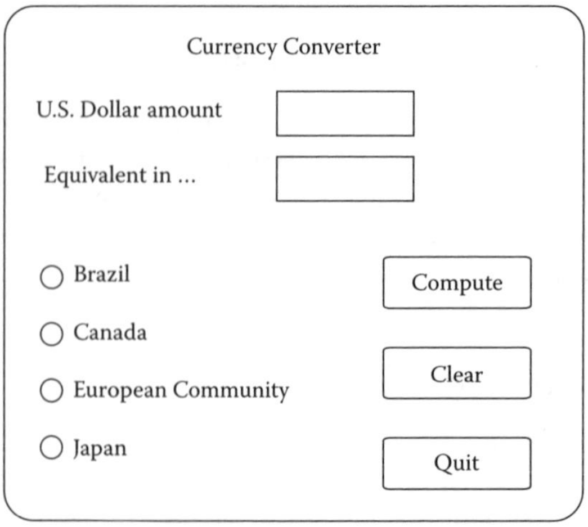

Figure 20.1   Currency conversion user interface.

20.1.4 High-Level Use Cases

The use case development begins with a very high level view. Notice, as the succeeding levels of use cases are elaborated, much of the early information is retained. It is convenient to have a short, structured naming convention for the various levels of use cases. Here, for example, HLUC refers to high-level use case. Very few details are provided in a high-level use case; they are insufficient for test case identification. The main point of high-level use cases is that they capture a narrative description of something that happens in the system to be built.

HLUC 1	Start application
Actor(s)	User
Type	Primary
Description	The user starts the currency conversion application in Windows®

HLUC 2	End application
Actor(s)	User
Type	Primary
Description	The user ends the currency conversion application in Windows

HLUC 3	Convert dollars
Actor(s)	User
Type	Primary
Description	The user inputs a U.S. dollar amount and selects a country; the application computes and displays the equivalent in the currency of the selected country

HLUC 4	Revise inputs
Actor(s)	User
Type	Secondary
Description	The user resets inputs to begin a new transaction

20.1.5 Essential Use Cases

Essential use cases add "actor" and "system" events to a high-level use case. Actors in UML are sources of system-level inputs (i.e., port input events). Actors can be people, devices, adjacent systems, or abstractions such as time. The numbering of actor actions and system responses (port output events) shows their approximate sequences in time. In EUC 3, for example, human observers cannot detect the sequence of system responses 4 and 5; they would appear to be simultaneous.

EUC 1	Start application	
Actor(s)	User	
Type	Primary	
Description	The user starts the currency conversion application in Windows	
Sequence	Actor action	System response
	1. The user starts the application, either with a Run ... command or by double-clicking the application icon	2. The currency conversion application GUI appears on the monitor and is ready for user input

EUC 2	End application	
Actor(s)	User	
Type	Primary	
Description	The user ends the currency conversion application in Windows	
Sequence	Actor action	System response
	1. The user ends the application, either by clicking a Quit button or by closing the window	2. The currency conversion application GUI disappears from the monitor

EUC 3	Convert dollars	
Actor(s)	User	
Type	Primary	
Description	The user inputs a U.S. dollar amount and selects a country; the application computes and displays the equivalent in the currency of the selected country	
Sequence	Actor action	System response
	1. The user enters a dollar amount	2. The dollar amount is displayed on the GUI
	3. The user selects a country	4. The name of the country's currency is displayed
		5. The flag of the country is displayed
	6. The user requests a conversion calculation	7. The equivalent currency amount is displayed

EUC 4	Revise inputs
Actor(s)	User
Type	Secondary

Description	The user resets inputs to begin a new transaction	
Sequence	Actor action	System response
	1. The user enters a dollar amount	2. The dollar amount is displayed on the GUI
	3. The user selects a country	4. The name of the country's currency is displayed
		5. The flag of the country is displayed
	6. The user cancels the inputs	7. The name of the country's currency is removed
		8. The flag of the country is no longer visible

20.1.6 Detailed GUI Definition

Once a set of essential use cases has been identified, the graphical user interface (GUI) is fleshed out with design-level detail. Here, we implement the currency converter in Visual Basic and follow the recommended (Zak, 2001) naming conventions for Visual Basic controls, as shown in Figure 20.2. (For readers not familiar with Visual Basic, this design uses four types of controls: text boxes for input, labels for output, option buttons to indicate choices, and command buttons to control the execution of the application.) These controls will be referred to in the expanded essential use cases. As in Chapter 19, we omit the country flag images.

20.1.7 Expanded Essential Use Cases

The expanded essential use cases (EEUCs) are the penultimate refinement of the high-level use cases. Here, we add pre- and postcondition information (not part of the Larman flavor), information about alternative sequences of events, and a cross-reference to the system functions identified

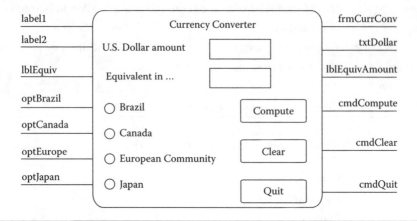

Figure 20.2 Visual Basic controls.

very early in the process. The other expansion is that more use cases are identified and added at this point. This is a normal part of any specification and design process: more detailed views provide more detailed insights. Note that the numeric tracing across levels of use cases is lost at this point.

The pre- and post-conditions warrant some additional comment. We are only interested in conditions that directly pertain to the expanded essential use case defined. We could always add preconditions such as "power is on," "computer is running under Windows®," and so on. As we saw in Chapter 15, threads (when expressed as EDPNs) interact via data places. The recommended practice is to record pre- and postconditions that will likely correspond to data places when the threads corresponding to expanded essential use cases are expressed as EDPNs.

EEUC 1	Start application	
Actor(s)	User	
Preconditions	Currency conversion application in (disk) storage	
Type	Primary	
Description	The user starts the currency conversion application in Windows	
Sequence	Actor action	System response
	1. User double-clicks currency conversion application icon	2. "frmCurrConv" appears on screen
Alternative sequence	User opens currency conversion application with the Windows Run command	
Cross-reference	R1	
Postconditions	Currency conversion application is in memory; txtDollar has focus	

EEUC 2	End application	
Actor(s)	User	
Preconditions	frmCurrConv is in run mode	
Type	Primary	
Description	The user ends the currency conversion application in Windows	
Sequence	Actor action	System response
	1. User clicks cmdQuit	2. frmCurrConv is unloaded
Alternative sequence	User closes frmCurrConv window	
Cross-reference	R2	
Postconditions	Currency conversion application in storage	

EEUC 3	Normal usage (dollar amount entered first)	
Actor(s)	User	
Preconditions	txtDollar has focus	
Type	Primary	

Description	The user inputs a U.S. dollar amount and selects a country; the application computes and displays the equivalent in the currency of the selected country	
Sequence	Actor action	System response
	1. User enters U.S. dollar amount on keyboard	2. Dollar amount appears in txtDollar
	3. User clicks on a country button	4. Country currency name appears in lblEquiv
	5. User clicks cmdCompute button	6. Computed equivalent amount appears in lblEqAmount
Alternative sequence	Actions 1 and 3 can be reversed, and consequently, responses 2 and 4 will be reversed	
Cross-references	R3, R4, R5	
Postconditions	cmdClear has focus	

EEUC 4	Repeated conversions, same country	
Actor(s)	User	
Preconditions	txtDollar has focus	
Type	Primary	
Description	The user inputs a U.S. dollar amount and selects a country; the application computes and displays the equivalent in the currency of the selected country	
Sequence	Actor action	System response
	1. User enters U.S. dollar amount on keyboard	2. Dollar amount appears in txtDollar
	3. User clicks on a country button	4. Country currency name appears in lblEquiv
	5. User clicks cmdCompute button	6. Computed equivalent amount appears in lblEqAmount
	7. User clicks on txtDollar	8. txtDollar has focus
	9. User enters different U.S. dollar amount on keyboard	10. Dollar amount appears in txtDollar
	11. User clicks cmdCompute button	12. Computed equivalent amount appears in lblEqAmount
Alternative sequence	Actions 1 and 3 can be reversed, and consequently, responses 2 and 4 will be reversed; actions 7, 9, and 11 can be repeated indefinitely, with corresponding responses 8, 10, and 12	
Cross-references	R3, R4, R5	
Postconditions	cmdClear has focus	

EEUC 5	Repeated conversions, same dollar amount	
Actor(s)	User	

Preconditions	txtDollar has focus	
Type	Primary	
Description	The user inputs a U.S. dollar amount and selects a country; the application computes and displays the equivalent in the currency of the selected country	
Sequence	Actor action	System response
	1. User enters U.S. dollar amount on keyboard	2. Dollar amount appears in txtDollar
	3. User clicks on a country button	4. Country currency name appears in lblEquiv
	5. User clicks cmdCompute button	6. Computed equivalent amount appears in lblEqAmount
	7. User clicks on a different country button	8. New country currency name appears in lblEquiv
		9. Previously selected option button is reset
		10. Currently selected option button is set
	11. User clicks cmdCompute button	12. Computed equivalent amount appears in lblEqAmount
Alternative sequence	Actions 1 and 3 can be reversed, and consequently, responses 2 and 4 will be reversed; actions 7 and 11 can be repeated indefinitely, with corresponding responses 8, 9, 10, and 12	
Cross-references	R3, R4, R5, R7	
Postconditions	cmdClear has focus	

EEUC 6	Revise inputs	
Actor(s)	User	
Preconditions	txtDollar has a nonblank amount OR a country has been selected	
Type	Secondary	
Description	The user resets inputs either to begin a new transaction or to revise existing inputs	
Sequence	Actor action	System response
	1. The user enters a dollar amount on the keyboard	2. The dollar amount is displayed in txtDollar
	3. User clicks on a country button	4. Country currency name appears in lblEquiv
	5. The user clicks on the cmdClear button	6. txtDollar shows the null entry
		7. The selected country option button is reset.
	8. The user enters a new dollar amount on the keyboard	9. The new dollar amount is displayed in txtDollar

	10. User clicks on a different country button	11. Country currency name appears in lblEquiv
		12. The selected country option button is set
	13. The user clicks on the cmdClear button	14. txtDollar shows the null entry
		15. The selected country option button is reset
Alternative sequence	Actions 8, 10, and 13 can be repeated indefinitely; responses 9, 11, 12, 14, and 15 will recur	
Cross-references	R3, R4, R6	
Postconditions	txtDollar has the focus	

EEUC 7	Abnormal case; no country selected	
Actor(s)	User	
Preconditions	txtDollar has focus	
Type	Hidden	
Description	User enters a dollar amount and clicks on the cmdCompute button without selecting a country	
Sequence	Actor action	System response
	1. User enters U.S. dollar amount on keyboard	2. Dollar amount appears in txtDollar
	3. User clicks cmdCompute button	4. A message box appears with the caption "must select a country"
	5. User closes message box	6. Message box no longer visible
Alternative sequence	n/a	
Cross-references	R3, R5	
Postconditions	txtDollar has focus	

EEUC 8	Abnormal case; no dollar amount entered	
Actor(s)	User	
Preconditions	txtDollar has focus	
Type	Hidden	
Description	User selects a country and clicks on the cmdCompute button without entering a dollar amount	
Sequence	Actor action	System response
	1. User clicks on a country button	2. Country currency name appears in lblEquiv
	3. User clicks cmdCompute button	4. A message box appears with the caption "must enter a dollar amount"

	5. User closes message box	6. Message box no longer visible
Alternative sequence	n/a	
Cross-references	R3, R5	
Postconditions	txtDollar has focus	

EEUC 9	Abnormal case; no dollar amount entered and no country selected	
Actor(s)	User	
Preconditions	txtDollar has focus	
Type	Hidden	
Description	User clicks on the cmdCompute button without entering a dollar amount and without selecting a country	
Sequence	Actor action	System response
	1. User clicks cmdCompute button	2. A message box appears with the caption "must enter a dollar amount and select a country"
	3.User closes message box	4. Message box no longer visible
Alternative sequence	n/a	
Cross-reference	R5	
Postconditions	txtDollar has focus	

20.1.8 Real Use Cases

In Larman's terms, real use cases are only slightly different from the expanded essential use cases. Phrases such as "enter a U.S. dollar amount" must be replaced by the more specific "enter 125 in txtDollar." Similarly, "select a country" would be replaced by "click on the optBrazil button." In the interest of space (and reduced reader boredom), real use cases are omitted. Note that system-level test cases could be mechanically derived from real use cases.

20.2 UML-Based System Testing

Our formulation lets us be very specific about system-level testing; there are at least four identifiable levels with corresponding coverage metrics for GUI applications. Two of these are naturally dependent on the UML specification; we saw the other two in Chapter 19.

The first level is to test the system functions given as the first step in Larman's UML approach. These are cross-referenced in the extended essential use cases, so we can easily build an incidence matrix such as Table 20.2.

Examining the incidence matrix, we can see several possible ways to cover the seven system functions. One way would be to derive test cases from real use cases that correspond to extended essential use cases 1, 2, 5, and 6. These will need to be real use cases as opposed to the expanded essential use cases. The difference is that specific countries and dollar values are used, instead of the

Table 20.2   Use Case Incidence with System Functions

EEUC	R1	R2	R3	R4	R5	R6	R7
1	X	—	—	—	—	—	—
2	—	X	—	—	—	—	—
3	—	—	X	X	X	—	—
4	—	—	X	X	X	—	—
5	—	—	X	X	X	—	X
6	—	—	X	X	—	X	X
7	—	—	X	—	X	—	—
8	—	—	X	—	X	—	—
9	—	—	—	—	X	—	—

higher-level statements such as "click on a country button" and "enter a dollar amount." Deriving system test cases from real use cases is mechanical: the use case preconditions are the test case preconditions, and the sequences of actor actions and system responses map directly into sequences of user input events and system output events. The set of extended essential use cases 1, 2, 5, and 6 is a nice example of a set of regression test cases; taken together, they cover all seven system functions.

The second level is to develop test cases from all of the real use cases. Assuming that the customer approved of the original expanded essential use cases, this is the minimally acceptable level of system test coverage. Here is a sample system-level test case derived from the real use case based on extended essential use case EEUC 3. (Assume the exchange rate for one euro is U.S.$1.38.)

RUC 3	Normal usage (dollar amount entered first)
Actor(s)	User
Preconditions	txtDollar has focus
Type	Primary
Description	The user inputs a U.S. $10 amount and selects the European Community; the application computes and displays the equivalent: 7.25 euros

Sequence	Actor action	System response
	1. User enters 10 on the keyboard	2. "10" appears in txtDollar
	3. User clicks on the European Community button	4. "Euros" appears in lblEquiv
	5. User clicks cmdCompute button	6. "7.25" appears in lblEqAmount

Alternative sequence	Actions 1 and 3 can be reversed, and consequently, responses 2 and 4 will be reversed
Cross-references	R3, R4, R5
Postconditions	cmdClear has focus

SysTC 3	Normal usage (dollar amount entered first)	
Test operator	Paul Jorgensen	
Preconditions	txtDollar has focus	
Test operator sequence	Tester inputs	Expected system response
	1. Enters 10 on the keyboard	2. Observe "10" appears in txtDollar
	3. Click on the European Community button	4. Observe "euros" appears in lblEquiv
	5. Clicks cmdCompute button	6. Observe "7.25" appears in lblEqAmount
Postconditions	cmdClear has focus	
Test result	Pass/fail	
Date run	August 8, 2007	

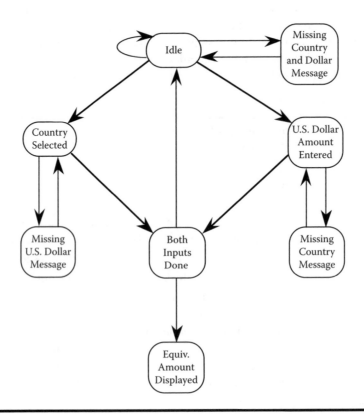

Figure 20.3   GUI finite state machine.

Table 20.3   Test Cases Derived from a Finite State Machine

State	TC1	TC2	TC3	TC4	TC5	TC6	TC7	TC8	TC9
Idle	1	1	1	1	1	1	1	1	1, 3
Missing country and dollar message								2	2
Country selected		2	2, 4			2			4, 6
U.S. dollar amount entered				2	2, 4		2		
Missing U.S. dollar message			3						5
Both inputs done		3	5	3	5	3	3		7
Missing country message					3				
Equivalent amount displayed		4	6	4	6				
Idle	2	5	7	5	7	1	1	1	1

The third level is to derive test cases from the finite state machines derived from a finite state machine description of the external appearance of the GUI, as shown in Figure 20.3 (repeated from Chapter 19). A test case from this formulation is a circuit (a path in which the start node is the end node, usually the idle state). Nine such test cases are shown in Table 20.3, where the numbers show the sequence in which the states are traversed by the test case. Many other cases exist, but this shows how to identify them.

The fourth level is to derive test cases from state-based event tables (see Chapter 19, Table 19.1 and Figure 19.2). This would have to be repeated for each state. We might call this the exhaustive level, because it exercises every possible event for each state. It is not truly exhaustive, however, because we have not tested all sequences of events across states. The other problem is that it is an extremely detailed view of system testing that is likely very redundant with integration- and even unit-level test cases.

20.3   StateChart-Based System Testing

A caveat is required here. StateCharts are a fine basis for system testing; we saw this in Chapter 19. The problem is that StateCharts are prescribed to be at the class level in UML. There is no easy way to compose StateCharts of several classes to get a system-level StateChart. A possible workaround is to translate each class-level StateChart into a set of EDPNs, and then compose the EDPNs as we did in Chapter 15.

References

Larman, C., *Applying UML and Patterns: An Introduction to Object-Oriented Analysis and Design*, Prentice-Hall, Upper Saddle River, NJ, 1998.

Zak, D., *Programming with Microsoft Visual Basic 6.0: Enhanced Edition*, Course Technology, Inc., Boston, MA, 2001.

MILLENNIUM TESTING VI

Chapter 21

Exploratory Testing

In the academic world, software testing was almost a dead research topic for much of the 1980s and 1990s. The new material in the second edition of this book dealt with advances due to the widespread adoption of the object-oriented paradigm. Part VI, "Millennium Software Testing," deals with the more recent initiatives in software testing. As a context for Part VI, we begin with a closer look at one of the four mainline schools of software testing identified by Bret Pettichord (2004): the analytic, quality, standards, and the context-driven schools.

In his STAR West presentation, Pettichord notes that his "schools of software testing" are more than just paradigms and techniques. More specifically, being a school implies existing standards of criticism, exemplary practices, and hierarchies of values.

Most of this book is exactly representative of Pettichord's analytic school. As the names imply, the quality and standards schools are driven primarily by those emphases. These two schools are focused more on the outcome of testing; they provide little guidance on how to actually *do* software testing.

21.1 The Context-Driven School

The context-driven school of software testing is closely associated with exploratory testing and agile programming. Andy Tinkham and Cem Kaner (2003) present a concise summary of the work (and people) that defined exploratory testing. They identify five essential characteristics of exploratory testing: it is interactive; it involves concurrent cognition and execution; it is highly creative; it intends to produce results quickly; and it reduces the traditional emphasis on formal test documents. The first two characteristics also describe a classical learning system. In testing terms, the exploratory tester learns about the system under test and uses this new knowledge to explore the system more deeply with more focused tests — very much like the professor giving an oral examination.

Because exploratory testing is also highly creative, it is difficult to describe the process precisely. It clearly depends on the attitude and motivation of the tester, but it also depends on the nature of the system under test, and on the priorities of the system stakeholders. One quick example:

imagine the differing priorities of a highly reliable telephone switching system versus the extreme time-to-market pressure of an e-commerce application. Such distinctions led to the establishment of the context-driven school of testing (Kaner, 2002). Members of this school have identified the following seven basic principles that define context-driven testing:

- *The value of any practice depends on its context.*
- *There are good practices in context, but there are no best practices.*
- *People, working together, are the most important part of any project's context.*
- *Projects unfold over time in ways that are often not predictable.*
- *The product is a solution. If the problem isn't solved, the product doesn't work.*
- *Good software testing is a challenging intellectual process.*
- *Only through judgment and skill, exercised cooperatively throughout the entire project, are we able to do the right things at the right times to effectively test our products.*

The first two apply to almost any endeavor — teaching, medical practice, automobile repair, and playing poker all come to mind. The third and seventh principles deal with effective teamwork, and as with the first two, they can apply to many human activities. The fourth, fifth, and sixth principles are more closely related to software testing — in fact, they almost characterize exploratory testing. Taken as a whole, the seven principles are pretty general. They might be the "motherhood and apple pie" of software testing.

21.2 Exploring Exploratory Testing

On the surface, exploratory testing seems to be a sophisticated alias for the special value testing discussed in Chapter 5. Here, pun intended, we explore exploratory testing, but first, we need to explore the metaphor. One sense of *explore* is to investigate the unknown. This sense conjures up images of a scientist in a laboratory, or of a world explorer. Both images are relevant — think about the contributions famous world explorers have made to the world body of knowledge. The Lewis and Clark expedition into the Louisiana Purchase is a good example. Thomas Jefferson wanted to know more about the sizeable chunk of North America that he bought from France. Lewis and Clark assembled a well-rounded team for their expedition, including army personnel, hunters and trappers, craftsmen, naturalists, and a first people woman, Sacajewea, who was familiar with much of the Missouri River basin.

In a letter dated June 20, 1803, Thomas Jefferson, president of the United States, wrote (Jackson, 1978):

> *The object of your mission is to explore the Missouri river, & such principal stream of it, as, by it's course & communication with the waters of the Pacific Ocean, whether the Columbia, Oregon, Colorado or an other river may offer the most direct & practicable water communication across this continent, for the purposes of commerce.*

> *Beginning at the mouth of the Missouri, you will take careful observations of latitude & longitude, at all remarkable points on the river, & especially at the mouths of rivers, at rapids, at islands, & other places & objects distinguished by such natural marks & characters of a durable kind, as that they may with certainty be recognised hereafter. The courses of the river between these points of observation may be supplied by the compass the log-line &*

by time, corrected by the observations themselves. The variations of the compass too, in different places, should be noticed.

The interesting points of the portage between the heads of the Missouri, & of the water offering the best communication with the Pacific ocean, should also be fixed by observation, & the course of that water to the ocean, in the same manner as that of the Missouri.

Your observations are to be taken with great pains & accuracy, to be entered distinctly & intelligibly for others as well as yourself, to comprehend all the elements necessary, with the aid of the usual tables, to fix the latitude and longitude of the places at which they were taken, and are to be rendered to the war-office, for the purpose of having the calculations made concurrently by proper persons within the U.S. Several copies of these as well as of your other notes should be made at leisure times, & put into the care of the most trustworthy of your attendants, to guard, by multiplying them, against the accidental losses to which they will be exposed. A further guard would be that one of these copies be on the paper of the birch, as less liable to injury from damp than common paper.

The commerce which may be carried on with the people inhabiting the line you will pursue, renders a knolege [sic] of those people important. You will therefore endeavor to make yourself acquainted, as far as a diligent pursuit of your journey shall admit, with the names of the nations & their numbers; the extent & limits of their possessions; their relations with other tribes of nations; their language, traditions, monuments; their ordinary occupations in agriculture, fishing, hunting, war, arts, & the implements for these; their food, clothing, & domestic accommodations; the diseases prevalent among them, & the remedies they use; moral & physical circumstances which distinguish them from the tribes we know; peculiarities in their laws, customs & dispositions; and articles of commerce they may need or furnish, & to what extent.

The Lewis and Clark expedition lasted 28 months and brought back much detailed information about the region. They got as far as the Columbia River in what is now Oregon, and they knew that from there the Pacific Ocean was within reach. Most people (with the exception of the first people) considered the expedition to be an enormous success. It certainly opened the way for waves of new settlers. The key part, as far as exploratory testing is concerned, is that their implementation of Jefferson's instructions is almost perfectly analogous to the goals and techniques of exploratory testing:

■ They knew what they were looking for (a route to the Pacific).
■ They had appropriate staffing and other resources.
■ They learned as they explored.
■ They were given plenty of time.
■ They were required to carefully document what they saw.

A second form of exploration illustrates the learning component of exploratory testing; it occurs when a professor gives an oral examination to a student. The first similarity is that the professor clearly has extensive domain knowledge. Second, the professor wishes to explore the extent to which the student has mastered the subject matter. The third, and most instructive, similarity is that when the student shows a weakness, the professor asks follow-up questions to explore the extent of the weakness; thus, knowledge gained from the answer to one question provokes a related question. This pattern is called adaptive testing.

These forms of exploration help explain the difference between special value testing and exploratory testing. As noted in Chapter 5, special value testing depends on the skill, insight, domain knowledge, and experience of the tester. The tester postulates test cases that seem to be important in that they might reveal faults. This is exploration, in a sense, but there is no feedback (other than pass/fail results of test case execution). Most often, the past experience of the tester is the greatest asset, as in the professor who gives an oral examination. By contrast, the exploratory tester is more focused and has better technology to help discover faults — much like the Lewis and Clark expedition. The essence of exploratory testing, per James Bach (2003), one of the originators of the term, is "simultaneous learning, test design, and test execution." According to Bach, an exploratory tester is most like the professor giving an oral exam. When an exploratory tester encounters suspicious behavior in a program, he or she will design and execute more tests to isolate the problem. The fault may reside in a normal part of the program that would not be found by special value testing. Results of some tests determine the nature of additional tests. It is the learning aspect that separates special value testing from exploratory testing.

21.3 Exploring a Familiar Example

The commission problem offers a chance to replicate exploratory testing. Suppose we know that a given implementation is faulty; the objective of traditional software testing is to simply verify the presence of faults. Exploratory testing goes a step further and tries to discover the nature of revealed faults. Recall that the commission problem deals with a salesperson who sells interchangeable rifle parts: locks, stocks, and barrels. The locks cost $45, the stocks cost $30, and the barrels cost $25; so a complete rifle costs $100. When our hypothetical salesperson reports monthly sales, the commission carries an incentive: 10% on the first $1000, 15% on sales between $1001 and $1800, and 20% on sales over $1800.

In the first few months, the neophyte salesperson never exceeds the $1000 goal, and the commission is correct. When sales finally reach the 15% level, however, the salesperson's commission is less than expected. And one month, when sales are nearly $2000, the commission is slightly more than expected. If our progressive salesperson had access to a spreadsheet, she would have seen something like Table 21.1:

Table 21.1 First Exploration

Case No.	Locks	Stocks	Barrels	Sales	Expected Commission	Computed Commission	Pass?	Expected Less Computed
1	1	1	1	$100.00	$10.00	$10.00	Pass	$0.00
2	8	8	8	$800.00	$80.00	$80.00	Pass	$0.00
3	10	10	10	$1,000.00	$100.00	$100.00	Pass	$0.00
4	11	11	11	$1,100.00	$115.00	$100.00	Fail	$15.00
5	17	17	17	$1,700.00	$205.00	$190.00	Fail	$15.00
6	18	18	18	$1,800.00	$220.00	$205.00	Fail	$15.00
7	19	19	19	$1,900.00	$240.00	$260.00	Fail	($20.00)

Table 21.2 Second Exploration

Case No.	Locks	Stocks	Barrels	Sales	Expected Commission	Computed Commission	Pass?	Expected Less Computed
1	10	0	0	$450.00	$45.00	$45.00	Pass	$0.00
2	0	10	0	$300.00	$30.00	$30.00	Pass	$0.00
3	0	0	10	$250.00	$25.00	$25.00	Pass	$0.00

The inquisitive salesperson began the exploration with four equations (locks, stocks, and barrels are, respectively, the numbers of each item sold):

1. Sales = 45*locks + 30*stocks + 35*barrels
2. Commission = 0.10*sales   (for $0 ≤ sales ≤ $1000)
3. Commission = $100 + 0.15*(sales – $1000)   (for $1000 < sales ≤ $1800)
4. Commission = $220 + 0.20*(sales – $1800)   (sales > $1800)

What could go wrong with equation 1? The sales column is correct, but maybe there were offsetting errors in the coefficients. So the second exploration is to see what happens when only one item is sold (see Table 21.2). The coefficients are clearly correct.

To explore equation 3, our intrepid salesperson wanted to devise sales near the $1000 commission incentive point. Conveniently enough, the coefficients lend themselves well to this task. The results are in Table 21.3.

Aha! reasoned our algebraic salesperson, the only thing wrong with equation 3 must be the amount subtracted from sales. Solving the two equations,

(3 should be) $100.75 = $100 + 0.15($1005 – $1000)

(3 computed) $85.25 = $100 + 0.15($1005 – x)

$$x = $1100$$

Table 21.3 Third Exploration

Case No.	Locks	Stocks	Barrels	Sales	Expected Commission	Computed Commission	Pass?	Expected Less Computed
1	22	0	0	$990.00	$99.00	$99.00	Pass	$0.00
2	21	0	2	$995.00	$99.50	$99.50	Pass	$0.00
3	21	1	1	$1,000.00	$100.00	$100.00	Pass	$0.00
4	21	2	0	$1,005.00	$100.75	$85.75	Fail	$15.00

The salesperson reasoned that, in fact, the calculation was

(3 faulty)   Commission = $100 + 0.15*(sales − $1100)

Our diligent salesperson reported this fault and was told that was the old policy and the commission program had not been updated.

21.4   Exploratory and Context-Driven Testing Observations

James Bach maintains that anyone who tests software does a certain amount of exploratory testing. It is more accurate to say that debugging one's own code is exploratory testing. Because the descriptions of these forms of testing are so general, it is difficult to draw precise conclusions about them. Here are mine:

1. Neither exploratory nor context-driven testing is appropriate in an agile programming environment. The whole idea of follow-up tests based on the outcome of previous tests presumes a completed application.
2. Both approaches are inherently dependent on the domain experience of the tester. By analogy, how effectively could a computer science professor conduct an oral examination for a history major?
3. Both approaches presume the tester is highly motivated, curious, and creative. A dull, disinterested tester will not be able to devise interesting follow-up tests.
4. Both approaches defy predictive measurement. This is true of any essentially creative activity, not just software testing. Even a very effective exploratory tester cannot estimate how much additional testing is needed, and it is theoretically impossible to determine how many faults remain. A conscientious exploratory tester can tell when no more faults are being revealed.
5. Management of both approaches is reduced to insistence on documented tests and results.
6. The effectiveness of both approaches is inversely proportional to the size and complexity of the system under test. Neither form easily lends itself to a team approach, and an individual will always have some threshold of system comprehension. An exploratory tester can certainly explore a large, complex system, but it will be difficult to keep track of all the follow-up tests.
7. Neither form of testing is well suited to identify faults of interaction (as in Chapter 15).

References

Bach, J., Exploratory Testing Explained, v. 1.3, April 16, 2003, available in PDF format at www.satisfice. com/articles/et-article.pdf.

Jackson, D., Ed., *Letters of the Lewis and Clark Expedition with Related Documents*, 2nd ed., 2 vols., University of Illinois Press, Urbana, 1978.

Kaner, C., The Context-Driven Approach to Software Testing, STAR East, Orlando, 2002.

Pettichord, B., Four Schools of Software Testing, STAR West, Anaheim, November 2004.

Tinkham, A. and Kaner, C., Exploring Exploratory Testing, 2003, available in PDF format at www. testingeducation.org/a/explore.pdf.

Exercises

1. Here is a true story (but the name is changed to protect the guilty):

    Ralph was the project manager of a small telephone switching system development. He started out as an electrical engineer, specifically as a logic designer. As his career progressed, he acquired solid domain knowledge of telephone switching systems. When the project prototype was completed, and when the first increment of software was loaded, Ralph signed up for three hours of scarce system test time. At the end of his session, he called the whole project team together and announced that the system was full of holes and that much work remained. When asked for more details, all Ralph could say was that he tried a bunch of things and most of them did not work. There was no record of faults found, no indication of the tests that were executed, and nothing was repeatable to help isolate the faults.

    Discuss the ways in which Ralph's testing conforms to and differs from exploratory testing.

2. If you look carefully at Table 21.1, there is another fault, this time in favor of our adjective-laden salesperson. Did she report the second fault, as an honest salesperson, or did she say nothing and become greedy? You can use the exploreCommission.xls spreadsheet to detect the other fault, (available on the CRC Press website).

Chapter 22

Model-Based Testing

> By my faith! For more than forty years I have been speaking prose without knowing anything about it.
>
> **Monsieur Jourdain in** *Le Bourgeois Gentilhomme*

I share the sentiment of Moliere's Monsieur Jourdain; in the second edition, Chapter 12, I wrote:

> *We also make a major shift in our thinking. We are more concerned with how to represent the item being tested, because the representation may limit our ability to identify test cases. Take a look at the papers being presented at the leading conferences (professional or academic) on software testing — you will find nearly as many presentations on specification models and techniques as on testing techniques.*

This is certainly part of what we now describe as model-based testing (MBT). Textbooks are beginning to appear (Utting and Legeard, 2006), and there is a Yahoo discussion group on the topic. Rather than repeat these discussions, in this chapter we describe the basic mechanism, discuss how to choose appropriate models, consider the pros and cons of MBT, and provide a short discussion of available tools. Actual examples of MBT are (and have been in the earlier editions) scattered throughout this book.

22.1 Testing Based on Models

The main advantage of modeling system behavior is that the process of creating a model usually results in deeper insights and understanding of the system modeled/tested. This is particularly true of executable models such as finite state machines, Petri Nets, and StateCharts. In Chapter 14, we saw that threads of system behavior, which are easily transformed into system-level test cases, are readily derived from many behavioral models. Given this, the adequacy of model-based testing will always depend on the accuracy of the model. The essence of model-based testing is the following sequence of steps:

1. Model the system.
2. Identify threads of system behavior in the model.
3. Transform these threads into test cases.
4. Execute the test cases (on the actual system), and record the results.
5. Revise the model(s) as needed, and repeat the process.

22.2 Appropriate Models

Avvinare is one of my favorite Italian words. It refers to a process that many Italian families perform in autumn when they bottle wine. After buying a demijohn of bulk wine, they rinse out the empty bottles that they have saved during the year. There are always small droplets of water clinging to the sides of a bottle, but it is really difficult to dry them. Instead, the Italians fill a bottle about half full of the wine and shake it up to dissolve the water into the wine. Next, the wine is funneled into the next bottle, shaken, and poured into another bottle. This continues until all the bottles have been rinsed with wine and are ready for bottling. *Avvinare* is the verb that refers to this entire process. How would you translate this word into English? I really do not know, but it would not be easy. Languages evolve to meet the expressive needs of their speakers, and this activity is not very common in the English-speaking world. To wax esoteric, this is where software engineering meets epistemology.

Because model-based testing begins with modeling, choice of an appropriate model determines the ultimate success of the associated testing. Making an appropriate choice depends on several things: the expressive power of various models, the essential nature of the system modeled, and the analyst's ability to use various models. We consider the first two of these next.

22.2.1 *Peterson's Lattice*

James Peterson developed an elegant lattice of models of computation (Peterson, 1981), which is summarized in Figure 22.1. The arrows in the lattice signify the "more expressive than" relationship between two models. In his text, Peterson carefully develops examples for each edge in the lattice. For example, he shows a semaphore system that cannot be expressed as a finite state machine. Four models in his lattice are obscure: vector replacement systems, vector addition systems, UCLA graphs, and message systems. There are scores of extensions to Petri nets; Peterson grouped these together for simplicity. Marked graphs are a formalization of dataflow diagrams, and Peterson shows them to be formal duals of finite state machines.

Peterson's lattice is a good starting point for model-based testing. Given an application, good practice dictates choosing a model that is both necessary and sufficient — neither too weak nor too strong. If a model is too weak, important aspects of the application will not be modeled, and hence not tested. If a model is too strong, the extra effort to develop the model may have been unnecessary. Of course, this is also dictated by the tools available to the model-based tester.

Unfortunately, Peterson developed his lattice before StateCharts were invented by David Harel. Where do they fit in Peterson's lattice? They are at least equivalent to, and probably more expressive than, most extensions of Petri nets. (I have no formal proof of this, but given

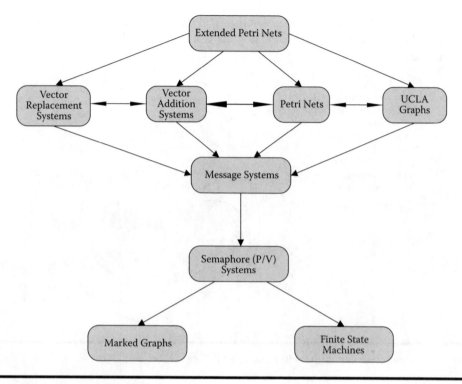

Figure 22.1   Peterson's lattice.

a relatively complex StateChart, I can always express it as an event-driven Petri net. However, the rich language associated with StateChart transitions will probably be difficult to express in most Petri net extensions.)

22.2.2 Expressive Capabilities of Mainline Models

There are two fundamental types of requirements specification models: those that describe structure and those that describe behavior. These correspond to two fundamental views of a system: what a system *is* and what a system *does*. Dataflow diagrams, entity/relation (E/R) models, hierarchy charts, class diagrams, and object diagrams all focus on what a system is — the components, their functionality, and interfaces among them. They emphasize structure. The second type, including decision tables, finite state machines, StateCharts, and Petri nets, describes system behavior — what a system does. Models of system behavior have varying degrees of expressive capability, the technical equivalent of being able to express *avvinare* in another language.

22.2.3 Making Appropriate Choices

Choosing an appropriate model begins with understanding the essential nature of the system to be modeled (and tested). Once these aspects are understood, they must be related to the various capabilities just discussed, and then the appropriate choice is simplified. The ultimate choice will always depend on other realities, such as company policy, relevant standards, analyst capability, and available tools. Always choosing the most powerful model is a simple-minded choice; a better choice might be to choose the simplest model that can express all the important aspects of the system modeled.

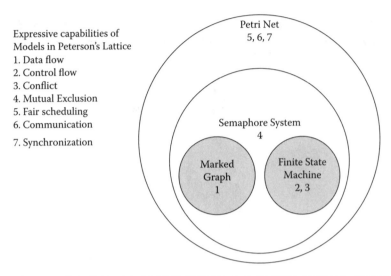

Expressive capabilities of
Models in Peterson's Lattice
1. Data flow
2. Control flow
3. Conflict
4. Mutual Exclusion
5. Fair scheduling
6. Communication
7. Synchronization

Figure 22.2   Expressive capabilities in Peterson's lattice.

Table 22.1   Expressive Capabilities of Selected Behavioral Models

	Decision Table	Finite State Machine	Event-Driven Petri Net	StateChart
Sequence	No	Yes	Yes	Yes
Selection	Yes	Yes	Yes	Yes
Repetition	No	Yes	Yes	Yes
Context-sensitive input events	Yes	Yes	Yes	Yes
Multiple causes of output events	Yes	Yes	Yes	Yes
Mutual exclusion	No	No	Yes	Yes
Concurrency	No	No	Yes	Yes
Deadlock	No	No	Yes	Yes
Event quiescence	No	No	Yes	Yes

22.3 Use Case-Based Testing

Given the widespread adoption of Unified Modeling Language (UML), and its newer derivative, SysML, these notations are the most common starting points for model-based testing. Here we just consider UML. (Much of the background on use cases is given in Chapter 20, along with an extensive example.)

Table 22.2a   Content of a Use Case

Use case identifier		
Narrative description		
Actors		
Preconditions		
Sequence	Actor inputs	System response
Alternative sequences		
Postconditions		
Function cross-reference		

Table 22.2b   Content of a System-Level Test Case

Test case identifier			
Narrative description			
Preconditions			
Event sequence	Port inputs	Expected port outputs	Observed port outputs
Postconditions			
Pass/fail?			

22.3.1 Deriving Test Cases from Use Cases

The detailed view of use case content is repeated in Table 22.2a. Deriving a system-level test case from a use case is almost a mechanical process; see the content of a system-level test case in Table 22.2b. At the simplest level, model-based testing based on use cases consists of this simple step, followed by running the derived test case and determining the pass/fail result. This process works reasonably well for systems in which there are no (or few) dependencies among use cases. For now, we might call these loosely coupled use cases.

It is easy to imagine systems in which dependencies exist among use cases. A common example: a use case that is a prerequisite for another use case, such as creating a password before using it. This is a system-level echo of the define/reference notion used in dataflow testing (see Chapter 10). As long as use case dependencies are of this nature, simple use case ordering (and corresponding test ordering) is sufficient. What if the dependencies are more complex? We consider that next.

22.3.2 Interacting Use Cases

If system-level test cases are derived from use cases, how can we identify the kinds of interaction discussed in Chapter 15? This is particularly problematic, because use case-based development is essentially (and intentionally) a bottom-up process. Recall that threads can interact in the four ways described by the directed graph concept of n-connectedness. We can apply this line of analysis to use cases by first translating use cases into event-driven Petri nets (EDPNs). Once expressed as EDPNs, recognition of n-connectedness is greatly facilitated. The simplest way is to use a database approach and relatively simple queries, but that is beyond the scope of this discussion.

Recall that an event-driven Petri net is comprised of port input and output events, data places, and transitions. Given a use case with content as in Table 22.1, the skeleton of an EDPN is derived as follows:

1. Preconditions are input places with indegree = 0.
2. Postconditions are output places with outdegree = 0.
3. Port input events correspond to the actor input sequence.
4. Port output events correspond to the system response sequence.

The only EDPN component missing is the set of transitions. For the purpose of determining EDPN connectivity, these can just be added with no derived names. (Usually, the transitions will correspond to atomic system functions that detect corresponding port input events.)

Given two (or more) use cases, we can determine their potential interaction in two ways. The first is to derive the corresponding EDPNs, compose them (as in Chapter 15), and visually inspect the resulting EDPN. In the process of composition, if there is ever a case in which an input event is used in two EDPNs, there is potential 1-connectedness. This is usually Petri net conflict. Similarly, if there is ever a case in which an output event is used in two EDPNs, there is the other form of 1-connectedness (ambiguous causes of an output). If there is ever a case in which the outdegree of a place is increased, the corresponding EDPNs are 1-connected with respect to that place (again, Petri net conflict). If there is ever a case in which the indegree of a place is increased, the corresponding EDPNs are 2-connected via that place. This visual process only works for small sets of use cases.

If there are too many use cases for the visual inspection approach, the composition can be performed by populating an appropriate database (see Figure 22.3).

With an actual database that implements the E/R model in Figure 22.3, the act of composing EDPNs becomes one of populating the database (which clearly scales up). Then the changes noted in the visual approach become changes in the number of appearances an entity has in various relations. For example, if a new EDPN is added to the database population and the number of appearances of a particular port input event increases in the portInput relation, then there is an instance of 1-connectivity with respect to that port input event. Recognizing all of the forms of n-connectedness, and hence potential interactions among EDPNs, is therefore reduced to making queries of a database.

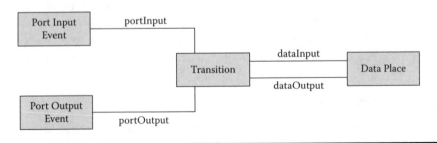

Figure 22.3　E/R model of EDPN interaction.

22.3.3 How Many Use Cases?

In addition to the problem of interacting use cases, there is the question of when a sufficient set of use cases (and hence derived test cases) has been identified. This question is inherent in the bottom-up nature of use case-based development, and it has both simple and elegant answers. The simplest answer is that in an agile programming development, the customer decides when the set of user stories (which extend to use cases) is sufficient. The customer can always add user stories. The answer is more complex in the top-down approaches. When the various top-down modeling approaches are done well, there is always a pattern of iteration — an analyst hardly ever "gets it right" on the first try. Fortunately, in the course of adding use cases, several lists can be developed:

- The port input events
- The port output events
- The set of components (procedures or classes)
- The set of system functions

Each of these can be put into an incidence matrix relating the list to the set of use cases, for example, the incidence of use cases with port input events. As additional use cases are postulated, the set of port inputs grows until, at some point, the existing set of port input events seems to support any new use case. Similar incidence matrices can be developed for the remaining lists. In each incidence matrix, a stopping point is always reached. Now, the incidence matrices can be reduced to smaller sets of use cases that cover all port input events, for example, and all port output events. This process happens to support an elegant notion of test coverage. We know, for example, that every port input appears in at least one test case derived from its corresponding use case.

22.4 Commercial Tool Support for Model-Based Testing

Alan Hartman (2003) separates commercial tools for model-based testing into three groups:

- Modeling tools
- Model-based test input generators
- Model-based test generators

According to Hartman, modeling tools such as IBM's Rational Rose and Telelogic's Rhapsody and StateMate provide inputs to true model-based test generators, but by themselves do not generate test cases. Model-based test input generators are a step up — they generate the input portion of test cases, but cannot generate the expected output portion. Full model-based test generators require some form of oracle to identify expected outputs. This is the sticking point for full test case generation. Present hopes (in 2007) are that domain-specific languages and practices will lead to full test case generation in limited applications. There are some existing university and company proprietary test generation systems, and a very few companies claim to have commercial tools available. Until this technology becomes commercially viable, note that use case-based testing provides the expected output portion of a test case.

Hartman's generalization is too sweeping — we know that full test cases, with expected outcomes, can be derived even from simple finite state machines (provided that the model shows the expected outputs). When the modeler is the oracle and provides expected outputs in any model, the model can serve as a full test generator.

References

Hartman, A., Model Based Test Generation Tools, 2003, available at www.agedis.de/documents/ModelBasedTestGenerationTools_cs.pdf.

Peterson, J.L., *Petri Net Theory and the Modeling of Systems*, Prentice-Hall, Englewood Cliffs, NJ, 1981.

Utting, M. and Legeard, B., *Practical Model-Based Testing*, Morgan Kaufman Elsevier, San Francisco, 2006.

Chapter 23

Test-Driven Development

"Pick a little, talk a little, pick a little, talk a little, pick, pick, pick, talk a lot, pick a little more."

From Meredith Willson's musical, *The Music Man!*

If we replace *pick* with *test*, and *talk* with *code*, the song captures the essence of test-driven development: write tests and code in small, incremental, alternating steps. A test case is written first, and in the absence of the corresponding code, the test case fails when executed. Immediately, just enough code is written so that the test case will pass. (*Nota bene*: *Pass* means the observed outputs are consistent with the expected outputs.) As code size increases, refactoring is permitted, but all the original tests must still pass (otherwise the refactoring is faulty). Test-driven development (TDD) has become very poplar in the agile programming community. Here we take a closer look at the process, using our standby example, the NextDate program.

23.1 Test-Then-Code Cycles

Test-driven development has matured to the point where there are both commercial and free tools to support the process. Two of the tenets of extreme programming are clearly present in TDD: doing just enough (the "You aren't going to need it" directive) and always having a working, albeit possibly incomplete, version of the program. Take time to follow the example carefully. The convention in the example is that source code in boldface font is what has been added to make the corresponding test case pass. Advocates of TDD are quick to claim that fault isolation is almost trivial in the TDD process. At any point in the process, all previous test cases must have passed. If a new test case fails, the fault can only be in the most recently added code. This is generally true, but it is not immediately obvious that it will always be true for "deeper" faults, such as those revealed only by dataflow testing.

Table 23.1   NextDate User Stories

1. The program compiles
2. A day can be input and displayed
3. An input month can be displayed
4. An input year can be displayed
5. A day below minimum can be detected
6. A day above maximum can be detected
7. A month below minimum can be detected
8. A month above maximum can be detected
9. A year below minimum can be detected
10. A year above maximum can be detected
11. Day = 31 in a 30-day month
12. Day = 30 in February (note: also need Day = 31 in February)
13. Day = 29 in February in a common year
14. Day = 29 in February in a leap year
15. A year divisible by 4 is a leap year (except for century years)
16. A year not divisible by 4 is a common year
17. A century year not divisible by 400 is a common year
18. A century year divisible by 400 is a leap year
19. Increment a non-last day of a month
20. Increment the last day of a 30-day month
21. Increment the last day of a 31-day month
22. Increment December 31
23. Increment February 28 in a common year
24. Increment February 28 in a leap year
25. Increment February 29 in a leap year

Test-driven development is guided by a sequence of user stories obtained from the customer/user. Table 23.1 contains the sequence of user stories developed in this section. One of the assumptions of all agile programming variants is that the customer may not know exactly what is desired, and that seeing an implemented (and tested) part of the eventual application often leads to additional user stories. The whole user story-driven process is very dependent on the order in which stories are given/received. In this example, the stories appear in an extremely bottom-up order — this is ideal for test-driven development, but it may not happen in practice.

There is a companion question of story granularity; this is deferred to Section 23.4.3.

In this sequence of user stories, only the most recent test is shown (to conserve space). In practice, all tests are present and run automatically. Here, the new code added to make the new test pass is in boldface font.

User Story 1: The Program Compiles

```
            Input: the NextDate source code.
            Expected Output: OK
```
Pseudo-Code
Program NextDate
End NextDate

User Story 2: A Day Can Be Input and Displayed

```
            Input: 15
            Expected Output: day = 15
```
Pseudo-Code
```
Program NextDate
 dim thisDay as Integer
 Input (thisDay)
 Output ( "day = ", thisDay)
End NextDate
```

User Story 3: An Input Month Can Be Displayed

```
            Input: 15, 11
            Expected Output: day = 15
            month = 11
```
Pseudo-Code
```
Program NextDate
 dim thisDay as Integer
 dim thisMonth as Integer
 Input (thisDay)
 Output ( "day = ", thisDay)
 Input (thisMonth)
 Output ( "month = ", thisMonth)
End NextDate
```

User Story 4: An Input Year Can Be Displayed

```
            Input: 15, 11, 2005
            Expected Output: day = 15
            month = 11
            year = 2005
```
Pseudo-Code
```
Program NextDate
 dim thisDay as Integer
 dim thisMonth as Integer
 dim thisYear as Integer
 Input (thisDay)
 Output ( "day = ", thisDay)
 Input (thisMonth)
 Output ( "month = ", thisMonth)
 Input (thisYear)
 Output ( "year = ", thisYear)
End NextDate
```

Refactor Code [this one is trivial, but it saves space]

```
Program NextDate
 dim thisDay, thisMonth, thisYear as Integer
 Input (thisDay, thisMonth, thisYear)
 Output ( "day = ", thisDay, "month = ", thisMonth, "year = ",
 thisYear)
End NextDate
```

User Story 5: A Day below Minimum Can Be Detected

```
          Input: 0, 11, 2005
          Expected Output:
          day = 0 is below minimum
          month = 11
          year = 2005
```

Pseudo-Code

```
Program NextDate
 dim thisDay, thisMonth, thisYear as Integer
 Input (thisDay, thisMonth, thisYear)
 If (thisDay < 1) Then
     Output ( "day = ", thisDay, "is below minimum")
     Output ("month = ", thisMonth, "year = ", thisYear)
 Else
      Output ( "day= ", thisDay, "month = ", thisMonth, "year
     = ", thisYear)
 EndIf
End NextDate
```

User Story 6: A Day above Maximum Can Be Detected

```
          Input: 32, 11, 2005
          Expected Output:
          day = 32 is above maximum
          month = 11
          year = 2005
```

Pseudo-Code

```
Program NextDate
 dim thisDay, thisMonth, thisYear as Integer
 Input (thisDay, thisMonth, thisYear)
 If (thisDay < 1) Then
     Output ( "day = ", thisDay, "is below minimum")
     Output ("month = ", thisMonth, "year = ", thisYear)
 Else
     Output ( "day = ", thisDay, "month = ", thisMonth, "year
     = ", thisYear)
 EndIf
 If (thisDay > 31) Then
     Output ( "day = ", thisDay, "is above maximum")
     Output ("month = ", thisMonth, "year = ", thisYear)
 Else
```

```
        Output ( "day = ", thisDay, "month = ", thisMonth, "year
        = ", thisYear)
 EndIf
 End NextDate
```

Refactor Code [Refactor the sequential tests of thisDay into a nested IF statement.]

```
Program NextDate
 dim thisDay, thisMonth, thisYear as Integer
 Input (thisDay, thisMonth, thisYear)
 If (thisDay >= 1) AND (thisDay <= 31) Then
        Output ( "day = ", thisDay, "month = ", thisMonth, "year
        = ", thisYear)
 Else
        If (thisDay < 1) Then
                Output ( "day = ", thisDay, "is below minimum")
                Output ("month = ", thisMonth, "year = ", thisYear)
        EndIf
        If (thisDay > 31) Then
                Output ( "day = ", thisDay, "is above maximum")
                Output ("month = ", thisMonth, "year = ", thisYear)
        EndIf
 EndIf
End NextDate
```

User Story 7: A Month below Minimum Can Be Detected

```
        Input: 15, 0, 2005
        Expected Output: day = 15
        month = 0 is below minimum
        year = 2005
```

User Story 8: A Month above Maximum Can Be Detected

```
        Input: 15, 13, 2005
        Expected Output: day = 15
        month = 13 is above maximum
        year = 2005
```

User Story 9: A Year below Minimum Can Be Detected

```
        Input: 15, 11, 1811
        Expected Output: day = 15
        month = 11
        year = 1811 is below minimum
```

User Story 10: A Year above Maximum Can Be Detected

```
        Input: 15, 11, 2013
        Expected Output: day = 15
        month = 11
        year = 2013 is above maximum
Program NextDate
    dim thisDay, thisMonth, thisYear as Integer
```

```
    Input (thisDay, thisMonth, thisYear)
    If (thisDay >= 1) AND (thisDay <= 31) Then
        Output ( "day = ", thisDay)
    Else
       If (thisDay < 1) Then
           Output ( "day = ", thisDay, "is below minimum")
       Else
          If (thisDay > 31) Then
             Output ( "day = ", thisDay, "is above maximum")
       EndIf
    EndIf
    If (thisMonth >= 1) AND (thisMonth <= 12) Then
        Output ( "month = ", thisMonth)
    Else
       If (thisMonth < 1) Then
           Output ( "month = ", thisMonth, "is below minimum")
       Else
          If (thisMonth > 12) Then
             Output ( "month = ", thisMonth, "is above maximum")
       EndIf
    EndIf
    If (thisYear >= 1812) AND (thisYear <= 2012) Then
        Output ( "year = ", thisYear)
    Else
       If (thisYear < 1812) Then
           Output ("year = ", thisYear, "is below minimum")
       Else
          If (thisYear > 2012) Then
             Output ("year = ", thisYear, "is above maximum")
       EndIf
    EndIf
End NextDate
```

At this point, the input data value ranges have been checked. The next iterations deal with impossible days in a given month. To save space, the data validity checking code is deleted. In TDD practice, of course, it would still be present.

User Story 11: Day = 31 in a 30-Day Month

```
               Input: 31, 11, 2005
               Expected Output:
               day = 31 cannot happen when month is 11
               month = 11
               year = 2005
Program NextDate
    dim thisDay, thisMonth, thisYear as Integer
    Input (thisDay, thisMonth, thisYear)
```

```
    ' data validity checking code would normally be here
    If (thisDay = 31) AND thisMonth IN {2, 4, 6, 9, 11}  Then
        Output("day = ", thisDay, "cannot happen when month is
        ", thisMonth)
    EndIf
    If (thisDay >= 29) AND thisMonth = 2 Then
        Output("day = ", thisDay, "cannot happen in February")
    EndIf
End NextDate
```

User Story 12   Day >= 29 in February
                       Input: 30, 2, 2005
                       Expected Output:
                       day = 30 cannot happen when month is February
                       month = 2
                       year = 2005

Pseudo-Code

```
Program NextDate
    dim thisDay, thisMonth, thisYear as Integer
    Input (thisDay, thisMonth, thisYear)
    'data validity checking code would normally be here
    If (thisDay = 31) AND thisMonth IN {2, 4, 6, 9, 11} Then
      Output("day = ", thisDay, "cannot happen when month is ",
      thisMonth)
    EndIf
    If (thisDay >= 29) AND thisMonth = 2 Then
      Output("day = ", thisDay, "cannot happen in February")
    EndIf
End NextDate
```

User Story 13   Day = 29 in February in a common year
                       Input: 29, 2, 2005
                       Expected Output:
                       day = 29 cannot happen when month is February
                       in a common year
                       month = 2
                       year = 2005
                       day = 29

Pseudo-Code

```
Program NextDate
    dim thisDay, thisMonth, thisYear as Integer
    Input (thisDay, thisMonth, thisYear)
    ' data validity checking code would normally be here
    If (thisDay = 31) AND thisMonth IN {2, 4, 6, 9, 11}  Then
        Output("day = ", thisDay, "cannot happen when month is ",
        thisMonth)
    EndIf
```

```
    If (thisDay >= 29) AND thisMonth = 2 Then
        Output("day = ", thisDay, "cannot happen in February")
    EndIf
    'Note: isLeap is a boolean function that returns true when the
    'argument corresponds to a leap year. Cannot run this test
    'case until Function isLeap is tested.
    If (thisDay = 29) AND thisMonth = 2  AND NOT(isLeap(this year))
    Then Output("day = ", thisDay, "cannot happen in February in
    a common year")
    EndIf
End NextDate
```

An anomaly occurs here. The developer postulated a Boolean function, isLeap, that responds with True or False, depending on whether the input year is a leap or common year. This function would have to be tested before the test "current" case. Possibly, this would be another point of refactoring. Function isLeap is the subject of the next few User stories.

User Story 14   A year divisible by 4 is a leap year (except
                     for century years)
                     Input: 2004
                     Expected Output: True

Pseudo-Code
```
Function isLeap(year) As Boolean
    dim year AS Integer
    '1812 <= year <= 2012 is given, and tested in main program
    'isLeap = False
    'MOD is the modulo arithmetic built-in operator in most
    'languages
    If (( year MOD 4) = 0) Then
        IsLeap = True
    EndIf
End isLeap
```

User Story 15   A year not divisible by 4 is a common year.
                     Input: 2005
                     Expected Output: False

Pseudo-Code
```
Function isLeap(year) AS Boolean
    dim year AS Integer
    '1812 <= year <= 2012 is given, and tested in main program
    isLeap = False
    'MOD is the modulus built-in operator in most languages
    If (( year MOD 4) = 0) Then
        IsLeap = True
    Else
```

```
        IsLeap = False
    EndIf
End isLeap
```

User Story 16 A century year not divisible by 400 is a common
                  year.
                  Input: 1900
                  Expected Output: False

Pseudo-Code
```
Function isLeap(year) AS Boolean
    dim year AS Integer
    "1812 <= year <= 2012 is given, and tested in main program
    isLeap = False
    "MOD is the modulus built-in operator in most languages
    If ((( year MOD 4) = 0) AND NOT(year MOD 100 = 0)) Then
        IsLeap = True
    Else
        IsLeap = False
    EndIf
End isLeap
```

User Story 17   A century year divisible by 400 is a leap year.
                  Input: 2000
                  Expected Output: True

Pseudo-Code
```
Function isLeap(year) AS Boolean
    dim year AS Integer
    '1812 <= year <= 2012 is given, and tested in main program
    isLeap = False
    'MOD is the modulus built-in operator in most languages
    If ((( year MOD 4) = 0) AND NOT(year MOD 100 = 0)) OR
            ((year MOD 400) = 0 ) Then
        IsLeap = True
    Else
        IsLeap = False
    EndIf
End isLeap
```

Comment: TDD shows a nice advantage in the development of Function isLeap. In a classroom experiment, only a few students were able to code the full condition (in user story 17) directly from the definition. The TDD build-up nicely simplifies this somewhat confusing condition. Now the user stories return to date validity tests.

User Story 18 Day = 29 in February in a leap year
                  Input: 29, 2, 2004
                  Expected Output: day = 1

```
                month = 3
                year = 2004
```

Pseudo-Code

```
Program NextDate
    dim thisDay, thisMonth, thisYear as Integer
    Input (thisDay, thisMonth, thisYear)
    ' data validity checking code would normally be here
    If (thisDay = 31) AND thisMonth IN {2, 4, 6, 9, 11}  Then
        Output ("day = ", thisDay, "cannot happen when month is
        ", thisMonth)
    EndIf
    If (thisDay = 30) AND thisMonth = 2 Then
        Output ("day = ", thisDay, "cannot happen in February")
    EndIf
    If (thisDay = 29) AND thisMonth = 2  AND NOT(isLeap(this
year))
        Then Output ("day = ", thisDay, "cannot happen in February
        in a common year")
        Else
            Output(day = 1, month = 3, year = this year)
    EndIf
End NextDate
```

The first 10 user stories checked to see that values of day, month, and year are in the appropriate ranges. User stories 11 to 18 dealt with valid and impossible dates. The remaining user stories deal with correct date increments. By now, the basic "test a little, code a little" principle should be clear. The remaining user stories are shown in Section 23.3.3, where the question of user story granularity is discussed.

23.2 Automated Test Execution (Testing Frameworks)

Test-driven development depends on an environment in which it is easy to postulate and run tests. To facilitate TDD, test execution frameworks have been written for most mainline programming languages. Most of these environments require the tester to write a test driver program that contains the actual test case data — both inputs and expected outputs. Section 23.3 contains a Java/JUnit example. Here is a partial list of TDD frameworks for various programming languages from wikipedia (http://en.wikipedia.org/wiki/XUnit) that demonstrates the variety of languages for which TDD frameworks are available.

> AUnit — A unit testing framework for Ada programming language.
> AsUnit — For ActionScript.
> AS2Unit — A unit testing framework for ActionScript 2.0.
> As2lib Unit Test — A unit testing framework for ActionScript 2.0.
> CUnit — A unit testing framework for C.
> CuTest — A cute unit testing framework for C.
> CFUnit — A unit testing framework for ColdFusion®.
> CPPUnit — A unit testing framework for C++.

csUnit — A unit testing framework for the .NET programming languages.

DBUnit — A unit testing framework for databases as a JUnit extension.

DUnit — A unit testing module for Delphi.

FoxUnit — A unit testing framework for Visual FoxPro®.

FRUIT — Fortran Unit Testing Framework.

fUnit — A unit testing framework for Fortran.

FUTS — The Framework for Unit Testing SAS.

GUnit — A unit testing framework for C with GNOME support.

HttpUnit — Testing framework for Web applications, typically used in combination with JUnit.

jsUnit — A unit testing framework for client-side (in-browser) JavaScript.

JUnit — A unit testing framework for Java.

JUnitEE — A unit testing framework for Java EE.

MbUnit — A unit testing framework for Microsoft .NET.

NUnit — For Microsoft .NET.

ObjcUnit — JUnit-like unit testing framework for Objective-C.

OCUnit — A unit testing framework for Objective-C.

OUnit — A unit testing framework for Ocaml.

PHPUnit — A unit testing framework for PHP.

PyUnit — A unit testing module for Python.

RBUnit — A unit testing framework for REALbasic.

SimpleTest — For PHP.

SUnit — A unit testing framework for Smalltalk (the original xUnit framework).

Test::Class — Another unit testing module for Perl.

Test::Unit — A unit testing module for Perl.

Test::Unit — A unit testing module for Ruby.

Testoob — An extended testing framework for use with PyUnit.

TSQLUnit — A unit testing framework for Transact-SQL.

VbaUnit — A unit testing framework for Visual Basic® for Applications.

VbUnit — A unit testing framework for Visual Basic.

23.3 Java and JUnit Example

The JUnit program is typical of the TDD test frameworks. Here is the Java code that corresponds to most of the example in Section 23.2.

23.3.1 Java Source Code

```
// class ValidDate checks if a date is correct, by Dr. Christian
Trefftz
public class ValidDate

{ public static boolean isLeap(int year)
    {if ( ((year%4)==0) && !((year%100)==0) || ((year%400)==0) )
      return true;
    else
      return false;}
```

```java
// validRangeForDay will return true if the parameter thisDay
is in the valid range
public static boolean validRangeForDay(int thisDay)
  { if ((thisDay >= 1) && (thisDay <= 31))
    {System.out.println("Day = "+thisDay);
     return true;}
  else {if (thisDay < 1)
              { System.out.println("Day = "+thisDay+" is below
              minimum.");
              return false; }
        else
          if (thisDay > 31)
                {System.out.println("Day = "+thisDay+" is
                above maximum.");
                return false;}
        }
    return false; }

// validRangeForMonth will return true if the parameter
thisMonth is in the valid range
public static boolean validRangeForMonth(int thisMonth) {
  if ((thisMonth >= 1) && (thisMonth <= 12))
    {System.out.println("Month = "+thisMonth);
     return true; }
  else
    {if (thisMonth < 1)
          {System.out.println("Month = "+thisMonth+" is below
          minimum.");
          return false; }
    else
      if (thisMonth > 12)
            {System.out.println("Month = "+thisMonth+" is
            above maximum.");
            return false; }
    }
  return false;}

// validRangeForYear will return true if the parameter
thisYear is in the valid range
public static boolean validRangeForYear(int thisYear) {
  if ((thisYear >= 1812) && (thisYear <= 2012))
    {System.out.println("Year = "+thisYear);
     return true; }
  else
    {if (thisYear < 1812) {
```

```
        System.out.println("Year = "+thisYear+" is below
        minimum.");
        return false; }
     else
       if (thisYear > 2012)
          {System.out.println("Year = "+thisYear+" is above
          maximum.");
          return false; }
       }
   return false;}

// validCombination will return true if the parameters are a
valid combination

public static boolean validCombination(int thisDay,int
thisMonth,int thisYear) {
   if ((thisDay == 31) && ((thisMonth == 2) || (thisMonth==4) ||
      (thisMonth == 6) || (thisMonth==9) || (thisMonth ==
      11)))
         { System.out.println("Day = "+thisDay+" cannot happen
when month is "+thisMonth);
         return false; }

   if ((thisDay == 30) && (thisMonth == 2))
      { System.out.println("Day = "+thisDay+" cannot happen in
      February");
      return false; }

   if ((thisDay == 29) && (thisMonth == 2) &&
    !(isLeap(thisYear)))
      {System.out.println("Day = "+thisDay+" cannot happen in
      February.");
      return false; }
   return true; }

// validDate will return true if the combination of the parameters
is valid

public static boolean validDate(int thisDay,int thisMonth,int
thisYear)
   { if (!validRangeForDay(thisDay))
    {return false; }
   if (!validRangeForMonth(thisMonth))
    { return false; }
   if (!validRangeForYear(thisYear))
    {return false; }
```

```
if (!validCombination(thisDay,thisMonth,thisYear)) {
 return false; }
 // If this point is reached, the date is valid
 return true; }}
```

23.3.2 JUnit Test Code

To test a Java unit, the tester must first write a test program such as the one that follows. This establishes a connection between the Java unit to be tested and the Junit framework. Actual test cases use the assertEquals method, where an assertion contains the pass/fail result of executing the called unit with test case values. For example, the assertion

```
assertEquals(true, ValidDate.validDate(29, 2, 2000));
```

asks JUnit to run the validDate method of ValidDate with the test case corresponding to Feb. 29, 2000. This is a valid date, and the expected JUnit response is "true". Similarly, the assertion

```
assertEquals(false, ValidDate.validDate(29, 2, 2001));
```

tests an invalid February date. Here is the actual JUnit test code.

```
//The test class ValidDateTest, by Dr. Christian Trefftz
public class ValidDateTest extends junit.framework.TestCase
{
    //Default constructor for test class ValidDateTest
    public ValidDateTest()
    { }
    //Sets up the test fixture. Called before every test case
    method.
    protected void setUp()
    { }
    //Tears down the test fixture. Called after every test
    case method.
    protected void tearDown()
    { }
      public void testIsLeap()
            {assertEquals(true, ValidDate.isLeap(2000));
            assertEquals(false, ValidDate.isLeap(1900));
            assertEquals(false, ValidDate.isLeap(1999)); }

      public void testValidRangeForDay()
            {assertEquals(false, ValidDate.validRangeForDay(-1));
            assertEquals(false, ValidDate.validRangeForDay(32));
            assertEquals(true, ValidDate.validRangeForDay(20)); }
```

```
public void testValidRangeForMonth()
      {assertEquals(false, ValidDate.validRangeForMonth(0));
      assertEquals(false, ValidDate.validRangeForMonth(13));
      assertEquals(true, ValidDate.validRangeForMonth(6)); }

public void testValidRangeForYear()
      {assertEquals(false, ValidDate.validRangeForYear(1811));
      assertEquals(false, ValidDate.validRangeForYear(2013));
      assertEquals(true, ValidDate.validRangeForYear(1960)); }

public void testValidCombination()
      {assertEquals(false, ValidDate.validCombination(31,
      4, 1960));
      assertEquals(false, ValidDate.validCombination(29,
      2, 2001));
      assertEquals(true, ValidDate.validCombination(29,
      2, 2000));
      assertEquals(true, ValidDate.validCombination(28,
      2, 2001)); }

public void testValidDate()
      {assertEquals(true, ValidDate.validDate(29, 2,
      2000));
      assertEquals(false, ValidDate.validDate(29, 2,
      2001));
      assertEquals(true, ValidDate.validDate(11, 10,
      2006));
      assertEquals(false, ValidDate.validDate(04, 30,
      1960));
      assertEquals(true, ValidDate.validDate(30, 04,
      1960)); }
}
```

23.4   Remaining Questions

23.4.1   *Specification Based or Code Based?*

Is test-driven development code based or specification based? In a sense, a test case is a very low level specification, so test-driven development seems to be specification based. But, test cases are very closely associated with code, so it has the appearance of code-based testing. Certainly, code coverage, at least at the DD-Path level, is unavoidable. Is it a stretch to claim that the set of all test cases constitutes a requirements specification? Imagine the reaction of a customer trying to understand a TDD program from the set of test cases. In the agile programming sense, however, the purpose of each test case can be considered to be a user story, and user stories are accepted by customers. It is really a question of level of detail, and this leads to a variant of test-driven development. Practitioners who object to tiny, incremental steps suggest that larger test cases, followed by larger chunks of code, are preferable. This has the advantage of introducing a small element of code design, and probably reduces the frequency of refactoring. The strictly bottom-up approach of "pure" TDD is complemented by top-down thinking.

23.4.2 Configuration Management?

Superficially, test-driven development appears to be a configuration management nightmare. Even a program as small as NextDate has dozens of versions in its growth from inception to completion. This is where refactoring comes in. Test-driven development forces a bottom-up approach to code development. At certain points, the conscientious programmer will see that the code can be

Table 23.2   User Story Granularity

Large-Grain User Stories	Fine-Grain User Stories
1. The program compiles	1. The program compiles
2. A date can be input and displayed	2. A day can be input and displayed
	3. An input month can be displayed
	4. An input year can be displayed
3. Invalid days can be recognized	5. A day below minimum can be detected
	6. A day above maximum can be detected
4. Invalid months can be recognized	7. A month below minimum can be detected
	8. A month above maximum can be detected
5. Invalid years can be recognized	9. A year below minimum can be detected
	10. A year above maximum can be detected
6. Invalid dates can be recognized	11. Day = 31 in a 30-day month
	12. Day >= 29 in February
	13. Day = 29 in February in a common year
	14. Day = 29 in February in a leap year
7. Leap years can be recognized	15. A year divisible by 4 is a leap year (no century years)
	16. A year not divisible by 4 is a common year
	17. A century year not divisible by 400 is a common year
	18. A century year divisible by 400 is a leap year
8. Valid dates can be incremented	19. Increment a non-last day of a month
	20. Increment the last day of a 30-day month
	21. Increment the last day of a 31-day month
	22. Increment December 31
	23. Increment February 28 in a common year
	24. Increment February 28 in a leap year
	25. Increment February 29 in a leap year

reorganized into something more elegant. There are no rules as to when refactoring should occur, but when it does, it is important to note that the original test cases are preserved. If the refactored code fails to pass all tests, there is a problem in the refactoring. Again, note the simple fault isolation. Refactoring points (once all test cases have passed) are good candidates for configuration management actions. These are points where a design object is, or can be, promoted to configuration item status. If later code causes earlier test cases to fail, this is another clear configuration management point. The configuration item should be demoted to a design object, which, by definition, is subject to change.

23.4.3 Granularity?

The sequence of user stories in the example in 23.3.1 uses a very fine grained level of detail. As an alternative, consider the enlarged granularity of user stories in Table 23.2. With larger user stories, a particular user story is broken down to a series of finer tasks, and code is developed for each task. In this way, the fault isolation is preserved. To distinguish between these granularity choices, sometimes the larger version is named story-driven development.

23.5 Pros, Cons, and Open Questions of TDD

As with most innovations, test-driven development has its advantages, disadvantages, claims, and unanswered questions. The advantages of TDD are very clear. Due to the extremely tight test/code cycles, something always works. In turn, this means a TDD project can be turned over to someone else, likely a programming pair, for continued development. Probably the biggest advantage of TDD is the excellent fault isolation. If a test fails, the cause must be the most recently added code. Finally, TDD is supported by an extensive variety of test frameworks, including those listed in Section 23.2.

It is nearly impossible, or at best very cumbersome, to perform TDD in the absence of test frameworks. There really is not much of an excuse for this, because the frameworks are readily available for most programming languages. If a tester cannot find a test framework for the project language, test-driven development is a poor choice. (It is probably better to just change programming languages.) At a deeper level, TDD is inevitably dependent on the ingenuity of the tester. Good test cases are necessary, but not sufficient for TDD to produce good code. Part of the reason is that the bottom-up nature of TDD provides little opportunity for elegant design. TDD advocates respond by claiming that a good design is eventually accomplished by a series of refactorings, each of which improves the code a little bit. A final disadvantage of TDD is that the bottom-up process makes it unlikely that deeper faults, such as those only revealed by dataflow testing, will be revealed by the incrementally created test cases. These faults require a more comprehensive understanding of the code, and this disadvantage is exacerbated by the possibility of the thread interaction faults discussed in Chapter 15.

Any new technology or technique has a set of open questions, and this is certainly true for test-driven development. The easiest question is that of scale-up to large applications. It would seem that there are practical limits as to how much an individual can keep in mind during a development. This is one of the early motivating factors for program modularity and information hiding, which are the foundations of the object-oriented paradigm. If size is a problem, complexity is even more serious. Can systems developed with TDD effectively deal with questions such as reliability and safety? Such questions usually require sophisticated models, but these are not produced in TDD. Finally, there is the question of support for long-term maintenance. The agile programming community and the TDD advocates maintain that there is no need for the documentation produced by the more traditional development approaches. The more extreme advocates even argue against comments in source code. Their view: the test cases *are* the specification, and well-written code, with meaningful variable and method names, is self-documenting. Time will tell.

23.6 Retrospective on MDD versus TDD

The first people of the North American plains have teaching stories based on what they observe in nature. When they speak of the medicine wheel, they associate animals with each of the four directions, and the animals have qualities that are seen in nature. One interesting pair is the eagle and the mouse. The eagle sees the big picture and therefore understands the important relationships among things. The mouse, on the other hand, sees only the ground where it scurries, and the grasses it encounters — a very detailed view. Living by the medicine wheel means that each view is honored — each view is needed to have better understanding.

It is unlikely that the first people ever thought much about model-driven development (MDD) and test-driven development (TDD), but the lessons are obvious: both are needed to have better understanding, in this case, of a program to be developed. This really is not too surprising. In the 1970s and 1980s, camps in the software community passionately debated the merits of specification-based versus code-based testing. Thoughtful people soon concluded that some blend of both approaches is necessary. To illustrate these two approaches, consider our Boolean function, isLeap, which determines whether a given year is a common or leap year. The definition of leap year is:

> A year is a leap year if it is a multiple of 4, but century years are leap years only if they are multiples of 400.

With this definition, the years 2000 and 2004 are leap years, and the years 1900 and 2006 are common years. A model-driven approach to developing isLeap would likely begin with a decision table showing the relationships among the phrases of the definition:

Conditions	r1	r2	r3	r4	r5	r6	r7	r8
c1. Year is a multiple of 4	T	T	T	T	F	F	F	F
c2. Year is a century year	T	T	F	F	T	T	F	F
c3. Year is a multiple of 400	T	F	T	F	T	F	T	F
Actions								
Logically impossible			X		X	X	X	
a1. Year is a common year		X						X
a2. Year is a leap year	X			X				
Test case: year =	2000	1900		2004				2006

The advantage of using a decision table for the model is that it is complete, consistent, and not redundant. Rule r1 refers to century years that are leap years, while rule r2 refers to century years that are common years. Rule r4 describes noncentury leap years, and rule r8 describes noncentury common years. The other rules are logically impossible. If we write isLeap from this decision table, we would get something like the following Visual Basic function.

```
Public Function isLeap(year) As Boolean
        Dim c1, c2, c3 As Boolean
        Dim year As Integer
1       isLeap = False
2       c1 = (year Mod 4 = 0)          ' leap years are divisible by 4
3       c2 = (year Mod 100 = 0)        ' but century years are common years
4       c3 = (year Mod 400 = 0)        ' unless they are divisible by 400
5       If c1 Then
6           If c2 Then
7               If c3 Then
8                       isLeap = True           'rule r1
9               Else
10                      isLeap = False          'rule r2
11              End If
12          Else
13                  isLeap = True               'rule r4
14          End If
15      Else
16          isLeap = False                      'rule r8
17      End If

End Function
```

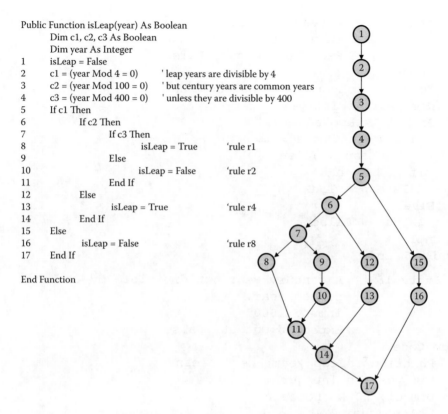

Notice that there are four paths from the source node to the sink node. The path through node 8 corresponds to rule r1, the one through nodes 9 and 10 to rule r2, and so on. Coding nested If logic three levels deep is probably not what the average developer would do, at least not on the first try. (And it is even less likely that a developer would get it correct on the first try. Score one for MDD.)

The test-driven approach results in a different form of complexity. The code for user stories 14 through 17 is rewritten here for a better comparison with the MDD version. The conditions c1, c2, and c3 are exactly what they were in the MDD example. As before, the new code for each test case is in boldface type. When it is copied to the next iteration, it is in plain type.

User Story 14 A year divisible by 4 is a leap year (except for century years)

                Input: 2004
                Expected Output: True

Pseudo-Code

```
    Function isLeap(year) As Boolean
    Dim year As Integer
    Dim c1 As Boolean
      c1 = (year Mod 4 = 0)
      isLeap = False
      If  c1 Then
        IsLeap = True
    EndIf
  End isLeap
```

User Story 15   A year not divisible by 4 is a common year.
                     Input: 2005
                     Expected Output: False

Pseudo-Code

```
     Function isLeap(year) As Boolean
     Dim year As Integer
     Dim c1 As Boolean
       c1 = (year Mod 4 = 0)
           isLeap = False
       If  c1 Then
         IsLeap = True
     Else
       IsLeap = False
     EndIf
   End isLeap
```

User Story 16   A century year not divisible by 400 is a
                     common year.
                     Input: 1900
                     Expected Output: False

Pseudo-Code

```
     Function isLeap(year) As Boolean
     Dim year As Integer
     Dim c1, c2 As Boolean
       c1 = (year Mod 4 = 0)
       c2 = (year Mod 100 = 0)
       isLeap = False
       If  (c1 AND NOT(c2)) Then
        IsLeap = True
     Else
       IsLeap = False
     EndIf
   End isLeap
```

User Story 17   A century year divisible by 400 is a leap
                     year.
                     Input: 2000
                     Expected Output: True

Pseudo-Code

```
     Function isLeap(year) As Boolean
     Dim year As Integer
     Dim c1, c2, c3 As Boolean
       c1 = (year Mod 4 = 0)
       c2 = (year Mod 100 = 0)
       c3 = (year Mod 400 = 0)
        isLeap = False
     If ( (c1 AND NOT(c2)) OR (c3)) Then
       IsLeap = True
```

```
      Else
        IsLeap = False
      EndIf
End isLeap
```

As a cross-check, here is the truth table for the compound (complex, actually) condition ($c1$ AND NOT($c2$)) OR ($c3$):

$c1$	$c2$	$c3$	NOT(c2)	c1 AND NOT(c2)	(c1 AND NOT(c2)) OR c3	Year
T	T	T	F	F	T	2000
T	T	F	F	F	F	1900
T	F	T	T	T	T	impossible
T	F	F	T	T	T	2004
F	T	T	F	F	T	impossible
F	T	F	F	F	F	impossible
F	F	T	T	F	T	impossible
F	F	F	T	F	F	2006

Notice that the same test cases and impossible entries occur in the rows of the truth table and the columns of the decision table; therefore, the two versions of isLeap are logically equivalent. Looking at the program graphs of the two implementations, the MDD version seems to be more complex. In fact, the cyclomatic complexity of the MDD version is 4, while that of the TDD version is only 2. From a testing standpoint, however, the compound condition in the TDD version requires multiple condition coverage. Both versions end up with the same necessary (and sufficient) four test cases.

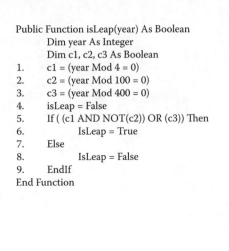

```
    Public Function isLeap(year) As Boolean
        Dim year As Integer
        Dim c1, c2, c3 As Boolean
1.      c1 = (year Mod 4 = 0)
2.      c2 = (year Mod 100 = 0)
3.      c3 = (year Mod 400 = 0)
4.      isLeap = False
5.      If ( (c1 AND NOT(c2)) OR (c3)) Then
6.          IsLeap = True
7.      Else
8.          IsLeap = False
9.      EndIf
    End Function
```

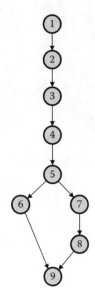

What, if any, conclusions can we draw from this? The MDD approach yields the eagle-eye view of the full picture. We know from the way decision tables work that the result is correct. We had to do a little more work to reach the same level of confidence with the TDD approach, but in the end, the two implementations are logically equivalent. The apparent difference in cyclomatic complexity is negated by the need for multiple condition coverage testing. The nested If complexity is moved into condition complexity — it does not disappear.

Any weaknesses? The MDD approach ultimately depends on the modeling skill; similarly, the TDD approach depends on testing skill. No significant difference there. What about size? The MDD version is longer: 17 statement fragments versus 9, but the TDD process requires more keystrokes. No significant difference here either.

The biggest difference would seem to be maintenance. Presumably, the modeling would be more helpful to a maintainer — the eagle again. But the test cases from the TDD approach will help the maintainer recreate and isolate a fault — the mouse view.

Chapter 24

A Closer Look at All Pairs Testing

All Pairs testing is extremely popular. According to James Bach and Schroeder (2003), over 40 journal articles and conference papers have been written about the technique, and it continues to be discussed in recent books on software testing. It is tempting to say that more has been written about All Pairs testing than is known. In this chapter, as the title implies, we take a closer look at the All Pairs testing technique, answering these questions:

- What is the All Pairs technique?
- Why is it so popular?
- When does it work well?
- When is it not appropriate?

The chapter ends with recommendations for appropriate use.

24.1 The All Pairs Technique

The All Pairs testing technique has its origins in statistical design of experiments. There, orthogonal arrays are a means of generating all pairs of experimental variables such that each pair occurs with equal probability. Mathematically, the statistical technique derives from latin squares (Mandl, 1985). The National Institute of Standards and Technology (NIST) papers by Wallace and Kuhn (2000, 2001) captured the attention of the software development community, particularly the agile community. They concluded that 98% of the defects in software-controlled medical systems were due to the interaction of pairs of variables. Given a program with n input variables, the All Pairs technique is a way to identify each pair. Mathematically, this is commonly called the number of combinations of n things taken two at a time, and is computed by the formula

$$_nC_2 = (n!)/((2!)(n-2)!)$$

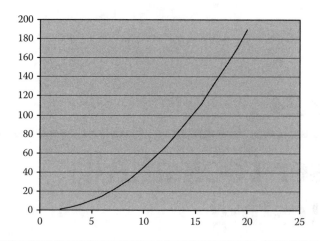

Figure 24.1 The combinatorial explosion.

which is the basis for the well-known combinatorial explosion. The first 20 values of $_nC_2$ are graphed in Figure 24.1. With the All Pairs technique, for example, the 66 pairs of interactions among 12 variables are exercised in a single test case.

Perhaps the most commonly cited example of All Pairs testing was developed by Bernie Berger and presented at the STAR East conference in 2003 (Berger, 2003). His paper contains a mortgage application example that has 12 input variables. (In a private e-mail, he said that 12 is a simplification. The actual application can be found at http://mortgage02.chase.com/pages/shared/gateway. jsp.) Berger identified equivalence classes for the 12 variables, varying in number between seven classes for 2 variables to two classes for 6 variables. The cross-product of the equivalence classes results in 725,760 test cases. Applying the All Pairs technique, this is reduced to 50 test cases — quite a reduction.

The All Pairs technique is supported by a commercial tool, the Automatic Efficient Test Generator (AETG) system (Cohen et al., 1994). It is also supported by a free program that is available from James Bach at his Web site (http://www.satisfice.com). The technique makes the following assumptions:

- Meaningful equivalence classes can be identified for each program input.
- Program inputs are independent.
- There is no order to program inputs.
- Faults are due only to the interaction of pairs of program inputs.

The necessity of each assumption is demonstrated (with counterexamples) next.

24.1.1 Program Inputs

As we have seen in earlier chapters, program inputs can be either events or data. The All Pairs technique refers only to data; that is, inputs are values of variables, not events. It is useful to distinguish between physical and logical variables, as in Table 8.1. As a guideline, physical variables are usually associated with some unit of measure, such as velocity, altitude, temperature, or mass.

Logical variables are seldom associated with units of measure; instead, they usually refer to some enumerated type, such as a telephone directory number or an employee identification number. It is usually easier to identify equivalence classes for logical variables.

As a counterexample, consider the triangle program. The three sides, a, b, and c, are all integers and are arbitrarily bounded by $1 \leq side \leq 200$. (*Nota bene*: The upper bound is arbitrary, but the lower bound is not.) The sides are physical variables, measured in some unit of length. What equivalence classes apply to a, b, and c? Only the traditional ones that deal with valid and invalid input values of a side:

EqClass1(side) = {x : x is an integer and x < 1}	(invalid values)
EqClass2(side) = {x : x is an integer and $1 \leq x \leq 200$}	(valid values)
EqClass3(side) = {x : x is an integer and x > 200}	(invalid values)

The actual Notepad input file to Bach's allpairs program is:

```
side a              side b              side c
a < 1               b < 1               c < 1
1<= a <= 200        1<= b <= 200        1<= c <= 200
a > 200             b > 200             c > 200
```

An interested tester might postulate equivalence classes such as one in which exactly two sides are equal, but such classes are on triples of triangle program inputs, not on individual variables. Table 24.1 contains the allpairs output generated for these equivalence classes; the actual test cases are in Table 24.2.

As expected from the allpairs.exe output, there is never an opportunity to choose values for the sides that correspond to an actual triangle. Because six of the nine equivalence classes deal with invalid values, this only exercises data validity, not correct function with valid values.

Table 24.1 allpairs.exe Output

Case	Side a	Side b	Side c	Pairings
1	a < 1	b < 1	c < 1	3
2	a < 1	1 <= b <= 200	1 <= c <= 200	3
3	a < 1	b > 200	c > 200	3
4	1 <= a <= 200	b < 1	1 <= c <= 200	3
5	1 <= a <= 200	1 <= b <= 200	c < 1	3
6	1 <= a <= 200	b > 200	c < 1	2
7	a > 200	b < 1	c > 200	3
8	a > 200	1 <= b <= 200	c < 1	2
9	a > 200	b > 200	1 <= c <= 200	3
10	1 <= a <= 200	1 <= b <= 200	c > 200	2

Table 24.2 Triangle Program Test Cases Generated by allpairs.exe

Case	Side a	Side b	Side c	Expected Output
1	–3	–2	–4	Not a Triangle
2	–3	5	7	Not a Triangle
3	–3	201	205	Not a Triangle
4	6	–2	9	Not a Triangle
5	6	5	–4	Not a Triangle
6	6	201	–4	Not a Triangle
7	208	–2	205	Not a Triangle
8	208	5	–4	Not a Triangle
9	208	201	7	Not a Triangle
10	6	5	205	Not a Triangle

24.1.2 Independent Variables

The NextDate function violates the independent variables assumption. There are dependencies between the day and month variables (a 30-day month cannot have day = 31) and between month and year (the last day of February depends on whether the year is leap or common). The day, month, and year variables are logical variables, and they are amenable to useful equivalence classes. In Chapter 7, we had the following equivalence classes and we used a decision table to deal with the dependencies. Table 24.3 is an extended entry decision table; it is the result of algebraically reducing the complete decision table in Chapter 7. It is canonical in the sense that it exactly represents all the combinations of valid variable values. The dependencies among day, month, and year are all expressed in the canonical decision table for NextDate.

Table 24.3 Canonical Decision Table of Valid NextDate Variables

	rule1	rule2	rule3	rule4	rule5	rule6	rule7	rule8	rule9	rule10
Day	D5	D4	D6	D5	D6	D5	1D1	D2	D2	D3
Month	M1	M1	M2	M2	M3	M3	M4	M4	M4	M4
Year	—	—	—	—	—	—	—	Y1	Y2	Y2
Day =1		x		x		x		x		x
Day++	x		x		x		x		x	
Month = 1						x				x
Month++		x		x				x		
Year++						x				

For day: $D1 = \{1 \le day \le 27\}$ $D5 = D1 \cup D2 \cup D3$

$D2 = \{28\}$ $D6 = D1 \cup D2 \cup D3 \cup D4$

D3 = {29}
D4 = {30}
D5 = {31}

For month: M1 = {30-day months}
M2 = {31-day months except December}
M3 = {December}
M4 = {February}

For year: Y1 = {common years}
Y2 = {leap years}

The allpairs.exe test cases for NextDate are given in Table 24.4. Note that the 10 canonical test cases are only partly present in the 20 All Pairs test cases. Because the All Pairs algorithm does not merge decision table rules, some of the generated test cases correspond to a single rule in the canonical decision table. For example, All Pairs test cases 1, 3, and 15 all correspond to rule 1; cases 2, 4, 16, and 18 correspond to rule 3; and cases 6, 8, 12, and 14 correspond to rule 5. The redundancy is understandable. The more serious problems are the missing test case (for rule 8) and the invalid test cases (cases 7, 9, and 19). The missing test case consists of the interaction of

Table 24.4 All Pairs Test Cases for NextDate

Case	Day	Month	Year	Pairings	Valid?	DT Rule
1	1–27	30-day	Leap	3	Yes	1
2	1–27	31-day	Common	3	Yes	3
3	28	30-day	Common	3	Yes	1
4	28	31-day	Leap	3	Yes	3
5	29	Feb.	Leap	3	Yes	10
6	29	Dec.	Common	3	Yes	5
7	30	Feb.	Common	3	No	
8	30	Dec.	Leap	3	Yes	5
9	31	30-day	Leap	2	No	
10	31	31-day	Common	2	Yes	4
11	1–27	Feb.	~Leap	1	Yes	7
12	1–27	Dec.	~Common	1	Yes	5
13	28	Feb.	~Common	1	Yes	9
14	28	Dec.	~Leap	1	Yes	5
15	29	30-day	~Common	1	Yes	1
16	29	31-day	~Leap	1	Yes	3
17	30	30-day	~Leap	1	Yes	2
18	30	31-day	~Common	1	Yes	3
19	31	Feb.	~Leap	1	No	
20	31	Dec.	~Common	1	Yes	6

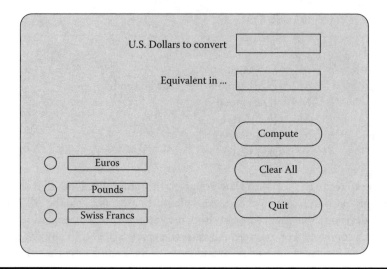

Figure 24.2   Currency conversion GUI.

all three variables, so the All Pairs algorithm cannot be expected to find this one. The invalid test cases are all due to dependencies among pairs of variables; these demonstrate the necessity of the independent variable assumption.

24.1.3 Input Order

Applications that use a graphical user interface (GUI) frequently presume that inputs are entered in particular orders. Figure 24.2 is a simple GUI for a simplified (from Chapters 16 and 19) currency converter. A user can enter a whole U.S. dollar amount up to $10,000, select one of three currencies, and then click on the Compute button to display the equivalent amount in the selected currency. The Clear All button can be clicked at any time; it resets the U.S. dollar amount and any selected currency. Once a U.S. dollar amount has been entered, a user may perform a series of currency conversions by first selecting a currency type, then clicking on Compute, and then repeating this sequence for other currencies. The Quit button ends the application.

Because there is no control of the sequence of user input events, the Compute button must anticipate invalid user input sequences. It produces five error messages:

> Error message 1: No U.S. dollar amount entered
> Error message 2: No currency selected
> Error message 3: No U.S. dollar amount entered and no currency selected
> Error message 4: U.S. dollar amount cannot be negative
> Error message 5: U.S. dollar amount cannot be greater than $10,000

Clicking on the Compute button is therefore a context-sensitive input event, with six contexts — the five that result in the error messages and an input U.S. dollar amount in the valid range. The data contexts of an input event are clearly pairs of interest to a tester, so the All Pairs technique should be appropriate.

Table 24.5   allpairs.exe Input for the Currency Conversion GUI

U.S. Dollar	Currency	Operation
No entry	Euros	Compute
<$0.00	Pounds	Clear all
$1 <= $ <= $10,000	Swiss francs	Quit
>$10,000	Nothing selected	

At first glance, the currency conversion GUI seems to lend itself nicely to the All Pairs technique. The following equivalence classes are derived naturally from the description and are shown in Table 24.5:

> USdollar1 = {no entry}
> USdollar2 = {USdollar < $0.00}
> USdollar3 = {$1.00 <= USdollar <= $10,000.00}
> USdollar4 = {USdollar > $10,000.00}
> Currency1 = {Euros}
> Currency2 = {Pounds}
> Currency3 = {Swiss Francs}
> Currency = {nothing selected}
> Operation1 = {Compute}
> Operation2= {Clear All}
> Operation3= {Quit}

The first four columns of Table 24.6 are the allpairs.exe program outputs. The (tester-provided) expected outputs are in the last column. The "~Compute" in test cases 15 and 16 is an allpairs output that directs the tester to pick an operation other than Compute. (It is an extension of the "don't care" entry in decision tables.) Notice that only error messages 1, 4, and either 2 or 5 are generated. Test case 9 generates a fourth context, in which the equivalent currency in pounds is computed. This is the only actual computation — the All Pairs test cases never check the conversion of dollars to euros or to Swiss francs.

There is a more subtle problem with the All Pairs algorithm — the order of inputs can make a surprising difference, even though it should be irrelevant. Table 24.7 just changes the order of U.S. dollar inputs, and the resulting test cases are in Table 24.8. With just this slight change, two currency conversions are performed (to pounds and Swiss francs), but only error messages 3, 4, and 5 are generated. The change is caused by the way in which the algorithm picks pairs of variables. The early test cases contain the greatest number of pairs, and the last ones contain the fewest. This means that a potential All Pairs tester needs to be clever about the order in which classes of a variable are presented to the algorithm.

24.1.4 Failures Due Only to Pairs of Inputs

By definition, the All Pairs technique only potentially reveals faults due to the interaction of two variables. The NextDate counterexample showed that faults due to interaction of three variables

Table 24.6   allpairs.exe Test Cases for the Currency Conversion GUI

Case	U.S. Dollar	Currency	Operation	Expected Output
1	No entry	Euros	Compute	Error message 1
2	No entry	Pounds	Clear all	Pounds reset
3	No entry	Swiss francs	Quit	Application ends
4	<$0.00	Euros	Clear all	U.S. dollar amount reset, euros reset
5	<$0.00	Pounds	Compute	Error message 4
6	<$0.00	Swiss francs	Compute	Error message 4
7	<$0.00	Nothing selected	Quit	Application ends
8	$1 <= $ <= $10,000	Euros	Quit	Application ends
9	$1 <= $ <= $10,000	Pounds	Compute	Equivalent in pounds
10	$1 <= $ <= $10,000	Swiss francs	Clear all	U.S. dollar amount reset, Swiss francs reset
11	>$10,000	Pounds	Quit	Application ends
12	>$10,000	Nothing selected	Compute	Error message 5 or 2
13	>$10,000	Euros	Clear all	U.S. dollar amount reset, euros reset
14	No entry	Nothing selected	Clear all	No change in GUI
15	$1 <= $ <= $10,000	Nothing selected	~Compute	?
16	>$10,000	Swiss francs	~Compute	?

(e.g., February 28 in a common year) will not be detected. This cannot be an indictment of the All Pairs technique — the advocates are quite clear that the intent is to find faults due only to the interaction of pairs of values. Orthogonal arrays can be used to find interactions among three or more variables. As long as the program tested uses logical variables, there is not too much risk. If a program involves computations with physical variables, some insight will likely be needed. Suppose, for example, a ratio is computed and the numerator and denominator are from different classes. There may be no problem with nominal values, but a very large numerator divided by a very small denominator might cause an overflow fault. Worst-case boundary value testing would be a more likely method to reveal such a fault.

Table 24.7   allpairs.exe Input in Different Order

U.S. Dollar	Currency	Operation
<$0.00	Euros	Compute
$1 <= $ <= $10,000	Pounds	Clear all
>$10,000	Swiss francs	Quit
No entry	Nothing selected	

Table 24.8   allpairs.exe Test Cases (note differences with Table 24.6)

Case	U.S. Dollar	Currency	Operation	Expected Output
1	<$0.00	Euros	Compute	Error message 4
2	<$0.00	Pounds	Clear all	U.S. dollar amount reset, pounds reset
3	<$0.00	Swiss francs	Quit	Application ends
4	$1 <= $ <= $10,000	Euros	Clear all	U.S. dollar amount reset, euros reset
5	$1 <= $ <= $10,000	Pounds	Compute	Equivalent in pounds
6	$1 <= $ <= $10000	Swiss francs	Compute	Equivalent in Swiss francs
7	$1 <= $ <= $10,000	Nothing selected	Quit	Application ends
8	>$10,000	Euros	Quit	Application ends
9	>$10,000	Pounds	Compute	Error message 5
10	>$10,000	Swiss francs	Clear all	U.S. dollar amount reset, Swiss francs reset
11	No entry	Pounds	Quit	Application ends
12	No entry	Nothing selected	Compute	Error message 3
13	No entry	Euros	Clear all	Euros reset
14	<$0.00	Nothing selected	Clear all	U.S. dollar amount reset
15	>$10,000	Nothing selected	~Compute	?
16	No entry	Swiss francs	~Compute	?

24.2   A Closer Look at the NIST Study

Most introductory logic courses discuss a class of arguments known as informal fallacies. One of these, the fallacy of extension, occurs when an argument is extended from a simple situation to an extreme one, where it is easier to persuade the point to be made. The conclusion is then brought back to the simple case. The fallacy of extension most commonly occurs when someone is asking for special consideration and the response is something like "What if we let EVERYONE have that exception?"

There is an element of the fallacy of extension in the myriad papers that emphasize how the All Pairs algorithm compresses an enormous number of test cases into a smaller, more manageable set. Although the popular papers cite the NIST study as the basis for the All Pairs technique, the NIST papers (Wallace and Kuhn, 2000, 2001) never stress this idea of compression; rather, they stress that faults due to more than two variables are relatively rare (2% in the examples they studied). Both papers are concerned with describing faults, identifying root causes, and suggesting fairly standard software engineering techniques to avoid similar faults in future systems.

The closest the NIST papers come to the dominant All Pairs emphasis on test case compression is when they discuss their analysis of 109 failure reports. They note (Wallace and Kuhn, 2000) that "only three of the 109 failure reports indicated that more than two conditions were required to cause the failure." Further, "the most complex of these [three failures] involved four conditions."

The conclusion of that part of the report is that "of the 109 reports that are detailed, 98% showed that the problem could have been detected by testing the device with all pairs of parameter settings." The report notes that most medical devices only have "a relatively small number of inputs variables, each with either a small discrete set of possible settings or a finite range of values." Then the fallacy of extension occurs. Quoting from Wallace and Kuhn (2000):

> *Medical devices vary among treatment areas, but in general have a relatively small number of input variables, each with either a small discrete set of possible settings, or a finite range of values. For example, consider a device that has 20 inputs, each with 10 settings, for a total of 10^{20} combinations of settings. The few hundred test cases that can be built under most development budgets will of course cover less than a tiny fraction of a percent of the possible combinations. The number of pairs of settings is in fact very small, and since each test case must have a value for each of the ten variables, more than one pair can be included in a single test case. Algorithms based on orthogonal latin squares are available that can generate test data for all pairs (or higher order combinations) at a reasonable cost. One method makes it possible to cover all pairs of values for this example using only 180 test cases [8].*

What is really perplexing about this is that they preface it with the note that most devices only have a few input settings, so the extension to 10^{20} cases makes little sense.

24.3 Appropriate Applications for All Pairs Testing

Figure 24.3 presents two considerations that help determine whether All Pairs is appropriate for a given application. The first consideration is whether the application is static or dynamic. Static applications are those in which all inputs are available before calculation begins. Such applications are sometimes called transformational because they transform their inputs into output data. Classic COBOL programs with their input, processing, and output divisions are good examples of static applications.

Dynamic applications are those in which not all of the inputs that determine the ultimate path through a program are available at the onset of calculation. The term *reactive* to conveys the fact that these applications react to inputs that occur in time sequence. The difference between static and dynamic applications is analogous to the difference between combinatorial and sequential circuits of discrete components. Because the order of inputs in important, dynamic applications is not very appropriate to the All Pairs technique, there is no way to guarantee that interesting pairs

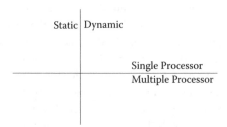

Figure 24.3 Partitions of the application domain.

will occur in the necessary order. Also, dynamic applications frequently contain context-sensitive input events in which the logical meaning of a physical input is determined by the context in which it occurs. The currency conversion example in Section 24.1.3 contains context-sensitive input events.

The second consideration is whether the application executes on a single or multiple processors. The All Pairs technique cannot guarantee appropriate pairs of input data across multiple processors. Race conditions, duration of events in real-time, and asynchronous input orders are common in multiprocessing applications, and these needs will likely not be met by All Pairs. Therefore, applications on the dynamic side of the partition, whether in single or multiple processors, are not appropriate for All Pairs.

The remaining quadrant, static applications in a multiple processing environment, is less clear. These applications are usually computation intensive (hence the need for parallel processing). If they are truly static, within a processor, All Pairs can be an appropriate choice.

24.4 Recommendations for All Pairs Testing

All Pairs testing is just another shortcut. When the time allocated for testing shrinks, as it frequently does, shortcuts are both attractive and risky. If the following questions can all be answered yes, then the risk of using All Pairs is reduced.

- Are the inputs exclusively data (rather than a mix of data and events)?
- Are the variables logical (rather than physical)?
- Are the variables independent?
- Do the variables have useful equivalence classes?
- Is the order of inputs irrelevant (i.e., is the application both static and single processor)?

Because the All Pairs algorithm only generates the input portion of a test case, one last question:

- Can the expected outputs for All Pairs test cases be determined?

References

Bach, J. and Schroeder, P.J., Pairwise Testing: A Best Practice That Isn't, presented at STAR West, 2003.

Berger, B., Efficient Testing with All-Pairs, presented at STAR East, 2003.

Cohen, D.M., Dalal, S.R., Kajla, A., and Patton, G.C., The Automatic Efficient Test Generator (AETG) System, in *Proceedings of the 5th International Symposium on Software Reliability Engineering*, IEEE Computer Society Press, 1994, pp. 303–309.

Mandl, R., Orthogonal latin squares: an application of experiment design to compiler testing, *Communications of the ACM*, Vol. 28, No. 10, 1985, pp. 1054–1058.

Wallace, D.R. and Kuhn, D.R., Converting System Failure Histories into Future Win Situations, 2000, available online at http://hissa.nist.gov/effProject/handbook/failure/hase99.pdf.

Wallace, D.R. and Kuhn, D.R., Failure modes in medical device software: an analysis of 15 years of recall data, *International Journal of Reliability, Quality, and Safety Engineering*, Vol. 8, No. 4, 2001, pp. 351–371.

Chapter 25

Epilogue: Software Testing Excellence

Finishing a book is almost as hard as beginning one. The ubiquitous temptation is to return to "finished" chapters and add a new idea, change something, or maybe delete a part. This is a pattern that writing shares with software development, and both activities endure small anxieties as deadlines near.

This book started as a response to Myers's *The Art of Software Testing*; in fact, the original working title was "The Craft of Software Testing," but Brian Marrick's book with that title appeared first. In the years between 1978 (Myers's book) and 1995 (the first edition of this book), software testing tools and techniques had matured sufficiently to support the *craft* motif.

Imagine a continuum with art at one end, leading to craft, then to science, and ending with engineering. Where does software testing belong on this continuum? Tool vendors would put it all the way at the engineering end, claiming that their products remove the need for the kinds of thinking needed elsewhere on the continuum. The process community would consider it to be a science, arguing that it is sufficient to follow a well-defined testing process. The context-driven school would probably leave software testing as an art, due to the need for creativity and individual talent. Personally, I still consider software testing to be a craft. Wherever it is placed on the continuum, software testing can also be understood in terms of *excellence*.

25.1 Craftsmanship

First, a disclaimer. The more politically correct *craftspersonship* word is unnecessarily cumbersome. Here, *craftsman* uses the gender-neutral sense of the *-man* suffix.

What makes someone a craftsman? One of my grandfathers was a Danish cabinetmaker, and that level of woodworking is clearly a craft. My father was a tool and die maker — another craft with extremely stringent standards. What did they, and others recognized as craftsmen, have in common? Here is a pretty good list:

- Mastery of the subject matter
- Mastery of the associated tools
- Mastery of the associated techniques
- The ability to make appropriate choices about tools and techniques
- Extensive experience with the subject matter
- A significant history of high-quality work with the subject matter

Since the days of Juran and Deming, portions of the software development community have been focused on *quality*. Software quality is clearly desirable, but it is hard to define, and harder still to measure. Simply listing quality attributes, such as simplicity, extensibility, reliability, testability, maintainability, etc., begs the question. The *-ability* attributes are all similarly hard to define and measure. The process community claims that a good process results in quality software, but this will be hard to prove. Can quality software be developed in an *ad hoc* process? Probably, and the agile community certainly believes this. Do standards guarantee software quality? This, too, seems problematic. I can imagine a program that conforms to some set of defined standards yet is of poor quality. So where does this leave the person who seeks software quality? I believe craftsmanship is a pretty good answer, and this is where *excellence* comes in. A true craftsman takes pride in his work — he knows when he has done his best work, and this results in a sense of pride. Pride in one's work also defies definition, but everyone who is honest with himself or herself knows when he or she has done a really good job. So we have craftsmanship, pride, and excellence tightly coupled — recognizable, yet difficult to define, and hence to measure — but all are associated with the concept of best practices.

25.2 Best Practices of Software Testing

Any list of claimed best practices is subjective and always open to criticism. Here is a reasonable list of characteristics of a best practice:

- They are usually defined by practitioners.
- They are "tried and true."
- They are very dependent on the subject matter.
- They have a significant history of success.

The software development community has a long history of proposed solutions to the difficulties of software development. In his famous 1986 paper, "No Silver Bullets," Fred Brooks suggested that the software community will never find a single technology that will kill the werewolf of software development difficulties. Here is a partial list of best practices, each of which was intended as a silver bullet. The list is in approximate chronological order.

- High-level programming languages (Fortran and COBOL)
- Structured programming
- Third-generation programming languages
- Software reviews and inspections
- The waterfall model of the software development life cycle
- Fourth-generation programming languages (domain specific)

- The object-oriented paradigm
- Various replacements for the waterfall model
- Rapid prototyping
- Software metrics
- CASE (computer-aided software engineering) tools
- Commercial tools for project, change, and configuration management
- Integrated development environments
- Software process maturity (and assessment)
- Software process improvement
- Executable specifications
- Automatic code generation
- UML (and its variants)
- Model-driven development
- Extreme programming (with its odd acronym, XP)
- Agile programming
- Test-driven development
- Automated testing frameworks

Quite a list, isn't it? There are probably some missing entries, but the point is that software development remains a difficult activity, and dedicated practitioners will always seek new or improved best practices.

25.3 Top 10 Best Practices for Software Testing Excellence

The underlying assumption about best testing practices is that software testing is performed by software testing craftsmen. Per the earlier discussion, this implies that the tester is very knowledgeable in the craft and has both the tools and the time to perform the task with excellence. There was an interesting discussion at the QA&TEST conference in Bilbao, Spain (October 2006) as to whether a tester should be a talented programmer. The consensus was an emphatic yes. (As a craftsman, programming is clearly part of the subject matter.) Other attributes include creativity, ingenuity, curiosity, discipline, and, somewhat cynically, a "Can I break it?" mentality. My personal top 10 best practices are only briefly described here; most of them are treated more completely in the indicated chapters.

25.3.1 Model-Driven Development

Model-driven development (MDD) has emerged as a powerful possibility for large, complex applications. Among the extensive commercial products, some produce reasonable code, while others only produce code skeletons. Either way, the developer has a good start at a system that is tightly coupled with its definition. This takes discipline — changing code without updating the underlying model is self-defeating. One of the main advantages of MDD is that models, if used well, can provoke recognition of details that otherwise might be ignored. Also, the models themselves will be extremely useful for maintenance changes during the application's useful lifetime. Ideally, MDD should include a product that supports the notion of an executable specification, along the lines of Petri nets or StateCharts.

25.3.2 Careful Definition and Identification of Levels of Testing

Any application (unless it is quite small) should have at least two levels of testing — unit and system. Larger applications generally do well to add integration testing. Controlling the testing at these levels is critical. Each level has clearly defined objectives, and these should be observed. System-level test cases that exercise unit-level considerations are both absurd and a waste of precious test time.

25.3.3 System-Level Model-Based Testing

If an executable specification is used, a large number of system-level test cases can be automatically generated. This in itself greatly offsets the extra effort of creating an executable model. In addition, this enables direct tracing of system testing against a requirements model. Because executable specifications are provocative, the automatically generated system test cases include many possibilities that otherwise might not be created.

25.3.4 System Testing Extensions

For complex, mission-critical applications, simple thread testing is necessary but not sufficient. At a minimum, thread interaction testing (as in Chapter 15) is needed. Particularly in complex systems, thread interactions are both serious and difficult to identify. Stress testing is a brute-force way of identifying thread interaction. Many times, just the sheer magnitude on interactions forced by stress testing reveals the presence of previously undiscovered faults (Hill, 2006). Hill notes that stress testing is focused on known (or suspected) weak spots in the software, and that pass/fail judgments are typically more subjective than those for conventional testing. Risk-based testing is a shortcut that may be necessary. Risk-based testing is an extension of the operational profiles approach discussed in Chapter 14. Rather that just test the most frequent (high-probability) threads, risk-based testing multiplies the probability of a thread by the cost (or penalty) of failure. When test time is severely limited, threads are tested in terms of risk rather than simple probability.

25.3.5 Incidence Matrices to Guide Regression Testing

Both traditional and object-oriented software projects benefit from an incidence matrix. For procedural software, the incidence between mainline functions (sometimes called features) and the implementing procedures is recorded in the matrix. Thus, for a particular function, the set of procedures needed to support that function is readily identified. Similarly for object-oriented software, the incidence between use cases and classes is recorded. In either paradigm, this information can be used to:

- Determine the order and contents of builds (or increments)
- Facilitate fault isolation when faults are revealed (or reported)
- Guide regression testing

25.3.6 Use of MM-Paths for Integration Testing

Given the three fundamental approaches to integration testing discussed in Chapter 13, MM-Paths are demonstrably superior. They can also be used with incidence matrices in a way that parallels that for system-level testing.

25.3.7 Intelligent Combination of Specification-Based and Code-Based Unit-Level Testing

Neither specification-based nor code-based unit testing is sufficient by itself, but the combination is highly desirable. The best practice is to choose a specification-based technique based on the nature of the unit (see Chapter 8), run the test cases with a tool to show test coverage, and then use the coverage report to reduce redundant test cases and add additional test cases mandated by coverage.

25.3.8 Code Coverage Metrics Based on the Nature of Individual Units

There is no "one size fits all" test coverage metric. The best practice is to choose a coverage metric based on the properties of the source code.

25.3.9 Exploratory Testing during Maintenance

Exploratory testing is a powerful approach when testing code written by someone other than the tester. This is particularly true for maintenance on legacy code.

25.3.10 Test-Driven Development

The agile programming community has demonstrated success using test-driven development (TDD) in applications where an agile approach is appropriate. The main advantage of TDD is the excellent fault isolation capability.

25.4 Mapping Best Practices to Diverse Projects

Best practices are necessarily project dependent. The software controlling a NASA space mission is clearly distinct from a quick-and-dirty program to develop some information requested by someone's supervisor. Here are three distinct project types. After their description, the top 10 best practices are mapped to the projects in Table 25.1.

25.4.1 A Mission-Critical Project

Mission-critical projects have severe reliability and performance constraints and are often characterized by highly complex software. They are usually large enough so that no single person can comprehend the full system with all its potential interactions.

25.4.2 A Time-Critical Project

Although mission-critical projects may also be time critical, this section refers to those projects that must be completed rapidly. Time to market and the associated loss of market share are the usual drivers of this project type.

25.4.3 Corrective Maintenance of Legacy Code

Corrective maintenance is the most common form of software maintenance. It is in response to a reported fault. Software maintenance typically represents three-fourths of the programming activity in most organizations, and this is exacerbated by the pattern that maintenance changes are usually done by someone who did not create the code being changed.

Table 25.1 Best Testing Practices for Diverse Projects

Best Practice	Mission Critical	Time Critical	Legacy Code
Model-driven development	x		
Careful definition and identification of levels of testing	x	x	x
System-level model-based testing	x		
System testing extensions	x		
Incidence matrices to guide regression testing	x		x
Use of MM-Paths for integration testing	x		
Intelligent combination of specification-based and code-based unit-level testing	x		x
Code coverage metrics based on the nature of individual units	x		
Exploratory testing during maintenance			x
Test-driven development		x	

Reference

Hill, T.A., Importance of Performing Stress Testing on Embedded Software Applications, Proceedings of QA&TEST Conference, Bilbao, Spain, October 2006.

Index

T